Armed and Dangerous! On first heari
This is in fact a 'Southern', an extrem
leading figures in the last chapters of ⸻⸻ in South Africa.

This is not a book about heroes and heroines, though many mentioned in it did in fact perform heroic deeds. This is a tale about how ordinary men and women, who driven by their consciences and by necessity became involved in the fight to overthrow White domination and apartheid in Southern Africa.

Ronnie Kasrils came to the liberation movement incensed and horrified by the brutal slaying of 69 protesters by the apartheid regime's police in 1960. After joining the ANC-allied South African Congress of Democrats, he became ever more deeply involved in the liberation struggle, rising to become Head of Military Intelligence in Umkhonto weSizwe (MK) in 1985. This highly readable tome offers a rare insight into the internal life of the liberation movement by a person who has filled many roles over the past sixty years of his involvement. From recruit in 1960, Ronnie Kasrils became a founding member of MK, went into exile and trained in the USSR before taking up a central position in coordinating the revival of the liberation inside South Africa. A government Minister until 2008, Kasrils' experience is notable for its breadth and longevity.

Armed and Dangerous is a good and valuable read. Enjoy!

Pallo Jordan

This gripping narrative of our struggle for freedom against enormous odds makes one laugh and weep and marvel at the fortitude and resilience of the human spirit captured in the book. It ought to be required reading for our youth who need to be armed with an understanding of what we have overcome and the values we need to protect and cherish as we struggle to create a just society. It ought to be at the bedside of every politician from the President to everyone wielding power and bearing responsibility to remind them that their sacred trust is to serve the people – and that it is a dangerous betrayal to deviate from that duty.

Archbishop Desmond Tutu

Front cover photographs:
Bottom right, author aged 20, after a beating by the police
Bottom left, author aged 23
Top right, author aged 26, from wedding photo
Top left, Minister Kasrils in 2008, aged 70

It is most appropriate that Ronnie Kasrils has dedicated this latest edition of Armed and Dangerous to the "born-frees". These are the millions in our country who were either too young or were not born during the years of struggle to defeat the pernicious apartheid system.

Armed and Dangerous is an important historical record of what were vital elements of that struggle, as well as some of the early steps during the process of the establishment of our non-racial democracy. Accordingly, it communicates the vital message especially to the "born-frees" that – freedom was not free!

A deep understanding of this is critically important at this time when all of us have an urgent obligation to act to defend the victories of our historic democratic transition. This is particularly so as we have to use those victories to achieve new successes as we strive to build South Africa into the winning country all of us want it to be.

It may be fashionable among some in our country to assert that 'yesterday was another country', and therefore that we should forget the past and concentrate only on the present and the future.

However, we must resist the pressure of 'fashion' to dictate that the captivating story Ronnie Kasrils tells in Armed and Dangerous belongs to 'another country'. It is very much our story, which celebrates the values of selfless service to the people which must continue to inspire us if we are to succeed in our continuing effort to reconstruct, remake and develop our country.

The young in our country, including the "born-frees", are quite correct to claim – the future belongs to us!

Armed and Dangerous will tell them that they would never have had that future if the heroic and principled struggle recorded in this book had not happened. It will tell them that for them truly to make theirs and ours a better future, they will have to take ownership of the history it tells, rightfully claiming it as their own.

Thabo Mbeki

We are fortunate enough to have, in their books, the revelation of the conviction and courage of the individuals who, in the struggle against apartheid have written of personal experience of that great battle overcome by their sacrifice and conviction that justice must be gained for all of us, any colour, race, in South Africa.

Ronnie Kasrils, one of them in the Struggle, now active in that other Struggle we didn't expect: facing the past for transformation to a free, just and equal opportunity of life in South Africa. *Armed and Dangerous* was how apartheid described him. To the oppressed he was one of those rightfully, courageous. He has now written his book to open South African minds to the reality of the responsibility we have beyond the time of arms, to the struggle within ourselves to create in conviction the absolute need of a new South Africa to become our country. A zestful and thought-provoking work.

Nadine Gordimer

This thrilling insider's account of the formation and activities of Umkhonto we Sizwe is essential reading for anyone wishing to understand the history of the armed struggle against apartheid. The chapters detailing Kasrils' experiences as a minister of defence and then water affairs and forestry offer equally riveting testimony to the challenges of governing. A new introduction to this edition sets out with stark clarity the ethical and practical dilemmas that confront a new generation of political activists in this complex society. Highly recommended for students, youth, general public – and any academic who writes or lectures on the subject.

Anthony Butler, Professor of Political Studies, University of Cape Town

Kasrils delivers a riveting testimony to our times. The razor-sharp 2013 introduction becomes the prism of hindsight through which the long road from struggle, through rose-tinted optimism at the transition, to a polity dominated by a comprador class with 'snouts in the trough' is lived. Ironies and despairs now jump off the pages of Kasrils' memoir of the time of liberation struggle. Offered by a timeless revolutionary, it sheds important new light on the continuous struggle for a liberated South Africa.

Susan Booysen, University of the Witwatersrand, author and academic

This timely fourth edition of Ronnie Kasrils's classic South African memoir shows the enduring vitality of the word as a weapon in the struggle for justice and equality and in what Milan Kundera calls 'the struggle of memory against forgetting'. Kasrils reminds us of where we have come from and of the long and challenging road that still lies ahead.

Darryl Accone

Armed and Dangerous is an amazing and honest story of the struggle for freedom of South Africa. This book acquires special importance now, when those who were outside of the liberation movement or even opposed it are trying to rewrite history and to hide the truth.

Prof Vladimir Shubin, Institute for African Studies, Russian Academy of Sciences

When I read *Armed and Dangerous* the first time, I was gripped by Ronnie Kasril's derring-do but, more importantly, intensely moved by his humanity and challenged by his commitment and courage. Reading it again now with its new introduction about the state of the country he fought for, I feel a renewed admiration for his humanity, his commitment and his courage. Kasrils draws the lines between the past and the present in ways that, while often distressing, are vital and energising too. His book is as bracing and necessary as it was a decade ago.

Mark Gevisser

This new edition of one of the classic books of the South African liberation struggle should be a key text for the young generation of South Africans. They are born into a transformed society, but that is now too often taken for granted instead of treasured.

Armed and Dangerous is an exciting read which is hard to put down, but most importantly it is a reminder of how courage and resistance developed against repression and tyranny, and of the great price paid by previous generations. The violent deaths, the arrests and torture of close colleagues, and the tragic betrayals, run through these pages. They illustrate the daunting responsibility that Ronnie Kasrils and his wife and colleagues took on for the sake for the dignity of all South Africans half a century ago. The challenges of the new generation are different, but Ronnie Kasrils' book is calling them to face responsibilities for creating the just society that the men and women he writes about lived and died for.

Victoria Brittain – British author

The story of a South African freedom fighter who rode on the Cold War stage with warm panache.

John Carlin

A classic account of the determination, integrity and sacrifice of those who fought for our freedom. Today and future leaders must not deviate from those qualities by courting corruption and self-interest. In its fourth edition, 'Armed and Dangerous' is a must read for young scholars who would like to go beyond the mundane history books and documentaries by obtaining a more personalised account of the liberation struggle.

Dr Renee Horne, University of Johannesburg Lecturer and Researcher

ARMED AND DANGEROUS

'To be is to do and to know is to do.'
Spinoza

'Hitherto the philosophers have interpreted the world;
the point however is to change it.'
Marx

'Those who make peaceful change impossible
make violent change inevitable.'
J.F. Kennedy

'The time comes in the life of any people when
there remain two choices; to submit or to fight.'
1961 Manifesto of Umkhonto we Sizwe

ARMED AND DANGEROUS
From Undercover Struggle to Freedom

Ronnie Kasrils

First published in the United Kingdom by Heinemann Educational in 1993

Updated edition published by
Jonathan Ball Publishers (Pty) Ltd in 1998 and 2004

This edition published by Jacana Media (Pty) Ltd
First and second impression 2013
Third impression 2016
Fourth impression 2017
10 Orange Street
Sunnyside
Auckland Park 2092
South Africa
+2711 628 3200
www.jacana.co.za

ISBN 978-1-4314-0795-8

Cover design by publicide
Set in Adobe Garamond 10.5/14 pt
Printed and bound by CTP Printers, Cape Town
Job no. 003157

See a complete list of Jacana titles at www.jacana.co.za

IN MEMORY OF ELEANOR, MY LATE WIFE & COMPANION
OF 48 YEARS
and all who sacrificed their lives in the struggle to liberate our country

THIS BOOK IS DEDICATED TO THOSE 'BORN FREE'
The generation born after the attainment of a democratic South Africa in 1994,
to help them understand the struggle and carry on where we left off
to make South Africa a better place for all who live in it

'I think continually of those who were truly great,
Who from the womb, remembered the souls history.
What is precious is never to forget
The names of those who in their lives fought for life,
Who were at their hearts the fire's centre.
Born of the sun, they travelled a short while towards the sun,
And left the vivid air signed with their honour.'
Stephen Spender

CONTENTS

PART III:
Home, 1990–93

PART IV:
Freedom and Government, 1994–2004

ACKNOWLEDGEMENTS

I AM DELIGHTED THAT JACANA MEDIA has decided to reprint this new edition of *Armed and Dangerous* because it covers those struggle years which laid the basis for today's South Africa. It will hopefully not only assist a new generation to understand the struggle but will explain to those of an older generation who were ignorant of or simply unclear about what drove us on. It will hopefully also assist those who, like all mortals, myself included, struggle with memory against forgetting. I believe the book has relevance for all generations.

Armed and Dangerous was first published in November 1993, by Heinemann (Oxford), several months before our first democratic election. It was one of the earliest struggle memoirs – certainly the first to deal from a personal perspective with the formation and development of MK, and the remarkable role it played in helping to bring about the downfall of apartheid.

The book proved popular in our country and abroad. So much so that Jonathan Ball acquired the rights and brought out two further editions: one in 1999 which added coverage of our first democratic election and my service as Deputy Minister of Defence (1994–99); and the second in 2004 which included my work as Minister of Water Affairs and Forestry (1999–2004). *Armed and Dangerous* has been translated into German, Spanish and Russian – and done remarkably well in those countries and in Cuba where it first appeared in the Spanish language.

The book has recently been published in Spain's Basque country which has seen its share of violent struggle over that region's claim to self-determination, and where I attended the book's launch. It has sold particularly well in Ireland with its tradition of anti-colonial struggle and use of revolutionary violence. It also has an appeal in Britain where many of us lived in exile and developed important clandestine links with South Africa. I am indebted to all the publishing houses, editors and translators who have enabled this book to reach a South African and international readership. My appreciation to the dedicated staff at Jacana, in particular Bridget Impey, Maggie Davey, Russell Martin, Kerrie Barlow and Megan Southey, who as ever are a delight to work with.

This Jacana edition includes some additional observations and the provision of the real names of those not previously revealed which it is now possible to do. I considered updating this volume but decided, with my publisher, that the period post-2004 – quite a dramatic time indeed, which poses huge questions and dilemmas – must await the writing of an entirely new volume. The lengthy Introduction to this new edition attempts a cursory analysis of some of those fundamental problems.

My gratitude to friends for their encouragement and suggestions and to those who, by providing refuge during difficult times, made this book possible. Parts I–III were written during the first half of 1993 and published by Heinemann at the end of that year. Part IV was written by snatching time late at night or over weekends in 1998 in between government duties. To do so required the support and calming essence of Eleanor, my late wife, to whom I am especially grateful.

As I cannot thank everybody personally, I would like to thank everyone concerned with this project and acknowledge the following:

Pietermaritzburg Sabotage Trialists 1963–64:
Natvorlall Babenia, Alfred Duma, Ebrahim Ismail Ebrahim, Dorsamy Kisten, George Naicker, Billy Nair, David Ndawonde, Curnick Ndlovu, Bernard Nkosi, Riot Mkwanazi, Shadrack Mapumulo, Matthew Mayewa, Zakhele Mdlalose, David Mkize, Kisten Moonsamy, Siva Pillay, Sonny Singh, Joshua Zulu.

Fellow MK Commissars, Angola 1978–79:
Edwin Mabitsela, January Masilela (Che), Vumile Ngculu (James), Jabu Nxumalo (Mzala), Chris Lungile Pepani (S'bali), Alec Tshabalala (Arthur).

MK High Command at its creation in 1983:
Commander – Joe Modise; Chief of Staff – Joe Slovo; Commissar – Chris Hani (1983–86); Chief of Operations – Lambert Moloi; Ordinance – Job Thabane; Communications – Jackie Molefe; Logistics – Bogart Soze.

Hani succeeded Slovo in 1986, and Steve Tshwete became Commissar. Rashid Patel succeeded Job Thabane as Ordinance Chief in 1987. (I was Chief of Military Intelligence from 1983–8.)

Fellow publicly revealed Vula operatives, detainees and fugitives 1987–1991:
Pravin Gordhan, Farida Jadwat, Raymond Lalla, Janet Love, Mac Maharaj, Christopher Manye, Tsotsi Memela, Yusuf Mohammed, Catherine Mvelase, Billy Nair, Charles Ndaba (murdered), Siphiwe Nyanda, Charles Nqakula, Max Ozinsky, Dipak Patel, Ivan Pillay, Mpho Scott, Jeremy Seebers, Moe Shaik, Solly Shoke, Jabu Sithole, Anesh Sunker, Mbuso Tshabalala (murdered), Vuso Tshabalala, Susan Tshabalala.

Chapters 32 and 33 cover the period 1999–2004, and were written at the suggestion of the publisher for the third updated publication.

Lyrics from 'The Harder They Come' by Jimmy Cliff are used by kind permission of Island Music Ltd, Media House, 334–336 King Street, London W6 ORA. Photocopying of the above copyright material is illegal.

INTRODUCTION TO THE
JACANA EDITION

THIS BOOK IS DEDICATED TO THE 'Born Frees', born after our first democratic election of April 27, 1994 – the dawn of South Africa's hard-won freedom – so they can understand what the sacrifices were and what lies behind where we are today. Understanding the past is to explain the present and help strategise and work for an even better future. Kierkegaard put it so elegantly: *'We can only live life forward but view it backwards.'*

This book is essentially about the sung and unsung heroes and heroines who fought the apartheid system and often sacrificed their liberty and their lives. It is about the courage to stand up and fight white supremacy. It is about the dangerous secret missions that were undertaken by ordinary people, young and old, male and female of every race, who in the process of struggle discovered they possessed extraordinary qualities. It is about human ingenuity in outwitting apartheid's ruthless security forces; daring to leave home and cross borders in the dead of night for military training abroad; of facing a brutal enemy in battle; of dedication and betrayal; of deaths in detention and long terms of imprisonment; of triumphs and tears. Above all it is about the values and principles that propelled those who resisted and made so many invincible in the interrogation chambers, behind prison walls, under internal restriction or in exile.

It is about those like the young Solomon Mahlangu who on the morning of his execution in Pretoria, April 4, 1979, told the priest: *'Tell my mother and my people that my blood will nourish the tree of Freedom.'* Fifteen years previously, Vuyisile Mini, Port Elizabeth dockworkers' leader, sentenced to death like Mahlangu for Mkhonto weSizwe (MK) activities, had walked tall with his fellow comrades Khayingo and Mkaba to the gallows singing freedom songs. Mini's daughter Nonkhosi, an infant at the time of her father's death, joined MK after the 1976 uprising and was assassinated by apartheid agents whilst on a secret mission to Maseru in 1985. The ANC's representative in France, Dulcie September, died in Paris in 1988 from the bullet of a cowardly assassin. Another ANC representative, Joe Gqabi, was similarly murdered outside his Harare office a few years earlier. Legendary struggle veteran Ruth First, wife of Joe Slovo, was murdered by a parcel bomb in Maputo in 1982 where she was working as writer and researcher for the Frelimo government. Jackson Sibanyoni fell in combat in Zimbabwe in 1967 whilst holding back advancing enemy forces to allow his comrades to retreat. In that same campaign against Ian Smith's Rhodesian forces Basil February was, like so many others, to fight to the last bullet. Young Ashley Kriel similarly shed his blood over twenty years later, not in the Zimbabwe bush but in the urban warfare jungle of Cape Town. Barney Molokwane died in action, fighting like a lion on the Swazi border in 1986, after his second attack on the Sasol refinery complex near Vereeniging. Phila Ndwandwe, barely twenty-one, was abducted from Swaziland in 1988, kept naked in a farm dungeon near Pietermaritzburg, and, because she refused to divulge information about MK, was murdered in cold blood. Many died in apartheid torture chambers over the years such as Looksmart Solwandle, Imam Haroon, Steve Biko and Neil Aggett. Babla Saloojee and Ahmed Timol, who carried out underground work for the ANC and communist party, were both hurled to their deaths from Security Police interrogation rooms in Johannesburg, in 1964 and 1972 respectively. Others died in SADF raids on Maseru, Matola and Gaborone. Griffiths and Victoria Mxenge, Matthew Goniwe and David Webster were amongst those murdered by apartheid's death squads inside South Africa.

These are just some of the names of those who served in the ranks of the ANC, MK and the liberation movement. So many more from various political formations such as the PAC, Azapo and the Black Consciousness movement died or languished for long years in prison. Massacres of our people were the order of the day and un-named thousands were killed. A heavy price indeed was paid for the freedom we have won. The regime's repression could not halt resistance. The struggle of the masses, reinforced by MK's actions and supported by international solidarity and the anti-apartheid movement, intensified over the years. The apartheid enemy was punished on countless occasions and many a time their police and soldiers ran from the battle. MK operations increased spectacularly over the years, rising to over 250 operations in 1988.

The psychological impact on the racist oppressor was devastating – MK's blows and the people's mass struggle put fear into their hearts – and together was the driving factor that pressurised F.W. de Klerk to seek a peaceful solution through negotiations. It was either that or a bloody revolution which he and his entourage needed to deflect at all costs.

Those who joined MK did so voluntarily and did not expect the promise of future positions or material gain. They were not mercenaries fighting for pay. The courage and values of service for the people that they displayed stemmed from the simple fact that they fought for a just cause. That was why they occupied the moral high ground. The slogan was: "We serve the people of South Africa!"

The motives and values of those who served in the struggle need to be clearly understood by every generation of our people. The target was the apartheid system, its symbols, its power grid and communication lines, and of course in a war their security forces and collaborators. The weapons carried were utilised to remove oppression and establish justice, peace and equality. Those who might in their youthful zeal have thought that killing was to be glorified or used for personal motives were disabused of such wrong-headed concepts through the political education and revolutionary morality that was a by-word for MK and our movement. Resorting to demagogic language and opportunistic attitudes to whip up support was unacceptable. The need for discipline and maturity in politics is an abiding necessity that has its relevance today.

Let us provide an example from recent times, for our history can never be relevant, our heroes can never be properly recalled, without placing past sacrifices within the context of our current struggles for justice today – struggles against the persistence of social and economic inequality even after racial apartheid has been conquered.

A young black man prone to make demagogic speeches, Julius Malema, stated in 2008 when Jacob Zuma's future was still undecided that he would 'Kill for Zuma'. Rather than recognising that the era of armed struggle in the South African fight for justice was over, and that supporting anyone's ambitions for presidential office should not be framed around a willingness to kill for them, Malema spouted fire. With the young man at his side Zuma told the crowds that Malema had the qualities to one day become President of the country. Malema and the ANC Youth League had in fact helped Zuma topple Thabo Mbeki as party leader at the ANC's 2007 Polokwane Conference. Malema later went on to upset the ANC applecart by daring to call for the nationalisation of the mines. This was a relevant demand but one that frightened the government and even its communist allies, who having failed to open the debate in the first place, left a void for demagogues like Malema to exploit. It is history that when Malema had served his purpose he was dropped like a hot coal by his friends in power, was expelled from the ANC and without media attention has disappeared – for the time being at any rate – into the political wilderness.

In July 2008 when Malema was still a force to be reckoned with, I was asked by the Gauteng ANC to deliver a lecture on Job Tabane (alias Cassius Make) murdered by apartheid agents in Swaziland in 1987. This coincided with the return home of his remains for reburial. Malema's glorification of violence and appeal to sections of frustrated youth led me to deal with what had motivated the young Job Tabane to take up arms and join MK in 1961 at the age of sixteen.

Why was revolutionary violence appropriate at that time? What is to be learnt about revolutionary values and conduct and today's choices? The historic decision to establish MK and take up arms by the Mandela leadership in 1961 was not simply a decision to kill. It was rather the need to utilise modern arms as a means to liberate our people when no other possibilities for change existed. For almost fifty years from its inception in 1912 the ANC and its allies had attempted to achieve equality and rights for the dispossessed and disenfranchised African majority through peaceful non-violent means. The brutality of the apartheid regime, as illustrated by the Sharpeville massacre and outlawing of the ANC and the PAC in 1960, signalled that there was no possibility of change through non-violent means alone. That was a time when the ballot did not exist for black people and the bullet was part of the answer. 'Part of the answer' because it was understood that political power did not come from the barrel of a gun alone – or even primarily from arms – but as part of reinforcing the mass political struggle. Deciding to take up arms had to be carefully weighed up within the context of place and time. Job Tabane understood that in a democracy where peaceful change was possible there would be no need to resort to warfare. Neither was the enemy simply seen in terms of skin colour. It was emphasised that the enemy was not colour but the system of apartheid that served the narrow interests of a white minority but in particular the economic power of the mining, energy, agricultural and manufacturing sectors of the country and the overseas investors making super profits. That implied that once we had toppled the apartheid system we would replace it with an infinitely superior humane, non-racist, non-sexist, democratic system – a system ensuring social and economic rights and the control of the country's bountiful riches – which would serve the needs of all and especially the multitudes who had borne the brunt of racist oppression and exploitation.

Those 'Born Free' are fortunate not to have endured the cruelty of apartheid as their parents did. They were not consigned by white supremacy, like previous generations, to forever remain 'hewers of wood and drawers of water' and in the racist advocacy of Dr Hendrik Verwoerd, grand architect of apartheid, the shutting of the doors of knowledge: 'What is the use of teaching them mathematics when they are never going to need to use it?' African youth today can enjoy the dignity and opportunities of having been born into a democratic society of equality for all with the right to vote and choose who shall govern. Yet without doubt we do not have a perfect society where full equality exists – embracing social and economic equality and control of the country's wealth, which remains in the hands of a few – and new challenges and frustrations arise. We were always firmly of the view that whilst equality at the racial level was extremely important, there would never be full equality if the economy, the mines, mineral resources, land, financial system and banks remained in the hands of a few domestic and international shareholders – even if some blacks were admitted as junior partners.

Struggle veterans are frequently asked in the light of disappointment: was the sacrifice really worth it? Whilst my answer is decidedly affirmative, I must confess to grave misgivings too – for I believe we should be doing far, far better. We owe it to our moral conscience, to our people and the 'Born Free' generation to carry forward the banner of those who so unstintingly and bravely gave their lives for a better life for all.

There are many bridges to cross. Twenty years into freedom, the more pernicious obstacles cannot any longer be blamed on the apartheid legacy. As citizens we expect the government we have elected to do everything in its power within the available resources to solve the people's problems. In a democracy, when those in power fail in their duties we have every right to peacefully protest to make our concerns and demands known in a disciplined and vigorous way and use our vote to make it count.

Without seeking laurels, for I have my own failings, I took a strong position within the SACP from at least 2005 about the pervasive culture of corruption and greed we were sliding into. Of Zuma, and the Party's clear preference to see him as President of the ANC and country, I was at pains to point out that I had known him for years in the struggle, before many of them, and not only the younger comrades, had heard his name. I found him warm, brave and engaging, but he had many weaknesses. Amongst these was a rural, ethnic conservatism and a sexual impropriety which his rape trial demonstrated. He was, I stressed, '*no working class hero*' as they were making him out to be. I certainly paid the price for being prepared to speak frankly, for I lost my positions on the Party's Central Committee at its July 2007 Port Elizabeth Congress; and on the ANC's NEC at the Polokwane Conference of December that year. At these elective conferences the king-makers have regressed into circulating lists of the preferred candidates they wish to see voted onto the top leadership structures – an anti-democratic practice that was anathema in the old days.

When the ANC's newly elected Polokwane NEC acted to recall Mbeki as

President of the country in September 2008, I was among the twelve ministers and deputies who resigned in solidarity with him and in disgust at what was in fact a *putsch*. That must be the subject of another book but at the time of Polokwane and Mbeki's dismissal I had cause to reflect on words that Bob Hughes, British Labour Party MP and leader of the Anti-Apartheid Movement, had once said to me on a tour of his country's parliament. Pointing out where the ruling Labour Party front-benchers sat, he remarked that opposite was the opposition and behind his Party's leaders 'the enemy' – the Party's own back-benchers, ever waiting the chance to supplant them.[1] Little did I imagine that in our democratic South Africa those who had fought for freedom would have to watch their own backs as the inner-party struggle for positions took hold in the run-up to Polokwane. But then as the saying goes: 'Revolution devours its own children'. That does not have to be the case. Our commitment today should be to make sure such a statement no longer applies to our revolution.

I turn now to the South Africa of the here and now; the country where the 'Born Frees' are growing up, in whose hands the future of our people lies. There have been impressive achievements since the attainment of freedom in 1994 – in building houses, crèches, schools, roads and infrastructure; the delivery of water and provision of electricity to millions; free education and health care; increases in pensions and social grants; financial and banking stability; and a slow but steady increase in economic growth, up to the 2008 international melt-down at any rate. These gains, however, have been offset by a breakdown in service delivery resulting in violent protests by poor and marginalised communities; gross inadequacies and inequities in the education and health sectors; the ferocious rise in unemployment; endemic police brutality and torture; unseemly power struggles within the ruling party that have grown far worse since the ousting of Mbeki in 2008; an alarming tendency to secrecy and authoritarianism in government; the meddling with the judiciary; and threats to the media and freedom of expression. Even Madiba's privacy and dignity are violated for the sake of cheap photo opportunism by the ANC's beaming top echelon.

Of utmost concern is the increasing dysfunction of the state machinery, maladministration and incompetence at national, provincial and municipal levels because of the practice of appointing unqualified cronies into senior posts. Lack of leadership is starkly illustrated in such matters as sections of the police out of control; such scandals as the non-delivery of textbooks to schools; the wasteful expenditure of over 200 million rand on security alone at the President's Nkandla home; the manner in which the Gupta family from India, current favoured transnational corporate pals of our President, are making South Africa look like a banana republic as they lord it over their ANC and government contacts. Add to this the extravagant ministerial expenditure on luxury limousines and hotels and the enormous graft linked to the manipulation of tenders and awarding of state contracts to cronies and cousins. The list is depressing and endless. Crony capitalism and corruption as a way of life stare us in the face!

Most shameful and shocking of all, reflective of how far the ruling party and government have lost their way, came on Bloody Thursday, 16 August 2012, when the police massacred 34 striking miners at Marikana platinum mine owned by the London-based Lonmin company. It was the Sharpeville massacre in 1960 that prompted me to join the ANC. I found Marikana more distressing for this occurred in the democratic South Africa we had sacrificed for and which was meant to bring an end to such barbarity. To compound it all, the President's hand-picked, newly appointed police commissioner, with no previous security record or experience, defended the police, commended their actions and stated: 'This is not the time to point fingers.' Her refrain was instantly echoed by the President and his ministers locked into a culture of denialism and panic-stricken cover-up. Incredibly, the SACP, my Party of over fifty years, did not so much as condemn the police. I wrote an article castigating the police, stating that it was indeed time to point fingers, and asking who had given the command to those squeezing the triggers, and the green light for such punitive action on behalf of the mineowners. Everyone at the top denies responsibility. As with the Gupta family's flagrant use of an air force base to land their guests from India for a wedding junket at Sun City, it is the foot soldiers and state employees who are made the scapegoats by their cowardly superiors.

Our liberation struggle had reached a high point but not its zenith when we overcame apartheid rule. How much further along the revolutionary road could we have proceeded under the conditions we inherited? Our hopes were high that we could make the necessary advance given South Africa's modern industrial economy, range of strategic mineral resources (not only gold and diamonds), the unprecedented upsurge of the masses and a working class and organised trade union movement with a rich tradition of struggle. That optimism overlooked the resources and tenacity of a powerful international corporate capitalist system with the ability to seduce and corrupt on a grand scale. That was the time from 1991–1996 that the battle for the soul of the ANC got underway and was lost to corporate power and influence. That was the fatal turning point. I will call it our Faustian moment when we became entrapped – some today crying out that we 'sold our people down the river'.

Just as Faust, in the classical German tale, became captive of the devil, so we became prisoner of the neo-liberal global economy. Faust's pact with the devil was surrendering his soul in return for the devil's promise of wealth and success.

Faust surrendered his moral integrity and was irrevocably corrupted and descended to hell. We took an IMF loan on the eve of our first democratic election and had already imperceptibly succumbed to the guile and subtle threats of the corporate world which had been chipping away at revolutionary resolve for some years. That loan, with strings attached that precluded a radical economic agenda, was considered a necessary evil at the time, as were the concessions to keep negotiations on track and take delivery of the promised land for our people. We walked into that in the misguided belief that there was no other option. Doubt at that time had come to reign supreme: doubt that there was no other way; doubt that we had to be prudent and cautious since by 1991 our once powerful ally on whom we had relied so much – the Soviet Union, bankrupted by the arms race – buckled, collapsed and disappeared. Perhaps more inexcusable for us than that was losing faith in the ability of our own revolutionary masses to overcome in united action, with correct theory and reliable leadership, all obstacles. With those masses who were so fundamental to destroying apartheid we would arguably have had the means and the resources to press home the huge advantages the revolution was gaining at the time. Moving to control the heights of the economy would have placed us in a position to truly turn things around. Whatever the threats to isolate a radicalising South Africa, the world cannot do without our vast reserves of precious strategic minerals – platinum, palladium, chrome, uranium, titanium, vanadium.

To lose nerve, go belly-up, was neither necessary nor inevitable. The leadership needed to remain determined, disciplined, united and free of the taint of corruption – and above all with the strong revolutionary will that had brought us so far. Instead we chickened out. We needed to assiduously avoid embracing the ostentatious trappings and luxuries of personal power. Above all it required that the ANC did not stray from its noble principles and objectives and especially from its commitment of serving the people. This would have given it the hegemony it required not only over the entrenched capitalist class that ruled the economic roost but over emergent elitists, many of whom would seek wealth through black economic empowerment (BEE), corrupt practices and selling political influence – a comprador rentier class greedy for personal wealth at all costs: comprador because they would be the lackeys of corporate business; rentier because they create no value but live off shady commissions, bribes and payouts akin to receiving rental for doing nothing.

Kwame Nkrumah, in his quest for Ghana's independence, stated that first came the 'political kingdom' (i.e. the right to rule) and then the 'economic kingdom' (economic control and development). The ANC Alliance had always criticised the disconnection. Political without economic independence would see the political power weakened in its ability to serve people's needs.

An untrammelled colonial-capitalist system of production and social relations with its comprador lackeys would inevitably gain the upper hand. The way we had achieved political power in South Africa with compromises regarding the sanctity of private property – particularly of the heights of industry and finance, mining and energy resources, banking and land ownership – and postponing key economic goals of the Freedom Charter such as nationalisation, held these inherent threats and dangers – and inevitably led to our Faustian moment – that devil's pact with corporate capitalism. The need to break the back of apartheid rule, however, presented by the possibility of negotiations, rather than a supposed bloody insurrectionary path and civil war, was an option too good to be ignored. At that point in time, however, the masses of our people, led by the working class, were disciplined and powerful, the balance of power was with the ANC, conditions were favourable for more radical change at the negotiating table than we ultimately accepted. It is by no means certain that the old order, apart from isolated rightist extremists, had the will or capability to resort to bloody repression of the nightmare scenario envisaged by Mandela's leadership if we had held our nerve and stood up to the corporate blackmail. My belief is that we could have pressed forward without making the concessions we did. That with the masses, at that time, we could have neutralised the counter-revolution. Attempts within the ANC to voice such views were imperiously put down by Mandela, who firmly believed the opposite and by then was used to getting his way. In this he was markedly different from Oliver Tambo, his predecessor, who had always allowed full and open debate.

History will judge whether we lost a golden opportunity to press on then rather than make the concessions we did regarding economic control. It has become a debatable issue whether Mandela and his economic advisers buckled under pressure from the IMF and corporate business to follow a 'prudent' economic course. This implied not embarking on what they would have termed radical socialist measures in an attempt to robustly address the poverty of our people.[2] I do not want to be self-serving here. I was as guilty as others in focusing on my own responsibilities and government portfolios and leaving the economic issues to the ANC experts. That was a dire error and I believe we are paying for such a lapse at huge cost. Too often both the revolutionary soldier and political activist leave economic affairs to the specialists. My greatest mistake is having neglected economic study. Would-be revolutionaries need to wake-up every morning and exclaim: 'It's the economy, stupid! Understand it.'

Palestinian writer Rashid Khalidi sums this up in his critique of how the Palestinian Authority has become co-opted and emasculated by the hopelessly flawed Oslo negotiating process and leverage of Western economic preferences, and writes: 'Embracing neo-liberalism results in the creation of a constituency for normality and risk aversion which puts brakes on the struggle for national independence and social emancipation.' Most of us never quite knew what was happening with the ANC's top-level economic discussions, which eminent Stellenbosch professor and analyst Sampie Terreblanche reveals in his sensational critique, a book aptly entitled *Lost in Transformation*. He was party to intimate talks between the economic gurus of the ANC and South African and big business interests from the late 1980s which developed into a far more intimate discourse outside the Transitional Executive Council's operations where the politicians, including myself on the military sub-committee, were hammering out the 1994 democratic dispensation.[3]

According to Sampie Terreblanche's thesis, by late 1993 big business strategies and manipulation, which had two years previously started at financial and mining mogul Harry Oppenheimer's Johannesburg residence, were crystallising in secret late-night discussions at the Development Bank of South Africa. Present were South Africa's mineral and energy leaders and in the wings the bosses of American and British companies with a presence in South Africa. Their protagonists were young ANC economists schooled in Western economics. The latter were certainly reporting to Mandela and were either outwitted or gradually frightened into submission by hints pertaining to the dire consequences for South Africa's economy should an ANC government prevail with what were considered ruinous, unworkable and flawed Soviet-era forms of economic development. The aim of corporate big business was to circumscribe the ANC's future economic policies. The objective on the ANC side was to open the path to the political kingdom.

All means to effectively eradicate poverty, which was Mandela's and the ANC's sworn promise to the 'poorest of the poor', was lost in the process. Nationalisation of the mines and heights of the economy as envisaged by the Freedom Charter was of course first to be consigned to history. The vast apartheid-era debt, which should have been cancelled, was an undertaking that an incoming ANC government was bullied into agreeing to accept responsibility to pay off. The idea of imposing a wealth-tax on the super-rich so as to help pay for developmental projects was set aside. The exoneration of the domestic and international corporates of apartheid-era enrichment without having to make financial reparations was a generous ANC concession. Extremely tight budgetary obligations were instituted which would tie the hands of any future government's redistribution plans; obligations to implement a free-trade policy and abolish all forms of tariff protection in keeping with neo-liberal free trade fundamentals were accepted (which greatly weakened our economy and brought de-industrialisation in its wake). Allowing big corporations the privilege of shifting their main listings abroad was yet another nail in the coffin of South

Africa's desired capital accumulation. The consequent massive outflow of long-term capital followed. All these and more constituted the deal as unpacked by Sampie Terreblanche's diligent research. In his opinion these constituted 'treacherous decisions that are going to haunt South Africa for generations to come.' In his view: 'As long as the white corporate sector remains untouched for the apartheid crimes they committed ... the South African social problems – of poverty, unemployment and inequality – will remain unresolved and will become even more severe.'[4]

Agreement at the level of secret negotiating and endorsement in very broad terms later by an ANC-SACP leadership eager to assume political office (myself no less than others) sealed our Faustian moment. Those late-night deliberations were never revealed to the ANC's collective leadership at NEC level nor to the SACP for that matter. Joe Slovo, SACP chairman and leading theoretician, engrossed with the 'sunset clause' golden-handshake pension pay-off for the racist old-guard, knew nothing to my knowledge of the night-time shenanigans and certainly did not raise any alarm bells. We readily accepted that devil's pact and are damned in the process. It has bequeathed to our country an economy so tied in to the neo-liberal global formula and market fundamentalism that there is very little room to alleviate the dire plight of the masses of our people. Little wonder that their patience is running out; that their anguished protests increase as they wrestle with deteriorating conditions of life; that those in power have no way of finding adequate solutions. Indeed the scraps that are left go to the emergent black political and business elite. There should be no surprise that corruption has taken root as the greedy and ambitious fight like dogs over a bone.

To be sure the SACP, following the deaths of Chris Hani and Joe Slovo, provided a critique of the government's economic growth path (Growth, Employment and Reconstruction strategy, adopted by the Mandela Administration in 1996), which the Party referred to as the 'Class of 1996'. This was aimed primarily at attacking Mbeki, seen to be the author of Gear. The Party later placed its wholehearted, uncritical support behind Zuma, and lapsed into effective silence once he elevated many members to posts as ministers and deputy ministers in his government. They serve loyally, as did the far lesser number of SACP members in the Mandela–Mbeki cabinets; however, their once outspoken critique of the Gear economic trajectory, which is still in place, is barely audible.

What has happened in once-revolutionary Angola carries dire warnings. Today that oil-rich country is plagued by corruption, its MPLA leaders basking in luxury with the masses living beyond the margins of poverty. The daughter of President Dos Santos is the wealthiest woman in Africa. The watchword of the revolution had been in the words of Angola's outstanding leader, Agostinho Neto, 'solving the people's problems'. Neto's closest comrade-in-arms, Lucio Lara, who unlike Neto lived to see the demise of that once-revolutionary state, explained:

> *I don't have illusions about many things anymore. In the Angolan struggle perhaps we didn't have philosophers or sociologists, but we had those words of Neto's: 'The most important thing is to solve the people's problems.' Once in the Council of Ministers I heard someone say that we should stop using this phrase. I thought maybe he was right because no one spoke against him. In my opinion that was when the Party began to collapse. The leaders felt they had the right to be rich. That was the beginning of the destruction of our life.*[5]

I elaborated on this in an article on corruption within the ANC entitled 'Personal Wealth or Real People's Power'.[6]

We live in a world where one per cent of the population has amassed 40 per cent of all wealth. A fraction of that one per cent own the transnational corporations that control the global economy and finance system; run and overthrow governments; make colossal profits from conflict and aggressive wars; own the mainstream media and control our lives. Two-thirds of the world's people live in poverty. Sampie Terreblanche provides the following insight into the relationship between government power and corporate power in the unequal distribution of domestic income in the United States:

> *In 1928 the richest 1 per cent received 23,5 per cent of total income. Roosevelt's New Deal policy and the social democratic approach in the post-war world reduced the share of the richest 1 per cent to 9 per cent in 1976. After Reagan's neo-liberal counter-revolution on behalf of the corporate sector, the share of the richest 1 per cent increased again, to almost 24 per cent in 2008. From 1976 until 2008, the share of the poorest 50 per cent in the US declined from 17 per cent to 12 per cent.*[7]

Regarding the distribution of income in South Africa in 2008, the top 20 per cent or 10 million received 74.7 per cent of total income, while the poorest 50 per cent (or 25 million individuals of which 23.7 million were Africans) received only 7.8 per cent of total income. Whilst 83 per cent of the whites (3.7 million) were among the top 20 per cent of income receivers in 2008, only 11 per cent of Africans (4.4 million) were in that top category – beneficiaries of BEE measures.

The fact that the Gini coefficient (an international formula expressing income variables) increased from 0.66 in 1992 to 0.70 in 2008 indicates that the gulf between rich and poor in South Africa is widening and the country had reached the top position in the world. Income has become much more unequally distributed since the end of apartheid.[8] This contradiction between extreme wealth and abject poverty is an irreconcilable contradiction that cannot last forever – whether globally or in South Africa – without serious repercussions. The statistics conceal unmitigated human suffering and helplessness for the 'poorest of the poor' – fifty per cent of our South African population. Little wonder that the country has seen such an enormous rise in civil protest and discontent. This is a ticking time-bomb. Our future cannot lie with solutions imposed by the corporate world.

Lest it be said that I raise doubts now with the taste of sour grapes in my mouth, I can only assert that I am not motivated by personal pique but by concern for where our country is going and refer to the final words of the 1993 edition of this book. After a hospital visit to a woman wounded in the Bisho massacre I found strength in her bravery:

> *I realised that it was me, not her, who needed reassuring. 'Leaders come and go, but the masses are always there,' J.B. Marks [SACP and ANC leader] used to tell us. There will be mistakes and setbacks, and some of us will not survive to see freedom. Those who hold the reins of power, regardless of their slogans and their political colours, must understand that unless they serve the interests of the people, they will never succeed.[9]*

In today's South Africa I have no hesitation in identifying the type of leaders produced by the increasingly bitter struggle for a better life. They are products of the masses, and follow in the footsteps of the courageous activists who sacrificed to overthrow the apartheid regime – those like Andries Tatane, community leader in Ficksburg who was savagely attacked and murdered by police in July 2011; and Mgcineni Noki, the man in the green blanket, who led the Marikana miners' strike for better conditions and pay and along with 33 others, was shot to death by the police acting on behalf of the mine bosses on Bloody Thursday, 16 August 2012.

The 2004 edition of this book ended with the death in 2003 of one of our most outstanding leaders, a man of unimpeachable integrity, Walter Sisulu. Speaking at a memorial meeting I said his life was about bringing people out of the cold and into the light, and helping them to stand upright. I added the optimistic words: 'that was exactly what the ANC government, was achieving. South Africa's progression radiated as a beacon of hope to the world.'[10] For this

Jacana addition I have added the words: 'Writing now, almost ten years since I wrote the above paragraph the gloss has worn off and South Africa, in the eyes of many, has lost its way. Now as we approach twenty years of freedom and democracy in 2014 the challenge for those who govern is to serve the people and not themselves – and that is how we must ultimately be judged. For if we fail to focus all our strength on solving the people's problems we will continue to fall prey to corruption, avarice and delusional theories to explain all our mishaps instead of facing up to reality and there will be an inevitable descent into darkness and decay.' I believe it is a revolutionary duty to maintain hope and optimism. There is that quip about the pessimist regarding a glass as half-empty whilst the optimist says it is half-full. Well, perhaps as a country we are presently hovering between the light and the dark.

A descent into darkness must be curtailed. I do not believe the ANC Alliance is beyond the pale. There are countless good people within the ranks. A revitalisation and renewal from top to bottom is urgently required. The ANC's soul needs to be restored; its traditional values and culture of service and sacrifice needs to be reinstated. The ANC house must be put in order in the interests of the whole country. In some versions of the Faustian tale the chief protagonist manages to escape eternal damnation. What is required is a reversal of the pact with the devil – which requires a Revolution within the Revolution.

At present the impoverished masses do not see any other hope on the horizon than through the ruling party, although the ANC's ability to hold those allegiances is deteriorating. For the masses the effective parliamentary opposition reflects big business interests of various stripes, and whilst the country needs a strong parliamentary opposition to keep the ANC on its toes, the majority of voters want socialist policies, not measures inclined to serve big business interests, privatisation and neo-liberal economics. This does not mean it is only up to the ANC, SACP and Cosatu to rescue the country from crises. There are countless patriots and comrades in existing and emerging organised formations vital to the process. Civil society is an essential force for defending and developing democracy, as has been demonstrated by the Treatment Action Campaign on Aids, the Right2Know protests against the Protection of Information Bill (so-called Secrecy Bill), Cosatu's resistance to e-tolling, the uprising of Western Cape farmworkers along with that of the powerful mineworkers' strikes for a living wage, and the consistent demands by striking workers and angry communities throughout the land, which show how pressure from the streets – with good leadership and discipline – can achieve victories. Above all, these manifestations signal the urgent need for fundamental change. Then there are the legal avenues and institutions such as the Public Protector's office and Human Rights Commission, and the ultimate appeal to the Constitutional Court to test, expose and challenge injustice and infringement of rights. Organised, carefully thought-out strategies and tactics at trade union, civic, community, faith-based, gender, student, youth, cultural, professional and grassroots level – non-violent, dignified, disciplined, militant action – signpost what needs to be done and the way ahead. These are the creative methods in the current context where space and freedom to express one's views, won through decades of struggle, are available and need to be developed. All who love our country and our people can contribute in different ways. Above all we must ensure that the economy is placed under strategic public control and made to work for the many, not the few. We look to the workers and the 'Born Frees' as the future torchbearers.

PS: What was an infinitely greater blow to me personally than losing political positions and becoming marginalised, was the sudden death of my beloved wife Eleanor, fellow comrade and companion of forty-eight years. This agonising blow occurred at the end of 2009 – when we were just beginning to enjoy a new chapter of our lives. She was a wonderful wife and mother who actively participated in the struggle and I can claim, for the first time here, that she was the first female operative of MK to participate in actual operations. I wrote an award-winning book in tribute to her entitled *The Unlikely Secret Agent* which Jacana published in 2010. Life goes on and I was fortunate to have found companionship with Amina Frense, the journalist who had introduced me to the media at the Mike's Kitchen meeting in 1990 when I was on the run from the police. I had encountered her on a Right2Know protest march in 2011 against the government's draconian legislation aimed at curbing information. We married a year later.

26 May 2013

Southern Africa, featuring key locations in the book

WANTED: ARMED AND DANGEROUS

November 1990

'THE POLICE ARE APPEALING TO members of the public for assistance in locating Mr Ronald Kasrils and three other members of the African National Congress and South African Communist Party.' I had just tuned in to the South African TV news to be confronted by a picture of myself. 'The four are wanted in connection with Operation Vula, the plot to overthrow the government by force. They are also being sought for the alleged illegal importation of arms, ammunition and explosives.' After giving details of the names, ages and aliases of all four fugitives, and indicating that an unspecified reward was offered for our capture, the announcer concluded with a police warning: 'Kasrils and his associates are armed and extremely dangerous.'

If I was armed, it was only for self-protection. If I was considered dangerous, then it was by a government that had practised apartheid for over 40 years. I considered that an honour. It was November 1990. Not for the first time in my life, 'wanted' posters had been posted by the South African security police for my capture.

To survive the difficult – even dangerous – transition process through which the country was going, I would have to exercise all the skill I had acquired in thirty years of clandestine activity. The ANC and SACP had been unbanned in February 1990. Most of our leadership were functioning legally, beginning the delicate negotiation process with the then Government. I was in no man's land, caught up in a hinge of history, between two distinct eras.

LOOKING OVER MY SHOULDER

Early 1990
Return to South Africa

AT THE END OF 1989, I BOARDED AN international flight, at a busy Mediterranean airport – destination Johannesburg. After 27 years in exile, over half my life, I was homeward-bound.

I was just over 50 but appeared older. Not that the intervening years had been unkind, it was my disguise that aged me. I looked like a businessman, possibly Greek or Italian, with my hair dyed black, a well-cut suit and the regulation briefcase. With the advancing years I had put on weight, almost reaching the 200 pounds of a childhood ambition but, alas, far short of the six-foot height. My hair had thinned on top, and I had accentuated the balding process by shaving the hairline well back. I had grown a moustache and trimmed my distinctive eyebrows.

'You must slow down your movements once you've changed identities,' had been Eleanor's parting advice, when I left in my normal persona from London's Heathrow airport on the first leg of my trip. 'You've got to become a 60-year-old at the next stop – remember.'

My wife, Eleanor, had been living in London with our two sons, while I had been working for the ANC from its Lusaka headquarters. Experienced in clandestine activity herself, she well knew the risks I was about to take. We embraced briefly, not wanting to draw attention to ourselves in public. We were not sure when we would next meet, and had tried to hide the anxiety from each other.

My journey had its origins several months earlier in the small Lusaka office of Oliver Tambo, then President of the ANC.

The headquarters of the organisation were located in a cramped, single-storey building in the downtown area of the Zambian capital. Tambo sat at a large desk neatly stacked with papers and files. His office was filled with photographs, certificates and souvenirs presented to him on his world trips spanning three decades.

Tambo was making alterations to a document. His concentration was impressive whether he was writing or listening. His absorption gave me the chance to glance at his familiar features, his grey sidewhiskers and distinctive moustache. His cheeks were identically scored by several vertical lines, an Mpondo clan tradition, cut into the skin at infancy and said to bestow strength on the individual. He was an ascetic person living a frugal lifestyle, and the ethnic shirt he was wearing was his sole compromise with anything elaborate.

He looked up and gave me a warm, almost fatherly greeting. We shook hands and exchanged pleasantries. I thought he had called me to get a progress report on a document I was preparing for him. I began giving him an update.

'No, no, it's not about that,' he said in a quiet voice. His eyes moved restlessly, a characteristic mannerism when he had something urgent on his mind and was searching for the right words. After a long pause, he waved his finger around the room, intimating, as he always did if the conversation was going to be sensitive, that we might be bugged.

He wrote on a clean sheet of paper: 'Operation Vula', and looked up at me. He wrote: 'Underground leadership group at HOME.' He underlined 'HOME' several times. (*Vula* means 'open' in Zulu and is short for *Vulindlela*, or 'open the road', which was the full name of the project.)

Tapping at the piece of paper he continued aloud: 'There's a group in place, doing good work. The messages we receive from ...' and he wrote 'Mandela' (who was still in prison), 'reach us through their communication lines.' He looked up: 'They're asking for you.'

I had been waiting for this moment. For years we had been striving to strengthen our underground structures and develop the armed struggle against a powerful, efficient adversary. We had often debated that what we lacked was a senior leadership inside the country, capable of taking decisions on the spot and linking up with the emergent mass movement. Although the possibility of negotiating with the Pretoria government was arising, expectations of progress were generally uncertain and the ANC remained banned. With popular protest soaring, most in our ranks argued that underground leadership was more necessary than ever.

Tambo wanted to give me time to think things over. But I insisted I was ready. I had to agree, however, to wind up my current projects first. Tambo was delighted with my response and embraced me warmly. It was an unforgettable moment.

Not long thereafter he had suffered a severe stroke after a gruelling tour of several African states. He had been briefing governments on possible negotiations and the preconditions the Pretoria regime would have to meet.

From Heathrow I had taken a flight to Europe, met up with friends at a safe venue and with their assistance undergone a physical transformation. From being a South African refugee with a stateless United Nations document issued by the British Home Office, I had become a respectable passport-holder from an EC country.

To this day, those who assisted me prefer to remain anonymous. They watched from the shadows as I made my way through passport control.

At last the plane took off. It was a non-stop flight. We were due to land at Johannesburg's Jan Smuts airport early the next morning. I settled back in my seat, high above the African continent, comforted by the hum of the aeroplane and the chit-chat of the passengers. I managed to have a reasonable night's rest and set aside two miniature bottles of whisky, courtesy of a solicitous stewardess, for consumption the next morning. I have no pretensions to having nerves of steel and, without overdoing it, had long discovered that 100 gms of alcohol settled me nicely in special circumstances. My impending arrival at Jan Smuts airport was definitely one of those circumstances.

'*Sto gramme vodka*' (100 gms vodka) was the Russian prescription, taken by their troops half an hour before battle. Some joked this was the secret of their victory over Hitler. My Russian friends were always very precise about this: it had to be 100 gms and it had to be taken exactly half an hour beforehand.

Johannesburg and the dun-coloured mine dumps of the Witwatersrand (the mining area to the east and west of Johannesburg) looked unreal as they rose from the flat highveld landscape and we descended out of a clear sky. The problem was that I had miscalculated the time of arrival. Instead of imbibing in a civilised way, strictly half an hour before arrival, I had to gulp down the Scotch at the last moment.

As we disembarked I felt both tense and elated, as though I was about to appear on stage before an audience. I kept thinking of my opening lines for the passport official. I remembered to slow down my movements, as Eleanor had instructed and, with considerable relief, had my passport stamped, no questions asked.

'*Welkom in Seth Efrika*,' said the woman official, smiling sweetly beneath an elaborate hair-do.

I picked up my baggage, placed it on a trolley and moved through customs. A pimply-faced customs official stopped me. He was so young I thought it must have been his first day on the job. He motioned to my briefcase and asked what was inside. 'Just some papers and magazines.'

He looked carefully through the contents, a mixture of business and tourist literature. The question uppermost in my mind was whether this was a routine check, or whether a rigorous search was about to follow. If they were simply having a sniff at me, I reasoned, surely they would not use such an inexperienced kid? It was at this moment, my chest tightening while I sought to appear nonchalant, that I wished I had jumped the border fence instead. In the end, satisfied that I was not smuggling in banned material – I guessed he had probably hoped to uncover a copy of *Playboy* magazine – I was allowed to continue on my way.

I was soon in a taxi, aglow with excitement but glancing through the rear window for any signs of a tail. The city skyline, coming in from the airport along a busy motorway system, suited my optimistic mood. In the distance was the phalanx of glass and concrete towers of downtown Johannesburg, framed by stony ridges and *koppies* (hillocks) and the mine dumps like sand dunes in the sunlight. With a sense of triumph, I picked out the Yeoville *koppie* where I played as a child. The speed of the traffic, the high performance cars, the dizzy interchanges, the gigantic power lines and impressive buildings that flashed past, indicated the development that had taken place. I looked from the mine dumps to the skyscrapers and thought how no other city in the world was so visibly tied to its economic roots.

At my out-of-town hotel I found a public telephone. I dialled a London number and reported my safe arrival on an answering machine. A call from London would be made to my undercover contacts in Johannesburg. This would trigger a rendezvous for the next day. In the meantime, I needed to check for surveillance to be as sure as possible that I was not being followed. The best way of doing that was to go for a long walk. I would kill two birds with one stone and look round Yeoville, my childhood stomping ground, which I was longing to see again.

After a rest and a change into casual clothes, I took a taxi to Yeoville. Away from the motorway system, many of the less fashionable parts of Johannesburg were substantially unaltered. The superstructure in Yeoville's narrow main road, Rockey Street, was still much the same. The tramlines were gone, but not the municipal swimming baths. The nearby sports ground had been converted into a park, part of the surrounding wall still in place. For years that wall had borne the slogan: 'An attack on communism is an attack on you.'

I alighted at the park and paid the taxi. The art of counter-surveillance is never to look over your shoulder. You have to provide yourself with situations which naturally allow you to look around. Like stopping someone and enquiring 'Could you tell me the way to Rockey Street?'

I had a good view of the departing taxi as we half-turned to face one another. The young boy I had stopped readily replied: 'It's jist along thet way, sir. It's the striet with all the small shorps. O-kay hey?' It was the once familiar accent, an uncultured nasal whine, music to my ears. He could have been any one of my childhood pals. He could have been me.

I settled down on a bench to become accustomed to the people in the park. I needed to pay special attention to those who arrived after me. I found myself re-living the football games we had played when I was centre forward for Yeoville Boys' soccer team. Then there were the races I had run on the track that once formed the perimeter of this very ground. In those days the only black people to be seen in Yeoville, or any white suburb, were domestic workers. There were plenty of black people about now, some with children, enjoying the sunshine, sitting on benches which, in the not so distant past, had been reserved for whites.

A frumpy lady with shopping bags, in need of a rest, sat down beside me, sighing heavily. As one white to another, she complained: 'My aching feet, thank heffens, you know you cawn't always git a seat these days with all the *swartzes* [blacks] about.'

I made the mistake of catching her eye, which encouraged her. The words came out in a rush: 'And the kewz in the soopamawket? So many *swartzes*. And the gerl at the chack-out? Vot a cheeky *shiksa* [black woman]. The mouthful she gayf me about my chaynch? From ver did they learn to git so obshtreperis?'

Her appearance on the scene was not unwelcome. If I was under surveillance, it could draw out whoever was tailing me. But nobody sauntered by trying to eavesdrop. After putting up with her grievances a while longer I took my leave. But I could not resist a bit of my father's homespun philosophy. 'Well, after all, madam, what can we do? We're on this planet together, so live and let live.'

Around the corner, the orthodox shul where I had my barmitzvah, once an unrivalled centre of Jewish life, appeared deserted. I walked away from the shopping area into the quieter suburban streets where any car or pedestrian following in my tracks would be easier to spot. I noticed that many fringe establishments had proliferated, catering for ultra-orthodox sects.

Most of these had been converted from ordinary houses. I walked into one of them. A young man in a dark coat and hat, with beard and long sideburns, *payas* in Yiddish, was seated at a desk. I pretended to be looking for the previous owner of the house. After a pleasant conversation in which he asked whether I was *baal te shuvah* – a repentant Jew wanting to return to the fold – and proselytised about 'the need to be sure of one's identity in these troubled times', I bade him *shalom* and left.

The street was quiet. My visit to the house would certainly have drawn anyone watching me. I could have expected a loiterer across the road, or another lurking at the corner. I was particularly on the lookout for young men of any race, physically fit and casually dressed. Men, or perhaps young women, who would avoid eye contact and pretend to be engaged in some innocuous activity like tinkering with a car or window shopping. A car full of devout Jews drove by. Not the type to be conducting surveillance on behalf of the South African security police.

I made my way back to Rockey Street. Window shopping would provide other possibilities to uncover a tail. Shop mirrors and plate glass windows would obviate any need to glance over my shoulder.

Once unfashionable, the neighbourhood had become cosmopolitan with a shabby trendiness. The prim stores catering for lower middle-class custom had largely vanished, to be replaced by a variety of mouldy craft shops, music dens, coffee bars, clubs and food outlets. Black and white couples, dressed in hippy style, ambled by as though apartheid had never existed. Yeoville might look seedy, but it was a pacesetter with regard to the collapsing race barriers.

On the corner of Rockey and Raymond streets, a stone's throw from where I grew up, a motley crew hung about, looking like they dealt in dope. Nearby, street urchins sniffed glue. Just the kind of place that invited police scrutiny. I decided I had seen enough of Rockey Street.

There in Raymond Street was Albyn Court, the building where I had lived for the first 16 years of my life. Just two storeys high, but a full block in width, it was almost palatial in comparison to the jerry-built flats around it. Admiring the clean, functional lines of its 1930s design – certainly not regarded as special by the tenants of my time – I was flooded with memories of all who had lived there.

I visualised my mother and father in our first-floor apartment. Like all the other adults in the building, they were the offspring of Jewish immigrants who had arrived in South Africa at the turn of the century. My grandparents had come from Lithuania and Latvia fleeing from the Czarist pogroms. The family name, it was claimed, stemmed from a Jewish *shtetl* (settlement) in Lithuania called Kasrilevka, celebrated in the stories of Shalom Aleichem. My paternal grandfather, Nathan, was an early prospector on the Kimberley diamond fields, and brought his wife, Sarah (née Sachs), out to South Africa in 1900, soon after my father's birth. My grandfather set up a jewellery business and later was the first owner of Albyn Court. By the time he died in 1938 – the year of my birth – he had lost his money on the stock market. Family recollections have revealed that Nathan Kasrils was an avowed anti-imperialist who had a loathing for Churchill and Cecil John Rhodes. An elderly cousin of mine citing documentary evidence said that he served the Boers as a sharp-shooter and acted for them as a spy.

My father, whose name was Isadore – Issy for short – was a reserved, trimly-built man. Like most of the men in the building, he worked as a commercial traveller for a factory. He dressed conservatively in a suit and tie and always wore a wide-brimmed hat, the conventional style of the times. He drove a 1947 Plymouth and I sometimes accompanied him 'on the road' during school holidays. I saw how hard he worked, driving along dusty township roads, visiting the largely Indian or Chinese shopkeepers who were the factory's main customers. It was then that I saw the crowded shacks and squalid conditions in which black people lived. My father had a good relationship with his customers and the polite greetings he exchanged with them made me proud of him. In common with most of his friends he was a chain smoker, and his incessant coughing at the wheel of the car alarmed me. He died in 1963, shortly after I left the country.

Years later, in exile, I met the secretary of the Commercial Travellers' Union, Eli Weinberg. He had known my father and considered him a 'socialist'. This surprised me, as my father had not appeared to be interested in politics. Eli explained that the majority of the Union's members were highly individualistic Jews with an anarchistic temperament, who blew hot and cold and were difficult to handle. I recollected the tenants of Albyn Court – poker-playing, horse-racing fanatics. 'Your father was down to earth and understood the right course to follow in disputes with employers,' he said.

My maternal grandparents, Abraham and Clara Cohen, lived in a semi-detached house just around the corner from Albyn Court. They had owned a Hillbrow delicatessen when my mother was a child.

My mother, Rene, was a vivacious brunette, with a dazzling smile and fine figure. In contrast to my father, she was sociable and extroverted. They got on well together as long as she kept the rummy or canasta parties within limits. When my father met her she was doing secretarial work. Later, after the birth of my sister, Hilary, she took on part-time jobs in order to make ends meet. With the death of my grandmother, Clara, grandfather Abe came to stay with us. He became a commercial traveller too, and in the absence of his wife, who had been a restraining force, became the most popular gambler in Yeoville.

Although I was an energetic and somewhat unruly youngster, absorbed in sports and neighbourhood games, the attitude whites displayed to blacks did not pass me by. It was wartime and I constantly questioned my mother about the fate of the Jews in Europe. In many ways she was a simple, even naive, woman. But when I drew parallels between Jews in Europe under the Nazis and the way black people were being treated in our country, I found she was prepared to agree. This honest response to her son's questions left its mark.

Surveying the scene, I remembered the afternoon when I had been kicking a ball around in the street with my friends. One of the boys had embarrassed me by passing a foul remark about a black man who had been hit by the ball while walking by. 'Don't swear at me and don't call me "boy",' was the man's reply. 'In 20 years' time things are going to be very different in this country.' It was now 40 years later. The prediction, if delayed, was at last coming true.

Most of my generation of Yeovillites – or Yeoville boykies as we were called – went into the professions or business and had long moved on to the prosperous northern suburbs. Quite a few, like Ali Bacher, the Springbok cricketer, had become famous sportsmen. A large percentage, fearful of the country's future, had joined the brain-drain and emigrated. I wondered if any of those who remained would be prepared to help me if I came knocking on their door.

I had become so engrossed in the past that it was only when I noticed one of the present residents of Albyn Court peering at me from a second-floor window – where Jock Silver the bookie had lived – that I woke from my reverie. I had all but forgotten the other purpose of my stroll.

PART I

BEGINNING
1938–63

ONE

SHARPEVILLE MASSACRE

Johannesburg
21 March 1960

My PRIMARY SCHOOLING AT YEOVILLE Boys was enjoyable. It was my sporting ability that won me a place at KES – King Edward VII High School – in 1951. Although still exclusively white, this was a different world from the one in which I had grown up. Yeoville Boys was a typical lower-income, concrete and tarmac school. KES aspired to the standards of an English public school. In a leafy setting, the Edwardian-style main building had a clock tower which surveyed numerous playing fields. We wore smart green blazers – a crown insignia on the breast pocket – with grey flannel trousers and, on special occasions, straw boaters.

On the first day of school the small group of Yeoville boykies who had gained admission were sneered at for arriving in long trousers. 'It's obvious you're a bunch of Jews,' we were told by a senior boy. 'Can't you wear short pants until second year?' I found that this element of anti-Semitism was rooted among some of the boarders from the East and West Rand mining towns. They led a miserable life, having to fag for masters and prefects alike, and some of the more ignorant looked for any excuse as an outlet for their frustrations.

Although I did well on the sports fields, especially in athletics, I clashed with teachers and prefects alike. It was not that mine was a conscious rebellion, but I could not contain my contempt for the haughty attitude of those in authority.

My favourite teacher was 'Boetie' van der Riet who taught us Afrikaans and coached us on the rugby field. He was straight, direct and approachable, so that when he whacked us with the cane we did not mind. One day during lessons a senior boy came to Boetie's door. After conversing outside, Boetie returned to tell us that the *kêrel* (youngster) he had been talking to was making a terrible mistake by leaving school prematurely. 'He thinks he can make a living playing golf,' Boetie said, visibly upset. The *kêrel* was Gary Player, world-famous golfer-to-be.

3

The school principal was an angular individual with a high forehead and a bald head, St John B. Nitch. He was referred to by masters and boys alike as the 'Boss'. Perpetually unsmiling, he reminded me, in his black gown, of a medieval monk. As we intoned the Lord's prayer at his assemblies and murmured 'Our Father who art in heaven...' I wished that the Boss too was 'up there'.

Most teachers used the cane to effect discipline, but the Boss was the Lord High Executioner. Recidivists like me were well acquainted with the procedure. He would order you to bend over a chair in his office, while he selected a cane from his cabinet. You heard him swishing it around, testing its suppleness and psyching himself up.

The first time I was a victim – for whistling at a newly employed school secretary – I made the mistake of turning around to see why he was taking so long. I found him bearing down on me in full stride. He could not check himself and I received the blow partly on my legs and hands. 'Will you stay down,' he hissed, while I wrung my hands in pain. When he had finished, you were curtly ordered to 'get out'. It was a matter of honour not to show that you were *bang* (intimidated) – nor to utter a sound or show the pain.

If you held your head high, your classmates would gaze in awe on your return. The caning caused welts and bruising which lasted for weeks. I discovered at an early age that corporal punishment was a negative way of dealing with a problem. In fact, I learnt that by accepting the punishment stoically, the battle was won. Instead of being humiliated, you drew admiration. This created a vicious circle between school authority and myself as I stubbornly sought to show that I would not toe the line.

It was Teddy Gordon, history teacher in my senior school years, who aroused my interest in studies. My class was an assortment of laggards, solely interested in sport. We barely scraped through each year and studied geography instead of Latin. Teddy, bird-like and keen-eyed, had served in the Royal Navy as a young man during the Second World War. He was regarded as the school's liberal. He lectured us on the French Revolution and drew vivid pictures of peasant suffering and aristocratic cruelty. For me, the parallels with apartheid South Africa were clear.

Gesturing out of the window, he asked us to consider what effect the slogans of the Revolution would have on the wealthy residents of nearby Houghton compared to those of the black townships. Probably for the first time in high school I was giving every word my total attention.

During the holidays I was invited with a few friends to stay at the farm of one of our classmates. His father was a wealthy potato king in an area where farmers were later exposed for subjecting farm workers, supplied by the police, to conditions akin to slave labour. Not that we noticed anything amiss. We had a carefree time – swimming, playing tennis and riding horses. But we debated politics late into the night. When I forced my friends to accept that black people were mistreated, they responded that it was impossible to overthrow white rule. I argued passionately – if romantically – that just as the French peasants had risen with pitchforks and scythes, so too would black South Africans.

After writing a test on 'The Causes of the French Revolution', I received the highest mark in the school and had the unaccustomed experience of being asked, by those derisively called the 'Latin swots', what reading I could recommend. Among the swots was Tony Bloom, who became a friend of mine, and later, as Chairman of Premier Milling, one of the saner big-business voices in the country. He was part of the first such group that met Oliver Tambo in Lusaka. Another was Richard Goldstone, who became a judge and later headed the important Goldstone Commission into political violence. A sombre, impassive boy, he refereed a fist fight I had with a school prefect.

I surprised both my teachers and myself by obtaining a reasonable matric pass. So, after many vicissitudes, I left KES on a high note, even managing to part on good terms with the Boss. As I shook hands with him, he appeared to have softened, indicating his pleasure that I had gained a university entrance pass. I suspect, however, that his relief arose from the fact that the war between us was at last over. KES for me had been a battlefield. I came out of it bearing no grudges, fairly self-confident, prepared to stand up to authority, and with my cerebral faculties aroused. But I was so relieved that it was over that I burnt all my notes, except Teddy Gordon's. Those were seized a few years later by the Special Branch.

My father was preoccupied with earning a living, and my mother with my sister's marriage and the young children she was producing. They hoped I would settle down and find a job as they could not afford to send me to university. I first worked as an articled clerk for a firm of attorneys, attending law school at night. I thought the legal profession would orientate me to the plight of black society. But I found the studies boring. Worse still, my clerical duties were centred on glorified debt collecting through the courts.

Most of what I learnt came from the firm's messenger and so-called 'tea boy', July Marishane. He introduced me to clerical procedures in the lower courts – how to register summonses and writs of attachment. One day he was arrested within a block of our office because he had left his 'pass book' behind. The policemen refused to allow him to fetch the identity document, which was in his desk drawer. Fortunately we managed to secure his release after being informed by a client who had witnessed July being bundled into a Black Maria. Otherwise he might have disappeared into the potato fields.

July had worked for our employer from an early age as a gardener, after arriving from the countryside in search of work. He was a tall, gangling person with eyes that never ceased to open wide with wonder when he learnt something new. He had learnt to read and write in his spare time and this decided our employer to take him into the law firm. Whenever there was time, I coached him in his studies. He was hoping to write an examination for a junior school certificate. He did not expect much from life and was appreciative of our boss, whom he described as 'a kind and generous man'. I found in July a humanism I came to see in most black people – which struck me as arising from the daily battles to survive. One day July told me that I was different from other whites. In what way? I enquired.

'They mostly show fridge faces to us blacks. Cold and frosty. They pretend we don't exist.'

Sometimes we would hear singing and chanting from the streets and, looking down from our office window, observe township demonstrators making their way to the City Hall. It was then that I saw the growing attraction of black protest. July would drop whatever he was doing, grab his jacket and run to join in. When he came back, he would give me an animated account of what had happened.

There was often racist violence in the city centre. It was most obvious when the pass raids were in progress. Police in civilian dress would lurk in ambush in the city's alley-ways and pounce on black males, demanding to see their pass books. If, as with July, the pass book could not be produced the individual would be violently bundled into a nearby van. When there were protests, batons would be drawn and black people would be scattered in all directions. I had seen barefoot street kids, begging outside the cinemas on cold winter evenings, dispersed with *sjamboks* (bull-hide whips) by laughing policemen. White people, standing in the queues, would look the other way. Even at international sports fixtures, where black spectators would be herded into the most obscure corner of the ground, the police would charge into them because of their exuberant support for the visiting team. Then the white spectators would join in, hurling empty beer bottles at their black counterparts. On one occasion, while I was still a Yeoville boykie, I had watched impotently as a group of white thugs beat a black man senseless in the town centre, while other whites hurried by. What I saw personally was nothing compared to the stories that sometimes appeared in the more liberal newspapers, revealing deaths in police cells and on the farms. Police brutality in the townships was seldom reported, and as far as most whites were concerned, could have been taking place on another planet.

I soon had my own personal brush with the law. Alongside droves of white teenagers, I was taken into custody following the showing of Bill Haley's *Rock around the Clock*. Caught up in the hysteria of the new musical beat we had poured out of a city cinema into lines of police. I was assaulted for being in the vicinity – easily identified as a rock fan by my blue suede shoes and hair style – and released after a weekend in jail, with a black eye and damaged nose. A charge against me was dropped when I threatened to sue the arresting officer for assault.

I had grown disillusioned with my work, unhappy about issuing summonses for bad debts on people who could ill afford their hire purchase goods – a sorry collection of black and white householders. Giving up my articled-clerk status meant dropping out of law school. I resigned from my job after two years, having become attracted to less conventional pursuits which suited my budding creative aspirations, and a search for identification across the colour line.

A friendship with an art student had drawn me into a bohemian circle based in the café society of Hillbrow, an upbeat cosmopolitan area. By day I had been a lawyer's clerk, at night and on weekends I listened to heated arguments about art, poetry, literature and music, while swigging wine amid clouds of *dagga* (hemp) smoke.

I tried the weed for a time but preferred to keep a clear head. I began writing poetry and prose and was soon meeting some of the creative people from the townships.

Black writers were making an impact through *Drum* magazine and a wealth of artistic talent was bursting onto the stage, notably through the musical *King Kong*. Those were the days of swinging multi-racial parties, called *jolls*, which made the city buzz. If the police raided the premises, all the blacks present grabbed soft drinks because it was illegal to serve them alcohol. There were liaisons across the colour line, which often ended with the unfortunate couples being arrested and charged under an Immorality Act forbidding sex between the races.

I enjoyed a brief relationship with Miriam Makeba, *King Kong*'s lead singer, who posed as a domestic worker so that we could meet secretly in a friend's flat. We had tender moments, overcoming the tensions of illegal love-making, until she soon left the country for stardom abroad.

At the end of 1958, with no job to worry about and some small change in my pocket, I left Johannesburg for Cape Town. There are times in life when romantic interests take priority and this was one such occasion. I was in pursuit of an attractive member of the Hillbrow circle, who had run away from a broken relationship with a talented painter. Her name was Patsy and she had lived with the artist from the age of 15. She was petite and volatile and nine years older than me. I tracked her down to a night club in the Cape Town docks called the *Smugglers' Den*. She was soon showing me the latest dance step from England.

She was staying at a run-down boarding house called *Water's Edge* in Bantry

Bay – years before the developers got busy and turned the area into a millionaire's preserve. It was owned by a drunken Irish couple and overrun by their cats.

She had befriended a fellow resident, a lanky American called Larry Salomons, who wore scruffy sneakers and jeans. He appeared to me to have stepped straight out of Jack Kerouac's beatnik novel *On the Road*.

On many occasions we would drive along the Cape Peninsula until we came to a suitable picnic spot. The scenery is breath-taking: thundering Atlantic surf and a backdrop of rugged mountains. Larry used to love nothing better than to smoke a joint and allow the vast landscape to overwhelm him. 'Greatest damn spot, in the world,' he used to enthuse. He loved South Africa for its 'three Ps'– Pot, Politics and Pussie.

Larry was five years older than me and for a while became my mentor. He had been born in Germany and was sent to live with an aunt in New York shortly before his parents were rounded up. He never saw them again. He was visiting South Africa on a scholarship, researching the growth of the labour movement. He was soon lending me his books about South Africa and giving me insights into American beatnik culture. He was no Marxist, but he was scathing about America's anti-communist phobia and the harm this had done to rational thought. Racist attitudes in South Africa never ceased to amaze him. A student at Cape Town University once told him that he had just run down and killed 'a coon' with his motor car. At first Larry thought he meant a 'racoon'. When he realised the student was nonchalantly referring to a black man, he was thrown into the depths of depression.

Patsy had friends in District Six, the pulsating Coloured ghetto, on the slopes of Devil's Peak next to Table Mountain. We spent many weekends there in the company of Zoot and Ma'am (short for Miriam), a couple who lived in an old cottage in one of the steep, narrow streets. While Ma'am cooked exotic Malay dishes, Zoot would roll his guests *zols* (joints). He bought his *dagga* at the *Seven Steps*, a fabled haunt in the area, where it was referred to as the 'tree of knowledge'. Zoot enjoyed brandy and Coke, so we contributed the liquor.

Zoot had been in Roeland Street Prison for receiving stolen goods. He amazed us with his tales about prison culture and how he smoked more pot inside jail than out. Among his friends were Alf and Isaiah – pronounced Eyezay – who appeared to be going through a course of left-wing political studies. Alf would amuse us by analysing any problem under the sun in a mixture of an Afrikaans patois called *tsotsi-taal* and high-sounding English: '*Nou sê vir my mense* [now tell me folks], what's the cause? What's the effect?' And then he would lean forward in mock sagacity, revealing his missing front teeth, and exclaim: '*En* in whose *blerry* interests anyway?' Like Ma'am, Isaiah neither drank nor smoked, and was a pillar of support to his family. I met up with

Isaiah Stein years later when he too was a political exile in England. His sons, Brian and Mark Stein, played first-division football for Luton Town, and Brian even played for England. Isaiah longed for a District Six that had since been bulldozed into oblivion by apartheid's forced removal policy.

Ma'am, dark and sultry-looking, was a member of the Coloured People's Congress, an ally of the ANC. One afternoon, their house full of the pungent fumes of *dagga*, panic broke out when some political colleagues arrived at the front door. One of these was Sonia Bunting, the first communist I ever set eyes on.

Larry had bought an old Beetle and was moving off to continue his research assignment in Johannesburg. I had the possibility of a job there and persuaded Patsy to return with us.

I began working as a script writer for a film company called Alpha Film Studios. We mainly produced commercials for the cinema, which required an exacting, concentrated skill. I enjoyed the work, and after a year was given the chance to direct some commercials. I was sharing a basement flat in Hillbrow with Larry but often stayed with Patsy, who was still having problems sorting out her life. She lived in a rented room above a jazz club nearby.

Although by my parents' standards, and those of my school friends, my life was decidedly unconventional, I had managed to settle down to a job and lifestyle that suited me. But more important, I believed I was living beyond the narrow and prejudiced confines of white South Africa. I felt that, because I had crossed the colour-bar frontier, I was a free individual.

I had met Robert Resha and Duma Nokwe, two ANC leaders, at a party. Resha had asked me to give an hour of my time a week to the ANC but I never got around to it. March 21st 1960 started off as a quiet day at Alpha. Nothing spectacular was happening. Then Lee Marcus, a senior script writer who worked part-time, came into the department, looking pale and drawn.

'Have you heard about the shootings?' she asked me, with troubled eyes.

'N-o,' I replied, sensing something dreadful.

'I've just heard on my car radio. Dozens of Africans have been shot by the police at Sharpeville...' Before I could ask, 'Where's that?' she added, 'It's a township near Vereeniging.'

'God!' someone interjected, 'those trigger-happy bastards.'

I wandered around Alpha's grounds in a state of anger. I tuned into the BBC for more reliable news. Africans had been demonstrating against the pass laws outside the Sharpeville police station and had been mown down without provocation. The final count was 69 dead and 179 wounded. The victims were men, women and children – all unarmed. Many had been shot in the back as they fled. There was an international outcry.

9

We could hear and see military spotter planes buzzing about the sky, and this added to my fury. The black workers were standing around, talking earnestly among themselves. I went over to commiserate. They told me: 'This is South Africa. *Amapoyisa yi'zinja* [the police are dogs].'

The white studio technicians, English- and Afrikaans-speaking artisans, were also gathered together. It was as though everyone realised a national crisis was imminent. They grinned inanely at me and jeered: '*Moenie worry boetie* [don't worry little brother] you'll be in the trenches with the rest of us. *Ons witous* [us white guys] have to sink or swim together.'

TWO

THE MOVEMENT

Durban and Johannesburg
April 1960–July 1961

IN THE DAYS FOLLOWING THE SHARPEVILLE massacre my mood turned impatient. One intense argument followed another: with family, friends and colleagues. Outside my immediate circle, few whites showed any sensitivity – the general view being: 'we should machine-gun the lot of them.'

The black workers at Alpha kept more to themselves than ever. It was some consolation for my sense of frustration when they showed me ANC leaflets denouncing the shootings and calling for nationwide protests and pass burnings. This made me feel part of some cause aimed at redressing the injustice. But I felt the impotence of the spectator when I saw the press photographs of Chief Luthuli burning his pass book before being arrested along with thousands of others. The government declared a state of emergency and banned the ANC and rival Pan Africanist Congress (PAC). Daily, I watched British-made Saracen armoured cars racing through the streets to the nearby Alexandra township, where Alpha's black workers lived.

What could be done? I was dismayed to discover that there were no answers forthcoming from my circle. Unfortunately, Larry Salomons had returned to the USA earlier in the year. The one change was that the drinking got heavier. I accused them of 'fiddling while Sharpeville and Alex burnt'. I realised I had been fooling myself. It was not possible to live life as a free and independent agent when atrocities like Sharpeville could occur at any time. I felt I had been basking in self-indulgent luxury. I cursed myself for not having responded to Robert Resha's request to give the ANC some of my spare time. I had no way of contacting him and supposed that he and Duma Nokwe, like Luthuli, had been rounded up.

It was Easter and I decided to claim holiday leave from work. I resolved to go to Durban, where I had a relative who had been an active communist. I needed guidance from someone who must know what could be done. Patsy wanted to accompany me and we hitched a lift down to the sub-tropical Natal coast. We stayed with an artist friend called Wendy who lived in a studio flat on the Berea heights overlooking the harbour.

She was in a state of excitement because the Royal Ballet Company was on tour from England. The very night of our arrival, Patsy and I attended a party for the ballet dancers at a leading socialite's home. Champagne flowed, and we were swept into a world where Sharpeville did not intrude.

The following day, as we nursed our hangovers, Wendy told me that one of her neighbours was 'a communist like you'. I jumped at the chance of an introduction, which was arranged for that night. In the meantime, events were speeding up. That very morning thousands of people had begun marching into the city from Cato Manor – a sprawling shanty-town behind the Berea. Their aim was to reach the city prison and demand the release of their leaders. Like a river, they split up into various streams to avoid the police. A group of marchers were blocked by a hastily erected police barricade right on our doorstep.

There were people of both sexes and all ages, poorly dressed and down at heel, unarmed save for a pitiful assortment of sticks carried by some of the men. Blocking their paths were lines of police with sten-guns pointed straight at them. There was silence from the people. They remained calm and dignified.

White suburbanites sheltered indoors, peering nervously from behind barred windows. A couple of white men, pistols in their belts, strutted out into the street and took up positions behind the police lines. A young black man with a beard, dressed in a ragged coat, parleyed with a police commander who towered over him. The police line gave the appearance of nonchalance but you could make out the nervous twitching of trigger-fingers. I debated whether to join the township people. Before I could decide, the crowd turned about and marched peacefully back to Cato Manor.

I learnt later that a white couple, Maggie and Harold Strachan, had done what I had only thought of doing. The main group of marchers had managed to reach the city prison, where they had been ordered to disperse. The couple, holding hands, had stepped forward in front of the police guns. It was said that this helped avert another mass shooting.

Another of Wendy's neighbours, a young woman with striking grey eyes, was nervous because her four-year-old daughter was stuck down the road at her nursery school. I calmed her down by pointing out that the marchers were peaceful. She too was shocked by the Sharpeville shootings but, as a young mother, was apprehensive. Wendy introduced her as Eleanor. After she left, in one of those ironies of life, I remarked to Wendy and Patsy how pretty she was. Wendy, who was gay, laughed and said that she had been unsuccessfully pursuing Eleanor for months. Little did any of us realise how closely interlinked

Eleanor's and my life would become.

Graham Meidlinger, a doctor, was the other neighbour. He listened patiently to my views. He enquired whether I knew anyone in what he called the 'Movement'. At first I thought he was referring to a dance group – was he talking about the Royal Ballet, I thought – but he explained, 'that's a collective noun for the ANC and its allies'.

I gave him the name of my mother's first cousin, Jacqueline Arenstein, whom I was hoping to locate. She had stood trial with Luthuli, Mandela and others in the 1956 Treason Trial, and my mother used to take her food during court appearances.

The following evening, Graham called to see me. 'I've got Jackie's husband, Rowley, in a car around the corner. The police are looking for him. Can you put him up? My place is unsafe.' I asked Wendy, who agreed that it would be okay, but just for the night.

Graham ushered in a lanky, almost ungainly, figure in a dishevelled suit. It was Rowley Arenstein, a bearded lawyer, who remembered me as a ten-year-old visiting Durban with my mother. As though he had just dropped in for tea, he enquired about her health and joked about her zest for life. We stayed up for hours as he told me about the Movement and the current crisis. He stressed that the black majority had potential power which could be achieved through organisation and unity. He startled me by predicting that the National Party government 'would not remain in power for six months'.

Rowley showed no sign of fatigue and seemed capable of continuing the discourse right through the night. Although he was way off the mark with his prediction – the government was to survive for well over 30 years – I never again came across anyone so willing to explain a situation, so fully, to a newcomer.

I volunteered to assist in every way possible. Since I was unknown to the police, and could be trusted, I was plunged into clandestine struggle at the deep end. For the next week I became his 'minder' and 'runner' much to the chagrin of Patsy, whom I totally neglected.

After that first night, I found him accommodation at another friend's place. There was an old Ford in the garage. We were given use of this but the key had been mislaid. I impressed Rowley by starting it up with a wad of silver paper. I ran messages between him and Graham and picked up a wig for Rowley from Graham's wife, Valerie Phillips. She was a well-known actress who had sent a cable of protest to Harold Macmillan over the Sharpeville shootings. I drove Rowley to 'safe' houses at night where he consulted others who were on the run like himself. At one such meeting he met Monty Naicker and J.N. Singh, who were leaders of the Natal Indian Congress. They laughed uproariously over each other's disguises before settling down to business.

I was sent on an errand to meet Jackie at an address in the Indian quarter of the city, but got lost. It was dark, with crowds on the pavements, and not another white in sight. I had forgotten the name of the street I was looking for and felt insecure. I stopped someone at random, who put me on the right track after I gave the name of the person whose flat I was trying to locate.

The person, a Mrs Ponnen, was obviously well known in the neighbourhood, because I was guided to her very door. I wondered nervously whether I had broken any security rules by asking a stranger where she lived. What if the person I had stopped was on his way to report to the police that a strange white guy was in the Indian quarter looking for her? The thought unsettled me.

My knocking was answered by a young Indian girl. Immediately afterwards, a grey-haired, white woman in her fifties, with piercing eyes and a stern expression, came to the door, gave me what could only be described as an icy 'once over' and enquired why I wanted Mrs Ponnen. When I told her I had come 'to see Jackie', she nodded and let me enter, identifying herself as Mrs Ponnen.

Even as a young boy I had been struck by Jacqueline's appearance. She had long black hair, penetrating eyes and an olive complexion. Her mother and my grandmother were sisters, and there was a strong family resemblance with my mother. Jackie was pleased to see me but showed signs of tension, smoking heavily. Her two young daughters, dark-eyed and pensive like her, played in the flat. Jackie was interested to know what had motivated me to 'become involved with the Movement'.

Vera Ponnen served tea and listened intently. Like Jackie, she chain-smoked. I discovered that Vera was a Cockney who had come to South Africa at the age of 18 and married George Ponnen, a trade unionist. While Jackie had a reserved personality and a polite choice of words, Vera, by contrast, talked in a rasping voice and swore freely. Between fits of coughing, her mood alternated between humour and anger. She told me straight out: 'I've been a communist since the age of 16. I fought Mosley and his fascist scum in Cable Street. This country's run by fascists who would've loved to see Hitler win the war. But I tell you...' – she was seized by a fit of coughing – '... I tell you the effing bastards have gone too far this time. The African people are on the move, they're not going to take this crap much longer.'

Jackie handed me a suitcase of clothing for Rowley and I departed, with Vera coughing in the bathroom as though she was about to expire.

Patsy and I accompanied Rowley to Johannesburg, where he needed to make contact with the Movement's leadership who had gone to ground. It was bitterly cold and I encouraged him to don the uniform of a Hillbrow bohemian – jeans and a heavy polo-neck jersey. For Rowley, who had shaved his beard, and normally dressed in suit and tie, this was a useful disguise. At a shop specialising in Persian carpets, we received instructions to wait on a street corner near the library gardens. At the appointed time a car stopped, the driver looked towards us, nodded, and we climbed in. The driver had a hat pulled down over his face and wore a coat with the collar turned up. I thought I was living through an Alfred Hitchcock movie. The driver managed a few nervous looks at Rowley and began to giggle uncontrollably.

'My gawd, Rowley,' he managed to blurt out, 'I thought I'd picked up a couple of tramps by mistake. Hell, man, I would never have recognised you.' I learnt later that our driver was Wolfie Kodesh, a veteran of the Movement who had painted the Communist Party slogan on the wall in Yeoville when I was a boy. We became lifelong friends. Wolfie took over my job of assisting Rowley and I went back to work at Alpha Films.

Rowley introduced me to the Movement in Johannesburg and I became part of an emergency committee of the Congress of Democrats (COD), an organisation of whites who supported the ANC. We began to meet clandestinely. Everyone in the group was much older than me, except an attractive Luli Callinicos, later to become a writer on labour history. I recognised the owner of the carpet shop who, together with some half-dozen others, made up the group's complement. I did not at first know their real identities and later, when I got on closer terms with them all, was surprised to discover that none was Jewish. I had laboured under the illusion that Jews were the only whites concerned about the racial oppression of blacks.

The hour a week that Robert Resha had asked me to give the Movement was escalating into virtually all my spare time. The COD committee drafted and secretly printed leaflets. I was given the task of distribution in the Hillbrow area. I drew in friends and we trudged the streets at night, slipping leaflets into letter-boxes and under doors. These demanded the release of all detainees, the lifting of the state of emergency and the replacing of apartheid with a democratic system. On some occasions we showered leaflets from the roofs of buildings into the city streets. We went out in teams, with brushes and paint, and put slogans up on walls. We had to be careful because the risk of arrest was high.

One of our number, Raymond Toms, was arrested when he carelessly tossed leaflets into the Hillbrow police station. We did not know the cause of his disappearance and I went to his flat to investigate. His father opened the door and, in an irate mood, tried to seize me. 'What have you got my son into?' he demanded. I tried to tell him to get hold of a lawyer, but he was intent on manhandling me, while his wife telephoned for the police. There was nothing I could do but flee from the scene.

I had found Durban exciting and when one of Alpha's clients, Lintas, an advertising agency based there, sought my services in their film and television department, I jumped at the offer. My relationship with Patsy had been a strained, on-and-off affair, partly owing to the nine-year difference in our ages, but more because she had had difficulties getting over her involvement with the artist who had dumped her. On an impulse I offered to marry her, and when family and former school friends tried to intervene and dissuade me – on many grounds, including the fact that she was a gentile – I simply became firmer in my resolve. Patsy's response was tentative, and we agreed to regard our marriage as a trial. We were married in the Johannesburg magistrate's court. After a typical Hillbrow *joll*, we departed for Durban.

We found a cottage in the same complex where Wendy and Graham Meidlinger lived. Eleanor was going through a divorce and had moved elsewhere with her young daughter.

The firm that employed me was an in-house agency for Lever Brothers, the manufacturer of soap and detergents. From our air-conditioned offices on Durban's Victoria Embankment, we could seek inspiration by gazing out over the harbour to the plant where the company's products were produced.

I became part of a team of copywriters and commercial artists devising campaigns to sell the products. My immediate boss, the Creative Director, who came from England, would use the phrase 'I've a feeling in my water' before passing judgment as to whether he thought an idea was good or bad. In the final analysis, however, all that mattered was whether the hard-nosed marketeers over at the plant approved the idea or not.

With the lifting of the state of emergency in September 1960, I began to meet many people who had been in prison, in hiding or simply lying low. Although the ANC, like the PAC and the Communist Party, remained banned, the other components of the Movement – the COD, Indian Congress and trade unions – resumed public activity.

I became friendly with a burly Afrikaner, Steve Nel, who ran a chemist shop across the road from the so-called black section of the University of Natal. The black students studied in dilapidated buildings while whites were based at a well-endowed campus on the hilltop. A group of ANC students made a back-room on Steve's premises their headquarters. Among these were future leaders of the ANC like Johnny Makhathini, who went on to represent the organisation at the United Nations, and Kgalakhe Sello, Rowley's articled clerk, who became a successful lawyer in Lesotho. Another was Ernest Gallo, also a law student, who lived with Steve Nel and family.

Ernest was from Cape Town. His parents had battled to put him through school and he had gone on to study law part-time. Like the others, he was several years my senior. He and I became close friends. Every Friday after work I teamed up with him to sell copies of the Congress-aligned newspaper, *New Age*, which had been delivered to Steve's shop. 'New Age! *i' phepha lomzabalazo!*' (*New Age!* the paper of the struggle!) we would cry out to the workers rushing for township buses and trains.

Vera Ponnen lived around the corner from Steve's shop. I finally met her husband, George, who had been in detention. He was a stocky individual who had pioneered trade-union organisation among the Indian sugar-cane cutters. He slowly considered questions put to him, held one's attention with a long gaze, and then delivered a down-to-earth reply. He liked to relax with a brandy and Coke at the end of a hard day's work. Vera, normally fierce and combative, would quieten down completely then, too. At COD meetings, where she sometimes had sharp disagreements with Rowley, she would quote 'Ponnen' – never referring to him by his first name – which, as far as she was concerned, settled the argument her way.

The only other individual to whom Vera displayed deference was Moses Kotane, veteran leader of the Communist Party and ANC, who stayed with the Ponnens when he was in Durban. I met him there one unusually cold day, and found the two of them in dressing gowns with scarves wrapped around their heads, drinking tea. It was difficult for me to suppress my amusement at the sight of Kotane, who was regarded as the country's most dangerous communist, looking like a *gogo* (grandmother).

New Age had its Durban office in Grey Street, the bustling Indian trading centre. It was run by M.P. Naicker, who commanded a great deal of respect. Under his tutelage, I began compiling reports for the newspaper. M.P., as he was called, was assisted by a young man, Ebrahim Ismail Ebrahim, who was of Moslem background, as the name implies. All the Indian comrades' names were abbreviated and Ebrahim was known as Ebe.

Just across the road from *New Age* was Lakhani Chambers, a dank, run-down building housing a maze of seedy companies. On one poorly ventilated floor were the cramped and overcrowded offices of the Natal Indian Congress (NIC) and the South African Congress of Trade Unions (SACTU). The place was like a railway station, with workers coming and going all the time. Billy Nair stood out as the most dynamic official and commanded tremendous respect. There were times when I had an urgent message for him and, if he was attending to a queue of workers, he would order me to wait. Afterwards he would explain that the union office was the one place where the workers must know they came first. He liked a tipple after work, and I sometimes popped in to an Indian pub with him to knock back one or two rounds of cane spirits, the drink popular with Indian workers.

Public meetings were again being held. The regular venue, the innocuous-sounding Bantu Men's Social Centre, was in the vicinity. Because most COD members, including Rowley, Vera and Jackie, were banned from addressing meetings under the Suppression of Communism Act, I was given the task of speaking at these meetings. The hall invariably overflowed with workers in militant mood, singing freedom songs in deep, melodious Zulu. 'We will shoot the Boers with cannons!' was the general theme of the songs.

I was introduced on the platform by Stephen Dlamini, SACTU President, who dressed formally in suit with red tie, and had impeccable old-world manners. With a group of Special Branch officers and policemen at the rear of the hall, he announced that he was not going to reveal my name because that would make their job too easy. A trade unionist named Jerry Khumalo had stepped forward to serve as my interpreter, so Stephen decided to christen me 'Khumalo'.

Later, when I wrote poems in exile, I used the pen-name, A.N.C. Khumalo. After my speech, however, some of the youth leaders gave me the name '*Vuka'yibambe*' – 'one who is ready to leap into the fray'. At the pace I was going, there was little time for married life. Patsy had not wanted to get involved in politics and, by mutual consent and without bitterness, she returned to Johannesburg. Our marriage had lasted six months. I felt that I had failed in my obligations to her but was consoled somewhat when Vera and Jackie, who had been counselling the two of us, told me that the relationship never looked as though it would work out. At least we had split up amicably without the complications of children. Patsy soon re-married and had a child, but I never saw her again.

At the end of May 1961, Dr Verwoerd, grand architect of apartheid, declared South Africa a republic. The ANC, led by Nelson Mandela, who had gone underground to organise resistance, called for a three-day protest strike. For weeks beforehand we had worked in top gear to make the call a success.

It was during this period that I renewed acquaintance with Wendy's erstwhile neighbour, Eleanor, who was working in a downtown bookstore. Born in Scotland, she had come to Durban as an infant. We found we had much in common and Eleanor was soon distributing leaflets with me. She had a number of liberal-minded friends who helped swell the ranks of the minuscule COD.

On the very eve of the strike, when we should have been involved in last-minute activities, a group of us gathered at Rowley's house to guard him. He had been receiving repeated death threats and we had a tip-off that a group of assassins were about to make their move.

I had been on the first shift with Johnny Makhathini. At 2 a.m. we were relieved from duty and flopped down in an upstairs bedroom. Hardly had we shut our eyes than shooting erupted in the garden, drawing war cries from our side. Our people were armed only with clubs. Dashing outside, I saw two cars driving off with our people in hot pursuit. Grabbing a brick, I gave chase, encouraged to see that one of the vehicles was having engine trouble. My speed brought me to the fore and, as the car jerked into action, I sent the missile crashing through the rear window. Almost simultaneously, I came under gunfire from a masked passenger. I felt a stinging sensation in my cheek and, when I put my hand to my face, I could feel the blood oozing out. I squeezed the skin and pulled out a sliver of lead – a fragment from a ricochet.

Windows at Rowley's house had been shot up. Fortunately there were no casualties. I learnt that six of the raiders, with stockings over their faces, had gone to the front and rear doors of the house. A seventh, skulking about in the garden, had come face to face with Ernest Gallo, who sounded the alarm. The police, who arrived on the scene within minutes but failed to apprehend the fleeing raiders, spread a story that we had been involved in an internal fracas. With the morning newspapers highlighting the attack, and referring to a 'bodyguard hit by bullet', I contacted my parents to assure them I was unharmed.

As for what my employers were going to make of the attack, I would face up to that after the three-day strike.

THREE

THE SPEAR

Durban
16 December 1961

THE THREE-DAY STAY-AWAY WAS ONLY partly successful. The government mobilised the army and, at bayonet point, forced people to go to work. The day of the new 'Republic', 31 May, took place under a dark cloud. White South Africa, and the Verwoerd government, were beleaguered at home and isolated internationally. The violence used by the state carried important lessons for the liberation movement. Activists throughout the country were questioning whether it was possible to advance the struggle for freedom by nonviolent methods alone.

Indeed, after the abortive attack on Rowley, I raised with Ernest the need for us to arm ourselves. As a white, I was able to obtain a licence for a firearm. My salary made buying a weapon possible and I was soon acquainting Ernest and others in the use of my new Browning 9 mm pistol.

My photograph on the front page of the *Natal Mercury*, and the graphic account of the assault on Rowley's house, alerted my employers to my political involvement. It was also clear that the Special Branch had become aware who my employer was and, as was their practice, warned them that I was a dangerous individual.

There were queries about my political involvement. The Creative Director was solicitous. 'You know, there's a saying in England: If you're not a communist at the age of 21 you have no heart. But if you are still a communist at the age of 31, you have no mind.'

Neither was the agency's Managing Director hostile, although it was evident that he was concerned. From his office, where we were discussing the issue, he gazed out over the harbour to the mother company's plant. He reminded me of the promising future I had with the firm. With an embarrassed clearing of his throat, he said he was asking, on behalf of the board of directors, whether I was a communist.

I was able to answer immediately, and honestly, that I was not a member of the Communist Party. 'What I'm interested in is democracy for this country. When I talk about democracy, I mean government by the people, for the people and of the people. President Kennedy's in the news these days. He stresses that the answer to present-day problems in the world is a democratic system. Please tell the board of directors that I would like to see President Kennedy's prescription applied to this country.'

Not long after, I joined the outlawed Communist Party. It was Vera Ponnen who approached me, and said she had been formally requested to ask whether I would be interested in becoming a member. She spoke about the commitment and discipline this would entail, and the dangers. She emphasised that the point of being a member of the Party was to serve the working class. I immediately responded in the affirmative, considering it an honour to have been approached.

The Party, as an outlawed organisation, had a mystique that drew me. It was clear that many of the most active and respected people in the Movement empathised with the Party and were probably members. The government, and the super-wealthy, clearly hated the Party, while it enjoyed great popularity among the disenfranchised blacks. Every time the Party was referred to, whether at mass meetings or in personal conversations with workers, there was a positive response. Whenever the Soviet Union was mentioned, there was a roar of approval.

Emotional revulsion for racism had drawn me into the Movement. My commitment extended to the removal of apartheid. But soon I was drawn into discussions about what would follow the removal of racial discrimination. The country had suffered gross inequalities and injustice before the apartheid government came to power in 1948. A colour-blind capitalism, if such a creature existed, would perpetuate social division and inequality. I had begun reading Marxist literature, and with the assistance of Rowley and Ernest Gallo, among others, began to develop something of a Marxist critique. Once I had joined the Party I found myself in an underground cell with Rowley, Vera, Sello and several black workers. We discussed Marxist theory, and secretly distributed Party leaflets. There was no conspiracy about controlling the ANC or the Movement. What was emphasised was the need for communists to lead by example. The Party's strategy was that the immediate objective, in alliance with the ANC, was the achievement of a democratic state through a national liberation struggle. This would open up the possibilities for advancing to a socialist stage.

Along with everyone else, I found myself susceptible to the pre-eminent position of Moscow. There were historical reasons for this, going back to the 1917 socialist revolution, which inspired the formation of communist parties throughout the world. The defeat of Hitler, in which the Soviet Union played a key role, and remarkable socio-economic achievements which had transformed a backward Czarist Empire occupying one-sixth of the world's land surface, added to this prestige.

Our Party never developed a critique of the Soviet Union, for several reasons. In the main, the historic role and the basic facts of achievement of the Soviet Union in its early stages sufficed for us. The isolation of South Africa from political and cultural thought abroad must also have played a role. Ideological development in our Party marked time at 1917, and then at 1945. This was reinforced by the nature of our leadership. The white leadership of the early 1920s was rooted in early Bolshevism. The black leaders who emerged in the 1930s, like Moses Kotane, J.B. Marks and Yusuf Dadoo, were similarly affected. Even the exposure of Stalin's crimes by Khrushchev in 1956 failed to shake the basic ideological position of the old guard. The Soviet Union had made mistakes and these would be rectified. This meant that there was no insight into the internal contradictions within the Soviet model, which later led to catastrophe. In my experience only Ruth First, Joe Slovo and Hilda Bernstein, of the older leaders, were to show signs of a critical attitude in the 1960s.

During July 1961, M.P. Naicker took me for a walk along the beach front. He confided that the Movement was about to change its strategy. The government's repressive policies had convinced the leadership that non-violent struggle alone could not bring change. We were forced to answer the regime's violence with revolutionary violence.

'I've been asked to approach you,' he said, above the roar of the surf smashing against the rocks, 'to sound you out. Are you willing to get involved?'

I became a member of the Natal Regional Command of Umkhonto we Sizwe (Zulu and Xhosa for 'the Spear of the Nation'; MK for short). The name harked back to the wars of resistance against British and Boer colonialism. The spear was a symbol of resistance.

The Natal Regional Commander was Curnick Ndlovu, Secretary of the Harbour and Railway Workers' Union. His beard, spectacles and agitational manner on a public platform conjured up the image of a Chinese revolutionary. Billy Nair was Curnick's deputy, and his presence on the command added to my confidence. Eric Mtshali, another trade unionist, physically strong and fit, appeared eminently suitable for the work in hand. We were looking for an additional member and, after considerable debate, chose a recent recruit into the Movement who had been showing promise in political-economy classes run by SACTU. This was Bruno Mtolo, full of charm and good intentions. To me, the fact that he had worked as an electrician and handyman was compelling enough reason. We were going to need those skills.

I was the only one who was not a trade unionist. When I enquired why none of the leading ANC members were part of the command, I learnt that the Natal leadership of the ANC was still debating the policy change. The national leadership, however, had instructed us to go ahead and recruit ANC cadres from the townships for the local command levels. Curnick and Eric were members of the ANC. At that stage, only Africans were members of the ANC. Billy and I belonged to the allied Congresses, but MK membership was open to all.

Within a month, Billy informed me that we were about to receive our first training from one of the most outstanding comrades in the Movement. He told me that our visitor had fought the Germans in North Africa and his nickname was the 'Desert Rat'. We drove to a small sugar-cane farm outside Durban, and gathered in an outhouse. Billy ushered in a man in an open-necked shirt and sports jacket.

Although a code name was used for introductory purposes, I recognised our visitor from a treason-trial photograph. He was Jack Hodgson, one of the leaders of the Springbok Legion, an anti-fascist, ex-servicemen's organisation that had opposed the National Party in the immediate post-war years. He was practical in his approach and demonstrated everything from how to use a soldering iron to grinding chemicals into fine powder.

He placed a chemical mixture with icing sugar into a spoon and carefully added a drop of acid with an eye dropper. The powder burst into flame and we were as impressed as pupils in a science class. The problem, of course, was how to achieve the result without directly applying the acid. For that one required a timing device.

With a huge grin he produced a condom: 'The English call this chap a French letter and the French call it an English raincoat. We're going to use it for something neither the English nor the French intended it for.'

First he placed a teaspoon of the chemical mixture into the condom. Next he produced a small, gelatine capsule – the kind that normally contained medicinal powder – and told us that these were obtainable from any chemist shop. Opening the capsule, he added a few drops of acid, carefully put the cap back on the capsule and dropped it into the condom. He told us that it normally took up to 50 minutes for the acid to eat through the capsule, with the time varying according to temperature and even altitude. While we waited for the result, he lectured us on the organising of what he called an 'operation' – stressing the need for thorough planning and reconnaissance before attacking a target.

We were so absorbed in his lecture that we forgot the condom. Suddenly there was a blinding flash, amid acrid smoke. It was amazing to see so much combustible energy released from a teaspoon of powder. 'Forty-six minutes,' our instructor remarked, consulting his watch, 'plenty of time to make a clean getaway.'

We later made our way to a field to test the effect of the timing device on a home-made bomb. The bomb was nothing more than a glass jar partly filled with a chemical mixture. The condom was prepared as before. It was tied with a knot, placed inside the jar, and the lid was closed tight.

We stood together like guests at a Guy Fawkes party, waiting for the fireworks to begin. I relished the sensation of the star-studded sky above us and the sea of sugarcane stretching in all directions. Although we would be a small band to begin with, I had total confidence in our mission.

While we waited, Jack reminded us that the actions we were about to embark on must not result in injury or loss of life. Our targets were to be inanimate objects. 'We'll see how things develop later on,' he said, 'but if anyone knows the stories of Damon Runyon you might be familiar with that opening line: "There's no better sight in the world than a dozen dead coppers lying in the gutter." Well, when the police act like fascists, I have to admit it's a sentiment I agree with.'

Billy chaffed him that he had better be careful, otherwise he would get into trouble with the leadership. For the first time I heard Jack Hodgson utter a phrase that I was going to hear him repeat countless times in the years to come: 'So let them shoot me down in flames,' he said with a broad grin.

He became serious again and cautioned us to stick to MK's policy and avoid taking life. He added, however, that if the government stuck to its present course, then, as was the case with many other struggles – Cuba and Algeria for instance – we would have to 'take the gloves off'. I thought of Alf's 'cause and effect', and saw the link between Sharpeville and the birth of MK. But were we aiming to simply put pressure on the government – to force it to change – or to overthrow it? If so, how? I perceived these questions only dimly at the time. In retrospect, from what Jack and other leaders told us, I came to realise that the strategy had not been clearly worked out. Uppermost in virtually all our minds was the need to hit back, and in so doing to demonstrate that apartheid rule could be challenged.

There was a blinding flash and a loud crack as the jar shattered. We expected a louder bang. 'Hell, no,' Jack explained. 'We don't want to attract unwanted attention.' He proceeded to explain how we needed to use stronger containers so that the chemical reaction would build up more powerful pressures than when a mere glass jar was used.

After Jack's visit we received instructions from the National High Command in Johannesburg. The date for launching MK's initial attacks was to be 16 December 1961. There were murmurs of approval as Curnick Ndlovu made the announcement. Popularly called 'Dingaan's Day', the date had been declared a public holiday by the government. It had been renamed the 'Day of the Covenant' in commemoration of the 'Battle of Blood River' where, on 16 December 1838, the Boers had inflicted a heavy defeat on King Dingaan's Zulu *impis* (warriors). They had vowed to God that they would sanctify the day if he delivered the enemy into their hands.

We were instructed to attack government offices, particularly those connected with the policy of apartheid, and were reminded to avoid loss of life. Night after night we ground chemicals in the back room of Steve's chemist shop. We needed about 20 kgs of Jack's mixture to make four bombs. It was pretty arduous work. It was easy to stain one's clothing and skin with the chemical, which left a distinct purple mark. So we had to be extremely careful to avoid leaving a trail of clues around.

At this time a photographer from Pietermaritzburg, who had become interested in the COD, was a regular visitor to Rowley's and Jackie's home, where I was lodging. His name was Tom Sharpe, who later became famous as a satirical novelist. I was always short of transport and Tom was quite happy to lend me his car. When we were just a few days from D-Day, I needed to transport the chemicals from one workshop to another. Tom was deep in discussion with Jackie about a play he was struggling to write and, as usual, obliged. I got back after midnight to Rowley's, where Tom had been patiently awaiting the return of his car. I gave him the keys and collapsed exhausted on my bed. He returned within minutes and enquired what I had been doing with his car.

The interior was covered in a fine dust from the chemicals, which must have leaked out during transportation. I made up an excuse about having moved a friend's painting equipment and hurried to help him clean up. I cursed myself for being careless and hoped the others were not repeating such mistakes.

By 15 December we were ready. We neatly wrapped each bomb in Christmas paper and delivered them to different combat units. I met up with Bruno and was unhappy to find that he had been drinking heavily. In answer to my question, he clicked his tongue in irritation and said he had only taken '*one dop*' (one tot). Our unit's target was a large government complex, from where apartheid officials exercised total control over thousands of Africans seeking the right to work or reside in Durban. The place was guarded by a squad of municipal policemen called 'black jacks' because of the colour of their uniforms. We had observed that late at night they grew bored and sat together around a fire, drinking beer. We had already left sandbags in long grass near the side entrance of the building. Just after midnight, our unit cautiously approached the building. Bruno had prepared our timing device and would add the acid at the last moment. I walked on the opposite side of the road carrying the Christmas present. A third saboteur was already crouching down near the sandbags, while a fourth kept a look-out. The 'black jacks' were engrossed in conversation on the other side of the building.

I removed the wrapping paper and placed the bomb we had manufactured next to the door. Bruno placed a capsule with acid into the condom, with its special initiating powder, and armed the bomb. The sandbags were placed behind the bomb so as to direct the explosive charge inwards, after which we melted off in different directions.

I went straight home. Rowley's place was in darkness. I flopped on the bed but could not sleep. I was acutely conscious that we were making history that day and wondered how the others had made out. I was relieved that our unit had carried out its mission safely, but success would depend on whether our explosives worked well enough.

'Surely they will,' I told myself for the hundredth time. 'The technique is so simple.'

Posters proclaiming the existence of Umkhonto we Sizwe appeared in the city streets simultaneously with the first actions. These stated: 'The time comes in the life of any people when there remain two choices; to submit or fight. That time has now come to South Africa. We will not submit but will fight back with all means at our disposal in defence of our rights, our people and our freedom.'

Banner headlines in the press reported successful bomb blasts at government offices in Johannesburg and Port Elizabeth. Durban was mentioned in a minor way.

Devices had been placed at the main pass office and at the Departments of Coloured and Indian Affairs as well as at the municipal offices. Some small fires had been started but the explosive charges had failed to detonate.

Billy and Curnick were particularly angry with Bruno, who had prepared the small amount of chemicals required for the timing devices. It looked as though there was something wrong with the preparation. When Bruno had delivered timing devices to them, just a few hours before the start of operations, they both observed that he had been drinking heavily. Bruno was admonished for drinking too much and warned that this would not be tolerated again.

He lapsed into a sulk. I had become quite friendly with him and sought to console him after the meeting. He denied the charges against him and said he would prove himself in the future.

Life became complicated for me. Rowley was completely against the Movement's change in strategy. Debates raged in his house about the 'adventurism' in the Movement. He was avidly consulting the texts of Lenin and produced screeds of criticisms which declared that the actions were 'anarchistic'.

When I argued that the policy of non-violence in the face of the government's brutality had demoralised the people he had cut in sharply:

'The people! That's just the problem. We fail to organise the masses, so we turn to using firecrackers. A group of conspirators will not give us the solution. Read Lenin on Blanqui. He gives a searing indictment of exactly this type of deviation.'

In the face of Lenin I felt the wind coming out of my sails, but dug deeper into my reserves: 'But Fidel Castro began with a small group. We've got to begin somewhere. We've got to show that there's a new way ...'

I had never seen Rowley so angry. But he displayed no animosity to me. He handed me the Lenin volume and suggested I read the essay on 'anarchism'.

Jackie strove to maintain the peace, serving tea and home-made cheesecake. 'Revolution depends on organising the masses,' Rowley expounded, in a calm, matter-of-fact tone. 'It is the masses who make revolution, not a bunch of conspirators.'

Eleanor and I visited the Ponnens. We found Vera elated about the bomb blasts. 'Jesus!' she exclaimed. 'When we got the morning paper I said, "Ponnen, the bloody revolution's begun!"'

Ponnen was sipping his brandy and Coke and looked at us with his liquid brown eyes: 'She got so excited she had to run and pee.'

Anxious to obtain their views on Rowley's critique, I tried to explain his exposition as accurately as possible. I thought I had become used to Vera's volatile temperament, but the ferocity of her reaction took me aback: 'Bloody 'ell! That's Rowley for you. Invariably against action. Always "the masses, the masses!" – like a bloody incantation! And he'll quote Lenin 'til the cows come home like a Talmudic scholar.'

Ponnen told her to cool down. She shook her head and continued in a quieter vein: 'Don't get me wrong. Reading Marx, Lenin, Rosa Luxemburg – even bloody Kugelmanshmugelman if you like – is very important. But none of them would've wanted us just to copy them – have blind faith in them, like a religion. We use them for guidance but we must begin with our own conditions. Theory grows out of our own reality – not so, Ponnen?'

'I don't know where Rowley gets this conspiracy theory from,' he began. 'The ANC and the Party are banned. We can't discuss things in public. Anyway, certain things can only be discussed in secret. As far as Vera and I know, there have been discussions within the Movement about changing our methods of struggle, departing from the exclusively non-violent approach. Some of our people have opposed this, but the majority view has had to prevail. As far as anarchism is concerned, that is disorganised and basically pointless violence. As I see it, Umkhonto is meant to be an organised and disciplined force. In our situation we can't have a mass army overnight, as the Bolsheviks were able to build. The Russian workers and peasants were already in the Czarist army and revolted. We do have to begin with small numbers, in secret, and gradually build up our forces.'

Ponnen took a long sip of his drink. Vera, Eleanor and I did not take our eyes off him. 'Rowley has a point about organising the masses, and it doesn't matter that he repeats it like a gramophone,' he chuckled. Vera nodded at this like a chastened child. 'Certain points do bear repetition,' he continued. 'We need armed actions. I hope this sabotage will lead to armed struggle proper, where we can challenge the regime's monopoly of force. But these actions must be part and parcel of the general resistance of the people. They must link with the mass struggle in the urban and rural areas. Achieving that might not be so easy. Time will tell.'

FOUR

DYNAMITE

Durban
1961–2

THEN I WAS ARRESTED. IT HAPPENED AT work. One morning the Creative Director, looking concerned, appeared at the door of my office and said: 'The police are here asking for you.'

Two of them were standing in his office. In their drab suits they looked out of place in the advertising world. The shorter of the pair introduced himself as Lieutenant Grobler. He was a wiry, diminutive individual, with ginger hair and moustache and restless eyes that conveyed an impression of volatile energy. He showed me a warrant for my arrest and said he was taking me in under the Pondoland Emergency Regulations. Natal COD had produced a pamphlet supporting an Mpondo rebellion against the imposition of government-appointed chiefs. Grobler's words came as a relief to me. My concern was about being arrested for sabotage activities, not leaflets.

'This is Natal,' I said. 'How can you arrest me under Pondo regulations?'

That cut no ice with him. I was taken to a police station, booked in, finger-printed and locked in a cell. There I sat in my ad-man's suit, looking as incongruous as Grobler had in the agency. I had heard that Grobler had been recently transferred to the security police from the murder and robbery squad, where he had earned for himself a reputation as an efficient and ruthless investigator.

I stood trial, in a country hamlet in Pondoland, alongside two other COD officials, Melville Fletcher and Graham Meidlinger. By then I was Natal secretary of the organisation and the three of us constituted the executive. Rowley secured bail for us, so when the trial began we put up at the hamlet's solitary hotel. It was crammed with members of the Special Branch from Durban. It was fascinating to study the 'SB', as we called them, close up. They were a sour-looking crew who played cards and drank heavily until late at night.

To my surprise, I discovered that they bickered a great deal with one another, mainly about pay disparities. This gave me a chance to relate to one of them, Frans Erasmus, who was most aggrieved about the salary differences. A friendly conversation ensued. His superior officer gave him a cold look, however, and he broke off the discussion.

Because of their rowdiness, the SB lost favour with the hotel manageress and her few regulars. By contrast with their behaviour, we three 'communists' were restrained in our manner.

During the trial, many witnesses came forward to testify that they had received our pamphlet through the post. The state case collapsed, however, when the judge upheld our argument that the Pondoland emergency regulations did not apply to our activities in Durban, from where the pamphlets had been posted.

In high spirits we took our leave at the hotel. The manageress and her regulars wished us good luck, having decided that we were not as dangerous or distasteful as they had first imagined.

Despite the successful outcome of the trial, I lost my job. I was given the option of resigning, but refused on principle. I had not kept my politics secret. Many members of staff were sympathetic. Quite a few had bought Congress booklets from me and attended house meetings which we held for whites interested in learning something about the ANC. The best of these was a young copywriter who had a most original mind and an outrageous sense of humour. His name was Barry Higgs. Together with his girlfriend, Sybilla – who worked in the same bookshop as Eleanor – he became an active member of our circle.

Attitudes about whites involved with the ANC verged on the paranoid. Like many others who were victimised for basic democratic beliefs, I came to experience the bizarre reaction that could be induced among those responsible for wielding power. At a human rights day rally in Durban, I spoke about our demand for universal franchise and ended my speech with the slogan: 'One man one vote!' The reaction of the Minister of Bantu Affairs afterwards was to rail against white communists in Durban for 'intoxicating the Bantu' with foreign ideas. I was served with a banning order, which prohibited me from attending public gatherings or meetings of more than three persons. Before long, the Congress of Democrats was banned under the Suppression of Communism Act. While there were members of the COD, like Rowley and Vera, who made no bones about their communist beliefs, the organisation had many non-communists in its ranks.

The government moved to extend its powers as a way of dealing with the wave of sabotage. They were seeking to pass a draconian act through Parliament, which would allow them to confine opponents to house arrest, detain suspects without charge or trial for periods of 90 days at a time, and introduce heavier sentences, including the death penalty, for sabotage.

In response to the gauntlet being thrown down by the government, the Movement called a special meeting on the Natal north coast. This was to enable Chief Albert Luthuli to participate. He had been banished to the village of Groutville, where he farmed sugar-cane.

The meeting took place on a farmstead in the area. Suddenly there was a hush and into the gathering stepped Chief Luthuli, a strongly built man, whose eyes were full of humour. In a checked shirt and dark trousers tucked into a pair of Wellington boots, he looked as though he had been working in the fields. He glanced around the room and greeted us all. There were warm embraces for old friends, such as Moses Kotane and Walter Sisulu.

Luthuli chaired the meeting, which he opened by leading us in singing the national anthem – *Nkosi Sikelel' iAfrika* (God bless Africa) – in a superb baritone voice. The meeting deliberated on the latest moves of the government. Much of the time was taken up with how to mobilise opposition and the need to adapt to the new situation. Kotane and Sisulu carefully guided discussion. There were points made about what new forms of underground organisation were required, including the need to strengthen our external mission. There was a report about Nelson Mandela's progress abroad and how he and Tambo were securing facilities of various kinds for the Movement. Nobody questioned the creation of MK.

During a break in proceedings, while everyone was eating, Billy pulled me aside. We walked along a path leading to a sugar-cane field, where we met Curnick and a stocky comrade who had slipped out of the meeting ahead of us. It was Joe Modise, a senior MK commander. We gave him a brief account of our activities. But instead of praising us, he chastised us for not being more active.

Curnick observed that MK units in the Transvaal were using dynamite. 'Can't you give us some?' he asked. 'There's a limit to what we can achieve with home-made bombs.'

Modise became irritated and growled: 'We're getting a few sticks from the mines. Use your own initiative.'

Before we could take up Modise's challenge, we were summoned to another meeting. Our entire command assembled in a Durban flat. We did not know what was on the agenda, until Billy arrived and ushered in Nelson Mandela. Dubbed the 'Black Pimpernel', he had just slipped back into the country.

Bearded, and in khaki trousers and shirt, he towered above us as he shook each one by the hand. Wearing a solemn expression, he looked every inch a commander. In well-measured tones, he stated that the initial acts of sabotage were the opening shots in a war that would grow into a guerrilla struggle, if the government failed to respond to our demands.

A few days later came the shock news of Mandela's arrest. His capture occurred on the national road, two hours' drive from Durban. A police roadblock had been erected and Mandela was found posing as a chauffeur in the car of Cecil Williams, after a tip-off from an informer.

Within days, Mandela appeared in a Johannesburg court. He was charged for leaving the country without a passport and for organising the 1961 strike. He was sentenced to five years' imprisonment and sent to Robben Island, the maximum security prison off Cape Town.

We mustered all MK's resources to register our protest at his capture. By then we had scores of units throughout Natal. We had been training these units in the use of home-made petrol bombs, and unleashed an offensive against goods trains, government offices and the large sugar-cane estates and wattle plantations. Fires raged throughout Natal and considerable damage was caused. But we needed more effective explosives.

One of our units reported a dynamite installation near a sleepy hamlet outside Durban. It had been set up by a construction company busy with road cutting. Eleanor packed a picnic basket and we drove out to investigate. With the sound of dynamite booming in the hills, we laid out a blanket for our picnic in the shade of a tree and then began our reconnaissance. Off the road was a solid, barbed-wire enclosure. Inside was a store room, painted red, which we concluded was the magazine for dynamite. We watched as two men arrived in a truck, unlocked a gate to get into the enclosure, and opened the door of the magazine. Without paying any attention to us, they loaded some boxes on to the truck and drove off.

'The only way to get inside that is with wire cutters,' I remarked.

'Easier if we had a key to the padlock,' she replied.

'Fat chance of that.'

'Not if we can get close and have a look at its brand name and serial number,' said Eleanor.

While no one was around, we sauntered innocently past the gate and Eleanor managed to get a good look at the padlock.

She spent several days exploring the hardware stores. I was doubtful that she would find what we were looking for, and had made up my mind to use wire cutters. Nevertheless she bet me a drink that she would succeed. A couple of days later we met at a favourite haunt. She was sitting at a table under a palm tree, looking cool and demure. As I joined her she handed me a key and said: 'I'll have a gin and tonic.'

One night a group of us parked a station wagon near the dynamite store.

We had established that a solitary watchman drank in a shebeen at that hour. I inserted Eleanor's key into the padlock and, as it clicked open, resolved to buy her roses the next day.

Bruno began to jemmy-open the door of the store room. Under his deft hand, the metal door sprang open with a loud crack. As swiftly as possible, we began carrying boxes of dynamite to the vehicle. We packed it so full that a couple of us had to lie on top of the boxes. 'Move!' we commanded the driver, who had remained by the car, unaware of the contents.

We careered wildly along bumpy tracks avoiding the highway. We had not anticipated such a large haul and had to find a bigger storage place than the one we had planned. It was the holiday period, so we ended up storing the load temporarily in a school to which we had access.

The next day, banner headlines in the press proclaimed: 'Dynamite Stolen Near Pinetown.' Our getaway driver spotted the poster and promptly drove through a red light into another vehicle. He had imagined we were picking up underground leaflets.

There was no time to celebrate the success of our haul. As soon as possible, I visited the public library and made a beeline for the Mining section. I found what I was looking for, a book in which there was a chapter dealing with the safe handling of dynamite. There were obvious precautions to observe, such as not striking matches in the vicinity of a magazine. I thought of Bruno's jemmy, striking metal, causing sparks to fly as he broke open the magazine. You were also not supposed to exceed 20 miles per hour when transporting dynamite. I thought of our wild getaway. But at least those things were in the past.

What worried me was the warning: 'Dynamite must be safely stored away from inhabited areas and in special magazines designed to maintain a moderate temperature.'

I envisaged the school being blown sky-high in Durban's heat. We overcame the immediate concern by installing a fan in the school storeroom. We were soon able to move our cargo. We had seized such a large quantity that we were able to supply Johannesburg and other regions. What we kept, we buried in caches around Durban.

The availability of powerful explosives meant our units were able to go on the offensive. Pass offices were demolished and railway lines cut. We continued to avoid any loss of life.

We decided on a special operation against Natal's power supply. I spent many days on a motorbike tracking the lines of electric pylons emanating from strategic power stations. It was fascinating work plotting the grid system on an operational map. We selected three key pylons, which we judged would cause the maximum disruption to the region's electricity supply.

Billy commanded one unit, Bruno another, and I the third. We had decided to strike simultaneously, soon after dark. I led my unit through thick bush, up the slope of a hill, to a large pylon. Eleanor, the getaway driver, remained in our car.

We carefully attached dynamite charges to each leg of the pylon. Each charge was composed of four sticks of dynamite, tightly wrapped together. A detonator with fuse was inserted into one of the charges. We strung out a length of cordex, which looked like electric cord, and linked up the four dynamite charges. Once the charge with the detonator exploded, a shock wave would travel along the cordex line and almost instantaneously detonate the three other charges.

When we had got everything in place, we filled a capsule with acid, dropped it into our condom timing device, and attached it to the end of the fuse. The powder for the condom had been prepared that day and had been checked to ensure it was dependable. We looked over our handiwork to make sure everything was in order, and withdrew to the car.

Within 40 minutes Eleanor and I were back home, having dropped our companions off on the way. I had moved out of Rowley's to share a cottage with her. The Special Branch had recently taken to raiding the houses of leading activists immediately after bomb blasts. That was to check on our movements as soon as they received a report of an action. We estimated that we had about five minutes to go before we knew how successful the night's operations had been.

We did not wait long. Our cottage was suddenly plunged into darkness. We ran outside to witness the extent of the black-out. Not a light was showing in the entire street. We ran a short way up a hill to a park with a good view of the city. From there it was possible to see the city centre, the beach front and the harbour. An eerie darkness had blotted out the entire town. We hugged one another and danced a jig in the park.

Remembering the Special Branch raids, we raced back to our cottage. Eleanor found some candles and we relaxed in their glow. Within ten minutes, a car screeched to a halt outside our front door. It was the friendly SB man whom I had talked to in the Pondoland hotel, checking that we were home. We enquired whether he knew what had happened to the lights.

He grinned. 'You'll read about it in the papers tomorrow,' he said.

FIVE

THROUGH THE TRAP DOOR

Durban
May 1963

NEWS OF THE DURBAN SABOTAGE MADE national and international headlines. The electric power to the city had been cut, and coastal and inland areas were affected as well. We decided to press ahead with an offensive, despite increasing Security Branch raids, round-the-clock guarding of strategic objects, and intensive police and army patrols. Jack Hodgson's words rang in our ears: 'When they have to guard everything that opens and shuts in the country, they'll have no one available to control the people.'

I continued to lead a double life and registered at the university for a degree course at the beginning of 1963. My interests were more in physical fitness than studies, so I competed for a place in the cross-country team and was soon representing the university. During one cross-country meet we came up against a police team. Members of the Special Branch were present as spectators and could not hide their surprise at my presence in university colours.

The government began serving house arrest orders on what it considered to be its most dangerous opponents. Helen Joseph was the first person to be placed under 24-hour house arrest, followed by Walter Sisulu, Govan Mbeki, Jack Hodgson, his wife Rica, and scores of others. Leaders like Moses Kotane and Joe Slovo followed Tambo into exile to organise from abroad. I was considered lucky, for I was simply restricted to the Durban magisterial district.

When Rowley received a dusk-to-dawn house arrest order, a group of supporters staged a solidarity demonstration outside his house. Ebe, Eleanor and Barry Higgs were among them. They were arrested and fined for 'causing a public disturbance'. Signs of an impending police swoop were increasing. I was having to report to a police station once a week in terms of my banning order.

One day, while I was signing the register, the duty sergeant glared at me and said: 'If you don't clear off to Israel we'll deal with you here!'

When I bumped into Erasmus, the one Special Branch man who had shown signs of not being hostile, he remarked that he was surprised I was 'still hanging around'.

I raised the question of going underground with M.P. Naicker and Billy who were, like Rowley, under 12-hour house arrest. 'We're sitting ducks,' I argued. It was clear that the moment the 90-day Act became law we would be rounded up. They hesitated about taking a decision but instructed me to organise a reserve MK command. Detention in the Treason Trial and going underground during the state of emergency had made them reluctant to forsake their families yet again. It was simpler for younger people like me who did not have so much to lose.

Eleanor, in particular, urged me to act. But because I had not been given firm instructions to 'go underground', I delayed the decision.

When I returned to our cottage later that day, I found her hard at work. We had discovered a trap door in the floor of our bedroom when we first moved in. It was under our bed, which Eleanor had pulled aside. We opened the trap door and shone a torch into the black hole below. There were plenty of spider webs, a dank smell and stone ground about one metre below the floorboards. I slipped into the hole and crawled about on my stomach. I had got down to the foundations of the cottage but to my disappointment found that there was no way out. I asked Eleanor for matches and burnt the cobwebs.

'Well, at least we've got a hiding place,' Eleanor remarked as she cheerily washed spider web out of my hair. We were extremely fond of one another to say the least and hid our anxiety as best we could.

A couple of nights later I paid a secret visit to Billy. Under our banning orders we were forbidden to communicate with one another. The 90-day detention clause had become law. The police were now at liberty to detain anyone they pleased, without explanation, and hold them in isolation for periods of 90 days at a time. According to the Justice Minister, John Vorster, the 90-day periods could be repeated 'this side of eternity'. Detainees had no right of access to lawyers or family.

Billy lived in a building called Himalaya House, near the central market. I remained in a side alley while a boy from the building went to call him. Billy was unperturbed and, as usual, in good spirits. He told me to do everything possible to avoid arrest. I had to ensure that the reserve command would still function in the event of a round-up. He and others would have to face detention. Nobody was going to break. If our people could 'stick out' the detention, as had been the case during the state of emergency, the government would be 'back to square one'. He seemed sure of himself but I had my doubts. We embraced and wished each other good luck. That was the last I saw of him for 27 years.

That night I was trying to catch up on university studies.

I was up late reading Dickens' *Great Expectations*. I was particularly able to relate to Pip's attempts to help his benefactor, the convict Abel Magwitch, escape from the authorities. 'Don't go home,' was the message Pip received from Mr Walpole, which alerted him to impending danger.

At 2 a.m. there was loud banging on the front door. I put down Dickens, while Eleanor quickly woke up. She helped me get through the trap door and then struggled to move the bed back over it. It was pitch black, musty and cold below the floorboards. I was pleased we had cleaned out the cobwebs. There were heavy footsteps above. It sounded as though several people were walking about.

The cottage was small. The entrance led into a sitting-room off which were a kitchen and our bedroom. The bedroom led into a bathroom. There was no back door. The briefest examination would show I was not in. The bed, which was just a few inches above the ground, gave no possibility of anyone hiding underneath it. So long as they did not think of examining the floorboards ...

But what if they took Eleanor down to the police station for questioning? There was no way I would be able to get out then. The thought chilled me more than the cold ground which was permeating my bones.

After what seemed an age the trap door was opened by Eleanor.

'It was the SB, alright. Four of them, led by Grobler, trying to sound casual. Said you should contact them in the morning.'

She was a little shaken, but well controlled. She had told them she would not be seeing me any more, because we had a row and I had left her. She had pointed to a framed copy of the Freedom Charter, signed by Chief Luthuli, which had fallen from the wall and been damaged. She told them she had broken it on my head.

It was time to go. I put on a cap and coat. We made last minute arrangements about future contact, and I was about to open the front door. Eleanor stopped me just in time. A vehicle was parked in the shadow up the road, four men sitting inside. So we sat in the cottage, talking in whispers, for the rest of the night.

About 6 a.m., just before dawn, the car started up and Eleanor saw the police driving off. She walked down the road to a telephone box, pretending to make a call, to draw any surveillance in case Grobler had left someone to observe the house. I watched, making sure nobody followed her, slipped over a wall and emerged into a side street. Keeping to the shadows, I walked swiftly away.

Hundreds of suspects had been rounded up in countrywide raids, including Billy and Curnick. Ebe and Bruno had been sleeping away from home and were safe. The other members of our reserve command, David Ndawonde and Stephen Mtshali, commanders of MK units in two important townships, and Abolani Duma, our rural organiser, were safe.

I had an advert inserted in the small columns of a newspaper: 'Reunion of Phoenix art group next Friday.' This was to trigger a meeting of our command. The time and venue had been pre-arranged.

I slipped into the city's botanic gardens on a wintry Friday at dusk. A friend had cut my hair very short and I was wearing glasses. The line of a moustache was already showing on my upper lip. From the shadows I watched David and Stephen enter the gardens and make for a bench, soon to be followed by Ebe. I walked over to join them.

We were delighted to see one another and exchanged news of the arrests and our own situations. We realised that the Special Branch would rely on solitary confinement and interrogation to obtain further information about MK, and all too easily believed that they would learn nothing from those who had been detained. The years of struggle had produced a camaraderie that created a great deal of faith in one another. Much would depend on David and Stephen for our future work. Both young and energetic factory workers, they were relatively unknown to the police and had good contacts in the townships. I reported that Bruno and Duma were safe and arranged a meeting at which all of us would be present.

With Eleanor's behind-the-scenes assistance, we set up our underground headquarters in the Kloof area. Kloof was a small hamlet 15 minutes' drive from Durban, off the highway to Pietermaritzburg. It was a rustic setting where prosperous whites maintained houses with rambling gardens and numerous servants. Eleanor's parents owned a vacant property in the locality. It was bounded by a thick hedge and contained some dilapidated sheds. There was no electricity, but there was a tap with running water in the grounds. The place was lush with sub-tropical flora, a paradise for birds. Eleanor's folks hardly ever visited the place. She asked them if a botany student could camp on the premises for the purpose of a field study. They were well disposed to such things and readily agreed.

I borrowed a van and we set to work cleaning out the sheds and bringing in rudimentary furniture. There was only one enclosed room, in which we slept. It grew dark by 6 p.m. and we used to talk by the light of a lantern. We cooked on a camper's stove and washed at the tap. We dug a latrine and for a fortnight lived a rough and ready life. We were in need of funds and were relieved to receive something from M.P. Naicker. He was sending Eleanor to Johannesburg to obtain more funds for us.

About that time disaster struck again. On 11 July 1963, the security police raided a farm in Rivonia on the outskirts of Johannesburg. There they arrested the top leadership of our Movement, including Walter Sisulu and Govan Mbeki. One of the Special Branch men boasted to Walter Sisulu: 'We've set you people back 20 years.'

We regarded the Kloof property as only a temporary haven. One morning, with my moustache at a respectable length, I spruced up, shaving the stubble off my chin. Dressed in a safari suit, I paid a visit to the local estate agent and, in the plummiest accent I could affect, said I was a writer on holiday from England, looking for a house in the area. An over-refined woman was assigned to take me to view some properties. I finally settled for a modest house in another rustic setting, just five minutes' drive from Kloof.

We were soon ensconced in our new residence, where we created the impression that Bruno was the gardener and Ebe a handyman in my employ. Bruno joked that the set-up was like the Rivonia farm and said we should name our place 'Little Rivonia'. I did not like the suggestion and told him not to tempt fate.

We had trouble furnishing the house. We had insufficient funds and simply concentrated on furnishing the entrance hall and living room. This would give the impression of respectability in case the estate agent or other unwelcome visitors arrived at the front door. Meanwhile, we slept on mattresses on the floor in the bedrooms.

Duma, a peasant who, unlike the others, spoke little English, returned to our base after a successful trip to rural Natal and we soon despatched him on another. We began to realise that insufficient attention had been paid to the rural areas, because most of our cadres were employed in the city. Yet Duma was beginning to recruit many members into MK and, for the first time, we began to sense the possibility of establishing a rural network. This would be invaluable for the development of guerrilla warfare.

David and Stephen reported good progress in reorganising the Durban network after the raids. We began to develop plans for a renewed sabotage offensive, to raise the morale of our supporters. At the same time, we arranged to have a meeting with M.P. Naicker and other political leaders to assess the changed situation and consider our strategy.

As usual we were down on funds. We despatched Eleanor once more to Johannesburg, expecting her to be back the same weekend with the money. It was an overcast Saturday morning in August, a strong wind blowing. I was up early chopping firewood with Bruno. A large locust, bright green and yellow, landed on the grass nearby. Impulsively, I swung the axe and cleaved it in two. Bruno was upset and remonstrated with me, saying that what I had done would bring bad luck. I felt ashamed and apologised. While I buried the insect, he looked on with fear in his eyes. I tried to tell him to put the incident out of his mind. 'After all,' I remarked, 'luck does not turn on something like this.' He immediately pointed out that I had been unhappy when he called our place 'Little Rivonia'.

Bruno was a complicated, intelligent individual and I regretted having upset him. He was meeting David and Stephen at noon at the Kloof property and was going to deliver timing devices to them. In keeping with 'need-to-know' rules, they did not know where we had moved to.

I tried to cheer Bruno up as I gave him a new disguise. I shaved his head and cut his eyebrows. He put on a pair of spectacles and a delivery man's coat. He looked slightly comical but very different. We had little cash left and not much food in the house. He took our last ten shilling note to buy some meat for our supper and off he went, the locust incident apparently forgotten.

By evening Ebe and I were beginning to grow uneasy.

Bruno should have long returned. The evening wore on, and there was still no sign of him.

Once a problem arises, apprehensions about an individual's reliability invariably come to the fore. We began to speculate that he must have gone to a shebeen and got drunk. Even the next morning, when he still failed to appear, we tried to put out of mind the possibilities of arrest. Not only had he got drunk, we fretted, but he had found a woman and spent the night with her.

All day Sunday we sat about hoping he would reappear. We had no money, no transport and were reluctant to move. In the end, we shut the house and retreated into the bush, to watch from relative safety. Just after dusk we heard a car entering our drive. I drew my pistol and cocked it. To our relief, it was Eleanor. 'There's been trouble at Kloof,' she reported.

When we told her about Bruno's disappearance, she immediately concluded that he had been arrested. On returning from Johannesburg that afternoon, she had visited her parents. The police, who had traced them through the local estate agent, had already contacted them, enquiring about a 'native boy' who had been arrested on their Kloof property.

The news meant we had to evacuate the house immediately. Eleanor drove us at high speed to Pietermaritzburg. We had a COD group there and were soon put up in a safe house. The meeting we had arranged with M.P. Naicker and several others was due to take place the next day. We had arranged to meet them at Kloof station. Since I was known to the estate agent whose office was nearby, and had become a familiar figure in the Kloof high street, Ebe undertook to go to the area and inform M.P. and the others that we were having to cancel the meeting. I bade Ebe farewell that morning as he caught a bus for Kloof.

Eleanor came to see me that evening with more alarming news. M.P. Naicker and scores of others had been arrested the night before. Many were important members of the MK network. There was some concern about Stephen Mtshali and David Ndawonde. Both were missing. It began to look as though Ebe had been arrested too.

There were instructions from Vera and George. I was to report to Johannesburg on the situation, and remain there as it would be safer for me. Apparently there were 'Wanted' posters about me in all the police stations, and they felt it would simply be a matter of time before the Special Branch caught up with me.

I objected and told Eleanor to tell them that she could go to Johannesburg and make the report. I felt I should remain in Pietermaritzburg, as a base from which we could reorganise.

At this point Eleanor gave me a sealed envelope. Vera had asked her to hand it to me if I was stubborn. It was a curt statement in Vera's hand: 'Comrade, orders are orders. There can be no debate. You are to go to Jo'burg at once – Vera.' There was a PS: 'Good luck and take care!'

I was concerned about Eleanor's safety, which could be jeopardised by the arrests. She told me that Vera was worried about her too. It was agreed that she would take time off work and sleep at friends. Vera and George wanted her to leave for Johannesburg in a few days' time to discuss her role with the leaders there. She had already placed her daughter, Brigid, with her parents out of harm's way. She strove to bury deep within her an all-consuming love for the child; a hope that the separation would only be temporary; that she was fighting for a better country for children to grow up in; and an optimism that the government could not last much longer in power. Eleanor was an extremely brave young woman whose genteel exterior, quick wit and sophisticated grace hid an inner strength and loathing of cruelty and injustice that had gradually compelled her to join me in the struggle for freedom and equality. Not only had she demonstrated her courage and skill as a getaway driver but creative innovation in obtaining the key to the dynamite enclosure. She proved her courage in working at my side in several other sabotage operations where we had posted a pipe bomb at night at the central Durban Post Office and another at the premises of the Durban Special Branch. Eleanor was the first woman in MK to engage in operations. She showed that whites were able to risk their world of security, privilege and sacrifice if need be in a just and noble cause. She was already showing a natural predilection for clandestine work and the bookstore where she worked had become an important point for underground activists to receive funds and messages through her. With the situation in the country growing even more precarious, the role of the likes of Eleanor was becoming even more vital if the outlawed organisation was to survive. No one would have guessed that this winsome, slender young blonde, a divorcee with a young child, was a secret agent working to topple the racist regime.

By the next morning Ebe had failed to return and we assumed the worst. I felt particularly depressed because it had been a case of him or me going to Kloof. I embraced Eleanor and we arranged to meet in Johannesburg. That, at least, was something to look forward to.

SIX

INTO EXILE

Johannesburg, Pietermaritzburg, Bechuanaland
August–October

ONCE IN JOHANNESBURG, I WAS reporting to Bram Fischer, an important figure in the underground. As a leading advocate from a prestigious Afrikaner family, he enjoyed respect from many quarters. In his mid-fifties, he was a courteous man, with a gentle smile and silver-grey hair. He enquired about Eleanor, who had been reporting to him on the situation in Durban. He clearly liked her and said she resembled his youngest daughter. In the following weeks, he visited me frequently. A great deal of his time was taken up with the Rivonia arrests. The blows to the Movement must have placed an immense strain on him, more particularly since it was clear that he was shouldering the burden of leading the rearguard action. Yet he remained composed, sprightly and witty during all the times he attended to me.

He was assisted by Hilda Bernstein, an accomplished woman in her forties, whose husband Rusty had been arrested during the Rivonia raid. Hilda, with large, expressive eyes, transmitted the same resilience as Bram. She was a veteran in the Movement. I had previously met her at Rowley's when she returned by way of Durban from a visit to China. I discovered that she, like the Ponnens, had no sympathy with his criticism of MK.

Eleanor arrived with her blonde hair dyed black. It made her look quite different. The Durban comrades thought that she was at risk and wanted to send her out of the country. After long deliberations, Bram asked her to consider going back to Durban because of the role she could play in the reconstruction of the underground. It was, admittedly, a risk, but without batting an eye she agreed. It was more the problem of re-dyeing her hair back to its original colour that bothered her. She was most preoccupied, however, about being separated from her daughter.

Not long after, the newspapers reported her detention at work under the

43

heading 'Blonde Divorcee Held in Durban under 90-Day Act.' I began to keep a calendar of Eleanor's detention, striking each day off last thing at night. The depression sat heavily on me and the time dragged. John Bizzel, one of our Durban recruits, was working in Johannesburg and helped to keep up my spirits.

One day he brought my parents to see me. I was relieved to find that although they were anxious about my safety there were no recriminations. In fact they were supportive. Ever since I had become politically involved my mother had given me more or less instinctive support. My father had sought to understand my position – not without strong arguments against – and had come to respect my views. My parents' main desire was that I should leave the country.

This was beginning to look a distinct possibility although I vowed to myself that I would never leave without Eleanor. According to Bram, the Durban comrades were recommending I be sent for military training as part of the growing force assembling abroad. Although he considered keeping me with him in Johannesburg, he was loath to disagree with their request.

The next time Bram visited me, he brought good news about Eleanor. She had managed to get herself transferred to a hospital and had found a way of smuggling out a letter. What was more, she thought she had a chance of escaping. He handed me her note:

Lieutenent [sic] Grobler and another SB arrested me at work. They wanted to know where R was. I was kept in solitary at the central jail. I was interrogated constantly. Where was R? Where were the explosives? I am sure Bruno is co-operating with them. He must have told them within 36 hours about the house because they raided the place shortly after we left. There are lots of indications that he is talking. They know virtually everything about our operations and some of the details about me which, as far as I can be sure, only R, Billy and Bruno were aware of. And Billy has not talked at all. The SB remark how stubborn he is. Ebe never talked either. All the investigating officers are new boys, not the ones we've come to know, except Grobler who is vicious. He threatened me on numerous occasions and pulled my hair in fury. He is anti-Semitic and rants on about how Jewish men misuse 'Christian' girls. After I was transferred here my father was allowed to visit me. He said the SBs boasted that 'the native caught at Kloof was singing like a canary' and they 'hadn't even laid a finger on him'.

Don't be alarmed that I am here – in Fort Napier – a mental asylum! I just had to get out of prison to find a way of warning you about Bruno. It was easy to feign a mental breakdown. They have been uncertain how to handle me. I refused to eat for six days and just allowed myself to appear depressed and ill. They brought in a psychiatrist who recommended I be transferred here. I'm in a lock-up with about 20 poor wretches. Some are completely round the bend but it's surprising how quickly one gets used to this sort of thing. I've made contact with some sympathetic people here, and it's possible to escape. I'll need transport to pick me up once I'm out of the grounds. I don't know how long the SB will tolerate my presence here. It's supposed to be temporary.

Bram looked keenly at me. There were two key questions on his mind. Firstly, did I think Bruno could have collapsed? Some comrades in Johannesburg, who had dealt with him, felt it was unlikely.

I pondered for a moment, finding it difficult to make a negative pronouncement about a comrade in detention who could be fighting for his life. I replied, however, that it was possible. I told him about Bruno's drinking problem, which we had largely ignored, and suggested it might have hidden unperceived weaknesses. The second question Bram put to me concerned Eleanor's escape plan. Could we rely on her assessment? I answered positively but indicated that the nervous breakdown worried me.

He called it a 'clever ruse'. She was only the second white woman to be detained under the 90-day Act and, in his view, the authorities were terrified something might go wrong. There were psychiatrists with integrity who would give someone the benefit of the doubt and have them removed from solitary confinement to hospital or a mental institution. He wound up by asking: 'You don't think there's anything strange about the letter, do you?'

'No,' I laughed, 'she's only spelt lieutenant wrong. She's normally a good speller.'

We began working with the Pietermaritzburg group to effect her escape. In the event, she carried it off virtually single-handedly. While they agonised over every detail of their preparations, she acted.

The first news I got was from John Bizzel, who came to celebrate with me. 'Great news about Eleanor!' he proclaimed joyfully.

When he saw my blank expression he exclaimed: 'Her escape! Haven't you seen the papers today?'

I had glanced through the Sunday newspapers but had missed a small item reporting the escape. It briefly indicated Eleanor had been in police custody but had disappeared. Roadblocks had been set up around Pietermaritzburg and police were searching for her. I was ecstatic with joy and longed to hold her again.

Some days later I heard a faint rustling at the front door of my flat. I was expecting Eleanor but remained dead quiet and listened intently. Then, unable to contain my impatience any longer, I flung open the door.

I was confronted by a boy in grey flannels and sports jacket, with pale face and dark hair under a cap. The tall, slightly-built figure gave me a start. But then I recognised the impish smile. It was a moment of triumph. Eleanor and I danced around the room.

When the excitement of our reunion had subsided, she related her story. It began with her arrest at work. She had attempted to dodge behind a bookcase and slip out the rear door, but the SBs were too quick for her. She was held in solitary, at the female section of Durban Central, and taken to an interrogation centre virtually every day by Grobler.

'He's desperate to get you. He brags that he always gets his man and that you're going to hang. He kept making obscene remarks about Jewish men – cursing me for going out with you.'

She talked about a crack unit formed to deal with MK. They appeared more efficient than the others but still relied on basic detection, building systematically from one clue to another, and relying heavily on interrogation. There was no speculation about our strategic aim other than: 'You people are out to ruin the country so that Russia can take over.'

From snatched conversations at the interrogation centre she knew that neither Ebe nor Billy had spoken. Billy had taunted them to kill him if they liked, but he was not going to open his mouth. After arresting Ebe at Kloof station they had taken him to a lonely spot and beaten him unconscious, without learning anything from him. It was Bruno and a few others who had collapsed. The SB boasted that Bruno started talking the day after his detention. They said they knew how to deal with a criminal, revealing that he was a thief who had served several years' imprisonment for breaking into railway property.

It was obvious why Bruno had displayed such skill breaking into the dynamite magazine. We had all too easily accepted his credentials, without really knowing him. If it had been only Eleanor's and my mistake, we might have concluded that the reason for the misjudgement was overcompensation born of some white guilt complex, resulting in an uncritical attitude about a black person's weaknesses. But Billy, Curnick and even senior Johannesburg comrades had been taken in by Bruno's charm and ability.

Eleanor had so much to get off her chest that she scarcely paused. It appeared that disaster first struck with the arrest of Stephen Mtshali's wife. There was some problem between her and Stephen, and she had informed the police where he was hiding. Perhaps the shock of his wife's betrayal affected his morale, for it emerged that he had led the SB to the Kloof rendezvous with Bruno.

Once she realised how desperate the situation was, Eleanor's mind turned to escaping. She began by refusing to take food and then allowed herself to start weeping. When she saw how this disturbed the SB, she 'opened the floodgates'. A psychiatrist was called in. He told the police that she was in no state to be interrogated and required hospital treatment.

They had driven her to Fort Napier, a large mental hospital converted from a 19th-century colonial fort and surrounded by high walls. As they drove through the main gate she was warned not to think she was 'so smart', because she was going to be locked up in the security section for the insane. This was a single-storey building which stood out from the others because of the bars and wire mesh on the windows. Waiting for the door to open had been a terrifying moment.

From within the building Eleanor could hear the sound of moaning and shrieking. Inside was a score of patients wandering aimlessly about. They were young and old, and dreadfully pale. One woman was trying to pull her hair out. Another was bumping her head against the wall so that a wound in her forehead began to bleed. Nurses ran to control her, and as she was pulled away, she screamed for her child. Eleanor, with her seven-year-old daughter Brigid very much in mind, looked around in horror for the infant. But as the woman was led away, she sobbed uncontrollably: 'Oh my baby Jesus! My sweet baby, why did they crucify you?'

The patients slept in large wards. Much to Eleanor's relief, she was taken to a single cell and locked in for the night. There was constant shuffling outside her door, and the eyes of patients peering at her through a grille. Next morning she was loath to leave her cell, and the nurses had to coax her out for breakfast. They told her the patients were harmless. This was the case. Many had been sedated for years. Some ignored her. Others were curious about the 'new girl', and stared and giggled. The more adventurous touched her. She began to help the nurses look after them, and discovered a few lucid women with whom she played cards. She was locked up in her cell every night, and mixed with the patients from breakfast every day.

One afternoon a week there was a dance for the patients in the open section. Eleanor pleaded with the sister in charge to take her along. This was agreed to when she promised not to run away. The female patients queued up to be dabbed with powder and lipstick by a nurse. Everyone wore their Sunday best. The men lined up on one side of the hall and the women on the other. The music was provided by an old gramophone player and, when a record began, the men raced across the hall to choose their partners.

'It was old-fashioned stuff,' Eleanor explained to me, '*tickey draai* (a Boer dance).' With one arm around an imaginary waist, she extended her other arm and pumping it stiffly up and down, waltzed around the room.

I had been horrified when I learnt she was in an asylum, believing she would be mentally scarred for life. It was a relief to find her in such good form.

Eleanor returned to the story of her escape. She had asked one of the more lucid patients to invite one of our COD colleagues for a visit. The woman agreed and together they wrote a letter to a student in Pietermaritzburg. Curiosity led him to respond, and he duly arrived at Fort Napier. He was not sure what it was about. At that stage the comrades outside did not know Eleanor was being detained there. While he was speaking to the patient, Eleanor walked past and slipped him two notes. One was for Bram and me, the other detailed the assistance she would need for the escape.

Some days later, while she was waiting for a response, she heard from one of the nursing staff that the police would be taking her back to Durban the following day.

That night Eleanor finalised her plans. She had cultivated a friendship with an African nurse who agreed to leave a crucial door momentarily unlocked just before breakfast the following morning.

Dressed smartly in clothing she had hidden, a scarf tied around her head, she was soon walking through the grounds of Fort Napier. It was the change of shift with members of staff, many out of uniform, arriving and departing. Nobody paid any attention to her. When she walked through the open gates the guards ignored her. Once out of the grounds she resisted the temptation to run. There was a nasty moment when one of the institute's ambulances drove past her on the way into town.

The comrades who helped her were taken aback by her sudden escape. They quickly fitted her out as a boy. Because the disguise was so good they decided to get her out of town as quickly as possible. Although Pietermaritzburg was ringed with roadblocks, the police paid attention only to vehicles with young women.

Eleanor's hair had been cropped very short. She put the cap back on for me and adopted a jaunty attitude. 'Good day to you, sir,' she said in an attempt at a masculine voice. We roared with laughter. 'Your mother wouldn't recognise you,' I joked.

The mention of family unsettled Eleanor. She became anxious for the first time: 'I'm so worried about my parents. My father was devastated when I saw him. And what will I do about Brigid?'

She looked distraught. I attempted to console her, saying that at least Brigid was in good hands. Once Eleanor was safely out of the country we would contact her folks and send for her. She desperately wanted to believe that was possible.

We were driven to the Bechuanaland border by Babla Saloojee. Slightly built, with a dashing moustache and merry eyes, he infected everyone with his ready wit. He had the reputation for being a daring and resourceful person. I gathered that he had made many runs back and forth to the border.

Eleanor had been fitted out in traditional Moslem dress. She wore an elaborate sequined dress over Punjabi trousers. Her hands and face had been smeared with a dark cream and she had on a long, black wig. She had grown very quiet as we travelled. I sensed she was extremely tense. I was made to look like a prosperous Indian businessman, in a suit and beard. Bram had given us letters and cards in the name of an Indian couple.

There were two elderly men with us. One was Julius First, father of the renowned anti-apartheid figure Ruth First. He was a taciturn man in spectacles who constantly smoked cigars, which did not help Eleanor's mood. He was having to leave the country because of his connections with the purchase of the Rivonia farm. Bram had asked me to take care of him. The other man was Maulvi Cachalia, who was helping Babla and was there to reinforce the conservative impression of our collective image. He had a long grey beard and wore traditional Moslem garb. He looked every inch a holy man and, as Babla explained, 'Maulvi' was not his first name, as I had supposed, but was the term for a priest.

Babla headed for the western Transvaal. Eleanor's tension seemed to affect the rest of us. We dreaded being stopped in a roadblock. Babla sensed the unease and informed us that comrades in a pilot car had undertaken the route ahead of us. They had telephoned to say the road was clear.

'In any event,' he said, 'if we do come across a roadblock just leave me to do the talking. They're seldom interested in the passengers and we look a respectable crew.'

After three hours on the road, we drove through Mafeking. Babla explained that we were in the northern Cape and, as we began to veer westwards, he announced that we were travelling parallel to the Bechuanaland border. We had under an hour to go before we reached the crossing point. We would get there just after daybreak.

At that stage, there was the possibility of us encountering a border patrol along the road, but Babla told us to remain calm. Along the border there were several shops with which he had contact, and he carried papers to prove it. 'So I'll just say we're taking the Maulvi to say some prayers.'

The countryside was dry and flat, with occasional rocky outcrops, scattered bush and small herds of goats. There were numerous homesteads along the road and we passed the occasional peasant driving a cart drawn by donkeys.

Babla pointed out a ridge to the north and informed us that we were almost at our destination. The road veered to the right and he began slowing down. I fancied I could make out a high fence a few hundred metres away. He came to a stop by a couple of thorn trees.

As we hurriedly disembarked he gave me directions, pointing out a red-roofed store on the Bechuanaland side, several hundred metres distant. We would find a wooden ladder at the border fence, a crossing point for the local peasants. Friends in a Land Rover would be on hand to meet us on the other side.

Julius First and Maulvi Cachalia were standing by the road dragging out their farewells. Eleanor called out in alarm that a vehicle was coming. I could see the dust cloud approaching just a mile away. Julius had two heavy bags. Eleanor and I had a hold-all between us. I picked up all three bags. Eleanor was going to have to support Julius.

At last Babla got Maulvi into the car and off they sped. Eleanor, who had changed out of the Punjabi dress and wig, took Julius by the arm and we ran for cover. Just as we got down behind some boulders, a police vehicle sped past. It seemed to be chasing after Babla. As soon as it was out of sight, we were on the move, hoping that Babla would be able to talk his way out of possible trouble.

Although we only had a few hundred metres to walk, it was up a gentle slope and we had to pick our way through several *dongas* (ditches). The cream on Eleanor's face was becoming a sticky mess. It had become very hot and Julius First was having trouble with his breathing.

At last we came to the ladder. There were homesteads nearby – on both sides of the border – and a couple of villagers stared at us in astonishment. I looked around anxiously, hoping nobody was going to challenge us at this final stage.

Eleanor went up the ladder first and waited at the top as I helped Julius follow her. She descended and then guided him down. The bags were too big to be passed through the wire. I had to heft them up the ladder, one at a time. Finally I got over myself, to see, against the northern skyline, a Land Rover arriving at the store with the red roof. Its arrival could not have been more perfectly timed.

We were on the soil of the British Protectorate of Bechuanaland. I never imagined that I would be relieved to see the Union Jack. It was the beginning of October, 1963. We expected that we would return as part of a victorious revolutionary army in a couple of years at the most. Not for a moment did we anticipate that we were going into exile for decades.

It would be many years later that I would obtain some insight into the security police files on me. In motivating the Minister of Justice to ban me in 1962 they reported me as delivering '*vurige toesprake*' (fiery speeches) which aroused 'non-white' audiences. I was a '*besliste gevaar*' (definite danger) to the safety of the state and consequently promoted the aims of communism. The speeches they wrote down showed youthful passion with declarations such as: 'The African giant has stirred and is awake! The ANC is banned but goes marching on! The youth of today will rule South Africa tomorrow!' (File 1032, National Archive.)

PART II

EXILE
1963–89

SEVEN

NORTHERN HIGHWAY

Bechuanaland, Tanzania, Odessa, London
October 1963 – September 1965

BY THE TIME WE REACHED THE STORE with the red roof, Eleanor's brown make-up was a sticky mess, Julius First was having palpitations, and my arms were seized with cramp. The comrades in the Land Rover relieved me of the bags and helped Julius and Eleanor into the vehicle.

The comrades who arrived so punctually were Batswana citizens who had joined the ANC in South Africa and were part of an efficient 'underground pipeline' established by Joe Modise. We drove to a township outside Lobatse and were carried into a house, wrapped in blankets. They explained that they had to be vigilant about South African agents. In fact, a charter plane for ANC fugitives had been blown up the previous month. We heard with relief that all was well with Babla. In order to travel safely on to Tanzania, where the ANC had its headquarters, we needed to report our arrival to the district commissioner.

While we waited outside the commissioner's door we had a foretaste of his character. A messenger arrived with mail and ceremoniously clapped his hands to gain admission. We found the commissioner to be a haughty individual, in old-style shirt and shorts. He looked disdainfully at us, sneering at Julius First for having to flee South Africa at his age. When he questioned us on where we had entered the Crown territory, we gave a different route from the one we had used. He enquired which way we had turned once we reached 'the tarred road'. Eleanor and I responded simultaneously – 'left,' she said; 'right,' said I. We could not conceal our mirth, and he turned scarlet with rage.

His young assistants, at least, were friendly and showed by their attitude that they were more in step with the 'winds of change' than he. We were granted political asylum and photographed.

Now that we were officially in Bechuanaland, the comrades suggested we book into a hotel under false names as tourists, because we would draw too much attention in the township. The hotel manager took us at face value and confided that 'those communists, Jack and Rica Hodgson,' had passed through a few weeks before, after jumping house-arrest orders. We spent a week, waiting for a charter flight, passing the time doing large jigsaw puzzles and playing cards.

We finally departed in a six-seater aircraft for Tanzania, which had just become independent. On departure we were automatically declared Prohibited Immigrants. Our pilot, an Afrikaner, turned out to be a sinister character. Within five minutes of being airborne he bragged that he had engaged in gun-running for Tshombe in Katanga, and was one of the few gentiles whose name was in the 'Golden Book of the Jews'. I sat right behind him, with a hunting knife in my pocket, eyes glued to the compass needle, while Eleanor was getting air-sick from the fumes of Julius' cigar.

Our first stop was Kasane on the banks of the Zambezi. The district commissioner there was even more hostile than the previous one. We were forced to spend the night in the police cells because he 'could not guarantee our safety'. The next day we overflew Northern Rhodesia for Tanzania.

We were in high spirits when we reached Dar es Salaam – Arabic for 'Haven of Peace'. Along with other liberation movements, the ANC had an office in the town and several transit camps. Among the senior leaders were two old friends – Moses Kotane and Duma Nokwe. Eleanor and I were accommodated in a guesthouse in the Arab quarter, opposite a mosque. We awoke in the mornings to the sound of the priests calling the faithful to prayer. One of our neighbours was Mosie Moolla who, like Eleanor, had escaped from police custody. We discovered, to our amusement, that he had been spirited out of the country by Babla, wearing Eleanor's wig and attire. Together with him, we licked stamps and answered the telephone at the ANC office. This was the ground floor of a shabby building, jammed between a row of struggling businesses. Cheap partitioning created a number of work places. The inner sanctum of the premises was a large room where the national leadership – house-hold names in South Africa – faced one another across old desks placed in a semi-circle.

My parents were overjoyed to hear on the radio that we had arrived safely in East Africa. But I soon received a letter informing me that my father had suddenly become ill and passed away. I was jolted by his death, and upset that I had not been present at his bedside. I was frustrated that I could not console my mother and be present at his funeral. Although I was not religious, I needed to say the traditional Judaic incantation for the dead. I visited the Israeli Embassy, where one of the officials assisted me in reciting the prayer. I was one of the first to experience the pangs of a family death in exile, and Eleanor and my colleagues rallied to comfort me.

When New Year's Day 1964 arrived, the ships in Dar es Salaam harbour sounded their foghorns. The harbour, the palm trees, the clammy heat, all reminded us of Durban and, with the mournful sound of the foghorns, Eleanor became depressed. She cried, fearing she would not see Brigid again. I tried to console her, but the absence of her child over the festive period had been weighing on her. She had tried to suppress the pangs of separation, and I had been oblivious to her suffering. During her hectic political initiation Eleanor, like so many others in the Movement, had responded to the pressing demands of the moment, and, for the sake of convenience and reasons of security, had left Brigid in the care of her parents. She now feared that her ex-husband would never allow Brigid to leave the country. What we failed to consider was the attachment her parents would develop for the child with whom they did not want to part. She began to wish that we had picked up Brigid and fled with her. We had considered this at the time but, on Bram's advice, had rejected it as being too risky.

Most of our colleagues were struggling with similar dilemmas. We were all beginning to feel the exile's bitter separation from loved ones. Mosie's wife and children had been left behind too, and it would be years before he saw them. We met up with Joe Modise who had also left his family behind. The same applied to Duma Nokwe and, of course, Moses Kotane. Many of the young people in our transit camps had left their homes without even warning their parents of their departures, so stringent were the security rules. Many were married and had young families. Few were consciously abandoning their responsibilities. Everyone expected to return home after completing training. Eleanor was beginning to have a premonition, however, that she would not see Brigid. That Brigid would grow up to have different values to her.

Back home, the Rivonia trial in Pretoria, and what was dubbed the 'Little Rivonia' trial in Pietermaritzburg, were starting. Nelson Mandela had been taken from Robben Island to join Walter Sisulu and others for having organised over 150 major acts of sabotage.

Among the more dramatic actions was the destruction by a powerful bomb of a cabinet minister's office in Pretoria. Electric pylons, transformers, railway lines, signal points, pass offices and other installations had been hit.

In Pietermaritzburg, Billy Nair, Curnick Ndlovu, Ebrahim Ismail, David Ndawonde and almost a score more were charged under the Sabotage Act. It was evident that Bruno Mtolo and Stephen Mtshali would be giving state evidence. Eleanor's assessment during her detention proved correct. We also felt depressed about being free while our comrades were facing possible death sentences. Many of our colleagues, fugitives like us, were in the same position.

Dar es Salaam, on the old East African slave route, and now the base of liberation movements, was a romantic place. We watched the Arab dhows sail in from the Persian Gulf and gazed at the exquisite carpets and other wares the crews unfurled on the town pavements. The *New Africa* hotel was a splendid colonial building – all wood and white paint, palm trees and verandahs – where the international diplomatic set and freedom fighters took refreshments and conspired. There we met some of the youthful leaders of the Mozambican Liberation Front (FRELIMO), including Joaquim Chissano and Marcelino dos Santos – later President and Vice-President respectively of Mozambique. A young woman I had known as a schoolgirl in Yeoville, Pam Beira, had fled South Africa and become part of our crowd. She later married Marcelino. We discussed co-operation between our organisations and analysed the situation in our respective countries over endless cups of coffee. If we had a few East African shillings in our pockets, and it was sundown, we would call out to the turbanned waiters: 'Tusker beer, *baridi sana* [very cold] *bwana*,' and acknowledge their service with that charming Swahili expression – '*asante sana* [thank you very much].'

Every week plane-loads of recruits from the various liberation movements travelled to North African and socialist countries for military training. By February it was my turn. Eleanor remained behind to work in the ANC office, She had decided to develop contact with her parents in the hope of sorting out Brigid's position.

I travelled to the Soviet Union with Joe Modise and Moses Mabhida. We were joining a group of 300 recruits who had already left for Odessa in the Ukraine. Modise was to be commander of the group and Mabhida, Luthuli's right-hand man in Natal, the commissar – or political officer. I had only recently met Mabhida, a proud-looking man with a Bismarck-style moustache. He had been extremely kind to Eleanor and sensitive to her problem. I discovered that he had an important quality of true leadership – compassion.

After all the accounts one had heard of the October Revolution and the building of socialism it was thrilling to land in a snow-clad Moscow. As we arrived Mabhida reminded us, with a deep-throated chuckle, that this was the state that a former leader of the ANC had dubbed 'the new Jerusalem' in 1927. We were met by a *polkovnik* (colonel) of the Soviet army in an imposing astrakhan hat. He dined us in an Uzbek restaurant filled with a hubbub of conversation and aromatic cooking. He toasted the success of our struggle. Following his example, we downed our vodkas in a single swallow. Mabhida raised his glass and toasted 'the land of Lenin'. With increasing aplomb, we again emptied our glasses, learning – Russian-style – to cope with the 'kick' by taking a salty morsel with our drinks.

We stayed the night at the Ukraine Hotel, one of Stalin's wedding-cake buildings. Snowflakes fluttered over the city as I gazed out of my window. I was struck by the quiet order that pervaded the scene. Snow-ploughs were already clearing the roads and there was a sense of peace and stability. I had seen no bread queues and, in fact, the people on the streets appeared well-fed and well-clad. Not only that, but the patrons in the restaurant and those in the bustling hotel foyer appeared in good spirits.

To my eyes, and those of my companions, the system which our enemies in South Africa projected as being on the verge of collapse, appeared to be prospering. I cannot say it struck any of us then that we were privileged visitors catered for by officialdom, and that reality for ordinary people in a territory one-sixth the size of the globe might be different. Perhaps we might have been more perceptive to the defects in the system had Western cold war propaganda been less hostile and hypocritical. While the West offered only pious statements about apartheid's evils, the Soviet Union gave practical support. It appeared that their interests in seeing the end of colonialism and racism in Africa were similar to ours.

The next day we arrived in Odessa, where we were to stay until November. Modise and Mabhida immediately took charge of the detachment. I joined a unit specialising in military engineering, under the command of a lively and irreverent character called Joel Klaas. He was later based in Lusaka, where for years he loyally served the ANC. To this day, I defer to him as *tovarish komandir* (comrade commander).

Joel was a young recruit from a village in the Eastern Cape. His father was a migrant labourer working ten months a year on the Rand mines. His mother struggled to find some work in the white farmers' kitchens. The family lived in a simple house and Joel used to walk ten kilometres in his bare feet to school each day. He had managed to get some work in a factory and was caught up in a strike. He was attracted to the ANC and readily agreed to leave the country for military training.

Joel was typical of most of the younger recruits, some of whom were only 17 or 18. The older cadres were in their mid-twenties or early thirties. They had been in the Movement for several years and were politically experienced. Whatever their age, however, unless they had related to leadership figures or the small group of COD members like myself, none had ever been in a white person's home. Virtually all of our contingent, therefore, were experiencing, for the first time in their lives, care and hospitality at the hands of white people. We were not only trained by Soviet officers, but male and female service personnel cooked for us, served us, kitted us out in military and civilian dress, provided medical care and generally fussed over us with motherly concern. For us, this was 'socialist solidarity' and 'proletarian internationalism' in practice. My colleagues also experienced non-racism for the first time in their lives. South Africa, and its capitalist system, did not bear comparison.

It did not occur to us that we were receiving special treatment. Years later, when I met one of the interpreters again, he told me how we had been provided with quality cigarettes in short supply to the Soviet officers. They had to make do with Papirosa, a cheap cigarette with a hollow tube.

The service staff were curious about my white skin and enquired '*pochemu byeli chelovyek?*' (how come you are a white person?), while the instructors were interested to know how I had become involved in the struggle. For my part, I had long stopped thinking of myself in colour terms and I believed my comrades no longer noticed my pigmentation – which was a liberating experience.

Some of the Soviet staff did ask what a '*prekrasni malchik*' (nice boy) like me was doing in a *chorniye* (black) army, and there were the odd fisticuffs with our comrades over the waitresses in the mess. Generally, fraternisation was good. Those were early days of co-operation between the USSR and students from Africa and elsewhere. It was later, in the 1980s, when the system began misfiring, that frustrations surfaced and relations between some of the common people and long-term visitors came under strain.

The doctor at the clinic, who gave us a medical check-up on arrival, was obviously Jewish. When I used the term '*shalom*' to greet him, he could not believe his ears. We had a cheerful conversation but, for whatever reason – whether fear or embarrassment – he politely asked me not to use the term again.

We were housed in a double-storey building which was part of a military training base. Our instructors were veterans of the war against Hitler – the Great Patriotic War as they referred to it. They were a tough, hearty breed who used a great deal of good humour and firmness to knock us into shape. They cut a splendid sight in their greatcoats, leather belts, karakul hats with the red star emblem, and Cossack-style boots. They would bark out their commands and encourage us with good humour. There was scarcely an individual we disliked. It was the big-boned physique, the directness and mirth, and a hardy quality, that came to remind us of the Boers at home.

We were kitted out in the same manner as Soviet conscripts. We wore tunics over our trousers, which were tucked into knee-high boots. Instead of wearing socks, we learnt how to wrap *portyanka* – a flannel cloth – around our feet and up our legs. This had been the tradition as far back as Czarist times. We discovered that this provided better insulation from the cold than ordinary socks. Around our waists we wore leather belts with brass buckles, on which were the hammer-and-sickle insignia. Out of doors we donned dove-grey fur hats (*shapkas*) and the traditional grey army coat. At night, or when the snow was falling, and we turned up the collars of our coats and turned down the earpieces of our *shapkas*, we were indistinguishable from the Soviet soldiers, more particularly since many among us soon became fluent in Russian.

There was a great spirit among us, and no higher than when we marched Red-Army-style, goose-stepping, with arms swinging across the chest, around the parade ground, singing our national songs. The most popular of these was *Sing amaSoja kaLuthuli* (Sing soldiers of Luthuli). Our own officers would bark out commands in Russian – '*Smyeerna!*' (attention), and '*Volna!*' (at ease) – and the kitchen staff would shout encouragement to the *chorniye Ruskiye* (black Russians) as we called ourselves.

One of the first exercises I participated in was at the shooting range. The detachment had been introduced to the famous AK-47 assault rifle. Designed in 1947 by a wartime veteran, Mikhail Kalashnikov, its uncomplicated design, accuracy under all conditions, fire power and durability made the 'Aftomat Kalashnikova' the most sought-after weapon of its type in the world. At the end of a day's firing a handful of us had scored sufficiently high marks to go forward to a more complicated exercise. I had done well because of all the years of practice with an airgun on Yeoville koppie. The others who distinguished themselves had undergone training in Algeria, Egypt and China. We were congratulated by the Soviet commander and allowed to shoot at pop-up targets at 200 metres. We shot these down as fast as they appeared, with the detachment cheering us on.

One of the most unforgettable of the Soviet officers was our political instructor, a swarthy Armenian by the name of Major Chubinikyan. He lectured us for the best part of the year without once referring to notes and took us through the history of the Russian Revolution, the basics of socialism and communism, the building of socialism, and the world revolutionary movement. He was scathing about Stalinism, trenchant about capitalist exploitation and often hilarious about revolution.

'Revolushin iz not rock en roll', was one of the phrases he liked to repeat in English and, later in the year when a new dance craze was sweeping the West, he replaced the latter phrase by 'the tvist'. Revolution was a 'tough prospect', not to be indulged in lightly, and he stressed that armed struggle should only be embarked on if no democratic liberties existed. He warned that revolution had its setbacks and defeats, but that development was always forwards.

He explained why the proletariat was the 'gravedigger' of the capitalist system, and why socialism was superior to capitalism. He liked to use the phrases, 'man to man as wolf to wolf' and 'man to man as friend, comrade and brother', to contrast the value system of the former with the latter.

He told us of the backwardness and poverty of the Czarist system and the strides made by the Soviet Union, the first country to put a man into space.

As an Armenian, he was proud to tell us that before the Revolution, Armenia was 'a nation of shoe-shine boys' and now had 'the highest per capita ratio of doctors and engineers in the world'. Khrushchev, the Soviet Premier, had declared that communism would be built by 1980, which greatly appealed to us. But I noticed that Chubinikyan preferred to suggest that it could be a longer process. He stressed that communism was impossible without the creation of an abundance of goods in a country. The communist principle of distribution – 'from each according to his ability to each according to his needs' – could only be introduced once there was sufficient wealth, According to the programme of the CPSU (Communist Party of the Soviet Union), 'the material and technical basis of communism' would be created in two stages. During the first stage, 1961–1970, production would be increased two-and-a-half times. In the second stage, 1971–1980, production would increase six-fold. By the end of that stage, the USSR would have the highest living standard in the world and 'the decisive victory would be won in the economic battle against capitalism'.

In retrospect, these goals were, quite frankly, unrealistic. At the time, however, we believed in them, as our Soviet friends did. It is difficult now to credit that anyone thought the USSR really could outstrip the USA in 20 years. But their economic growth at the time was impressive.

It was firmly believed that capitalism was in decay and that monopolistic contradictions would bring the system down. Those were the days of Khrushchev banging his shoe at the UN, and declaring 'we will bury you' to the West. With the help of the Soviet bloc, the former colonies would find a non-capitalist path to socialism.

The Sino-Soviet dispute was at its height. There were heated disputes within our ranks between a dozen or so who had undergone a short training course in China, and the rest. Mao Tse-tung had theorised that the so-called 'third world' was the new centre of revolution. He downgraded the role of the USSR and other socialist countries of Europe, and of the international working class. Both the SACP and the ANC opposed this view and shared the perception that Beijing was attempting to create splits within organisations in order to win support for the so-called 'China line'.

While there was no victimisation of the minority view within our ranks, Chubinikyan and the other Soviet officers denounced Maoism at every opportunity. Central to the polemic was the theory of 'peaceful co-existence.' According to the Soviet position, the alternative to the co-existence of socialist and capitalist camps was war, and this should be avoided. The socialist system would demonstrate its superiority by economic progress 'in peaceful competition' with capitalism. According to the theory, the capitalist economies would become progressively weaker because of the prolonged period of peace.

The Chinese, by contrast, were seen to be warmongers. They had fought India in 1962 and were determined to develop nuclear weapons at the cost of essential material progress. They advocated the idea that political power could only be attained 'through the barrel of a gun'.

China desired the Bomb because she wanted to become a world leader at any cost, Chubinikyan alleged. But the people had to experience the benefits of the revolution. It was no good being an 'atomic god' while your people went hungry.

The reasoning sounded plausible to us, particularly since the policy of peaceful co-existence allowed for Soviet assistance to national liberation struggles. It is ironic, however, that the very argument being used at the time against the Chinese is what finally led to the bankruptcy of the Soviet Union.

Following Khrushchev's denunciation of Stalin in 1956, the USSR seemed to be set on a course of economic advance which would incorporate greater freedom. We believed that Stalinist command system had been a consequence of Western attempts to crush the Soviet Union at birth and then its encouragement of Hitler's invasion: a war that accounted for 20 million Soviet citizens dead, 1000 large towns and cities destroyed, and 100,000 villages razed to the ground. Now that the Soviet Union had recovered, everything was possible.

From our leadership down, our Movement had unquestioning confidence in the integrity and capability of the Soviet Union, which, with the wisdom of hindsight, was a misjudgement. Even at that time, I sensed that revolutionary intellectuals like Marcelino dos Santos of FRELIMO were not as receptive as us. Later, when I first met Cuban comrades, I discovered that they were even more critical. But the SACP did not lay the line down for the ANC, as many of the Party's detractors have suggested. It was undoubtedly the moral and material support that the Soviet Union gave the Movement that engendered such close ties. It was Tambo who secured the training arrangements for our group.

Life on the streets of Odessa looked comfortable and stable. We had no way of comparing standards with advanced Western countries, although it was clear that the quality of consumer goods could not compare with South African shops. But then, we reasoned, those consumer items could only be purchased by a minority of the population. To my colleagues, the general level of life was so far in excess of the living conditions they had known that Odessa was paradise by comparison.

Although much of the housing was inadequate, we understood that this was a result of wartime destruction, and an ambitious construction programme was taking place before our eyes. Housing rent was less than five per cent of wages, and the cost of heat and electricity was barely one per cent. There were no beggars and few idlers on the streets, although there were plenty of hand-drawn cartoons and posters lampooning drunkenness. It was the older generation that looked as though it had experienced hardship, and there were many legless war veterans, propelling themselves about in antiquated wheelchairs. We saw alcoholism as a legacy of the war and the exceptionally low price of liquor. It was only later, when I became less naive about social problems in the Soviet Union, that I realised the extent to which boredom and frustration were contributory factors.

The only time the Soviet officers lost patience with us was when the odd comrade became so intoxicated on a Saturday night out on the town that he landed up in a police cooler to sleep it off. We began referring to such comrades as 'loose forces' – a phrase that became part of MK jargon down the years. So did the term *mgwenya*, which means pioneer or trail-blazer, by which the Odessa generation became known. With the passing of time the term took on the connotation of 'veteran', or 'old salt', to distinguish the 1960s recruits from subsequent generations.

The Xhosa word *qabane* came to be used for 'comrade', the 'qa' being expressed with an explosive Xhosa click sound. The word derives from the custom of washing your friend's back at the river.

My generation was easy to distinguish, not only by our age, but by the way Russian became incorporated into the *tsotsi-taal* patois we used. To the standard greeting, '*Hoe's it daar ma bra?*' (How are you my brother?), came the reply, 'It's *khorosho* (good) *pozhal'sta* (my pleasure).'

We attended dances at the Officers' Palace on Saturday nights, where we had the chance to meet the local girls. It was good, clean fun, with flirtatious gestures that to me seemed to come straight out of 19th-century Russian novels.

Some older comrades, well into their forties, became involved with war widows and enjoyed home comforts on Saturday afternoons and Sundays. These were discreet romances and I became aware of such developments only when one of our old stalwarts, Uncle Ngcapepe (Senzangakhona Ntunja), invited me out for Sunday lunch. When we arrived at his sweetheart's home – a woman of sixty like him – she gushed all over him, sitting him down in his favourite armchair, and providing him with a pair of slippers.

On one occasion, I was asked to address high-school students on the situation in South Africa. Joel Klaas accompanied me and, when I told them about the kind of schooling he had experienced, and how he had to study by candlelight, they were horrified and immediately wanted to raise funds for us.

On another occasion, a group of us descended on the university in search of company. We were soon in animated discussion with students in the English department, who were preparing a project on Robert Burns. I amused them by reciting the lines: 'Whisky and freedom gang well together.' We ended up buying *Sovietskoye Shampanskoye* and had a rip-roaring party. We made the mistake of pretending to be Cubans, because for security reasons we were told to conceal our true identities. As we left, they promised to include Spanish-speaking students the next time we visited. As a result we never returned.

In summer we did our stint on a collective farm – a *kolkhoz*. We harvested watermelons alongside students. We joked around with them during the lunch break and found them full of good cheer. It was when we were testing our political knowledge in Russian that not everyone agreed with conventional wisdom. We affirmed that the *rabochiy klass* (working class) were the leading force in society. They contradicted us, insisting that the *intelligentsia* were the vanguard. It was at the end of the day, at a splendid banquet, and during endless toasts, that we finally agreed that the laurels had to go to the *kolkhozniks* (collective farm workers).

There was a great deal of entertainment laid on for us. The opera house in Odessa is a splendid building and it was interesting watching my colleagues attending ballet and opera for the first time in their lives. The atmosphere of the opera house, its decor and elegance, was something that none of us had ever experienced. What also made an impression was that it seemed to be ordinary citizens who were attending and appeared to appreciate what we would have considered to be culture for the privileged.

As grand as the opera and ballet were, the Odessa zoo left us depressed. Used as we were to the vast space of Africa, we found a motley assortment of animals in cheerless confinement. One of our comrades, more unhappy for the citizenry of Odessa than the animals, averred that a free South Africa would provide plenty of lions and elephants for Soviet zoos.

When there were film shows in the school cinema my colleagues were at their liveliest. Watching Charlie Chaplin's *Modern Times* I saw the film maestro's powers of communication. The comrades shook with mirth at the antics of the little man in the bowler hat, and his struggles against authority.

After a year in which we had acquired the art of waging both partisan warfare and regular warfare, our course came to an end. We had become proficient in the use of small arms –including the pistol, AK-47 assault rifle and a variety of light and heavy machine guns. We went through a range of exercises and assault courses – in all conditions. We learnt to throw hand grenades and lay minefields. We learnt field craft and became adept at navigating in various terrains, by night and day, with and without a compass. We learnt how to sabotage installations, with military and home-made explosives, and we became skilled at laying booby-traps. Some of us specialised in mortars and heavy artillery weapons, while others concentrated on tactics, engineering, communications or commando tasks. We all learnt how to drive army trucks and, most exciting of all, T54 tanks.

In optimistic mood we travelled back to East Africa in batches of 20. When my group alighted at Cairo airport, I bumped into Joaquim Chissano who, like me, appeared to be escorting a group of guerrillas to some destination. '*Bon dia, camarade* Chissano,' I said. 'Do you know how Eleanor is?' He told me she was very well, still working in the ANC office. No, he did not know whether her daughter had joined her.

When we arrived at Dar es Salaam airport we climbed aboard a truck and travelled to 'Mandela camp' outside the city. This was simply a transit house, in the midst of tropical vegetation. We were completely in the dark about our further movement and believed that we might be on our way home. We had been largely cut off from news for most of the year and did not know what to expect. To make matters worse, the commander, Ambrose Makiwane, behaved ultra-conspiratorially about our situation and would give no information about our movements. We soon heard that we were going to move to a camp several hundred kilometres into the interior. We were not supposed to leave the residence, but I desperately wanted to contact Eleanor, and felt I had a duty to see her. With my colleagues covering for me, I slipped away and managed to find a telephone.

I reached her at the ANC office. It was a relief hearing her voice again. She had heard through 'radio potato' – the MK term for the grapevine – that I was back. From her I learnt that Ambrose was hoping to be appointed MK Commander over Joe Modise. She also told me that Oliver Tambo had arrived from London and was now based in Dar. She said he was strict, but fair, and most importantly had promised that we could meet.

I met Eleanor the next day. She was looking lovely, and speaking a passable Swahili. We sat on Banda beach, near where the *dhows* and the ocean liners glide into the harbour. We talked at length about Brigid. I had already sensed that the situation was not promising when she had refused to talk about the issue on the telephone. She had established contact with her parents, and the response had been 'there was no way Brigid could be sent to an African state'. Strain and despair were evident in Eleanor's face.

There was more distressing news. Babla Saloojee had 'fallen' to his death from the seventh floor of police headquarters while being 'interviewed' about his activities. We felt intense anger towards the Special Branch who, we were convinced, must have tortured him.

In the Pietermaritzburg trial, Billy Nair and Curnick Ndlovu had received 20-year sentences, Ebe 15 years and David 8 years. The other sentences ranged between 8 and 15 years. All the accused were in high spirits at the trial. The main state witness was Bruno. Stephen Mtshali had given damaging evidence as well. Bruno had also given evidence in the Rivonia trial, where Nelson Mandela and the others were sentenced to life imprisonment. We had received that news in Odessa. Eleanor informed me that Rusty Bernstein had been found not guilty and that he and Hilda had fled, passing through Dar on their way to London. Hilda had brought her greetings from Bram Fischer.

Our time together was all too short. When Ambrose informed me that I could see Eleanor, he had said with a leer that 'a soldier could do a lot in a single day'. What Eleanor and I needed, in fact, was time to work out what to do about Brigid. I was in low spirits, leaving her with a problem that was beginning to look much bigger than we had anticipated. We parted, unsure of our own future, and with no practical solution in mind concerning Brigid. I had never seen Eleanor so broken-hearted.

The following day, the occupants of Mandela camp awoke before dawn and piled into several trucks. Ambrose was on hand to tell us that we were on our way to a transit camp in the interior and this would be the first leg of our return home. The journey was broken at midday when comrades, with a few shillings in their pockets, were given a couple of hours' rest and recreation in a small town. I sat by myself in the truck, for the first time feeling estranged, as the comrades frolicked around the town. As much as I detested Ambrose for leering over my meeting with Eleanor the day before, I felt no animosity for my colleagues, most of whom had scant opportunity for sexual relief in the Soviet Union. As they returned to the truck, joshing one another in Russian and *tsotsitaal*, my spirits soon rose again.

I spent some time in the camp which was situated at Kongwa, a railway junction for the British groundnut scheme during the war. We were up before dawn, for physical exercises and a long run. During the day we were kept busy, constructing classrooms, barracks and a hall. Some comrades began questioning the permanency of the structures, since we had been told by Ambrose that our stay was to be temporary. He explained that this was so, but nevertheless it was logical to have a permanent structure for future needs. It became clear that he was not trusted. This was exacerbated by his evening trips to town where he drank until late with the local traders. When we got back from our early morning run we would see him walking about the camp looking ludicrous in dressing-gown and slippers. With my high expectations of what a guerrilla commander should be, I found myself disliking him more and more. In time the cadres became impatient over delays in returning home. The collapse of the underground made re-infiltration difficult. Ambrose was one of those leaders who, by creating false expectations, compounded the problem. He became so unpopular that he was later replaced by Joe Modise. There were some signs of authoritarianism creeping into our routine, especially with regard to the daily exercises which verged on the punitive. I was very fit, however, and shrugged off my concern, feeling that we were, after all, preparing for a rigorous guerrilla war.

We should have opened a debate on this at the time. Soviet instructors avoided drastic physical routines, and scientifically built up the strength of trainees. The tendency to stress the physical soon deteriorates into a macho cult, with its harmful effects. Something of this order crept into MK camp routine over the years.

One day Ambrose called me aside and said Oliver Tambo had informed him that a couple of us were needed in Dar es Salaam to work on a project. The following day I found myself travelling to Dar on the back of a truck with Chris Hani. Chris, who was 22, had been a member of the camp administration and was an activist back home. He was born in an Eastern Cape village, and had a background of hardship very similar to Joel Klaas. Somehow his family had managed to send him to the University of Fort Hare. Political involvement, as with me, had cut his studies short. I discovered that he had a passion for Shakespeare. We discussed *Julius Caesar*, which had just been translated into Swahili by Julius Nyerere, Tanzania's President. Chris had appeared to be somewhat taciturn in the camp but once he warmed up he became quite loquacious. When I began quoting the lines beloved by soldiers, 'a coward dies a thousand times…' he immediately cut in with, 'the valiant taste of death but once'. He appeared totally committed to the struggle. When he said he was unafraid of giving his life for freedom there was a ring of conviction in his voice. We talked about the universality of the power-struggle theme in the play and had fun suggesting who in our Movement had the potential to be Brutus, Cassius, Mark Antony, Octavius, etc. We joked about Ambrose, and Chris showed more than a superficial reading of Shakespeare's play by comparing him to 'that oaf Lepidus', Octavius's useful idiot.

As soon as we arrived in Dar we reported to Tambo. I had seen photographs of him, which showed a serious and dedicated leader.

He was brisk and businesslike with us, which impressed me after the laxity of Ambrose. At first, I thought his strict bearing had to do with his background as a teacher in a missionary school, his Christian faith – of which he never spoke – and his career as a lawyer. I came to realise he had a driving sense of mission. He had been left holding the flag abroad, after the imprisonment of Mandela and the internal leadership. Evidence of the personal burden he felt materialised for me almost three decades later, near the end of Tambo's life. After Mandela's release he could relax and allow his inner warmth and gentleness to shine through.

Tambo had a collection of books on guerrilla struggles and counterinsurgency warfare, which he wanted us to study and comment on. Chris remarked to me that, as much as he enjoyed studying revolutionary texts, he had secretly been hoping to use the time 'to plough through the works of Shakespeare'.

After receiving permission from the leadership, Eleanor and I were married at the end of 1964. At first the colonial registrar, who was still in place, stuck by the book and refused to marry us because we did not have our divorce papers. We knew the attorney-general, who wrote a curt note, ordering him 'to stop being obstructive'.

Our wedding ceremony was a simple affair at the Ilala Boma registry office. We were relieved the registrar was not officiating, a cheerful Tanzanian presiding in his place. Eleanor's hair had been styled for the first time since we had left South Africa and the comrades all remarked that she looked like a 'European lady'. She wore a simple dress and carried a bouquet of flamboyant flowers. Two ANC colleagues acted as witnesses, Maud Manyosi, a young trade unionist from Durban, and Flag Boshielo, from Sekhukhuneland. Flag became our best friend. He had been involved in the Communist Party in the late 1940s when, as a young man, he had come to work in Johannesburg as a 'garden boy'. He later became commissar of MK and was killed in an ambush in 1970, on his way back home to organise the underground.

There was a small party in Mendi Msimang's home, opposite the office. Only years later did we hear from his wife Agnes that it was Tambo who had come to her and said 'the children are getting married, we must have a celebration'.

Tambo asked J.B. Marks, one of the stalwarts of the struggle and later chairperson of the SACP, to make a speech. It was full of humour and wisdom and he said, paraphrasing from the MK manifesto, that the time came in the life of any young man when he had two choices. One was to remain indecisive, the other 'to stop being afraid of the lion lurking in the forest and seize its tail'. The 'lion' was not Eleanor, but the responsibility that went with marriage.

J.B. Marks was a large, warm-hearted old gentleman whom everyone approached with their problems. When trouble flared up at Kongwa camp over Ambrose's leadership, and later over the cadres' impatience to get back home, it was his sage-like temperament that defused the situation.

An unforgettable event occurred with the visit to Tanzania of the legendary Ernesto Che Guevara. He addressed 200 specially invited guests in the Cuban embassy. The leaders of all the liberation movements were present, along with many ordinary cadres.

It was exciting to see one's hero in the flesh and to hear him extolling the need for internationalism and socialist aims in guerrilla struggles. It was rumoured that Che, as we all called him, had been across the lake into the

Congo, where Cuban volunteers were secretly assisting in the fight for true independence. In fact he encouraged all the liberation movements to assist the 'Congolese comrades', and said we would gain good experience by fighting there. He advocated for Africa what he prescribed for Latin America, an alliance of the guerrilla movements, so that we could concentrate on freeing one colony after the other. It did not go down well with the ANC leaders, because it meant we would be last in the queue. I spoke to Marcelino dos Santos afterwards and, although he found the meeting stimulating, he too was critical of Che's thesis.

Present with the FRELIMO contingent was a certain Jonas Savimbi. He had resigned from Holden Roberto's FNLA (National Liberation Front of Angola) while in Cairo. FRELIMO was assisting him to reach Lusaka where he was to meet Agostinho Neto's MPLA (People's Movement for the Liberation of Angola). Within a week, people in Lusaka were informing Marcelino: 'This man is nothing but a tribalist.'

I was fortunate to meet Che while he was out walking in the streets. I was sitting by the harbour wall, eating freshly baked sweet potato, which vendors prepared on charcoal braziers on the pavement. A friend from the Cuban embassy was showing him the sights and introduced us. He was smoking a large Cuban cigar and was as relaxed as anyone on a sight-seeing tour. It was his striking features, almost feline, that set him apart from ordinary mortals. We shook hands and he tried some of the potato, saying it was indigenous to Latin America, and we bade one another 'good luck' in Spanish.

Another interesting figure who arrived on the scene was Malcolm X. This was shortly before his assassination. He was lanky, light-skinned, and had distinctive reddish hair. He was different from the image in the press, which portrayed him as arrogant and hot-tempered. In fact he was gentle and a good listener. What impressed me most about him, at a private party we attended, was the time he gave to a group of white, American peace corps women who were questioning him on his views.

Moses Kotane was the stern-faced ANC treasurer and general-secretary of the Communist Party. A self-educated man, he was of the old school, like Tambo and my father. He was taciturn, and expected hard work and sobriety from revolutionaries. He did have a sense of humour and could show a soft spot if he found he could rely on you. Our mutual friendship with Vera got us off to a good start. But he gave absolutely no favours and was even-handed with all and sundry. He had Eleanor drive him everywhere, and he entrusted her with the responsibility of depositing and drawing money from the bank.

The dismissal of Khrushchev in the Soviet Union came as a big surprise. I could not understand it, particularly since Major Chubinikyan had praised his fearless denunciations of Stalin to us. On the other hand, I had sensed some misgivings in the Major's predictions about the building of communism by 1980. *Malume*, as we called Kotane ('Uncle' in Zulu), received a briefing at the Soviet Embassy. He explained that Khrushchev's problem was his impulsiveness (like claiming that communism would be built by 1980) and his intolerance of the collective's views. The fact of his abrupt dismissal, though, was disturbing. Chris and I had misgivings about this, but we dispelled our doubts because our trust in the Soviet Union ran so deep.

By June 1965, a pregnant Eleanor, suffering from repeated malaria attacks and iron deficiency, was sent to England. From there we hoped she would have a better chance of seeing Brigid. In August, the leadership decided to send me to join Eleanor in Britain. My prospects of returning to South Africa in the immediate future were remote, and Jack Hodgson in London needed an experienced comrade to assist him.

EIGHT

LONDON RECRUITS

1966–76

Dr Dadoo shared a one-roomed office with Joe Slovo in a poky building in Goodge Street. Three old desks, a couple of odd chairs, nondescript carpeting, book shelves and a battered filing cabinet were the furnishings. Photographs of Mandela, Sisulu, J.B. Marks and Kotane hung imperfectly on the walls under a ceiling that sagged. A bust of Lenin and piles of 'Party' journals from Australia, Cuba, Czechoslovakia, the USA, Nigeria, Vietnam and the like, testified to our international links. The pleasant aroma of Dadoo's pipe pervaded the otherwise unremarkable setting.

It was there that Jack Hodgson and I would meet with Slovo and 'Doc' – as everyone called Dadoo – at 9 a.m. every Monday and Friday to discuss our programme. I would always be the last to arrive, bounding up the creaky staircase to the third floor. Invariably a few minutes late, I would find them glancing in an old-world way at their watches, ready to reproach me mildly. To this day, Slovo jokes with me when former underground contacts from a later period praise me for punctuality in the field – a quality I owe to those three old 'conspirators'.

'Well, let's get on with it,' Dadoo would suggest, with a polite nod to Slovo. The latter, cheerful, always with a witticism not far from his lips, would produce a bulging file from his briefcase. He would hand around typed copies of correspondence that had been received from underground contacts in South Africa, or from Tambo's assistants writing from Lusaka, or Dar es Salaam, or elsewhere in Africa.

The originals would have arrived at various 'safe' addresses in London or quiet country villages in the Home Counties. The original would be an apparently innocuous letter to someone's friend or relative. On the reverse side of the page would be a hidden text written in invisible ink. The form of address indicated what invisible ink had been used, and consequently, what developer was required to bring out the hidden message. 'My dear Aunt Agatha' would indicate one type, 'Dearest Aunt Aggie' another. We used a variety of chemicals, usually dissolved in alcohol or distilled water. The writer would use a clean pen to write out the secret text. Steam from a kettle would be applied to the paper to iron out any indentation marks left by the pen. After the paper had dried, the innocent text would be written or typed in.

Developers for our operatives inside South Africa could be as simple as an oven-cleaner lightly sprayed over the page. Within seconds, the secret writing would emerge. Other developers included a caustic soda solution and even a drop of blood dissolved in a few millilitres of distilled water. Soaked in a piece of cotton wool and lightly wiped over the page, the developer would reveal a vivid orange or yellow message.

Developing the invisible texts and compiling letters to our secret correspondents was a time-consuming and specialised task. This work was performed by Stephanie Kemp, married at the time to Albie Sachs. Stephanie had been imprisoned for sabotage activities in Cape Town.

In Dadoo's sparsely furnished office – with the Goodge Street traffic rumbling comfortingly outside and pedestrians, heads down, going about their everyday routine – a queer charade would be underway as we considered the weekly mail. Acting on the assumption that Dadoo's office was bugged, we conducted our meeting with a mixture of hand signals, code words and by writing sensitive details on blank sheets of paper.

'Right then,' Slovo would conclude a particular item on the agenda, 'we write to X to expect a courier on ...' and he would hold up a sheet of paper with the date scrawled on it, 'at the usual rendezvous point.' With Slovo blinking through his spectacles, I might act out a correction: 'The courier needs to give a bit of notice at work, we must add ... this number of days ... to that date.' And I would hold up the appropriate fingers like some pedantic judge at a dance contest.

At lunchtime we often went off together for a pub lunch, usually at Doc's favourite spot, the nearby *Valiant Trooper*.

After the death of J.B. Marks, 'Doc' became chairman of the SACP. He was highly respected in the Movement, and internationally, yet he was a modest man. He was tall and stately-looking, with receding forehead and wispy grey hair which he parted in a conventional style on the side. He was always formally dressed in dark suit and tie and invariably wore a red carnation in his buttonhole. He was an old-style communist, like Jack, for whom the Soviet Union was beyond reproach.

In my experience, communists like Dadoo, Slovo and Hodgson were people of great integrity. Over the years Dadoo must have handled millions, in dollars and pounds, for our Movement, without so much as a cent or penny going astray.

I often had to assist him to pick up or transfer crisp dollar notes in battered old briefcases. We jokingly referred to the money as 'Moscow gold'. On one occasion I met him surreptitiously in the transit lounge of Charles de Gaulle airport, Paris. We neatly executed a 'brush' swap of briefcases. He was nearly 70 at the time. Doc arrived off one international flight and I off another – mine out of Heathrow. We sat down with identical briefcases, without acknowledging each other. He sat sucking his pipe and reading a newspaper. I picked up his briefcase and sauntered off to catch a flight to Africa.

Joe, younger than the others by a decade, was the more open-minded and flexible thinker. His wife Ruth First, who was particularly critically minded, kept him on his toes and forced him to grapple with the thorny question of communist theory at a time when such probing was regarded as heresy. As a result, he became a theoretical and strategic trail-blazer in our Movement and internationally. He combined practical and theoretical gifts and was the driving force behind our work from London and the reorganisation of the Party. He was the antithesis of the perception of communists as being humourless and ruthless dogmatists. Warm and personable, he had a sense of humour and a witty turn of phrase. It was Joe who had dubbed Father Trevor Huddleston's Community of the Resurrection in Johannesburg, 'the Community of the Insurrection'. He had the ability to get a boring meeting to dissolve into mirth. He surprised me by declaring as early as 1966 that most of the East European Party representatives he met were not 'communists in the sense we were'. They were career-conscious 'functionaries' of the system. I noticed, however, that he did not use the derogatory term 'apparatchik', which was Ruth's preference.

Doc had immense regard for Joe, but at times was uncomfortable when his closest confidant criticised the official Marxist tenets. One such occasion was in 1974 when he published a controversial appraisal of the non-capitalist path.

When the Czechoslovakian Spring took place in 1968, I became impressed with Dubček. As pro-Soviet as I had been, I was affected by the popular groundswell for a new kind of socialism that he espoused. In the debates that took place I found all the older comrades, as well as my peers, disappointingly close-minded about the developments. I was finally persuaded, however, that the Soviet Union had no option but to check what most on our side saw as a slide into counter-revolution. I came to regret being swayed by an argument that mixed up Soviet interests with those of true socialism. But those two things were synonymous in those days. The course of action taken by Brezhnev only staved off the later crisis of socialism. Much could have been learnt in 1968, had

Dubček's reforms been allowed to take their course. I found that asserting an independence of mind could require more courage than facing enemy bullets.

Eleanor gave birth to our first son, Andrew, soon after my arrival in England. Our second son, Christopher, was born a couple of years later. We rented an inexpensive flat, above a shop in Golders Green high street, and were extremely happy.

The birth of our sons, who gave us great joy, did not deflect Eleanor from her desperate attempts to get Brigid to join us. Eleanor's parents had taken care of their granddaughter when Eleanor was in detention and on the run. But Eleanor could not get them, or her ex-husband, to agree to allow Brigid to join her. Our situation was not unique. Some of the most touching traumas of political involvement are not in the overtly political domain, but in the terrible wrenches that occur in personal lives. Some of these relationships have been irrevocably damaged.

Eleanor had to wait until Brigid was in her teens before she could communicate directly with her, by telephone to her boarding school, about their situation. Paranoid that the South African end of the line was bugged, she had to deflect Brigid's questions about politics. Within a week we received a letter, now much more serious than the previous correspondence between the two, wanting to know the difference between anarchism, socialism and communism.

South Africa was a long way off. The difficulties of exile were partly assuaged by the growing political community from home and our involvement in the Anti-Apartheid Movement. Among our closest friends were comrades we had known in South Africa like the Hodgsons, the Bernsteins and the Buntings. I became a particularly close friend of Wolfie Kodesh, who had driven Rowley and me around Johannesburg.

Rowley was serving a five-year prison sentence for his abortive attempt to set up a rival communist group with Maoist tendencies. Barry Higgs was called to give evidence in the trial and, unwilling to do so, skipped the country with his girlfriend Sybilla. They stayed with us for a while in Golders Green. Steve and Thelma Nel emigrated and established themselves in Muswell Hill, where we spent many happy hours. John Bizzel was summoned to give evidence in the trial of Bram Fischer, who had been arrested. Like Barry Higgs, John fled the country. He and his wife settled in Canada and became leading members of the Canadian Communist Party. Another Durban recruit, Ivan Strasburg, married Hilda's daughter Toni, and they left South Africa on exit visas. Ivan established himself as a leading TV and film cameraman in Britain. The saddest news was that Ernest Gallo, with whom I had sold *New Age* newspapers in Durban, fell ill in detention and died because of police neglect.

One day we received a newspaper clipping from Durban reporting 'the death by his own hand' of Lieutenant Grobler. The obituary outlined an illustrious police career, and reported that only I 'had evaded his long reach'. No mention was made of how Eleanor had got the better of him. Vera and George Ponnen went into exile too. I met them briefly at Heathrow airport on their way to Canada. Vera, hugging me warmly, paid me what I considered to be a compliment: 'You haven't changed. You're still the same.'

Both M.P. Naicker and Robert Resha lived in London, working for the ANC. Resha liked to joke that I was his protege, referring to the multi-racial jolls of the pre-Sharpeville period and his suggestion that I give 'an hour a week' of my time to the Movement.

My mother visited us in the summer of 1967. It was the first time I had seen her since my father's death and she had aged a great deal. Her father, my maternal grandfather Abe Cohen, had died the year after my father and she had been through a great deal of strain.

It was not difficult settling down in England. We learnt to refer to 'robots' as traffic lights, 'bottle stores' as off-licences, and 'stoves' as cookers. It was even possible to buy *boerewors* (a special South African sausage) at a butcher in Finchley. We learnt to live without Outspan oranges, Cape grapes and wine, and KWV brandy, although when an underground courier asked me whether I would like anything in particular from home, I opted for a bottle of the last-named.

I registered at the London School of Economics and for a few years studied sociology on a United Nations Fellowship. That was the hey-day of the students' movement, with the first sit-in taking place at the LSE in 1966. It was briefly declared an 'open' university, and I lectured on South Africa. Trotskyist-inclined students were the dominant force and, although I differed with them, I made some good friends. I made friends too with students from the USA, who were active on the Vietnam issue, and found their approach to politics fresh and lively, even if to them Marxism was not the crust of the earth.

A journalist, Gordon Winter, skulked around and took a sneak picture of me. Years later he confessed that he had been working as a spy for Pretoria and wrote his book *Inside Boss*. Winter claimed he was 'watching Ronnie and his pals at the LSE'. I was wary of him. Despite his surveillance, I managed to recruit LSE contacts to act as our couriers and none were caught. Winter misconstrued my 'lectureship'. For years, South African newspapers referred to me as 'a former President of Natal University's Students' Council and lecturer at the LSE'. This was a double elevation, since I had barely spent a full term at the Durban-based campus.

Those were years of exuberant protest. One demonstration, in which I was rather active, resulted in broken windows at South Africa House. My next-door neighbour, Ed Davoren, was arrested for hurling a rubbish bin through a plate glass window.

I gave evidence in his defence at the Old Bailey, referring to the Embassy as a racist symbol. He was acquitted by a sympathetic jury.

The first propaganda material we sent home was in 1967, soon after MK's incursions into the then Rhodesia. There were no direct borders for infiltration into South Africa. So our cadres joined with guerrillas of Joshua Nkomo's ZAPU (Zimbabwe African People's Union) in the hope of opening a trail to South Africa. The first material from London informed our people at home, among other things, of these MK activities.

Jack was an expert in building false bottoms in suitcases and a combination of South African and foreign tourists began ferrying clandestine leaflets into the country for us. At the same time, British dock workers stuffed our leaflets into ships' cargoes destined for South African ports and factories.

Britain's Young Communists were extremely helpful. I befriended the London district secretary, George Bridges, at a youth conference in Bulgaria. He was of the opinion that South Africa was one of the most difficult places in the world for communists.

He was puzzled when I disagreed and said that it was far more difficult in a country like Britain. I explained that, while it might be physically more dangerous, the issues in South Africa were very clear and the future for socialism, compared to Britain, much more promising.

While I was in Bulgaria I met Johnny Makhathini who was also representing the ANC and was based in France and Algiers. We reminisced about Durban days and the optimistic spirit at the time of his departure. The struggle inside South Africa in 1963 was at its lowest ebb. We agreed that it had been a victory to at least survive in order to regroup and prepare for the next round. The two of us were introduced to Yuri Gagarin, the Russian cosmonaut, who told us that the electricity output in the Witwatersrand region was *ochen yarki* (very bright) and could be seen from outer space. I told him how we were smuggling leaflets into the country and he said the next time 'he went up' he would take some with him.

Jack, in fact, was working on a project to put a rocket into the air that would do precisely what Yuri Gagarin had jokingly offered to do. Our rocket was improvised from a yacht distress signal. The idea was to jettison a load of leaflets from a respectable height by using a time-delay mechanism. For weeks we trudged around Hampstead Heath and Epping Forest in the damp and cold. On one occasion Aziz Pahad, a fellow exile, and I had to duck behind a tree as one of Jack's prototypes veered off its launching pad straight for us.

Jack and Rica lived in a small flat in Chalk Farm. While she was at work, I assisted Jack with his experiments. He was meticulous in ensuring that no mess was left to upset house-proud Rica. She was perfectly prepared to put up with the inconvenience of her bathroom and kitchen turned into a laboratory, but drew the line at the sitting-room. With the rocket project progressing, Jack decided that we needed additional space. He carefully laid sheets of paper out on the dining-room table. This was one of Rica's favourite pieces of furniture which she had purchased at Harrods. We were experimenting with a new quantity of propellant powder in the bottom of a hollow aluminium tube, with a cork stopper in the top. There was a touch-hole at the bottom of the tube to which he held a burning match. There was an unexpectedly violent reaction. The cork caught fire, bounced off the ceiling and lay smouldering on the table. We scurried around attempting to remove the burning cork and to dowse the fire in the tube. Rica was due home within the hour and there was an ugly burn mark on the ceiling as well.

While I scrubbed away at the ceiling, Jack attempted to remove the burn mark from the table. 'Oh well,' he grinned, 'at least we've found the propellant we need.'

Jack finally came up with a design which involved using a small explosive charge in the bottom of a bucket that launched a little wooden platform some 30 metres into the air. A pile of leaflets could be placed on the platform and these would waft down to the ground. A timing device was used to ignite the powder.

Early one morning we crept on to Hampstead Heath to try out our device. It was foggy, and we assumed the Heath was deserted. Our test was a success, but we had to move smartly off as scores of barking dogs and their curious owners unexpectedly emerged from every nook and cranny in response to the loud bang.

Another exile, Ronnie Press, whom we called 'the Professor', developed a compact electronic device which could function as a public address system. Consisting of a cassette player, electronic amplifier and car loudspeaker placed in a small box, it could broadcast a taped speech and freedom songs with a time-delay of several minutes.

On 26 June 1970 ('Freedom Day' in the Movement's calendar), leaflet bombs and street broadcasts were simultaneously activated in Johannesburg and all the main cities. It was the first major propaganda assault since the Rivonia arrests. The event was the lead story in every daily newspaper. Outside the *Rand Daily Mail* office in Johannesburg a photographer took a picture of a leaflet-bomb going off as a policeman bent to defuse it. The photograph was used the following year when there was a repeat performance of the event.

Street broadcasts, featuring a recorded speech by Robert Resha, were activated in several places. One operated from a parkade opposite the railway station in Cape Town. The device was chained to a railing with a fake 'booby trap' which deterred the police from immediately handling it.

'I've seen excited black crowds in my time,' an ex-Rhodesian policeman remarked to the Cape Town press, 'but never anything like the crowd outside the station.'

I did have time for other pursuits while in exile, particularly during the earlier years when the struggle at home was at a low ebb. I became very friendly with an acquaintance from my bohemian days in Hillbrow, Barry Feinberg. Barry had been a member of COD and, after Sharpeville, had elected to live in England. Barry offered me part-time work in a project he headed, compiling a detailed catalogue of the letters and writings of Bertrand Russell, the philosopher and leading exponent of nuclear disarmament and world peace.

Apart from augmenting my meagre income, it was fascinating work. A 1969 London *Sunday Times* review of our catalogue did us the favour of referring to it as 'one of the more fantastic documents of our age'. Our labour catalogued 100,000 items, over 70 books, 1000 essays and 25,000 letters, covering a period from 1878 to 1967. That many letters in the amount of time suggested, as Bertrand Russell himself remarked, 'that I have written one letter every 30 hours of my life.'

The association with Barry led to three books about Russell. The first was a selection of his correspondence with the general public, which we entitled 'Dear Bertrand Russell'. Russell replied to virtually all the letters he received, and we realised there were the makings of a book in a selection of his brief and witty rejoinders.

To an American correspondent who abused him for his 'peace at any price' psychology, and who believed that Russell was prepared to 'crawl to Moscow' rather than have England bombed, he replied:

> *The remark about crawling to Moscow is an invention of my opponents ...*
> *Nonetheless, if I thought that such a feat were within my powers at the age*
> *of 88 and would have any effect towards preserving my compatriots, or any*
> *human beings, from the imminent destruction by means of nuclear warfare,*
> *I should endeavour to do it, though I fear that I should also have to crawl*
> *to Washington ...*

I saw Russell, when he was 95, and was reminded of the face of Voltaire and the same 'ancient glittering eyes'. Our two other books were about his relationship with America.

Barry and I shared a common interest in writing poetry. This gave birth to a cultural group, performing poems and songs of the South African struggle. We called the group *Mayibuye*, meaning 'the land will come back'. Many of our poems were published in a book of South African freedom poems entitled *Poets to the People*, which Barry edited. Mayibuye was popular among anti-apartheid groups and we often performed at rallies in Britain and Europe.

One of our Mayibuye group was Pallo Jordan, an ANC member who had been studying in the USA. Pallo was a fiercely independent thinker, with a razor-sharp mind and memory, and a waspish temperament. He was politically unconventional in ANC circles because of his criticism of the Soviet Union. Some of those who could not match his intellect dismissed him as a 'Trotskyist'. There was a debate about whether he would be allowed to join our group and I argued in favour because what mattered 'was his loyalty to the ANC' and not whether he accepted 'the Moscow line'. He was a delightful companion on our trips and I soon came to refer to him affectionately as 'Zee Pee' from his initials. We had many fierce rows, the worst of all when he defended George Orwell's *Animal Farm* as an 'incisive prediction' of what had taken place in Eastern Europe. I dismissed it as crude, anti-communist propaganda. He liked me though, because I never used political differences in a personal way. He laughingly told me: 'The trouble with you, Khumalo, is you think you're a Stalinist but in fact you're not.'

One of the countries we frequently visited was the Netherlands. The driving force of the Dutch anti-apartheid movement was Conny Braam. She was a glamorous and exuberant young woman. I found the Dutch could particularly relate to our unfolding liberation struggle because of their wartime resistance against the Nazi occupation. I came to trust Conny and, as I cast my net wider for couriers and other assistance, relied on her to a great degree.

My favourite pastime in England was watching football. I have seldom been a neutral observer of life, preferring the cut and thrust of partisanship. I decided to support Arsenal football club because it was the nearest first division club to where I lived.

One of the friends with whom I used to watch Arsenal matches, Sean Hosey, was a member of the British Young Communist League. At the time, when Arsenal managed to pull off the 'double' – winning the 1970–71 League Championship and FA Cup in one season – some MK combatants had managed to slip back into South Africa. We received a secret communiqué requesting funds and identity books.

It was at Highbury's north end, behind the goal mouth, that I asked Sean if he would fly to South Africa and deliver the material. With the home crowd roaring on the Gunners in driving rain, 'Come on you Reds! Come on you

Reds!' it was difficult for Sean to refuse.

Sean was due back on a Saturday morning some weeks later. We had arranged to meet that afternoon at our usual place behind the north end goal mouth. Arsenal were playing Coventry, his home town team, and he was particularly keen to be back for the game. As the game progressed, Sean failed to appear. I sensed something terrible had happened. Even the victorious chants of 'Aaaarsenal! Aaaarsenal!' from the fans on the terraces began to sound ominous, not only for Coventry but for Sean Hosey.

Unknown to us, the writer of the MK communiqué requesting funds and IDs had been arrested. He had been compelled to write the letter to us by the police. Sean walked straight into a trap. The man he exchanged passwords with outside a store in a small Natal town turned out to be a black security policeman. After being brutally treated, Sean stood trial with the MK group and received a five-year prison sentence.

Losing a comrade in this way was traumatic. Such news never failed to throw me into the depths of depression.

Sean stood trial with another friend of mine – Alex Moumbaris. Alex was a plucky, taciturn Greek, with a stubborn temperament. Born in Egypt, he had grown up in Australia and had lived in France. He had been one of the 'tourists' carrying out propaganda tasks in South Africa. In 1971, Tambo and Slovo were part of a project aimed at landing a party of guerrillas on the South African coast. My task was information-gathering. Moumbaris was part of several reconnaissance units we despatched to South Africa to photograph and film the Indian Ocean coastline from Cape Agulhas in the south to Kosi Bay on the Mozambique border.

Jack and I spent long hours poring over topographical maps of the coast and books like *The African Pilot* – a manual for shipping which detailed the features of the African coastline.

Alex could not drive and neither could he use a cine-camera. I asked Stephanie Kemp to teach him to drive and Ivan Strasburg to teach him how to shoot a film. By the time he was due to leave he was accomplished with the movie-camera but had failed the driving test twice. He was resourceful, however, and at the last moment managed to obtain an international driver's licence from the Automobile Association. He was able to show that he had booked an official test with the Licensing Department and gave the AA a story about having to rush abroad in an emergency. They let him drive around the block, were satisfied, and issued him with one of their licences.

Alex understood that a cardinal rule of clandestine work is never to draw attention to yourself. He arrived in Durban, hired a car and drove to his hotel on the beach front. It took him a good ten minutes to reverse into a parking space.

When he got out of the car, exhausted and perspiring, a crowd of residents who had gathered on the hotel verandah applauded his achievement.

In London, Jack and I, with the aid of our photographs, film footage and shipping manual, managed to reduce 27 possible landing spots to a shortlist of six. Meanwhile Tambo and Slovo prepared the guerrillas in Somalia for their mission. An old boat, called the *Aventura*, was purchased and an international crew of leftist seamen recruited. Moumbaris was part of a reception party we organised to guide the landing craft from the mother ship into the Transkeian bay we had chosen.

Unfortunately the *Aventura's* engines seized up off Mombasa and the plan was aborted. I had to send Alex a cable which recalled him and others back to Britain. The message was: 'Regret to inform you mother has died.'

With the ANC it is a case of never say die. The freedom fighters were soon winging their way by international flight via Nairobi for destinations in Botswana (as Bechuanaland had become) and Swaziland. Moumbaris with his newly married French wife, Marie-José, was on hand to meet them. He would drop them near the border fence and rendezvous with them on the other side. Unfortunately one of their number surrendered himself to the police and Alex and Marie-José were arrested. Alex got 15 years and his pregnant wife was deported. I once again had the unenviable task of explaining things to shocked relatives.

By the time of Alex's and Sean's arrest, we were involved in training an increasing number of young South Africans who were volunteering for underground work.

We had already recruited some individuals by the late 1960s. Among these was an extremely brave young school teacher, Ahmed Timol, a close friend of Aziz and Essop Pahad. We were impressed as reports arrived from Ahmed, detailing progress in building an underground network. Then in 1971 disaster struck. Timol was arrested at a roadblock, with leaflets in the boot of his car. Within a week he had died in detention. As in the case of Babla Saloojee, the security police claimed that he had committed suicide. Ahmed plunged to his death from the tenth floor of police headquarters. Special Branch interrogators used to boast to other detainees about the 'flying Indian'.

Raymond Suttner was an earnest young law student studying at Oxford. He found his way to me via Albie and Stephanie Sachs. I was eager to show him how to manufacture our leaflet bombs, but he always had a ten-item agenda ready for me when I arrived at his cramped bedsit off Finchley Road. The whole morning would be spent in theoretical discussion and by midday he was always in need of coffee and Danish pastries, which we would consume at Lindy's, a cosy Hampstead coffee shop frequented by genteel womenfolk.

We would continue our discourse in undertones, with me striving to move the conversation from theory to the practical exercises. Around our conspiratorial heads the demure world of Hampstead revolved.

Our training course was basically developed out of our own experience. Subjects consisted of politics, secret communication, leaflet bombs, counter-surveillance, how to cope with interrogation, simple disguise, and what Jack termed 'the back door'. All this was designed to give our people the best chance to survive in a hostile environment while carrying out underground tasks. Jack's 'back door' was a plan for escaping from South Africa in an emergency. We insisted that the very first task every recruit had to sort out on arriving back home, before they became active, was an escape plan – disguise, funds, safe house, exit route.

There was a good mixture of theory and practice in all of this. There were books to read and discuss and not only on the history of our struggle. We made our recruits read Ruth First's *117 Days* and Albie Sachs' *Jail Diary* and other first-hand accounts of detention and solitary confinement.

The course in secret communications ranged from writing with secret inks to the use of Dead Letter Boxes (DLBs) and the variety of contact meetings used in underground work.

A DLB is a place or container for hiding material. It is used between operatives to pass on money, messages, documents, weapons – without coming into contact, and thus minimising risk. If we had used a DLB, Sean Hosey might not have been caught.

Contact meetings included the conditions to be observed and the safety rules for 'regular', 'reserve', 'emergency', 'brush' and 'blind' meetings and ways of triggering such meetings. A 'blind' meeting would consist of two strangers meeting for the first time and having to utilise recognition signals and exchange passwords at a pre-arranged rendezvous point.

As an exercise I would get Raymond, for example, to await his contact outside a supermarket in Hampstead at a precise time, reading *Time* magazine and holding a Woolworth's shopping bag – two recognition signals.

A comrade assisting me, whom Raymond had never met, would approach him with the passwords: 'Is this where they sell Danish pastries?'

Raymond would give the pre-arranged answer: 'No. You must be looking for Lindy's.'

'Ah, well then why don't you join me for tea?' would be the response and the two would walk off together.

This work could be fun and we would test the trainee by confusing the passwords. Raymond might be asked: 'Can you get Danish pastries at Woolworth's?' If he ignored the mistake and accepted the stranger's invitation to tea, he would have failed the exercise and be told that he had fallen into enemy hands.

These exercises, together with counter-surveillance, were the most interesting part of the training – giving ample scope for creativity and outdoor activity – especially after all the indoor discussions.

Hampstead, with its contrasts between busy shopping village and secluded residential area, its variety of colourful pubs, street markets, mews and lanes, its Heath, parks and playing fields, and the comfortable English attitude of 'do what you like, mate, as long as you don't interfere with me!' offered all the possibilities we required.

We would get our trainees to locate suitable places for DLBs, both indoors and out on the Heath, and see if we could successfully locate these on the basis of the diagrams we taught them to prepare. I would make them leave money in their DLBs, to ensure that they chose really secure, weather-proof locations. We taught them how to leave innocuous signals in public places which indicated when a DLB was 'loaded'. This could be a chalk mark on a lamp post, graffiti on a wall or a piece of coloured string tied to a fence.

We would also train our people to check for surveillance without looking over their shoulders – all the tricks I was to deploy on my return to South Africa in 1989. Tricks like glancing into shop mirrors and opaque windows, natural manoeuvres like stopping to ask the way or walking along a winding path, observing the street from the interior of a store, pretending to make a call from a public phone box – all these are ways of growing eyes in the back of your head.

After explaining how the surveillance section of the security police of any country operates, how to uncover whether you are being 'tailed' and how to 'cut the tail' and so on, the intrepid trainee would be given time to prepare for practicals.

By the end of the course, they would prepare for a 'blind' meeting. They would have to decide on the conditions for the meeting – time, venue, recognition signals, passwords. They would have to organise a 'check' route of several kilometres, along which they would travel by foot and bus, to ascertain whether they were being shadowed or not. In a real-life situation, if you uncovered a tail on the way to a secret rendezvous, the iron rule was to abort the meeting. We often used this exercise as the grand finale of the training at which the recruits would receive final instructions for their mission home. I would wait at the rendezvous point at the prescribed time, in a make-shift disguise, ready to play the role of the other party to the meeting. In Raymond's case he failed to turn up.

What was strange was that we had decided not to have anyone follow Raymond and yet, even though he had been meticulously punctual with all other meetings, there was no sign of him. What was particularly worrying was that he was due to leave for South Africa the very next day. I began to fear that he must have had an accident and began scouring the Hampstead streets for him. As dusk fell, my apprehension growing, I hastened to his bedsit.

Looking unperturbed he answered my impatient knocking. I soon established that he thought he had 'picked up a tail' and consequently aborted the meeting as instructed.

'But there was this guy in a white polo-neck jersey,' he insisted, explaining that he had used *Jack Straw's Castle*, a Hampstead pub, as one of his checkpoints, from where a man had all too obviously followed him. 'Not only that,' Raymond continued, 'he even tried to talk to me, which you said a tail would never do. So I thought it was one of your ruses.'

I burst out laughing, telling Raymond he must have attracted someone with 'other' interests. The place was a favourite haunt of gays.

No sooner had Raymond flown off to take up a position with Natal University's law department, than Brian Bunting was setting up a meeting for me with another graduate.

My contact would be sitting on a bench outside Hampstead underground station. 'How will I recognise him?' I asked Brian.

'Similar fellow to you, only ten years younger,' he answered benignly.

That was how I first met David Rabkin. From Cape Town originally, he had left South Africa as a schoolboy at the time of Sharpeville, when his parents, an enlightened couple, had decided to emigrate to England. Like Raymond, he was a brilliant and earnest intellectual who preferred to discuss theory and had difficulties with the technical side of things. Unlike Raymond, he never diverted me and patiently battled with the technical tasks I set him, after which he raised the theoretical questions.

I reported progress at our Goodge Street meetings and commented that David was one of the most impressive comrades I had prepared. Doc was always cautious about such enthusiasm and would laconically comment: 'Time will tell.'

With a couple of months to go before David's departure, he suddenly told me he was about to get married and hoped that his wife would be deployed with him. My heart sank. What would Doc and the others say when I announced this major development about an operative of whom I had seemingly known so much? I knew that Doc, without actually opposing married couples working together in the underground, was of the opinion that this did not often work.

I met David and his fiancée Sue Morris, a Londoner, at the *Bull and Bush* pub, off Hampstead Heath. She was, at the time, a bushy-tailed enthusiast who had expected to meet, as she put it, 'a black gentleman in a suit and bowler hat'.

The main impression she had of the ANC was derived from photographs of the founding fathers in 1912. I pitched up in jeans and anorak, with an unruly head of hair. David had warned her that she would not get details from me of any aspects of the underground they were joining that 'they needn't know'. When she asked me how large the underground was, I stalled her by asking whether she would be prepared to join 'even if you two were the only cell'. She nodded dutifully, and that was that.

Immediately after their wedding, David and Sue departed for Cape Town where he got a job with the *Cape Argus*, and she with the Open Space theatre. After a year we linked them with another recent recruit who had been studying philosophy at the Sorbonne – Jeremy Cronin.

Jeremy had also recently returned to Cape Town to take up a lectureship at the university. During training sessions with Jeremy in London and Paris I had been impressed by his intellect and the quiet inner strength he exhibited. I once met him by a bridge near Notre-Dame and increased his confidence in my security consciousness by suggesting we 'get away from all the tourists with their cameras'. We wandered along the left bank of the Seine talking about the mass actions of May 1968 that led to the resignation of De Gaulle and a near revolution. The events of 1968 made a strong impact on Jeremy.

For us, South Africa was a time-bomb nearing a similar point of explosion. Nevertheless, I took pains to stress to Jeremy, as with other recruits, the arduous times that lay ahead, the loneliness and dangers, particularly for those in the underground, and the fact (thinking of Doc's patient approach) that our revolution could take a long time yet – although I secretly believed otherwise.

How to get all this across to our recruits was always a delicate question. If we harped on too much about the dangers and the possibility of failure, there was the risk of inculcating paranoia and inactivity. On the other hand, if we glossed over the problems and pressed too hard for quick results, we might undermine the need for caution. Even with my bent for action, I do believe the correct balance was struck. I loathed the idea of the security police capturing any of our people.

About the time of the collapse of fascism in Portugal and, with it, Lisbon's colonial empire, another pair of would-be recruits from Cape Town sought us out. Tim Jenkin and Steve Lee were on a tour of Europe. They simply walked into the ANC offices, then based off Goodge Street, and saw Reg September. Reg had the good sense to get them out of the office as quickly as possible. He referred them to Aziz Pahad and me, and we met them in a pub. Because they had not been recommended by anyone, we requested they stay in London, so we could assess them. We put them through a long training course. I was delighted to discover in Tim a pupil who quickly progressed past anything I could teach him in the technical field. They stayed in London for almost a year in a Fulham squat, practising some of our propaganda ideas. Tim and Steve, who took a job as a London bus conductor, were so active that Fulham became covered in anti-Common Market graffiti. They returned to Cape Town where Tim took up a research job at the University of the Western Cape.

These were just some underground cells, all specialising in propaganda work, that we set up from London. We were kept busy maintaining communications with them. They were all active, despite the fact that the individuals had to keep up a public front, and expend a great deal of time on their careers. Whatever other energy they could muster went into the onerous hours of illegal activity. A growing impact was made by ANC and SACP propaganda after years of virtual silence. The Special Branch were having to devote considerable resources to hunting down the clandestine cells.

Not all would-be recruits were the genuine article. Craig Williamson, a puffy-faced, overweight student leader who claimed to have fled South Africa, offered his services. He had secured a strategic position with a Geneva-based student foundation. He struck me as a cold fish and, when we checked his background, discovered that previous colleagues did not trust him. We tested him with stale material, and when a South African newspaper, with security police links, reported our outdated booklets were surfacing in the townships, our suspicions increased. We kept him at arm's length but he maintained a strong nerve. He cleverly exploited his position to keep track of Swedish funding for anti-apartheid groups, until exposure led him to scuttle back to South Africa. He was promoted to the rank of major in the security police.

The overthrow of the Salazar regime in Portugal in 1974, when the armed forces finally revolted as a consequence of the colonial wars in Mozambique, Angola and Guinea-Bissau, was an auspicious time for Eleanor and me.

The date of the revolution, 25 April, was her daughter Brigid's 18th birthday. After almost 11 years of separation, mother and daughter were united when Eleanor's mother brought Brigid to London. The reunion was an occasion of joy and relief, although time was required to try to re-establish a confident mother-daughter relationship again. Brigid stayed on to live with us for a short while.

She all too soon married her Durban boyfriend, Garth Strachan, who followed her to England. Both developed a political commitment to the ANC. A couple of years later Garth was working for the Anti-Apartheid Movement in London and then for the ANC in Lusaka and Harare.

Eleanor's separation from her young daughter had been a shadow over all our lives and the source of anxiety and torment. The birth of our two sons and the fact that we managed, with minimal resources, to create a happy home above the shops in Golders Green, helped us cope with the problem. But there had been many an occasion when Eleanor had sobbed out her depression. She had been a loving young mother to Brigid and never expected that her parents would behave so cruelly as to keep them separated over those agonising years. They easily manipulated her ex-husband, who paid little interest in his daughter. Scars were left and never really healed after such a long estrangement. Brigid would have been given the impression that her mother had abandoned her and such doubts often surfaced. Eleanor became an activist through a process of involvement and by the time danger threatened, and the Movement desperately needed her skills, she sought to temporarily shelter her daughter at her parents' home, believing as we all did that the Apartheid regime would soon collapse. Our mentor, Rowley Arenstein, had predicted 'six months' – not that we would bet on that. But even the cautious Bram Fischer had thought that, with expected Western pressure and mass activism, it would take a couple of years.

Those were strange times indeed. For this edition of my book I am able to refer the reader to a work published in 2012 with the title *London Recruits* (Merlin Press) edited by Ken Keable who participated in the leaflet distributions in 1969 and 1970. It is a collection of some 33 contributions by courageous internationalists like him whose identities were kept secret for over forty years. We arranged a trip to South Africa for some of them in order to launch their book and they were acclaimed as heroes whose contribution was at last openly celebrated with them.

NINE

THE SOWETO GENERATION

East Germany
July 1977

IN JUNE 1976, A REBELLION BY BLACK school students shook South Africa. It started in Soweto and spread throughout the country.

The immediate cause was a government decree imposing Afrikaans as a compulsory language of instruction in black schools. When Soweto pupils organised a mass protest march on 16 June, the police opened fire. Twelve children died. But the show of brutality failed to subdue the anger of a generation that had grown up in a period of parental submission, Sharpeville and the Rivonia set-back. Youth resistance spread like wild fire throughout the country.

Street battles raged, with youngsters using dustbin lids as shields against bullets. Stones and petrol bombs rained down on the police and military. In the one-sided battles hundreds of young people died. Some estimates placed the figure at over 600 for the year. Many had only vaguely heard of the ANC and Umkhonto we Sizwe.

But recruitment into the ranks of MK, which had been at a trickle in the previous years, began speeding up and was soon a torrent. Youngsters were leaving South Africa in droves, heading for the neighbouring states in search of the ANC, with the single wish: 'To learn how to shoot, to get a gun and get back home to *moer* [finish] the Boers.'

The youth turned to the ANC as the most popular and persistent of the black organisations. As soon as resistance developed they found, among their parents' generation, ex-political prisoners to guide them. Most were veterans of the ANC and the sabotage campaign. The ANC had an infrastructure and training facilities. And it enjoyed close relations with guerrilla movements, such as FRELIMO and the MPLA, that had dislodged the Portuguese from Mozambique and Angola. The propaganda actions, planned in London, also

89

made an impact. Labour unrest had in fact predated the student revolt by three years.

The TV images of the street battles, of the heroism of youngsters facing armoured vehicles, of the first victim, 13-year-old Hector Pieterson, blood streaming from his mouth, being carried away in the arms of a boy in dungarees, stirred those of us in Britain to re-double our efforts.

At home our propaganda units worked round the clock. But not without risk. Raymond Suttner had been arrested, and sentenced to seven years in 1975, for distributing ANC literature. He was 30 years old and a senior lecturer in law at the University of Natal at the time.

We had teamed Jeremy Cronin with David and Sue Rabkin. Like other units, they worked at fever pitch. Tim Jenkin and Steve Lee were also operating in Cape Town. We prepared drafts of leaflets in London, and smuggled copies to them in innocuous presents. These were reproduced on cyclostyling machines in garages or back rooms, and then posted to thousands of addresses. Copies were distributed by leaflet bombs outside railway stations and bus terminals. Tim Jenkin proved to be our most adept operative in this respect. He sometimes placed up to eight bucket bombs at a time in a city centre. When Tim's bombs went off, I thought of Sue and her question about the strength of the underground. Tim, alone, would give her and the security police the impression that we had an army operating in Cape Town.

The leaflets we wrote from London breathed defiance. A leaflet distributed in Johannesburg in March 1976, after the South African army's abortive invasion of Angola, stated:

The conditions for developing our liberation struggle, smashing apartheid and winning our freedom, are greater than ever. Nothing can hide the fact that White South Africa is in irreversible crisis. Vorster thought he could send his army into Angola and place his stooges in power, but the MPLA thrashed him in battle and sent his White soldiers and stooges fleeing in terror.

Within days of the Soweto massacre, leaflet bombs were going off all over the country, scattering a message written by David Rabkin, saluting the Soweto martyrs. It exhorted our people to action and declared:

Vorster and his assassins have learnt nothing since Sharpeville, Once again he has called out his murderers to shoot down innocent people in the name of preserving 'law and order' ... demonstrate against the brutal murder of our children ... Demonstrate your opposition to the apartheid state and the massacre of our people.

Early in July, David and a pregnant Sue were due back in London, for the birth of their second child. I was looking forward to meeting them and receiving a first-hand report on the situation. But the day before their departure they, and Jeremy, were arrested.

We were puzzled over the cause of their arrest. Then it emerged that an original contact of Jeremy's had also been arrested. The contact, Anthony Holiday, a journalist, was inclined to talk loosely and we had put him on ice. Jeremy came to believe in prison that he was the weak link that led to the arrests. A security policeman, Mike Kennedy, told me years later, after we had won our freedom, that a similarity in the open, innocent text of the secret communication letters addressed to David and Jeremy had aroused suspicion by his section which monitored post from abroad.

The trial of Sue, David and Jeremy proved to be the speediest yet under the notorious Terrorism Act. Publicity in Britain over the plight of Sue, who was eight months pregnant at the time of sentence, sped things up. Her father, a famous paediatrician, cycling to South Africa House from rooms in Wimpole Street to join a vigil, no doubt helped.

David, aged 28, was sentenced to ten years and Jeremy, aged 26, to seven years. Sue was given an effective one month's imprisonment, during which time she gave birth to a baby daughter, Franny, and was deported back to Britain.

The security police achieved a further success when they arrested Tim Jenkin and Stephen Lee, in March 1978. They were charged with distributing 17 different pamphlets and detonating nearly 50 leaflet bombs in two years. They were also responsible for organising several successful street broadcasts. Tim was sentenced to 12 years, Stephen to eight.

The efforts had not been meaningless. Many of the 1976 generation were directly influenced by our propaganda actions.

The ANC sent some of us in London to attend to the political education of recruits undergoing training in East Germany – the former German Democratic Republic. The lecturers included Aziz Pahad and Pallo Jordan. We would lecture for a fortnight at a time.

I flew from Heathrow via Schiphol airport, Amsterdam, where I changed flights to board an East German Interflug flight for Schonefeld airport, East Berlin. On arrival I was taken to the VIP lounge by a dry-humoured fellow, wearing a tartan cap, whom I came to know through subsequent visits. I was keen to see the city, and of course 'The Wall', and he promised to show me around at the end of my trip. I was then whisked off by car. The drive lasted a couple of hours until I arrived at a training establishment in a forest.

It was a special school near the village of Tetrow where 40 of our recruits were put through a guerrilla warfare course every six months. The instructors were young East Germans. My assumption was that they were Party members from the armed forces. In their thirties, they were superbly fit and efficient. Like military instructors everywhere, they taught their charges with a mixture of humour and discipline.

I was curious to meet the new recruits, to compare them with my generation – the *mgwenya* of the 1960s.

That generation had received their experience in the non-racial politics of the Congress Movement. This generation was unacquainted with the ANC, which had been outlawed most of their lives. They were young and had grown up in a political void. The only whites they had known were arrogant school inspectors, township supervisors and swaggering thugs in uniform.

Now they were receiving instruction from German army officers, being catered for by a staff of elderly white women, and were going to be lectured to by me on the history of the struggle.

My experience in Odessa gave me some of the confidence I needed. Students were dressed in military fatigues and appeared on good terms with the instructors and dining-room attendants. The commander of the group was an easy-going young Sowetan called Seyiso. He put me at my ease with a warm welcome.

I had an advantage in that Pallo and Aziz had already visited the school, and had taken the students through the early history. My task was to deal with the formation of MK and its development.

I began by dealing with the impact of the Sharpeville massacre and the banning of the ANC at the end of March 1960. I sensed my audience's concentration increasing as we analysed the conditions that gave rise to the historic decision to embark on an armed struggle. I pointed out that the motivation was not hatred for whites and love of violence but the fact that apartheid rule, like all tyranny throughout history, had left our people with no alternative.

The comrades were interested in Marxism, which was included in the lectures, and they all strove to indicate a disdain for religion. I noticed during a game of volleyball, however, which they often played in the late afternoon after classes, that they were susceptible to superstitious beliefs.

A mischievous young character called Bob, who in discussions had shown some knowledge of rural culture, was on the losing side when his turn to serve came around. 'I'm going to *thakatha* [bewitch] you now,' he announced, waving his hand over the ball, 'I've got powerful *muti* [medicine].' His opponents started ridiculing him but he punched an unplayable serve over the net.

His teammates whooped in triumph as he prepared to serve again, confidently bragging that the *muti* was working. The next serve was a replica of the first and I detected a glimmer of fear in Seyiso's eyes as he strove to reorganise his team. Bob's next two serves put his opponents on the defensive too and, after some anxious scrambling to keep the ball in play, they lost both those points as well.

The match had taken on a tense air as Bob chortled to his teammates and proclaimed the power of his *muti*. He served, and an anxious Seyiso just managed to knock the ball up into the air. A furious battle followed for the point, with Seyiso rallying his forces and a confident Bob darting among his team for the final shot. With the ball bobbing high above the net, Seyiso rose above the rest and smashed it down to regain service.

Seyiso's team was ecstatic and threw lively insults at Bob's *muti*. The crisis over, they went on to win the match. The next day in class I introduced the topic of 'The Madala and the Sangoma' (The Old Man and the Wizard).

In brief, the story I unfolded was about a true incident involving a mixed contingent of MK and Zimbabwean guerrillas who had infiltrated Rhodesia from Zambia in 1967. After initial clashes with Ian Smith's forces, they sought sanctuary in the hills near a village.

They made contact with an old man, Madala, who agreed to help them. He began by providing food and information and agreed to nurse one of the wounded guerrillas in his hut in the village. He passed him off as a sick relative from town. Through Madala the guerrillas learnt that a famous *sangoma* would be visiting the village. The chief would be slaughtering a cow and providing beer for the occasion. Some of the guerrillas felt that at least one of them should participate in the traditional event with Madala and their injured comrade. They would receive the well-wishes of the chief and good luck from the *sangoma*. This suggestion, however, was met with firm opposition from the rest of the group, who felt it was a risk.

At that point I suggested a ten-minute break and told the class to be ready for the next session 'when you, as the guerrilla group in the hills, will decide what to do'.

The din during the recess, as the comrades debated the next step in the story, was deafening. The school's Director, whose office was down the corridor, emerged with a curious grin on his face, asking me what was going on. 'We're about to have an interesting debate between the protagonists of dialectical materialism and idealism,' I explained.

The debate got underway at a pace to rival the volleyball game. Bob and Seyiso were again on opposite sides. The protagonists were split down the middle, as had been the case in the actual event in Zimbabwe. There were those who argued that custom demanded that they should attend the function. A few, like Bob, were bold enough to argue that the sangoma's *muti* would help them defeat Ian Smith's soldiers.

The opposition argument was that the venture was extremely dangerous, that the *sangoma* could not be trusted, that there was no power in *muti* and that, as important as cultural tradition was, it had to be overruled by considerations of security.

I finally responded by telling them that their debate paralleled what actually took place in the Zimbabwe hills. There it had been decided that one comrade would accompany Madala and the injured comrade to the beer feast. They would say they were visitors from town. When they met the *sangoma* he took a long look at them and examined the injured comrade's wound. He told them he understood they had been through great danger. He then cast a spell, ensuring that the next time they were in trouble a thick mist would descend to hide them from their enemies. That night, after the function, Madala took the two comrades back to his hut.

'Early the next morning,' I continued, 'there was a commotion in the village as Rhodesian security forces arrived looking for the old man and his two friends.'

Madala had risen early to fetch firewood. From a distance, he saw the soldiers surrounding his hut and opening fire on the occupants. He fled for the hills to warn the guerrillas.

'Our comrades were alerted by the gunfire, and the sound of helicopters,' I explained. They saw Madala making his way up the slopes to their position, pursued by soldiers. Realising he could not outrun them, he changed direction to lead his pursuers away from the guerrillas. As he was crossing a stream he was hit by machinegun fire.

'That's what happened to Madala,' I concluded. 'He was a brave old man who gave his life for the liberation struggle.'

I paused, and there was a long silence, everyone saddened by the sacrifice of Madala, a story I had learnt first-hand from one of the survivors. The concluding part of the lecture was to emphasise the need for security, whether one believed in a spirit world or not.

This did not mean disrespect for the various cultures of our people. Traditional healers could be exceptionally skilled herbalists and psychologists. Modern medicine had a great deal to learn from them. But when it came to security, all other considerations had to take second place. One thing was clear. Magic could not bring safety. It was not possible to bring down a mist when you wanted one. There was no *muti* that could make you invincible. Victory depended not on *muti*, but on skill, preparation, and the fact that we were waging a just war.

I looked towards Seyiso and Bob, who were sitting next to one another, and said we should learn from real life. The previous day's volleyball game was an example. I referred to Bob's use of *muti*. I told them that Bob was a good psychologist. He almost succeeded in making Seyiso's team doubt their ability against his secret weapon. They had wavered when Bob played so well. But then Seyiso shook off his self-doubt and rallied his team. 'Not so?'

Everyone laughed and Seyiso nodded in agreement. But Bob, mischievous to the end, turned to the class and screwing up his eyes warned: '*Pasop* (watch out) for the *Umthakathi* (magician)!'

The comrades worked right through the week, sometimes spending the whole day and often part of the night in the surrounding woods. They specialised in tactics, springing ambushes on each other, and performing hit and run raids on mock targets. At one stage during the course, they lived in underground bunkers which they constructed themselves. There was a great deal more creativity and practical activity than I had experienced in Odessa. This appeared to be the result of experience gained over the last decade.

The Director took me out to examine the terrain, challenging me to locate the underground shelters. 'I can't see a thing,' I confessed, casting my eyes around the terrain. He knelt down to uncover the secret entrance to an elaborate Vietnamese-style tunnel system, that we had been standing above.

He explained that they began by teaching the comrades to construct simple caches to bury weapons in. These had to be at least one metre below the surface. They were shown how to pack weapons and explosives in weatherproof containers. They were warned not to leave any traces behind. One group, returning after a week to check on their work, had discovered that a cache had been dug up by wild animals. He laughed: 'The comrades who had dug the hole had been eating sweets and threw the paper wrapping into the hole.'

I was amazed that an animal could pick up the scent of a sweet wrapping through a metre of ground. It was something we would have to take very seriously in our countryside and border areas which were teeming with game.

I sat in on a lecture the Director delivered on security. He dealt with the problems a revolutionary movement faced as a result of infiltration by its enemies. He stressed that this was a greater danger than physical assault. Afterwards, drinking coffee in his office, I mentioned that this had become a growing headache for our Movement, particularly with the influx of so many unknown individuals. The problem was that in many instances, without hard facts, it was difficult to verify suspicions. 'In the final analysis,' I enquired, curious to put my question, 'what was the answer?'

He tapped his nose and sniffed the air, answering with a single word: 'Intuition.' This surprised me. 'Intuition?' I asked doubtfully. 'Isn't that getting into the realm of mysticism?'

He chuckled, his eyes bright and full of interest: 'Nein! Nein! First comes theory. On the basis of the knowledge we have practical application. Out of practice comes experience. Then ...' he stated triumphantly, 'out of much, much experience, emerges something that is like a sixth sense ...' He tapped his nose again, his eyes twinkling, '... intuition.'

All his instructors were strong-minded types like him. They gave the impression of being well drilled, in the subjects they taught, and in their ideological views. They were firm and self-confident about everything. None showed any sign of doubt. There was no 'well, maybe this' or 'maybe that'. This need for decisiveness arose from the threat of their big neighbour, West Germany. The shadow of the Federal Republic fell over all discussions. It was seen to be the inheritor of Hitler's anti-communism. It was a state that was 'soft' on former Nazis. It was bent on destroying the GDR, which was why 'The Wall' was necessary. What was wrong with having a border between two states, one extremely hostile to the other? It sounded convincing.

They relaxed in a small clubroom in the evenings after dinner. They drank beer and schnapps. They were lively company much like officers everywhere. They could unbend, and enjoyed trading jokes. Several of these were about the problems of building socialism. They liked rough, soldiers' jokes, and when I threw in the English variety, upper-class accent and all, they collapsed with laughter. One of these jokes used the word 'bugger', an English word they had not come across. When I explained its meaning they understood well enough. One of them said the German equivalent would never be used in public. It was too rough. To their amazement, the word was used in an avant-garde TV film we watched later that week. This evoked such amusement that it became a regular topic of conversation during the rest of my stay.

Weekend was the time for relaxation. On Saturday afternoon we played a game of football with a couple of instructors who stayed on over the weekend taking part. That evening there was a barbecue, with spicy German sausage and plenty of Czech beer and GDR brandy. It was a chance to relax and get to know one another better. A record player was brought outside and Seyiso began dancing to Bob Marley's hit 'No woman no cry'.

'I just love this song,' he told me, closing his eyes and miming the lyrics. Some of the other comrades began dancing and showed me the latest township bump and grind.

The instructors had come to know the comrades well and kept pulling their legs concerning their strong and weak points that had become evident in training: 'Don't close your eyes, Seyiso. Remember we told you to learn to sleep with one eye open.'

Some of the domestic staff came over to socialise. They had separate accommodation in the grounds. One of the cooks brought her teenage daughter across to meet the comrades and try out her English. She was soon surrounded by an admiring throng, including Seyiso, who began chaffing her. I hardly noticed the goings-on as the party got into full swing.

The next morning, Sunday, Seyiso asked me to attend a meeting of a leadership group. He looked worried. The others looked tense and angry. I asked what the problem was. The commissar of the group, an overweight figure called Ishmail, explained: 'There was too much liquor last night and comrades disgraced themselves with that schoolgirl.' He glared at Seyiso: 'Including the commander.'

For a moment I thought she had been physically molested. But when I enquired further, all Ishmail could complain about was a vague reference to unseemly behaviour. When I asked if any complaints had been lodged, there was a vague shrug of the shoulders. I promised to check with the Director the next day, and the meeting broke up.

Afterwards Seyiso, who was upset, claimed that 'no nonsense' had taken place between himself, or any of the comrades, and the girl. He said that there were a few individuals like Ishmail who took exception to alcohol being provided, even though it was only consumed at the weekends, and in moderation. 'It's a throw-back to the uprising,' he explained, 'when students set fire to the liquor outlets at home, because they objected to the way many of the adults drown their problems in booze.'

There was a cloud of depression over the comrades on the Sunday. Even the normally ebullient Seyiso was not keen to organise any games, and went around with an embarrassed expression.

It was a relief to learn from the Director, first thing on Monday morning, in response to my query, that there had been no complaints from the girl's parents or any of the staff. As far as they were concerned the comrades had behaved perfectly well. When I announced this in class it immediately cleared the air. Seyiso and the others were soon back to their cheerful selves. The incident made me aware of the contradictions that could easily rise to the surface, in what was a group of volatile young people still searching for stability in the world.

The last weekend with the comrades proved to be a most enjoyable one. We were taken on a trip to Thuringia, near the Czechoslovak border, where we visited historic spots associated with Goethe. Then there was a memorable trip to Wartburg Castle, where Martin Luther had translated the Bible into the German language.

I stayed in Berlin for the weekend. I was accommodated at the Party hotel. It was modest, but comfortable, and used by the ruling Socialist Einheidspartei (Socialist Unity Party) to put up guests. I spent the weekend sightseeing with my guide, and walking about on my own. There was a feeling of order and security in the streets. There was no criminal atmosphere, and no sign of beggars or down-and-outs. The Wall, without the strident musical accompaniment of cold war films, even looked pretty ordinary. There were impressive museums, statues, theatres and open squares, all rebuilt from the ruins of the war. We enjoyed a drink at the famous Opera Café on Unter den Linden, which ended at the Wall. Tourists, over for the day from West Berlin, appeared totally relaxed. There were modern buildings, and smart shops, which testified to the GDR's status as the fastest-growing economy in the socialist bloc. I quickly learnt to get about on the U-bahn, impressed that a ticket to any underground destination cost just a few pfennigs.

It was in meetings with East Berliners, friends of South African students, that I came into contact with a cynicism about the form of socialism being built. There was Monika, for example, and her circle, intellectual offspring of hardline communists, who were clearly dissatisfied with life.

Yes, the material advances for ordinary workers and farmers were impressive. The strides in health care and social security could not be matched by the West. But Monika and her friends could not bear the paternalism, the control of artistic freedom, the one-party line. They were supporters of the Prague Spring, and that at least appealed to me.

These were the views of young intellectuals, who had never had to struggle. But there were also the views of their parents, who had survived the concentration camps. Like the instructors at the school, the older generation argued that a firm economic base, and a strong socialist state able to defend itself against the West, was a prerequisite for the development of greater freedom.

The problem with the latter argument was the mechanical division between economic development and security on the one hand, and spiritual freedoms on the other. It is easy to see this in retrospect. My problem at the time was compounded by our lack of a critique of the contradictions within those East European states.

The debate in the GDR was whether they had achieved socialism or a more advanced model. Since they had been building socialism for over 25 years, and impressive economic advances had been achieved, it was decided they had reached the stage of 'mature socialism'.

Even my guide from the Party had joked about the vagueness of this. When I bade him '*auf wiedersehen*' at Schonefeld airport, I said they should beware of 'too much maturing', otherwise they might become 'over-ripe'. As we laughed, neither of us realised how prophetic the joke was to become.

TEN

ANGOLA

October–December 1977

WITHIN A FEW MONTHS I WAS trading pidgin German for the Portuguese counterpart. The ANC had asked me to teach politics for three months in our recently established Angolan camps. At the end of October 1977, I was on my way to Luanda from London. Coming in low over the Angolan capital I caught my breath at the sight of the red African soil, the sprawling townships, the skyscrapers lining a sparkling bay jammed with cargo ships, and a colonial fort on the hill-top.

'*Bon dia, camarade Khumalo*,' a young ANC cadre greeted me. He seemed to have a free run of the airport and took me through to the VIP lounge where Oliver Tambo, Joe Slovo, Joe Modise and other leaders were waiting to board the flight for Lusaka. Tambo thanked me for coming out to Angola and after a brief discussion with the two Joes, who were in charge of directing our military operations inside South Africa, I was whisked through immigration.

The city was bustling with people, traffic and noise. Soviet-made military vehicles of all descriptions vied with battered cars and myriad buzz bikes. The civilian population was generally young and alert-looking, dressed in casual clothing and easily mingling with uniformed men and women in police blue and military fatigues. There were slogans and murals depicting the historic change that had occurred in this diamond-, coffee- and oil-rich land. The red and black flag of the MPLA fluttered everywhere.

I learnt that the ANC had initially been using the residence of the former South African ambassador but had passed it on to the Polish diplomatic mission. We now had three residences in a former middle-class street, renamed Rua do Liberação (Street of Liberation), which housed offices of the OAU, SWAPO, ZAPU, ANC and Polisario – the movement for the liberation of West Sahara from Moroccan rule.

99

The ANC residence was a mixture of seaside boarding-house, back-street garage and military encampment. Our house was a moderate-sized, double-storey building with a palm tree dominating a small front garden and a couple of tents and a vegetable patch at the back. A military truck was being off-loaded with supplies by comrades in uniform. A couple in overalls were tinkering with the engine of a jeep. Other comrades in T-shirts and jeans were playing chess on the verandah and a group of young men and women in their late teens was busy at a table sifting through a pile of rice. I was taken up a spiral staircase to meet the ANC's personnel officer, Mzwai Piliso.

Mzwai, in his fifties, was a burly, no-nonsense figure, with a quiet presence. He had a wife and children living in Burnley. I had come to know him on his visits to the family in England and it was he who was instrumental in my coming back to Africa. A close confidant of Tambo, he was in charge of all Umkhonto we Sizwe camps and the training programme in Africa and abroad. He was a workaholic who concentrated his energy on improving every aspect of camp life – from the training programme, to supplies, medical service, construction, culture and sporting activity.

As chief personnel officer he was also responsible for attending to the vital area of security. He warned me to be on guard: 'Don't take anybody for granted. We're discovering a lot of infiltrators.'

Mzwai was referred to as '*Tata*' (Xhosa for father) by the young cadres and respected by the *mgwenya* scattered around the world. He never forgot their contribution and endeavoured to find deployment possibilities for them. He had left South Africa in the early 1950s to study as a pharmacist in Birmingham. When we traded anecdotes about life in Britain he used to take great pride in reminding me that he was once given a trial as goalkeeper for Birmingham City Football Club but ended up playing rugby for a local club instead. After Tambo's arrival in Britain in 1960 he met Mzwai and encouraged him to work full-time for the ANC.

Mzwai informed me that I would be leaving Luanda within a few days to teach at a camp in the east codenamed 'Thirteen'. When we concluded our discussion, he said he had a surprise for me and called out: '*Ngena dokotela*' (Come in, doctor).

A small, rotund woman came waddling in, her face beaming. She held out her arms and I hugged her with delight. It was Nomava Shangase, a friend of Eleanor's and mine from Tanzania. She had left South Africa in 1962, with a group of nurses, to work in the newly independent state as a gesture of solidarity from the ANC. Mzwai had been responsible for having her and others study as medical doctors in the Soviet Union. Like me, she had come to Angola to work for the ANC and was attending to the comrades' health needs in Luanda.

I had a couple of days to look around Luanda, meet the local comrades and swim in the sea. I wrote to Eleanor, the first of numerous letters over the years:

> *... It was the sight of the red soil, as we came in to land, that stirred my emotions ... we have been away from Africa for too long.*
>
> *I've been able to relax these few days and get my bearings ... everyone is a 'Camarade'. Angolans, Cubans and Soviets are allocated to assist us, and very proud to term themselves 'ANC militants'.*
>
> *The press and radio energetically project the ANC. I have been to the radio station with Pallo Jordan (in charge of ANC publicity), and found our young people compiling scripts and doing the broadcasting ... The Prime Minister – Lopo do Nacimento – made a statement in Moscow that Angola was going to be a base for Marxism-Leninism in Africa. Radio South Africa had hysterics over this last night ...*
>
> *Luanda is a striking city ... The Portuguese were trying to demonstrate that they would be here for years to come and had only recently put up some imposing hotels and banks ... night and day the streets are bustling and I've walked about without a care in the world being taken for Portuguese or white Angolan – until I've had to use my smattering of the language – and experienced no tension or shred of racism. Everyone, young and old, police, soldiers, hotel attendants addresses one as 'camarade' ...*
>
> *I walked around the bay which is dominated by a Portuguese fort in which Holden Roberto's FNLA forces holed up in those tense days around independence. Children were fishing and we watched flying-fish springing in and out of the water. It made me wish you were here, holding hands ...*
>
> *Our residence is comfortable although we sleep three or four in a room. My bed is a foot from Mzwai's and I don't care to say who snores louder. We are in an MPLA stronghold ... the gardens have been turned into small holdings ... a large black pig is tethered to a tree in the next-door house; goats, pigs and hens scratch about in the gardens and the streets ... we have a good vegetable patch, but the onions are doing poorly; we need your green fingers ... I've already done my share of the cooking; together with Pallo produced omelettes using onions and peppers from our garden ...*

Mzwai had me kitted out in military uniform and handed me a pistol. He had introduced me to my driver, whom he said he would trust with his life – a sedate-looking old man with receding hairline, called Sinatla Matome, *a nom de guerre*. We got into a Soviet jeep with two young MK soldiers armed with AK-47s in the back and were soon on the outskirts of Luanda.

I discovered that my driver was a lively companion once he had overcome an initial shyness. We passed a massive vehicle park with row upon row of Soviet military vehicles of every description. He told me the place was never empty. Every week it was cleared, and the vehicles replaced by more arriving by ship. Angola was a country on wheels. 'But you'll see the wrecks and breakdowns along the roads.'

'What's the cause?' I asked.

'In most cases reckless driving and lack of proper maintenance,' was his answer. But he added that there was a lot of deliberate sabotage too. The bandits might have been defeated but silent resistance was taking place. He said that even in our camps we had to exercise vigilance against sabotage by undercover enemy agents. He would not let anybody near his jeep.

Alongside the road leading north-east of the capital was a concrete pipeline. 'That's Luanda's water supply,' Sinatla gestured. 'The pumping station's along here, just 27 kilometres away, at a place called Quifangondo. It's the closest point the Boers reached at the end of 1975. Then they got hit by Cuban reinforcement ...' he laughed.

Sinatla was well into his stride, clearly enjoying recounting how the Cubans had saved the situation. 'Talking about the Cubans,' he went on, 'do you know that they're crazy about *mgulubi* – you know, pork? They say that when you're driving and a ball comes into the road you must slow down because a child will run after it. So if you see a pig you must also slow down because a Cuban will be chasing it.'

We had a good laugh, and he was eager to continue: 'Here's a question comrade: What's the quickest way to liberate Namibia? Answer: Chase all the pigs across the border and Namibia will be overrun by Cubans.'

We came down from the heights around Luanda and it became oppressively hot. We travelled through sugar-cane country and the small town of Caxito, with its tumbledown villas in pale chalky colours and tin roofs, dominated by a large pink-and-white church. Many of the buildings had been badly shot up and some had collapsed. We passed through a checkpoint manned by members of the Angolan People's Militia. These were ragged-trousered peasants with red armbands and green berets armed with AK-47s – a pregnant woman among them. They did not appear to be able to read our documents, but responded happily when we identified ourselves as ANC and handed around cigarettes.

A throng of children ran alongside us calling out 'Viva Cuba!' and the MPLA slogan: *Aluta* ... (the struggle ...) to which the comrades in the back of our jeep enthusiastically responded – *Continua!*

'A beautiful country,' Sinatla remarked, 'of AK-47s, pregnant women and hopeful children.'

A lopsided signpost indicated 'Luanda 50 kms – Quibaxe 146 kms.' Sinatla informed me that Quibaxe was our destination: 'That's where camp "Thirteen" is. The road ahead is typical guerrilla country, especially when we get into the province of Cuanza Norte, which is just ahead of us.'

The cassava plant, which provided the Angolan staple diet, and had been a feature of the vegetation, gave way to dense bush. After a while the road began ascending tortuous inclines. I learnt from Sinatla that he had trained in the Soviet Union. He pointed out features in the terrain which he assessed were perfect for ambush points. The comrades in the back of the jeep had long cocked their AKs and held them at the ready.

'When the Portuguese travelled along this road they used to rake the bush with machinegun fire to keep the freedom fighters at bay,' Sinatla said, 'but don't worry, there's been no trouble from bandits for some time.'

I had become intrigued about Sinatla's background. He was new to the Movement and it was rare to find a much older comrade among the recent exodus. In reply to my query about his recruitment he replied that he had joined the ANC on Robben Island. 'The comrades there gave me politics,' he stated proudly. 'They altered my life in a way the judge who sentenced me could never have imagined,' he laughed.

'How did you get there,' I asked.

'Armed robbery,' he replied. 'I was sentenced to 25 years in 1958. I was released by 1976 and began working with ex-Islanders like Joe Gqabi and John Nkadimeng.'

We were in coffee country, moving in low gear along steep hairpin bends. Groups of women in colourful *kitenge* (cloth wrappers) were weeding with hoes. Men were slashing the bush with Angola's national symbol – the machete. We passed the small villages of Cuso and Phiri, with their improvised checkpoints, huts, bullet-riddled buildings, some with 'Viva FNLA! Viva Holden Roberto!' slogans still scrawled on them. After a four-hour journey from Luanda, with the road becoming increasingly potholed, we arrived in the coffee-growing centre of Quibaxe.

Quibaxe was a quaint little town that had been hard hit by the war. Dilapidated villas and shops lined the single road that ran through it on the way to the Zairean border 350 kilometres distant. The predominant colours of ochre, white and pink that peeled off the buildings were offset by flamboyant trees and bougainvillaea that grew in profusion and hid the scars of war. We drove through a checkpoint of white painted drums, exchanging pleasantries with the militia. We passed an antiquated coffee-processing plant with a depot piled high with bags of the precious bean. We hooted as we proceeded past a garage where Angolan soldiers were filling up from a hand-operated diesel pump. We were cheered on by children at play in a school with broken windows.

In all of two minutes, the town was behind us and we turned off the tarred road on to a dirt track winding down a steep incline with an awesome drop into thick forest below. Now and again I glimpsed the bush stretching far into the distance like a green sea.

I had become used to the long English twilights and was surprised to find how suddenly dusk fell. It was dark when we arrived at the camp. We were stopped at a checkpoint by an MK soldier who shone a torch on our faces and greeted us in Zulu. There was the glow of camp fires and illumination in a few buildings which, I learnt later, came from a generator. We pulled up at a concrete building with a watch tower. A tall figure saluted as I alighted and shouted out:

'Detachment – *haatenshunnn!*'

It was my friend from East Germany, Seyiso. He was Chief of Staff in the camp. He took me into the command post, and introduced me to a group of uniformed comrades who comprised the camp administration. The commander had left for Luanda. We sat down to a welcome meal of tinned beef, rice and a thick gravy with some vegetables – much like our leaders were having in Luanda – washed down with black tea. The pleasant surprise here was the banana and pawpaw we had for dessert.

Seyiso explained that the area was fertile, with cassava and fruit growing in abundance. 'Mind you,' he went on, 'if you had arrived last week you would have found us eating python steaks.'

I asked what it tasted like.

'Delicious,' was the general response, 'it tastes a bit like chicken and a bit like fish, but it must be well done, otherwise it repeats on you.'

Seyiso went on to tell me about the camp.

'It's really a coffee estate with plantations all around. This little building must have been the supervisor's residence. There are four small rooms here which we sleep in. We use this room as an office and for eating. At the back is a small kitchen but our food comes from the main camp kitchen. There's also a small room with a diesel generator at the back. We use it to generate electricity for a few hours every evening.

'There's a couple of other dilapidated buildings which we are planning to repair and a barracks which must have housed the labourers. It has showers which you can use tomorrow. There's a water supply from a small spring up on the hill. There is a stream nearby and that's where we do most of our washing and bathing.'

The comrades who made up the administration were mostly young and had trained in the Soviet Union or East Germany. The camp commander who had left for Luanda was an *mgwenya* called Parker. Seyiso, as chief of staff, was acting as his deputy. Then there was the commissar, a personnel officer, a logistics officer and a medical orderly, another *mgwenya* called Barney.

We had a chat and he told me that he had been striving over the years to study medicine and still hoped to become a doctor like Nomava. Like many *mgwenya*, he had been living at an ANC settlement at Morogoro, Tanzania. The years of exile had not been easy and signs of weariness were evident in his voice and face. He was of a generation that left South Africa in the early 1960s and had expected to return home within a short time. They had not seen their parents in years. Those who had married young had left wives and young children behind. Many had inevitably developed relationships with local women and Barney told me that there was quite a mixed colony of our people both in Tanzania and Zambia.

Sinatla and I shared a small room in which were two iron bedsteads. We placed our bags on the floor next to several piles of books. Seyiso warned that the generator would be turned off within five minutes. I carefully laid my uniform out on a chair, my pistol within reach and my boots close by. It was pleasantly cool and I decided to sleep in a track suit. We were exhausted and fell fast asleep.

I became conscious of movement in the room and lay still trying to fathom out the noise. There was a crunching and scratching that made the hair on the nape of my neck stand up.

'Sinatla! Are you awake?' I whispered.

'Yes,' he hissed back, 'I think there's an underground worker in the room.'

'A what?' I asked.

I was relieved to hear him giggling. 'A rat,' he answered, groping for a boot.

After we dealt with the intruder I fell into a deep sleep again and then the alarm sounded. Barking sounds appeared to come from far away and I was convinced it was a dream. I was dreaming of Eleanor and London. Was that the sound of Rags, our pet dog, in Golders Green waking me up? I felt a hand shaking me and then the rata-tat-tat sound of gunfire close by. I heard a hoarse voice shouting in the distance and then another furious round of shooting.

'Wake up! Wake up!' Seyiso was telling me. 'We're under attack. We must get into the trenches.'

Seyiso was now outside bellowing: 'Evacuate to the trenches! Everyone to the trenches!'

Sinatla and I were desperately searching for our boots which we had flung at the rat. Seyiso was back in the room calling us to follow him. I gave up my futile search for the footwear and clutching my pistol followed him out into the pitch black night. We were soon with other comrades in the trenches peering into the darkness. It was 2 a.m. The bush outside the camp looked forbidding and was scarcely distinguishable from the night. Looking for the Southern Cross, I realised we were facing north.

Seyiso informed me in a low voice that one of the sentries at the barracks had seen intruders attempting to enter the camp and had opened fire. Others had joined in. I thought of the bandits from Zaire who must be out there waiting to attack and cursed myself for not putting on my boots. If we're overrun, I thought, and taken prisoner, I'll be walking barefoot all the way to Zaire.

We were perfectly quiet in our positions. A calm descended after the rude interruption of our sleep. I became sure that we would put up a good defence. The enemy would most likely attack at dawn.

Most of the comrades were young recruits with only a handful of trained and armed cadres among us. It seemed as though an age had dragged by when the first light began to break through. I became tense as the darkness began to fade, believing that the oncoming dawn would signal a ferocious attack on our positions.

The minutes passed and quite soon a brilliant dawn was upon us. The whitewashed buildings of the camp and our watch tower stood out clearly. Beyond our perimeter fence was the forest – a dull smudge of grey transforming into a lush green. Save for the sound of birds beginning to chatter, everything else was astonishingly tranquil. I had become so convinced of an impending attack that I could not quite believe that the foe had failed to materialise. The relief in everyone's faces was manifest.

Seyiso and a group of armed guards ventured out to investigate. The 'all clear' was soon sounded and everyone allowed to return to their quarters.

While we were breakfasting on sweetened black tea and dry biscuits a truckload of government soldiers and a group of tough-looking Cubans in civilian dress arrived from the town. The Cubans were agricultural specialists. They had heard the gunfire during the night and came to check up on us. We accompanied them down to the stream, but there were too many footprints about to show any sign of the intruders. The senior Cuban, who was introduced to me as Arnoldo, and whom everyone called 'Jefe' (meaning Chief), promised to loan to us a number of AK rifles and grenades, until we received more arms which were expected from Luanda.

It was during the course of the day that Seyiso informed me that there was growing doubt about the authenticity of the attack. The sentry who had started the firing had been arguing with his commander. He had tried to avoid guard duty by claiming he was ill. Ten minutes later he opened fire with an AK. He claimed that intruders had attempted to enter the camp by the north gate, where there was no sentry at night. He had fired off 30 rounds.

'We've decided to open an enquiry,' Seyiso said, 'and we want you to be part of it.'

The suspect's name was Jackson. He was a strong, solemn-looking individual with a beard, who had received a couple of weeks' preliminary training ahead of the main intake of recruits. There was nothing in his appearance that indicated any ulterior motive.

He coolly demonstrated what had occurred. The sentry point was the balcony of the barracks. This was a long, oblong, concrete building on the northern side of the camp, some 50 metres from the residence where I had slept.

'I heard a noise over there,' Jackson told us, pointing to the gate which led down to the stream and the forest beyond. 'I saw an armed group creeping up to the gate. One person took up a position at the gate and two others came through moving inside the fence towards the administration. That's when I started firing.'

He lifted his AK, which was unloaded, and clicked the trigger, pointing at the gate. 'I fired off six or seven rounds and then I jumped like this ...'

Displaying a remarkable athleticism he sprang from the balcony, rolled over on the hard ground several metres below and assumed a prone firing position. 'This is where I continued firing. At the two moving to the administration, at the man at the gate, and at the group beyond him. I finished a full magazine – 30 rounds. Other comrades started firing from the balcony and the enemy ran away.'

Seyiso remarked that Jackson had manoeuvred like a highly trained soldier, which was surprising since he did not have that kind of training. We interviewed a couple of comrades who had joined in the firing, but they had not seen the enemy. 'We wanted to demonstrate that we were vigilant,' we were told.

'It was pretty dark last night,' I said to Seyiso. 'There was no moon. Let's get Jackson to repeat his demonstration tonight.'

It was another dark night. A group of us assembled with Jackson on the balcony of the barracks. 'Although it's not 2 a.m. would you say the darkness is about the same as it was when you fired at the enemy last night?' we asked Jackson. He agreed.

'Okay,' we told him. 'We have placed comrades out there where you say you saw the enemy. Look carefully and tell us how many you can see and where they are.'

Together with Jackson we all peered towards the gate and the boundary fence. I strained my eyes and could not see further than five metres.

After a while Jackson said: 'There is someone standing at the gate.'

'Which side?' we asked.

'The left side.'

'Whose left side? Our left side as we face the fence or his?'

'Our left side.'

'Anyone else?'

'Yes, some people along the fence on the right towards the administration.'

'How far from the gate?' we enquired.

'About 30 metres,' he replied.

'Okay, comrades,' Seyiso called out, 'switch your torches on.'

Three lights came on. One just 15 metres from us in front of the gate and ten metres inside the camp. Both the other lights were situated well away from the positions Jackson had pointed out.

Jackson was clearly lying. It was decided to send him back to Luanda for further investigation into his background by the security department. While his behaviour could simply have arisen from disgruntlement, the skilful manner in which he had sprung from the balcony to take up a firing position raised suspicions that he might be an enemy agent. In fact this was later confirmed when another enemy agent provided information about him.

My first night in the camp had certainly proved eventful and I looked forward to settling down to my classes. These were conducted under a huge baobab tree and later under makeshift shelters of split poles supporting thatched roofs. My students sat on wooden benches and I used a home-made blackboard to spell out key words and ideas.

There were about 150 new recruits in the camp. They were going through a general induction course. From Quibaxe they would proceed to Novo Catengue, our main camp in the south of the country, for a course lasting six months.

The day began at 5 a.m. with physical exercises. By 5.30 comrades were busy washing by the stream. We had to abandon the showers because water from the spring ran out within weeks. Breakfast was served in an outdoor mess under a tin roof at 6.30. We had freshly baked rolls when flour was available. These were baked in simple ovens dug into the red clay earth. At times we had a maize porridge with sugar and the ubiquitous sweetened black tea. On odd occasions tins of condensed milk were provided which did much for the morale.

By 7 a.m. everybody fell in, with reports progressing military-style from platoon level through detachment commander to the camp commander: so many comrades on parade; so many on sentry duty; so many ill and so on. This was followed by the morning news announcement, compiled by an information unit which monitored the various radio stations.

The platoons marched off to their various classes, structured along the lines I had observed in East Germany. The instructors were all ANC cadres who had trained abroad. Classes lasted until 1 p.m. when a two-hour lunch and siesta break took place. As with the other instructors I gave six 50-minute classes throughout the morning with ten minute breaks in between. The timetable varied. If a platoon went into the bush for tactics or shooting it could be out of the camp for the entire morning. Subjects like weapons familiarisation, topography, engineering, first aid and unarmed combat might last two periods. Politics was considered a main subject, on a par with shooting and tactics, and could cover up to four periods at a time.

During the midday break the main meal would be served. When supplies were available in our Luanda stores and the transport functioned smoothly, this would be similar to the evening meal I had enjoyed upon my arrival. Supplies mainly came from the Soviet Union and the socialist bloc, Scandinavia and the Netherlands. These were brought to the camp by ANC trucks and were kept in a large barn-like building where the coffee must have been stored. We received powdered soup, sacks of maize meal, flour and rice, and tinned beef, pork and fish.

The most popular tinned meat was a pork stew from the Soviet Union, with '*Slava*'(Glory) printed on the label. Whenever it was delivered, those who spoke Russian invoked laughter by cheering: '*Slava Sovietskomu Soyuza!* (Glory to the Soviet Union!). Tinned fish from China was dubbed 'Mao Tse-tung' by the comrades. Supplies would arrive sporadically, so that at times we might only have 'Mao Tse-tung' and rice for days on end.

On one occasion at Quibaxe, supplies ran out and on one day all we had were mugs of boiled water. Supplies were a special responsibility of a comrade serving in the camp administration who was consequently referred to as 'Logistico'. When supplies were low, Logistico would buy ground cassava from the peasants which, when cooked, produced a stiff porridge. The peasants, however, were loath to sell their livestock, which was what most interested us.

Meals were enhanced by the inclusion of red pepper in the cassava, rice or meat and sometimes by fresh vegetables. What comrades missed most was red meat which everyone referred to as '*inyama*'. I soon came to learn of the cult of *inyama* when I heard some of my students complaining that they had not had meat for ages.

'But we've been eating *Slava* all week,' I retorted, 'and that's your favourite.'

'*Eish!* That's not *inyama*, comrade Khumalo,' they scoffed. '*inyama* doesn't come out of tins. We mean real meat.'

Hunting expeditions were organised. I discovered that in forest terrain game was difficult to locate, because the animals followed a solitary existence. The peasants dug pits and one day Seyiso nearly broke his neck by falling into one.

After an afternoon's rest, when the oppressive heat was lifting, comrades carried out camp duties between 3 and 5 p.m. These consisted of collecting firewood, cleaning the camp, constructing dug-outs and classrooms or other buildings. I would spend this time preparing my lectures for the following day and looking forward to the sports hour between 5 and 6 p.m.

Football was by far the most popular pastime, enjoyed by both players and spectators. There were six teams in the camp each with a manager whom I came to realise was something of an authoritarian figure. The group of managers made up the football association and their word was law. There were those with political names such as the Mandela United, Bram Fischer Eleven and People's Club. Then there were popular teams from the South African football league – Kaizer Chiefs, Orlando Pirates and Moroka Swallows. I joined Pirates, whose manager was a nuggety fellow with a shaven head, called Ross. We practised during the week and played matches on Saturdays and Sundays. Unfortunately, after a few weeks the only ball in the camp burst. It had already lost all its surface leather owing to the hard ground.

While we played soccer, other comrades engaged in jogging around the camp perimeter, or exercising with home-made weights. These were made from various-sized tins in which concrete had been set with a steel rod between. There was even a karate club in action.

The evening meal would consist of a powdered soup with home-made bread or tinned biscuits and black tea. A favourite to go with the tea was a dumpling made of flour called '*magunyas*' in township jargon. It was forbidden to pick fruit for individual consumption. Fruit was shared out when it ripened, although there were so many bananas these were available on a daily basis. It soon became clear that some comrades were picking pawpaws and the precious pineapples for themselves. The camp commissar had to issue stern warnings about the immorality of this.

The rank of commissar used in all the southern African guerrilla movements originated in the Russian Red Army from the time of the Civil War. At that time, it was a necessity because the new socialist state had to rely on Czarist officers. The commissar represented the Party and had to ensure that the commander adhered to the Party line and did not betray the Revolution. The commissar had also to counter any tendency of the commander to behave despotically.

Evenings, after dinner, were an active time in the camp too. Comrades revised the day's lessons on a collective basis. The emphasis was on assisting those who were having difficulties with their studies. On certain evenings platoons held political meetings and discussions. There was also choir and drama practice, because on Saturday nights and public holidays concerts would take place. Instructors and the camp administration would also hold meetings when necessary. Later at Quibaxe, as at Novo Catengue and all other camps, we established a library, an indoor games room and an adult education class. Mzwai Piliso was the dynamo behind all this and, with our international contacts, the camps were well supplied with everything from chess and Scrabble sets to wall charts, maps and books of all kinds. There was invariably a group of talented artists in any camp and, with the necessary equipment donated through the ANC network abroad, we were even able to hold exhibitions and decorate the camp with the portraits of our leaders. Most of my time in the evenings was occupied in conducting special classes for a handful of comrades whom I was preparing as political instructors.

By 10 p.m. the generator which had been in operation since dusk was switched off, and it was lights-out for everyone except the sentries. If necessary the administration would continue to meet by lamplight.

The relationship between the administration and recruits appeared to be good. The instructors, fresh from the Soviet Union and GDR, adopted a sound approach in their courses. Even in relation to physical training, and tactics in the field, I observed that they were careful not to overextend the trainees. This was in contrast to the macho period of Ambrose at the Kongwa camp in Tanzania. Notwithstanding concern about enemy infiltrators, I also noticed that the administration of discipline was mild. Those who malingered, when it came to guard duty or camp labour, were spoken to by their commissar and encouraged to correct their ways. Those who were found to be stealing fruit might be given some extra light duty, by way of punishment.

The recruits came from all corners of South Africa, both male and female. I learnt the slogans of our struggle in Zulu, Xhosa, Sotho, Tswana, Sepedi, Tsonga, Shangaan and Afrikaans and a smattering of greetings in all. Comrades spoke in a mixture of the vernacular languages and English. *Tsotsi-taal* was popular, especially during leisure hours. I first heard it being used in class when, at the start of a lesson I asked, as usual, for an interpreter. After beginning, I paused for interpretation, and was surprised to hear the colourful flow of the Afrikaans-township patois.

'You surprise me, comrades,' I exclaimed. 'I thought you had started your revolt against racism because of your rejection of *die taal* [Afrikaans].'

My students outdid each other in emphasising that it was not *die taal* they were resistant to but its forced imposition. As in East Germany I immediately felt at ease with them and sensed I was accepted not only because I was living among them but because the views I projected were the views they could relate to. I was constantly amazed at their lack of racism and the natural ease by which they came to understand that the basis of our struggle united all forces opposed to oppression and injustice. The culture this created was reflected in a joie de vivre and vitality that I had not found in all my travels. The exuberance of my students and colleagues such as Seyiso and Sinatla inspired me.

Not that they were without tensions, which ranged from worries about their families at home, love problems, psychosomatic anxieties and friction with their colleagues.

After class one day, a lanky, doleful-looking cadre who went by the name of Duke asked to speak to me. (There was a Runyonesque political and geographical flavour to the *noms de plume* they assumed, which ranged from Duke, Walk Tall, and Joe My Baby to Lenin, Nikita, Brezhnev, Castro, Samora, Mugabe and Inkululeko (Freedom), through to place names like London, Belgium and Tokyo.)

Duke looked awkward and was a trifle tongue-tied. 'What is it, Duke?' I enquired, giving him an encouraging prod.

He rolled up his sleeve. 'Do you know what this is?' he asked, revealing a crude-looking tattoo. 'Sure,' I said. 'A tattoo.'

'I don't think you understand, comrade Khumalo,' he continued. 'It's the mark of a prison gang. You see I belonged to that gang in jail.'

I told him not to feel ashamed. The apartheid system had made so-called criminals of many good people. Some were in the ANC.

'Not like me,' he answered. 'You see the police released me with instructions to infiltrate the ANC. When I agreed I didn't understand anything. I've been following your lessons and beginning to understand what the ANC is about. I don't want to work for the Boers.'

I congratulated him on his honesty, and assured him that he could feel at home in the ANC.

ELEVEN

DEFIANCE

Quibaxe, Angola
Christmas 1977

WEEKENDS WERE THE TIME FOR sport, cultural pursuits and sheer relaxation. I liked to carry my air-bed down into the lemon grove and laze in the shade with the citrus perfume wafting in the breeze.

Two of my students, Frank (Oscar Mbete) and Ashok (Krish Rabilal), liked doing the same thing. I used to have enjoyable conversations with them, learning about current life in South Africa. They were both from Durban. Oscar had been born in the African township of Umlazi. He had been expelled from Fort Hare University because of his role in a student strike. Ashok, from the Indian working-class area of Merebank, was of slight build. From different communities, they explained how racial oppression and the poverty of their parents had similarly shaped them and brought them into the ANC.

Oscar had worked at Natal University, Durban, as a laboratory technician. His sister was Baleka Mbete, future Chairperson of the ANC and Speaker of the democratic Parliament in a free South Africa.

'Do you know Logan's Bookshop up on the campus?' I enquired.

'Sure do,' he replied coolly. 'That's where we nick our books.'

'Shame on you, Oscar,' I chided him, 'the Logans are my parents-in-law.'

'Oh, they're nice people,' he replied, a touch embarrassed, 'but you know how hard being a student is.'

Oscar and Ashok took me on a walk across the stream, through a dark section of the forest to the edge of a hill on which our camp was situated. I had not realised we were at such a height and it explained the coolness of our location and why our camp was often shrouded in mist. I caught my breath at the beauty of the scenery that stretched before my eyes.

The side of our hill was part of an escarpment. The cliffs were steep and a dramatic red colour. Below was a sheer drop of 200 metres. Beyond was a

113

spectacular valley of thick bush through which a river meandered. So much for my fears of an attack on the camp from the north side!

First thing Sunday morning, I would join Seyiso and the commissar down at our stream for a swim and to wash our uniforms. They taught me how to 'iron' clothes without electricity or labour. The clothing was carefully laid out on sheets of newspaper under our air-beds. The 'ironing' was done while we slept. The next morning you found your uniform neatly pressed.

I never took to python steaks (I found they gave me indigestion regardless of how well they were done) but developed a taste for *mfeni* (baboon). There were plenty of the creatures around and shooting them was one way of obtaining real *inyama*. The meat had to be well cooked – roasting was best – and with red pepper and seasoning tasted like mutton. Some comrades, however, would not dream of eating *mfeni* because they regarded them as human. I found this strange because in my lectures the idea that met with the greatest resistance was that human beings descended from the apes.

I sensed this was partly due to the way racists the world over spoke of blacks as having 'only recently descended from the trees'. Consequently, when I came to explain evolution to my students I would open my shirt and, exposing my hairy chest, state: 'As you can see, comrades, white people are closer to our ape ancestors than black people are.'

My students, who according to Dr Verwoerd should have been taught only to be 'hewers of wood and drawers of water', had an inexhaustible thirst for knowledge and I was inundated with questions during and after lessons. Their unfamiliarity with international events and the history of our struggle was evidenced by the fact that nobody in a class of 30 knew who Ho Chi Minh was and only two had heard of Vuyisile Mini, one of our foremost leaders, executed in 1964. They were astonished to hear about the widespread resistance to apartheid in the early 1950s and '60s and could not understand why their parents had kept so quiet about this.

I explained that after the ANC's banning people were intimidated. Talking about the ANC could mean arrest. There was the incident of the factory worker sentenced to two years' imprisonment for scratching 'Free Mandela' on his mug. After the 1976 uprising many people began recalling the old days. Parents would say they had been in the ANC.

The topic they were most interested to learn about was communism, which undoubtedly stemmed from the pathological attacks on everything to do with communism that emanated from South Africa's apartheid masters. The leadership of the ANC had decided to introduce Marxism as a subject because there was such a demand to know about it. I pointed out that you did not have to be a Marxist to belong to the ANC.

They were fascinated by the version of South African history they received in the ANC. Accounts of the brave resistance put up against colonial invaders filled them with pride. They laughed uproariously when I told them that Jan van Riebeeck, the Dutch founder of the Cape settlement, had been found guilty of fraud in Holland and was sent to the Cape by the Dutch East India Company as punishment.

The training programme was going extremely smoothly, with everyone looking forward to celebrations which would take place on Christmas Day, New Year's Day and – most important of all the holidays – 8 January, the anniversary of the founding of the ANC.

One moment I was feeling fine and the next I was stricken low with malaria. Despite having taken anti-malaria tablets, I had a particularly severe bout. No amount of chloroquine injections seemed to work. For a week I lay on my air-bed, alternately shivering under layers of blankets and sweating with a high fever. I could not keep food down and rejected the brackish water we drank. Dehydrated, I craved ice-cold Pepsi Cola. I began hallucinating about Pepsi Colas. I began calculating how long it would take to get an urgent request to Eleanor in London. And how long it would take her to despatch a case of Pepsi, back to me, by air freight.

I became so demoralised that I nearly threw in the towel. I began thinking I was crazy ever to have left London for the African bush.

In the end I was carted off to hospital by Mzwai Piliso. Twenty-four hours on a glucolin drip had me back to normal.

Just before Christmas, the ANC's chief representative in Angola, Cassius Make (Job Thabane), paid us an unexpected visit. 'I've brought you 14 characters from Novo Catengue,' he told the administration. I pricked up my ears. When someone was referred to as a 'character' in the Movement it generally meant they created problems. Cassius explained that after their training course was over they insisted on immediately being sent home to fight the enemy. This was not possible, and they had refused to obey orders by way of protest. Modise and Mzwai were out of the country, and Cassius was leaving the group with us until their return.

Cassius had loyally served the ANC from the Odessa days, when he was one of the youngest recruits among us. He did not tolerate 'problem people' easily and was a person of few words. He had just made the longest speech I had ever heard from him. He was never one for ceremonies and immediately prepared to return to Luanda.

I reminded him that our generation had also 'kicked up dust' about getting back home. Were these cadres serious or just trouble-makers?

'I'm not at all sure,' he replied. 'Some could have been misled and

115

manipulated but some are really hard nuts. Just you wait and see,' he added with a dry chuckle. It was all right for him to chuckle. He had simply passed the problem on to us.

The administration, led by Parker, the commander, called a meeting with the group. We had already decided to take a conciliatory line. This amounted to accepting them in the camp, excusing them from all study classes, but expecting them to assist with camp duties. We were prepared to assign them to a tent and provide them with food, until the leadership decided their future.

We assembled under the baobab tree. The fourteen were in civilian dress and stood close together. They eyed us suspiciously, listening to Parker in silence. He was an exceptionally polite man, already in his fifties, wore the same burnt-out look as Barney and the older *mgwenya* who had seen it all before, and was at his happiest at the wheel of a truck or tinkering with machinery. I thought he put our position across well, even though he was not a forceful individual. A good thing that he was not a confrontational type, in the circumstances, I thought.

The group asked for the equivalent of 'time out' and went into a huddle. We waited patiently, then a spokesperson stepped forward. I was optimistic they would co-operate with us.

He gave his name as Dan Siwela. He was on the small side, dark-skinned, hard-looking, and wore a black leather jacket. He tilted his head at an angle and screwed his eyes up as he concentrated. He spoke rapidly in Zulu, in a harsh tone, and his voice carried weight and confidence. I caught snatches of what he was saying: *Siyafuna hamba ikayi-manje! manje! manje!* (We want to go home now! now! now!),' and he punctuated the *manje* by pointing his finger accusingly at us as though we were the barrier.

He ended with a flourish and turned his back on us in apparent disgust. It was Parker who now needed the 'time out'. He said that they should return to their tent and be ready for our response in an hour.

The rejection of our offer could undermine the order and authority that had been established in the camp. It was decided to give them a choice. Either they carried out basic camp duties or they would be locked up in the *kulakut* (cooler), a large basement below the barracks, where some stores were kept. It was considered adequate for the purpose.

We met under the baobab tree again. After Parker had put the ultimatum to the group, I sensed some wavering. They whispered together. A lanky fellow with a shaven head, called Leslie, said he was prepared to accept our offer. Several others agreed, but most were undecided. They requested more time to sort out the problem. This was agreed to, and they returned to their tent. Within an hour we were meeting them again. This time Dan did all the talking.

No, there would be no co-operation at all. Not from a single one of them. They would not move until the leadership sent them home. If we attempted to put them in the *kulakut*, they would resist.

I was impressed, but depressed, by Dan's leadership qualities and firmness. He was a tough nut all right and, if genuine, the kind of soldier we needed. But he was confused and frustrated, and clearly had a strong hold over the others.

The camp was restless and tense. The group had become a centre of attraction, and both students and some of my fellow instructors were fraternising with them. The fact that some instructors were behaving this way disturbed me. 'There are bad elements among those instructors,' Parker remarked. 'They gave trouble at Novo Catengue and were transferred here.'

This was news to me. I was unhappy that no one had informed me about these problems. I noticed, in particular, a tactics instructor, who had always been over-polite to me, deep in conversation with Dan.

A plan was proposed whereby we would apprehend Dan after dark and place him in detention. A group of trained cadres had recently returned from East Germany. We decided to deploy a group for the task.

Dan was told to pack his bag, which he did without any fuss. As he was being marched through the camp to the basement, a group of comrades materialised and asked what was happening. The instructor I had noticed talking to Dan earlier was among them. Parker saw this and hurried over. An argument erupted, and Dan hurled himself at the commander. They rolled over in the dust and one of the guards, coming to Parker's assistance, struck Dan in the small of his back with a rifle butt. This caused pandemonium among a score of comrades who were by now milling around.

I rushed over to try and calm down an obviously ugly situation.

'Cool it, comrades!' I yelled and received a push in the back.

The guards pointed their weapons to the sky as though ready to fire into the air. 'Don't shoot! Not even warning shots!' Seyiso ordered. 'Let's pull back to the administration.'

We assisted Parker to his feet and let Dan go free. All armed comrades were ordered to fall back to our headquarters. There was confusion in the camp. Although the order for rest time had long gone, many comrades were gathering about in animated groups, some shouting insults at the administration and the 'fascists' from East Germany. I wryly noticed that Ross, the manager of my football team, was an active presence. He and others built a fire which they sat around in voluble discourse for most of the night. We noted, however, that not more than 20 comrades appeared to have been involved in the fracas and perhaps twice that number were ignoring the usual routine. The rest soon retired, although an uneasy atmosphere descended over the camp. The strident voices of Ross and others continued well into the small hours of the night.

After a restless night, the camp woke to a surprising calm. Some comrades were beginning to stir, walking about bleary-eyed and attending to their washing. We decided to suspend the normal programme. It was agreed that breakfast would be organised and then the entire camp, apart from the fourteen, would be called to an assembly.

'Khumalo, will you speak on our behalf?' Parker asked me. 'We need your powers of persuasion.'

I faced the formation of comrades. Everyone was in a serious mood, and I judged that quite a number appeared to be shamefaced.

'Comrades,' I began, drawing a line in the dust with my boot, 'the difference between anarchy and order is as easy as crossing this line. You have to decide on which side of the line you want to be.'

I spoke about the need for discipline and order in the ANC and MK, which we had often discussed in class, pointing out that this was not like the orders from the racists, intended to keep people suppressed. I spoke about the fourteen sitting in the tent, defying orders because they wanted to go home to fight. I pointed out that they had no hope of surviving the journey without adequate preparation. It could be frustrating waiting to return home after training, but the leaders had made no secret of the problems. We were not like the Zimbabweans, with a single border to cross from a friendly state. We were very far from home, and had to move secretly through several countries. I concluded by pointing out that if only some of us followed the rules we would have confusion.

'With confusion and anarchy we will never succeed in our aims. No army or organisation can win unless there is discipline and order in its ranks.'

The speech went down well. It was a Saturday and we declared the remainder of the day a rest day. With the situation back to normal, Leslie, the lanky individual with the shaven head, approached us with a request from the group of fourteen: 'We are asking to be sent back to Luanda. We don't want to cause problems here.'

Perhaps too easily, the administration agreed. I must confess to a sense of relief as they departed that afternoon in a truck bound for the capital. A dark cloud had lifted from Quibaxe.

The next day had been set aside for an athletics competition. The mood had totally changed. A young comrade called 'Master' (Sandile Sizani) astonished me. We had dug a long-jump pit and I was judging the competition. He ran up to the mark in his bare feet and took off, almost clearing the pit with a leap well over 20 feet in length.

I halted proceedings so that we could lengthen the pit. His next jump was even longer. He went on to surprise me further by easily jumping over six feet in the high jump, and winning the sprint events. All this in his bare feet and on an uneven, rock-hard surface. I had never come across such a natural athlete in my life and was convinced he could have been an Olympic star with the proper opportunities in a non-racist society.

The sports day was a success. It was business as usual at Camp Thirteen.

Some days later the leadership arrived from Luanda. They came in a convoy with the group of fourteen. The camp was called to formation and Joe Modise sternly announced that a tribunal would be held to deal with the group's defiance. He told the camp that disobedience from any quarter would not be tolerated. The fourteen were subdued.

The leadership left and a few days later a tribunal of four senior comrades, headed by the deputy chief representative in Angola, began hearing evidence about the group's defiance at Novo Catengue and Dan's assault on Parker.

One of those giving evidence was the chief of staff from Novo Catengue, an exceptionally handsome individual. His MK name was Thami Zulu (Muzi Ngwenya) and he looked every inch a soldier. Thami proved to be approachable and intelligent. His view was that most of the fourteen had been manipulated by cleverer, disgruntled elements at his camp.

'They're quite simple, genuine guys,' he told me, 'and have been used, either by agents or by ambitious types who have an axe to grind with those in authority. The camp administration generally becomes the target. I'm talking about characters who are after positions and feel they've been overlooked by the leadership.'

The tribunal completed its work and sentence was passed on the fourteen. Seven were sentenced to one month's detention, six to two months' and Dan Siwela to three months', because of his attack on Parker. All were ordered to carry out labour tasks during the day, as deemed fit by the Quibaxe command. The fourteen accepted sentence without protest and in fact looked quite relieved when the case was over.

The basement, or *kulakut*, had been examined and was deemed fit as the place of detention. It was a large, cool room with the same concrete floor as other buildings in the camp, but it had no windows. It had a heavy iron door with a wire mesh, which testified to its use as a 'lock-up' during the colonial days. It was decided that the door could be kept open at night to improve ventilation if the occupants desired. They were given air-beds and bedding and the same food as the rest of the camp.

I was interested to get to know those serving sentence. Sinatla and I exercised with one of the platoons behind the barracks every morning. Some of the basement's new occupants exercised outside their door-way. The most energetic was a remarkably fit-looking character with a shaven head and beard that gave him an oriental look. He spent a lot of time shadow-boxing and throwing punches. I learnt that his name was Ben 'TNT' Lekalake, a former Transvaal junior lightweight boxing champion. In fact, Seyiso had been a close friend of his in Soweto.

I invited Ben TNT to join us, which he did, bringing Leslie and some of the others into our group. I was soon shadow-boxing with him. 'I'm going back to England soon and will arrange for boxing gloves and other sporting equipment to be sent here,' I promised him.

I was interested in getting to know what made Dan Siwela tick. He kept his distance, however, and did not exercise. In response to my query about this Ben said matter-of-factly: 'Well, you see, he is a peasant and would not bother exercising. He is naturally fit and conserves his energy for the tasks we've been given – digging the trenches and dug-outs here.'

The near mutiny was never mentioned in my classes, which were back to normal and going ahead at full speed because I was due back in London at the end of January. I wrote a lecture, however, based on the experience, which was to be used as an introduction into the army for all new recruits. Seyiso and others suggested I include in this an explanation of the roles of camp administration and of commander, and of the need to obey orders. I illustrated the difference between an army based on harsh discipline, the officer's baton, and spit and polish, and one guided by a discipline that came from the awareness of the cause one served.

The fourteen served out their sentences without complaint or incident. Ben TNT later worked with me in Angola and Lusaka. He told me that when his sentence was over, and he had to leave the basement, he objected 'because it was the coolest place in the camp'. Dan, Leslie and most of the others distinguished themselves in combat operations on the home front.

Fifteen years later a South African advocate, R. Douglas, and a prominent newspaper editor, Ken Owen, accused me of persecuting and torturing the group. Douglas had presided over a right-wing, virulently anti-communist-sponsored commission, into abuses of prisoners in ANC camps.

It was alleged from an anonymous quarter that I had allowed fumes from a diesel motor to almost suffocate the 14 inmates of the basement at Quibaxe. Douglas readily accepted this allegation, and on that basis Ken Owen described the basement as an 'African equivalent of the Black Hole of Calcutta'.

Quibaxe was at peace when I left. Armchair critics like Ken Owen, looking to swallow any anti-communist allegation, were the last thing on my mind, as I sprang into Sinatla's jeep and we sped off for Luanda, the first leg of my journey back to London. Years later, back in South Africa, I managed to locate most of the 14, who corroborated my version of the event.

TWELVE

UNIVERSITY OF THE SOUTH

Angola
1978–79

My PRIORITY BACK IN ENGLAND was organising material support for ANC camps and solidarity for the Angolan government. This was facilitated by the extensive ANC network, made up of exiles and anti-apartheid supporters.

Our sons, Chris and Andrew, were ten and twelve at the time. I had a close relationship with them. The nature and hours of my work enabled me to be at home ahead of Eleanor, who worked as a geology technician at a London college. I helped the boys with their homework, prepared afternoon tea, and spent many happy hours playing football and cricket with them on family rambles with our dog Rags on Hampstead Heath.

Our favourite place for holidays was Cornwall. We would drive down in an old Morris 'shooting-brake', which we had purchased for £150, our dog in the back.

The boys considered themselves one hundred per cent English. They were aware we regarded ourselves as South Africans and that we owed our first loyalty to the ANC rather than 'the English Queen'. We took care to ensure that our allegiance should not force divided loyalties on them. Eleanor was a wonderful mother, wife and home maker. The glue that kept the family together. She treated our sons with the care and love she once had bestowed on Brigid – and still hoped to do.

Our football team, Arsenal, had made it to Wembley for the cup final against Ipswich! To get a ticket was something of a feat. It entailed collecting numbered coupons from your side's home programmes – a different coupon per match. There were 22 home matches in the league, plus several cup and other fixtures. Once your team made it to Wembley you wrote to the club with your collection of coupons. Information was that, unless you had a minimum of 22 coupons, you need not bother. I had taken the boys to a number of home fixtures and, as we progressed through the initial knock-out rounds of the cup, had begun optimistically buying up as many old programmes as I could lay hands on.

With our cup prospects increasing with each successive victory a roaring trade was taking place outside the Highbury ground. The boys were frantically trading coupons at school as well. With the deadline running out, and our collection at little more than 15 each, I drew in the ANC network. Our phone rang incessantly as comrades and friends rallied to our cause. We finally had three sets of 22 coupons and one of 20. Eleanor had never been interested in 'watching 22 grown men chase a piece of leather around a field' so we said we would take Garth Strachan along if we qualified for four tickets.

I posted our collection to the Arsenal Club Secretary, including Eleanor's name as part of our application. 'They'll give us special consideration,' I assured the lads, 'because we're a family.' An envelope from Arsenal FC with the Highbury N5 post-mark duly arrived.

'Hurrah!' we all shouted as I waved four tickets to Wembley over the breakfast table.

About that time Tambo and Piliso requested that I return to Angola on a full-time basis.

They were sensitive about my separation from Eleanor, but promised that opportunities to travel to England would arise.

Eleanor and I had long discussions about this request during walks on Hampstead Heath. We had always remained conscious of our good fortune in escaping from South Africa and being able to start a family abroad, while Billy Nair and our other close friends had been languishing in prison since 1963. Babla Saloojee, who had helped us and others flee, had paid for it with his life. I had trained David Rabkin and others in London and now they too were separated from their loved ones by prison walls. We were intimately affected by this all the time. Sue Rabkin, with her two young children, was a close friend of ours who had made a considerable sacrifice as a young mother not unlike Eleanor, and we saw her regularly.

From the time I had joined Eleanor in London, we had lived with the possibility of the ANC making this request. When the news reached us in 1967 of MK's incursions into Rhodesia, as it was then, I had felt guilty that I was not a participant. The fact that there had been tasks to perform from London had been some compensation.

Now, after over a decade of settled family life in North West London, which we regarded as home, the ANC was requesting my presence elsewhere. Both Tambo's and Piliso's families resided in England, the former in Muswell Hill and the latter in Burnley, and they had been based in Africa since the 1960s. It was a joint decision that Eleanor and I had to take. We could have said no, and without much loss of face I could have carried on with my duties in London. But our consciences dictated otherwise. We decided that I would become a 'migrant worker'.

Had Eleanor not been reunited with Brigid (albeit all too briefly), and had we not enjoyed a happy and stable family relationship, the wrench would have been impossible to cope with. It was in fact Eleanor's commitment to the cause we served, and the support she provided as the main breadwinner of the family, that made my departure possible.

A victory for Arsenal at Wembley, that glorious summer's day in May 1978, would have provided just the tonic to offset the sadness of my imminent departure for Angola. The Gunners' star player and inspiration was Chippy Brady, who was unfortunately off form that fateful day. Plunged into the depths of depression (as only a football fan can know it) we watched a lacklustre Arsenal side struggle against an inspired Ipswich and go down by a solitary goal in a boring, uneventful final.

Riding back to Golders Green, in a bus full of crestfallen Arsenal supporters, was like going to a funeral. On top of it all, we had to put up with the jeers and hoots of derision from Arsenal-loathing kids as we travelled through hostile territory. Promising talk from Garth and myself – 'just wait until next season' – simply made matters worse, and tears rolled down Andrew's and Christopher's cheeks.

There is nothing quite like the humour and irrepressibility of the Londoner, in the face of a setback. A wag began singing a song from a current TV commercial for Heineken lager. The advert featured the losing cup side's delight over their defeat because it meant that instead of drinking champagne they could console themselves in the dressing-room with Heineken beer. When we reached the Golders Green terminal the entire bus was rocking with the refrain:

We lost the cup,
We lost the cup,
Ey aye addio –
We lost the cup.

By the time I was ready to depart, I was loaded with useful material for Angola. I had been to the Natural History Museum in Kensington and bought copies of their excellent wall charts, depicting the evolution of man, the creation of the solar system and so on. I had a number of lotions and sprays to wage war against malaria. Last, but not least, I had a book on card tricks given to me by Andrew, whose hobby was magic. I had found time to polish up a few deft tricks under his masterful eye, anticipating that I would have some fun with the comrades.

About the time I had been participating in the Wembley spectacle, South African jets were dropping bombs on a SWAPO refugee camp at Cassinga in southern Angola. The bombardment took place on 4 May 1978. Paratroopers followed the bombs and, by the end of the day, 867 refugees had been slaughtered. Pretoria claimed that Cassinga was a training base for SWAPO 'terrorists'. Both the UN High Commission for Refugees and the World Health Organisation reported that the majority of the corpses were those of women, children and elderly people.

One day I was participating in a demonstration outside South Africa House, opposite Trafalgar Square in London, in protest at the Cassinga massacre. The next day I was in Luanda.

At a meeting at our residence, Mzwai told me that we were having to step up our security and that underground shelters were being constructed in all our camps.

I learnt that the group of fourteen, having completed their sentences, were prepared to accept orders. Some had been deployed, while others were undergoing specialised training. My friends Seyiso and Sinatla had been deployed to the 'home front'.

'As for your friend Jackson,' continued Mzwai, referring to the man responsible for the shooting incident at Quibaxe, 'the disturbance he caused is one of the tactics used to unnerve recruits. A study of the initial biography he wrote after joining us showed some important differences with a biography we got him to write after the Quibaxe shooting.'

'What exactly?' I enquired.

'In the first version he says that he was recruited into the ANC at home and then left the country. In the later version he claims he simply joined a group that went to Swaziland in search of the ANC.'

'You think that by the time he came to write the second version he had forgotten some of the earlier details which he may have invented?'

'Exactly. The details of his route out also differ.'

'So where is he now?' I asked.

'Here in Luanda. We've got him working with a group, off-loading cargo in the docks. We'll just have to be patient and keep him under observation,' Mzwai responded, with a resigned shrug of his shoulders. The best solution when suspicions of this kind arose was to check up on an individual's story in their home-town neighbourhood. There it was possible to verify a story, learn about the individual's credentials and so on. Our weak contact with home and the absence of a fully developed underground, however, made this difficult.

In order to cope with such problems, the ANC had a security structure headed by Mzwai called 'Nat' (National Intelligence and Security) which was preoccupied with screening all recruits and investigating suspicious individuals. This applied not only to our camps but to the 'forward areas' on South Africa's borders, as well as Zambia, Tanzania and even Britain. Our leadership regarded political education as the main way by which to secure the loyalty and discipline of the cadres. Mzwai emphasised this role to me in combating the threat of infiltration. He told me that I was being posted to our main camp, Novo Catengue, in the south of the country near Benguela.

I stayed at our residence in Benguela for a few days waiting to be transported to our camp. The commander was a gruff old man called Dlokolo who had trained in Egypt in the early 1960s. He was nick-named 'Ranger' because of the stringent commando course he and others had undergone there. He was assisted by a carefree individual called Nikita who, having lived in Mozambique for some years, spoke fluent Portuguese. This had been a thriving area, with the Benguela railway line linking the nearby port of Lobito to the Katanga and Zambian copperbelts. Unita rebels under Jonas Savimbi, from their South African-supplied base on the Caprivi Strip in the south of the country, kept cutting the strategic line.

There were numerous visitors to Dlokolo's residence. One was a young Cuban, aged 20, teaching geography at a local school. He was passionately interested in South Africa, firing all manner of questions at me. When I acknowledged that I knew the various cities and provinces he enquired about, he reacted as though I had been to the most exotic places in the world.

An Angolan army major dropped by and we had an interesting chat. He had joined the MPLA in 1962, lived in exile in Kinshasa and then across the Congo river in Brazzaville, after Mobutu had turned on the MPLA and nearly wiped them out. He had fought the Portuguese and was now the commander of a crack anti-bandit unit.

He showed great understanding of the South African struggle and the fact that we were up against a powerful enemy. He kept emphasising the popular slogan: '*Angola trinchera firme da revolução em Africa* (Angola is a firm trench of the revolution in Africa)' and declared that the MPLA Government would always support the ANC.

There were two white Angolans in their early twenties, serving under the Major – like him dressed in camouflage uniform. They were brothers, whose parents ran a grocery shop and shebeen in the local township, and we were invited around.

I had discovered that many of the offspring of the older generations of Portuguese settlers had become thoroughly integrated in Angola, intermarrying with the African people and proving to be MPLA loyalists. The brothers were no exception. I wrote to Eleanor about the hospitality I experienced in their company:

> *They live communally, with their wives and parents, in a tumble-down old villa, part grocery shop and part shebeen – with tables and chairs in the yard where snacks and drinks are served. In civilian life the brothers are motor mechanics, so part of the yard is littered with old wrecks they are working on. We were served a local cane spirit and were joined by their father, an alcoholic on his last legs, whom they tenderly look after but denounce as a reactionary. They argue with him heatedly about politics. He thumps the table, objecting: 'Não! Não! Não!' They thump the table, responding: 'Si! Si! Si!' The mother is a huge-bosomed, Portuguese woman, who supports the revolution and is known as Mama Paquitta. The father-in-law of one of the brothers arrived on the scene – a Cape Verdean with several teeth missing, sporting an elegant white moustache. The Cape Verdean was full of 'Viva Fidel!' and 'Viva Neto!' slogans but unfortunately, as far as the brothers were concerned, a 'believer'. The debate centred on religion and became heated. The Cape Verdean will only say: 'Viva socialismo!' His son-in-law, like an inquisitor, insists: 'Viva socialismo scientifico!' – drawing out the 'sci-en-tifico!' The womenfolk sat around on their haunches, looking after the kids, smoking and gossiping, ignoring us men and spitting into the dust. The father passed out and was carried off to bed. The Cape Verdean produced a bottle of home-brewed cane. After one glass we decided to call it a day and hurried back to the residence to recover ...*

Our camp at Novo Catengue was over an hour's drive from town. The camp was on the Benguela railway line on the way to Angola's second city, Huambo, in the interior. The camp had been used by the Portuguese army to guard the strategic rail so there were a number of well-constructed single-storey barracks, administration buildings and other quarters. There were over 500 MK recruits undergoing training and a large contingent of Cuban officers and men in the camp. They were in charge of the training programme and the logistics supply. The terrain was of dry scrubland and bush with low hills on three sides of the settlement and a river running alongside the railway line. Whenever a train rolled past, wagons laden with supplies for the central interior, our comrades would whistle and wave at the heavily armed soldiers riding at strategic points, and shout: *Hamba kahle amajoni!* (Go well soldiers). The international press, in its wisdom, had long reported that the Benguela railway line was not functioning.

The MK commander was an *mgwenya* like me, who had trained in Odessa, fought in Rhodesia and was called Julius. We stood outside his small office as he pointed out the camp's features to me while chewing on a Cuban cigar. *Mgwenya* like Julius, having lived for 15 years in Tanzania and Zambia, were exceptionally homesick. London had many links with South Africa and I had brought books and magazines from home, including the new literary journal, *Staffrider*. Julius was delighted when I showed him a copy. He proceeded to demonstrate what a 'staffrider' did.

'When the train comes into the station,' he explained excitedly, 'there are passengers who skip on and off along the platform like tap dancers, man ... on and off ... on and off ... like this ...' He skipped along, his boots rat-tap-tapping on the cement floor outside a row of offices. An image from my youth instantly came to mind of the township commuters jumping on and off the packed trains with the nimble step of Fred Astaire. The term 'staffrider', Julius explained to me, derived from the fact that railway staff skipped expertly on and off trains to save time.

'Geewizz!' he exclaimed, 'what a *lekker* (good) name for a magazine,' and he bounced along the cement floor rata-tap-tap ... rata-tap-tap ... I looked up at the Cuban officer in olive-green uniform, cap low over his brow, cigar in mouth, striding towards us.

'Ah, Colonel Rodrigues, *buenos dias*,' Julius smiled, swiftly regaining his composure. 'This is comrade Khumalo, our political instructor, who has just arrived.'

It was pleasant being in a camp with the Cubans. They were full of fire and passion and reminded me of the Red Army officers who had trained us in Odessa. They referred to themselves as *internationalista*, who were performing their fraternal duty by training us to fight the *racista*. Their presence in Angola had been as a result of the request from Agostinho Neto and the MPLA, to help defend independence at the time of the South African invasion at the end of 1975.

I was issued with a Cuban uniform, and the Colonel himself gave me a thickly quilted military jacket for the evenings. Although it was hot during the day, by the evening a cold wind would regularly blow up. This was the effect of the cold Benguela Current, that had fascinated me in school geography. At a precise time – you could check your watch by it – the cold air which had formed over the Atlantic would come howling in over the land.

The ANC administration included Thami Zulu, who had been a witness at the Quibaxe tribunal. He was Chief of Staff. He and Julius were delighted that I had brought wall charts, maps and books.

'We're building a good library here,' they told me proudly, 'and we're busy creating an indoor games room too, thanks to the contributions from international support groups. Our artists are producing portraits of our leaders to hang on the walls.'

An *mgwenya* called Banda liaised with the Cubans over the training programme. He had a special liking for red meat, *inyama*, and spied on the Cubans with binoculars to see when they were slaughtering cattle. When *inyama* was on the menu he would be in the dining-room ahead of us.

On one occasion when we had gone without *inyama* for some time, our hunters had bagged *mfene* (baboon). I took special interest in supervising the cooking, using chilli, lemon juice, seasoning and oil as a marinade. Banda was down with malaria and off his food. The aroma of the *inyama* brought him, red-eyed with fever, from his sick bed to the nearby dining-room.

'What's that?' he enquired, eyeing the pieces of roasted meat on elongated bones.

Knowing that Banda regarded the monkey family as being close to human beings, I mischievously answered: 'Goat. Do join us.' He picked up a long, narrow limb and tentatively gnawed at the meat. His face was a perfect study of enjoyment turning to disgust. 'Ugh! that's not *inyama*, that's from the trees.'

The cooking required special supervision. This was because of the mass poison episode that had occurred in September 1977, known as 'Black September'. Everybody had a story to tell of how violently ill they had been that day. 'Fortunately the Cubans had their own cooking facilities,' Julius explained, 'so they were unaffected. Every one of them was mobilised to give us injections, which enabled even the worst affected among us to recover.'

The recruits who had trained the previous year had graduated at a special parade, with Oliver Tambo present, and had been named the 'June 16th Detachment'. Some had gone abroad for specialist training, many had been deployed in the forward areas and the home front, while some remained in the camp as commanding officers, political instructors and cooks, or in defence posts manning anti-aircraft and other positions. The 500 new recruits were undergoing a six-month basic training course.

The person in charge of running the political classes was virtually a legendary figure in our Movement. Jack Simons had been a leader of the Communist Party before it was outlawed in 1950. He had been a foremost theoretician and was a retired university professor. He was already in his seventies, had a rigorous intellect and a sharp wit, and was generally loved and respected in the Movement. He lived with his wife, the trade union and communist veteran, Ray Alexander, in Lusaka. His readiness to face the rigours of bush life in Angola was an inspiration to everybody. Jack was a vegetarian and everything possible was done to provide him with a reasonable diet. He could not abide anyone fussing, so any extra labour had to be discreetly managed.

Jack had produced a brilliant series of Marxist lectures on South Africa's stages of development, from the pre-colonial period through colonial conquest to capitalism. He was exacting in his lectures, so that the students were kept on their toes but were also treated to his irreverent brand of humour.

'So, comrades,' he would ask, 'what are the basic conditions for life that human beings must first satisfy before they can develop their culture, their politics and other pursuits?' Up would shoot a forest of hands. 'Marx and Engels would specify the need for food, shelter and clothing,' was the pat answer.

'Comrades, if Marx and Engels omitted the sex drive – people's need to reproduce themselves – they would be forgetting the most essential need,' Jack would respond, to howls of delight.

On one occasion we discussed the issue of Soviet 'dissidents'. His comments surprised me.

'Unconventional thought is a force for development. It is wrong to suppress it. The likes of you and me were thrown to the lions in Roman times and burnt at the stake in the Middle Ages as heretics. We would be labelled dissidents if we lived in Eastern Europe,' he said to me quietly.

Such a view was seemingly at odds with the basic demands of the Movement. Our life and death struggle demanded unity and vigilance. Again there was the tension between security and personal choice, which mirrored the contradiction in countries attempting to build socialism. Intellectuals like Jack Simons and Ruth First, and to a lesser degree myself, might see the dangers of suppressing independent thinking, but virtually everyone else took what is generally referred to as a 'hard line'. And this did not stem from the Party, where the role of the intellectuals was considerable. It arose from the intolerable oppression that was the life experience of the black comrades, leaders and rank and file alike. For them the unconventional attitudes espoused by Jack were a luxury of bourgeois society. It was for this reason that many black comrades, particularly workers, continued to sympathise with Stalin's tough practices.

When Jack was thinking through a political argument he was single-minded about it. Wolfie Kodesh, working for ANC logistics in Luanda and Lusaka, told me how he had visited the camp and late in the afternoon accompanied Jack on his regular walk. Wolfie had made the mistake of interrupting Jack's train of thought by remarking that the sunset was spectacular. 'Oh damn your bloody sunset!' Jack exploded, 'what I'm trying to explain to you is far more important!' Perhaps the most impressive aspect of Jack's work at Novo Catengue was the dynamic group of instructors he had produced. Mzwai had induced him to return to Zambia after nearly a year in the camp, where he had suffered from several bouts of malaria, and I was taking over from him. I was most fortunate to be working with his products. Among them were Jabu Nxumalo (Mzala),

Chris Pepani (S'bali) and Edwin Mabitsela, all destined to play an important role in the ANC in later years. Another product was a young man with an engaging smile whose *nom de guerre* was Che O'Gara (January Masilela).

My attention was drawn to Che the morning after my arrival, when I heard him addressing a company of trainees. He was the company commissar and was stressing the need for military discipline. I realised that he was quoting from a book I knew well. It was a piece from *Volokolamsk Highway*, a Soviet novel about the Second World War, by Alexander Bek. Che delivered his address in confident, ringing tones and concluded by saying: 'Comrades, that is why we have no hesitation in claiming that "Discipline is the mother of victory".'

Every evening after classes, I conducted seminars, as Jack had done, with a specially selected group of instructors and commissars, Thami Zulu, Che, Mzala and S'bali among them. They were a lively group, and the high standard of training at Novo Catengue inspired me to dub it 'the University of the South', much to their delight.

One of the promising young comrades, Ntima Segole, a bright youngster with a quiet but firm disposition, suddenly became ill. One evening he was participating in our seminar, the next evening I was told he had fallen ill and had been taken by ambulance to the hospital in Benguela. News of his death from a collapsed kidney reached us a few days later. He was buried in Benguela and we had a memorial parade at Novo Catengue. The ANC flag was hoisted and a gun salute fired in his memory.

The month of July was a lively one. Celebrations took place on 18 July, Nelson Mandela's 60th birthday, and on the 26th, a major date in the Cuban revolutionary calendar. It was the 25th anniversary of Fidel Castro's attack on the Moncada Barracks during the days of the Batista dictatorship and marked the launching of the armed struggle and establishment of the 26th July Movement.

On Mandela's birthday we were up by 5 a.m., ready to climb a nearby hill and plant the ANC flag on its peak. Later in the day we played soft ball against the Cubans and a 10-kilometre race was held, called the 'Mandela Marathon'. Mzwai, who was visiting us, and I spoke about the significance of the day at a meeting, followed by a concert that evening.

On the eve of 26 July, I typed a letter to Eleanor about the impending celebration, with my small room full of my fellow instructors dancing to taped music I had received from her.

'Dearest El,' I wrote, *'We're on the eve of a big event here ...*
There's been much preparation and the occasion gets going in exactly two
hours' time, at midnight, with a huge bonfire. Tomorrow there'll be athletics,
football, baseball, a meeting and a concert in the evening. Not to mention

a banquet of pork, fried chips made from banana (Cuban style) and other specialities such as Havana Club rum, beer and soft drinks. The Cuban comrades are full of vitality. With them it's not simply 'socialism with a human face' but 'socialism with cha-cha-cha'.

Mind you, talking of oomph, our comrades are hard to beat. They've repaired my tape recorder and seem to be able to repair almost anything. So much for job reservation. Last Sunday evening there were about twenty of us in the instructors' club room listening to the tapes you sent. Bob Marley, Sonny and Brownie, Jimmy Cliff, Bob Dylan and Pete Seeger have all gone down extremely well. They're keen to know about the Reggae scene and the politics of folk singing. At this moment, while I'm hitting the typewriter keys, Jimmy Cliff's 'The harder they come' is blaring and the comrades are singing:

I'd rather be a free man in my grave
than live as a puppet or a slave
for as sure as the sun will shine
I'm going to get it, what's mine
and then the harder they come
the harder they fall, one and all.

Anyone who thinks our politics is all heavy, hard-line Stalinism should take in this scene ... If I'm sounding a bit manic, it's because the festivities will soon be starting and excitement is mounting ... yet I must complete this letter to have it taken to Luanda tomorrow to be posted ...

When we received news of MK actions in South Africa there would be a surge of excitement in the camp. Operations against installations, such as electricity transformers and railway lines, had been steadily increasing since the 1976 uprising. Although only amounting to twenty or thirty a year they were of enormous psychological importance, demonstrating to our people that we had the capacity to hit back against the oppressive regime and that such operations would steadily increase.

Those undergoing training understood that these actions were being carried out by small units which had infiltrated back into the country. Solomon Mahlangu, one of the first cadres to complete training, had been captured in central Johannesburg and sentenced to death as a result of a white civilian having been killed in a shoot-out. His brave demeanour during his trial had made him into a hero. Early in August we received news of an engagement near Rustenburg, in the western Transvaal, between an MK unit and the security forces. An ANC communiqué announced that 'ten racist soldiers' had been killed and many injured. One of the most outstanding of MK combatants, Barney Molokoane, a young Sowetan, was the commander of this unit. He went on to carry out many daring raids, including the June 1980 sabotage of the Sasol oil plant, before falling in battle in 1985. Morale would rise in the camps in response to news of MK successes. You could measure this by the volume of the singing. One of the most popular songs, composed by MK cadres, was *Mayebizwa Amagama Amaqhawe*, which went:

> *When the names of the heroes are called*
> *My name too will be there.*
> *How will it be, when we are sitting with Tambo*
> *Telling him about the fallen Boers?*

By November the course was completed and preparations were underway for Tambo's arrival to officiate at the graduation. The ANC President and Commander-in-Chief of Umkhonto we Sizwe duly arrived in a convoy which included top Cuban and Angolan guests. Tambo, in a smart camouflage uniform, looked fit and proud, as he addressed the graduates and took the salute at the passing-out parade. There was a buzz of excitement as he announced the name of this, the third detachment in MK's history: 'In honour of the support we and Africa have received from the Cuban internationalists, their people and revolution, you shall be known as "The Moncada Detachment".' After the graduation ceremony, Mzwai Piliso sent me to Lusaka for a couple of weeks to work with Jack Simons. We were putting together a manual for political instructors. For the first time since 1963, I was in southern Africa.

I wrote to Eleanor:

> *Physically, it is like being in South Africa again. I feel at home and elated. The climate is mild, unlike the enervating humidity of Dar es Salaam and Luanda ... jacarandas are in bloom. Then there are the images: Asian shops with Coca Cola and Vaseline adverts in so-called 'second class' business districts; the crowded townships abuzz with life and hawkers selling everything from boot polish to bananas and single cigarettes; the suburban houses with large gardens and 'Beware of the Dog' signs; walls with jagged glass along the tops to deter the 'kabalalas' (burglars); South African railway wagons with the SAR-SAS logo in English and Afrikaans; schoolkids in neat European-style uniforms ... In other respects, this place reminds me of a Transvaal dorp (country town), with its small central business area and main road crossing the railway line. Politically things are quite different of course. Zambia is not unaffected by the existence of revolutionary governments in Mozambique*

and Angola and is smack in the front line struggle against Rhodesia and Pretoria, giving us and ZAPU full support. Geo-politically this country is placed at the strategic crossroads of the battle to liberate southern Africa, and Kaunda is foursquare behind us ...

I'm working with Jack Simons, and learning a great deal from him. He is in his seventies and has amazing reserves of energy. He works himself up into a passion – like Magnus Pike on BBC TV – and you can't help laughing at his irreverent remarks about some of our leaders or positions. After months in the bush, it's pleasant relaxing in a house with a large garden laden with fruit trees. Jack is a vegetarian and prepares appetising vegetable dishes and fruit salads. ANC logistics delivered supplies for me – eggs, bread, vegetables and some cash to buy meat. Jack was in a fury, not about the meat allowance but because he feels the delivery was unnecessary since he and Ray can cater for me. I told the comrades who delivered the eggs that I was going to boil them all and take them back to Angola. I haven't seen eggs in ages!

Early one morning we heard the sound of distant explosions. I rushed to the ANC office, which was in downtown Lusaka, and heard that Rhodesian planes had dropped many bombs on a ZAPU camp outside the city. Within the hour, ambulances, trucks and cars – including ANC vehicles – were ferrying the dying and wounded to hospital. Smith's forces had struck as the cadres were mustering on parade before breakfast. Over 600 people were mercilessly struck down by bombs, rockets and machinegun fire.

On my return to Angola I wrote to Eleanor:

The situation in Zambia became depressing and tense. We were nearly shot by drunk soldiers who were supposed to be guarding the road to the airport. The worst episode of the Rhodesian attacks was on a ZAPU women's camp in the north. The swine sneaked up on the camp and captured a female instructor. At gunpoint they demanded to know how she summoned the trainees, since with a general security alert everyone had dispersed in the bush. She told them she blew the whistle tied around her neck. They blew the whistle and about 90 women emerged from the bush. The instructor was handed a weapon and ordered to open fire on her comrades. She refused and promptly had her brains blown out. The killers then turned their weapons on the women and mowed them down. They scoured the area and despatched another 60. How does one characterise this barbarism? Words are inadequate.

I again waited in Benguela a few days for camp transport. I bathed for hours in the sea, resting my traumatised nerves after the unspeakable killings in Zambia.

We were going to need to continue improving our camp security, for Novo Catengue was not beyond the reach of South Africa.

I decided I needed a haircut. It was hot and I had grown a full beard and suddenly felt my hair was much too long. Sitting in a small barber shop I became entranced by the way the natty Portuguese owner sheared a burly, sunbronzed prospector-type and shaved him with a cut-throat razor. On impulse I decided to follow suit.

I wrote to my sons:

I've had the shortest haircut in my life and the smoothest shave, in an old-fashioned barber shop with a red, white and blue pole outside – none of your unisex business out here. I feel like a lad of twenty. At first no one recognised me. My Cuban friends were particularly approving. Fidel's beard is admired as a symbol of their revolution. But most Cubans prefer to be cleanshaven, apart from a moustache. The barber smoothed my hair with oil and combed it straight back. Tell Eleanor that I look like a smoothie out of a 40s movie!

Nikita had a new friend called Da Silva. He ran a business and Nikita bought supplies from him. We had a chat with him over a drink of cane spirits and I found that I did not like him. His praise for the ANC had a hollow ring and he appeared to me to be the type who was simply after a fast buck. Perhaps it was the experience of the Zambian bombings that was making me paranoid, but I felt the need to express my concern. 'I think we need to be careful of that guy,' I remarked to Nikita. 'Has he any idea where the camp is?'

'No, comrade Khumalo. No way! No idea!' Nikita answered, and I felt that he was over-responding. It left me with a nagging feeling which I tried to shrug off as paranoia, but the unease stuck in my mind.

The next responsibility Mzwai Piliso had for me was the organisation of a commissariat for Angola. The number of our camps had increased and he wanted me to co-ordinate the political classes and the cultural activities. We allocated our best commissars such as James Ngculu, Chris Pepani and Che O'Gara to the various camps, and I was appointed Regional Commissar. It was a position that carried much responsibility. I travelled around the country by road and by air, supervising the programme, I convened monthly meetings of the camp commissars and we rotated our gatherings from camp to camp. While the commissariat was an important structure for promoting the ANC's policy, it also served to ensure that open debate and differences of opinion were tolerated. It was important, too, in ensuring that disciplinary abuses and authoritarian practices did not take place. The commissars enjoyed the respect of the cadres, who saw in them approachable figures, responsive and sympathetic to all manner of problems. There were some tensions between commissars and commanders, and commissars were sometimes scoffed at for believing too much in talk. My presence, as a leading figure, undoubtedly gave muscle to the commissariat. We particularly sought to counter a macho tendency in training, which often expressed itself in an overzealous physical programme.

Andrew Masondo, an ex-Robben Islander who had served twelve years for sabotage, was the National Commissar. Based in Lusaka, he was a regular visitor to our camps. He lacked original thought, made the recruits recite the Freedom Charter like a conservative teacher and I found him overbearing.

Among the commissars who formed the Regional Commissariat was Jabu Nxumalo (Mzala), an energetic young man, with a restless manner and intense eyes, who had a scar from a bullet wound on his left cheek. He became my secretary and was based in Luanda, where he also performed duties as commissar in charge of our residences.

Mzala was militant even by June 16 standards. He was a powerful orator who kept his audience riveted with his denunciations of the enemy and by witty turns of phrase. He had been expelled from the University of Zululand and was scathing about the Inkatha leader Prince Mangosuthu Buthelezi, whom he regarded as a danger to the liberation movement. Mzala was ready to argue politics until late at night and often debated with Joe Slovo and Andrew Masondo over what he felt was the ANC's soft line regarding the Zulu chief. Mzala was one of the young cadres who later joined me in the forward areas. His polemical qualities and searching mind led him to write a book about Buthelezi entitled *Chief with a Double Agenda*. He was the son of schoolteachers from Vryheid, Natal. He died in London of Aids in 1990 at the tragically young age of 33 but was never sexually promiscuous.

There were several outstanding camp commanders too. The commander of the Funda camp, just outside Luanda, was a young man of sparkle and wit. His *nom de guerre* was Obadi, and he epitomised for me the style and dash of the Soweto generation. We often shared a room together and I travelled with him by jeep or Land Rover, which he drove with speed and skill. He spoke fluent Portuguese and had many Angolan friends who called him *Prima* (cousin). His deputy was a lanky individual called Rashid (Abubaker Ismail), who later organised audacious special operations from the forward areas.

'Let's see if Rashid is on his toes,' Obadi said to me mischievously one day in Luanda. He had arranged for an Angolan-piloted Mig 19 fighter to swoop low over the Funda camp in mock attack.

We jumped into his jeep and, nearing Funda, observed the Mig 19 executing several low dives. On arrival we found Rashid covered in swamp mud from top to toe. Most of the other comrades, however, were perfectly dry.

'What happened?' Obadi asked, with a broad grin.

Rashid gave an account of the Mig's appearance and told how he had yelled to the comrades to get into the trenches. Funda was near swamp land, however, and the trenches were oozing with mud and slime. Comrades were tentative about getting into them and chose to head into the bush. Rashid, something of a perfectionist, decided to lead by example and plunged into a trench which swiftly filled with water.

Early in March 1979, the South African airforce struck at Novo Catengue. Three Mirage jets and two Canberra bombers hit the camp at 7.15 a.m. when comrades should have been assembling on parade after breakfast. Tons of bombs flattened the camp, which was strafed by rocket and machinegun fire. The raid lasted five minutes.

Two MK members and one Cuban comrade died. There was a handful of injured. The attackers were driven off by fierce ground fire from ZKU anti-aircraft guns. A Mirage was seen to be hit, smoke erupting from a wing. It immediately disengaged and flew out to sea. The raiders had come in low and this had made hitting them difficult. Our Strella heat-seeking, ground-to-air missiles failed to operate on targets coming in so low, otherwise we would have succeeded in bringing several aircraft down. The enemy were lucky. They had in fact flown into a well-prepared ambush.

We had received information some weeks before that Pretoria was preparing an air attack on a target in Angola. Our camps had been placed on alert. At Novo Catengue we had dispersed into the bush and spent the day in huge underground shelters or in several deep culverts under the Benguela railway line. Jack Simons had been with us again and Mzwai had pressurised him to leave just days before the attack. Both his room and mine, in a row of rooms behind the main administration block, were reduced to rubble, along with our seminar room and library.

Most of the buildings received direct hits, including our armoury (the contents of which we had prudently carted off into the bush). This, together with the timing of the attack, pointed to first-hand information on the part of the enemy. If we had not possessed prior warning of the impending attack, we would have been massacred.

A small group had been on duty in the camp. One of the comrades killed was the chief of the kitchen staff called Guerrilla. With him was Nomkozi (Mary) Mini, daughter of Vuyisile Mini, who slipped into a dug-out and emerged unscathed. Another casualty was a popular instructor called Chairman who had been on duty at the command post. He panicked, and instead of sheltering in a nearby dug-out, ran across open ground towards a shelter outside the camp. Comrades in the culvert under the railway line saw him running towards them, with machinegun fire from a Mirage cutting him down as it swooped over the camp. The house used by the Cubans as their command post was demolished by one of the first bombs, with a young lieutenant inside who had gone to fetch some papers.

We had taken great pride in establishing and developing our 'University of the South' where over 1000 MK cadres graduated. It had been flattened within five minutes but we considered ourselves fortunate that the casualties were so light. During that month Pretoria and Rhodesia stepped up their attacks into southern Angola and killed many ZAPU and SWAPO combatants in their training bases, as well as Angolan civilians.

Benguela was abuzz with news of the attack on our camp. When I saw Nikita he gave a vivid description of the Mirage we thought we had hit and claimed that 'it fell into the sea near here'. I again had the feeling that he was exaggerating. It did not surprise me, therefore, when Mzwai informed me some time later that information had been received that Nikita was a spy for Pretoria.

After being confronted with the facts, he admitted his guilt. He had been involved in a smuggling racket between Mozambique and South Africa and been pressurised into working for the enemy or going to prison. His arrest and confession led to a whole network of Unita and Pretoria spies being uncovered in Benguela – Da Silva among them.

We evacuated the comrades and vast stores of equipment from Novo Catengue to the Quibaxe area. A new camp, with Thami Zulu as commander, was established on a coffee estate called Pango. It was on a higher plateau than the Quibaxe camp and consequently was cooler and under heavy mist at times. For a while, it became our main training camp. Thami often used to host meetings of the commissariat at his camp. We would end our meetings, which would last a couple of days, with a shooting contest between the commissars and his administration. The commissars were always determined to show that they could shoot as well as talk, so the event was highly competitive.

There were ominous signs that Unita was beginning to spread its operations to the north of the country. There were two ambushes that particularly upset me.

My friend Arnoldo, the Cuban agricultural expert, was killed with three companions, close to Pango in broad daylight as he drove to one of the coffee estates. Thami's forces combed the bush for several days but failed to pick up the trail.

Then, just three kilometres from Quibaxe camp, we lost one of our best instructors, an *mgwenya* from the Odessa days, whose real name was Gilbert Tseu. His MK name was 'Pasha' and he cut a proud, military figure in smart uniform and black beret – which was something of a trademark. He excelled in marching drill and the cadres loved to be put through their paces by him.

He was riding in the passenger seat of a Soviet Gaz truck with a section of heavily armed comrades on the back. As the vehicle came over the brow of a hill it drove into a hail of bullets. A rocket was fired and struck the bonnet but fortunately failed to explode. The driver was hit in one arm but managed to engage reverse gear and pull back behind the hill. The enemy attempted to advance, aiming to wipe out the comrades and seize the truck's supplies, but were driven off by fierce resistance – two falling in their tracks.

We found Pasha dead on the spot, slumped in the cab, pistol in hand.

A senior ANC delegation consisting of Tambo, Moses Mabhida, Slovo, Modise and Piliso visited Vietnam to learn from the experiences of a guerrilla struggle which had defeated both the French and Americans. The emphasis was on a combination of political and military struggle. The organisation and mobilisation of the masses was the prerequisite for the development not simply of military operations but of a fully-fledged people's war. In our situation this required both the strengthening of an underground network and the formation of broad-based mass organisations. At the time I was in London visiting Eleanor. Years later, the same advocate who claimed I had tortured people at Quibaxe, claimed I was on this trip. In fact he went so far as to allege that the delegation was visiting Pol Pot to study his barbaric techniques of repression. And this at a time when he was at war with our close ally, Vietnam. Pol Pot was regarded as a criminal by us. It was a laughable allegation.

Comrades like Obadi and Rashid had already been transferred to the forward areas to concentrate on military operations. Tambo was instrumental in the decision to transfer me to Maputo in Mozambique at the end of 1979. New structures were being set up and he wanted me to concentrate on strengthening the underground.

The year ended on a particularly high note with news of a sensational escape from Pretoria's top security prison. My friends Alex Moumbaris, Tim Jenkin and Steve Lee managed the unthinkable, by breaking out of their cells and through 14 locked doors to freedom. They had made duplicate keys out of wood in the prison workshop. When the trio reached Lusaka they issued a defiant statement that the struggle against apartheid continued even behind prison walls. They were speaking for the thousands of political prisoners all over the country from Robben Island to Pretoria. It was a reminder that the struggle was multi-pronged incorporating those behind prison walls and the exiles, those involved in trade union and political mobilisation in the country, with those in the underground at home and those in MK, whilst others organised international solidarity work.

THIRTEEN

FRONT LINE

Mozambique and Swaziland
1980–83

I ARRIVED IN MAPUTO, THE CAPITAL of Mozambique, in March 1980. Maputo, Lourenço Marques in Portuguese times, had been a tourist paradise for white South Africans with its tropical climate, lovely beaches, elegant hotels and night life. It was a place where a class of white South Africans, frustrated with the narrow Calvinistic morals of their country, yet unconcerned by the harshness of Portuguese colonial rule, could let their hair down. The revolution had put an end to that.

I stayed the first night at Sue Rabkin's. She had been single-minded in her efforts to move from London and live closer to her adopted country. She lived with her children in a spacious flat with a fabulous view of both the Indian ocean and the harbour. Both children, Jobie aged six and Franny barely four, had been travelling to Pretoria with their grandparents to visit David, their father, in prison.

After a lively update from Sue about the children's visits to David, and how underground work was conducted from Maputo, I went to sleep at an unearthly hour. Early the next morning I was awakened by melodious singing and the sound of boots striking the tarmac. Standing on Sue's balcony, overlooking Avenida Julius Nyerere, I observed ranks of Mozambican soldiers, stripped to the waist, jogging along the road in disciplined order.

They were singing, in rich and exultant tones, about the electoral victory of the liberation forces that had just been announced in Zimbabwe. Mozambique had rendered invaluable assistance to the Zimbabwean freedom fighters and particularly to Robert Mugabe's ZANU (Zimbabwe African National Union), absorbing heavy retaliatory raids.

The ANC had a closer historical alliance with Joshua Nkomo's ZAPU which operated out of Zambia. This was mainly because of the late formation

139

of ZANU, regarded for some time as a splinter group. Influenced by our close ties with ZAPU, most of us in the ANC expected Nkomo to take the majority of seats. I had stopped over in Lusaka on my way to Maputo and received a briefing there at ZAPU headquarters on their high expectations. I wrote to Eleanor from Lusaka predicting a big majority for ZAPU, with ZANU in second place.

A letter from Eleanor arrived care of Sue, commenting on the election results:

> *In politics, my dear, it is best not to be absolutely certain about anything – or so you've always advised. It seems that the* Guardian *in London had a far clearer expectation of the outcome than you in Lusaka. In future, take heed of your own advice.*

Enclosed was an editorial from the *Guardian* which stated that ZAPU was expected to get all 20 of the seats in its Matabeleland stronghold, and Robert Mugabe's ZANU (PF) by far the majority of the 60 seats in the Shona-speaking parts of the country, where it had waged the 'bush war'. The question, according to the *Guardian*, was how many seats Bishop Abel Muzorewa, who had aligned himself with Ian Smith, and Ndabaningi Sithole's breakaway ZANU, would manage to scrape together. In the event they obtained a paltry three between them.

The victory for African majority rule in Zimbabwe was a major boost for the struggles in South Africa and Namibia. As much as the forces for change were being strengthened in our favour, however, the apartheid state was far too powerful for Mozambique to be able to provide the open assistance to the ANC that had been the case with ZANU. Consequently, although the ANC had a public office in Maputo and received support and encouragement from FRELIMO, we had no training camps in the country and could not operate directly across the borders into South Africa.

The understanding was that we would operate in an undercover manner. For this purpose we utilised a score of safe houses for our operatives rather than base camps. This provided greater personal freedom for our cadres than they were used to in Angola. It made Maputo and the other Frontline areas favourite choices for deployment.

The easier-going lifestyle was facilitated too by the presence in these areas of ANC personnel employed in government institutions, long-term South African refugees, and sympathisers from abroad working on government contracts. Within days of my arrival, I was attending a party where MK cadres were interacting with Chilean, British, Portuguese and Italian aid workers and members of the local community.

It was a good opportunity to relax with comrades recently arrived from Angola, like Obadi and Rashid. Leslie, the lanky, shaven-headed defier from Quibaxe, was enjoying himself too and was soon leading everybody in a *toyi-toyi* – a new-style war-dance learnt in the ZAPU camps, which was soon to become a craze among activists in South Africa.

Leslie, body erect, running on the spot, knees raised as high as possible, bellowed out in rhythmical slang, to a circle of followers:

Slaan *(strike) the Boers*
Tambo says 'Victory or death'
Slovo says 'No middle road'
Mugabe says at Lancaster House
'No strings attached'
Hup hup hup
guerrillas coming
AKs talking
Sasol's burning
Free Mandela
Slaan *the Boers*
Free the Nation
Hup hup hup ...

More sedate was a dinner invitation to the home of Marcelino do Santos. My old friend Pam had organised a 50th birthday party for her husband, now the Vice-President of Mozambique. I sat opposite Joaquim Chissano, the Foreign Minister, and reminded him of the time we bumped into each other at Cairo airport. He enquired about Eleanor, whom he fondly recalled. I found my FRELIMO friends unaffected by the positions they occupied. Pam, in particular, remained natural and down to earth. The socialising was a far cry from the Angolan camps. I was to experience the tensions of undercover work in the Frontline States, and I came to appreciate the need for our cadres to relax. This was a necessity but it could lead to lapses of discipline.

The route home from Mozambique was through the tiny, land-locked kingdom of Swaziland. It took over an hour to travel the 80 kilometres over a poorly maintained road, through a couple of check-points, to the highland town of Namaacha on the Swazi border. Cadres moving between the two countries would jump the well-patrolled border fence by a number of routes. We conducted our planning in Maputo, while our operations were launched from Swaziland. The kingdom served as the main point for infiltration into South Africa and as the forward base for our operational units.

Partly as a result of the trip to Vietnam, but also because we were encountering problems in linking our armed operations with the mass struggle of our people, the ANC had embarked on the restructuring which had brought me to Maputo. A unified political-military command had been created in each forward area under the Revolutionary Council (RC) in Lusaka. Tambo arrived in Maputo to inaugurate our regional command, which was termed the 'Senior Organ' (SO). He encouraged us to be as creative as we wished, and to feel free to change established structures in any way we deemed fit.

The Senior Organ consisted of a group of interesting people, including Joe Slovo, who was now living with his wife Ruth First in Maputo. The chairperson was John Nkadimeng and the secretary Jacob Zuma. They were both ex-political prisoners who had helped reconstruct the underground in Soweto and Durban respectively, soon after their release in the mid-1970s.

Nkadimeng was a middle-aged worker and trade unionist, first active in the 1950s. He was respected for his honesty and firm commitment to the struggle. He had been recruited into politics by my old friend of Dar es Salaam days, Flag Boshielo. He liked to recall how the latter had impressed him by walking miles every Saturday to sell the Party newspaper. Nkadimeng's family lived in Swaziland and Seyiso was his bodyguard. It was a great joy meeting up with Seyiso, but I received the distressing news that Sinatla had died in a car accident.

'Are you sure it was an accident?' I asked, recalling Sinatla's concern about enemy agents. 'Could someone have tampered with the controls?'

'The car overturned on a hillside,' I was told. 'It was completely wrecked, so it was impossible to tell.' Death was constantly at our heels.

Jacob Zuma had grown up in the Natal countryside. I had known him in Durban in the early 1960s when he was a young factory worker with no formal education. He was an early recruit into MK and had been arrested with a group attempting to leave the country for training in 1962. Robben Island became his school. He learned to read and write, master English, develop tremendous political acumen and, by the time he left twelve years later, he had attained a Standard Six pass. Alas his formal education ended there, for unlike others he did not persevere.

I worked closely with Zuma and Nkadimeng in developing the underground political structures. The best young cadres from the camps had been deployed in military operations which, by nature, were episodic. Experience pointed to the need to build a strong underground as a foundation from which armed actions could be sustained.

One of the reasons for ZANU's spectacular success was the emphasis on commissars moving into the countryside and preparing the ground through political work. ZANU's military commander, Tongogara, fully imbibed Mao Tse-tung's analogy of 'the fish in water' for the guerrilla and the people, and after training in China returned to Africa preaching the need for political commissars to 'mass mobilise' amongst the people, particularly in the countryside.

Our combatants had been doing much the same as the Zimbabwean freedom fighters before they followed Tongogara's dictum. Small units would infiltrate the country, carry out operations, and withdraw back to the neighbouring states. We were inflicting blows, such as the dramatic sabotage of the Sasol oil refinery in June 1980, but were not satisfied with the progress. We had many sharp debates about how best to solve the problem which centred on the advisability of maintaining separate political and military implementing machineries. While Zuma and I favoured unifying all structures, it was not easy to win the debate. We decided to concentrate first on strengthening the underground base.

It was obvious that, if we could succeed in creating a strong and enduring underground network throughout the country, it would have the capacity of providing the necessary safe reception and assistance to the trained cadres. It would also be able to link them with the people. This had been the idea already in the 1960s. What stood in our way was the ruthless efficiency of the security forces and the problem of infiltration into our ranks. Another factor was that the majority of our recruits were young students from the townships. We could never have achieved what we did without the heroic Soweto generation, but their bravery and audacity could not make up for crucial limitations. The reason why Tongogara was so successful in developing bush war was because of ZANU's peasant base. The factor missing in South Africa was a massive peasantry. While MK's operations never rose to full-scale guerrilla warfare, these, nonetheless, succeeded in inspiring resistance in a way not seen in many other countries and played a huge psychological role. It was these operations that made the ANC such a popular force, particularly in the cities, and drew people to our side. What I only came to realise later, and saw for myself after I returned to South Africa, was that, until 1990 at any rate, we had not sufficiently reached out to politicise the rural people.

The political structures had been operating as second cousins to the military. The first requirement was to strengthen them with effective cadres who had both political and military skills. We began by bringing some promising cadres I had spotted in Angola to work with us such as Jabu Nxumalo (Mzala), James Ngculu, Phumla Williams (Flo), Charlotte Mabaso and Vuso Tshabalala (Paul). They joined Sue Rabkin, Indres Naidoo and Sonny Singh, the latter had been imprisoned for his courageous activity as an MK combatant with Eleanor and myself in Durban.

With mass activity at home on the rise, I wrote several letters to Eleanor about my new work:

The first weeks here were overpowering. I kept my mouth shut and antennae extended in order to absorb all dimensions of a complicated situation. It took a while to get things into focus because so much is going on, and one is assaulted by views from comrades who all claim to have the answers ... I've been so busy I scarcely have time to relax. Sometimes we work 18 hours flat – and all this can be where we sleep and eat. And meetings nonstop – what was it Mayakovsky said? – 'Long live the convention to end all conventions!' We've been involved in some heated debates and have to be clear on our approach ...

I did not mention the sharp debates with Joe Slovo and the testiness of Mac Maharaj with his inflated ego.

A memorial meeting was held in Maputo in honour of Lilian Ngoyi, the veteran women's leader who had just been buried at a mass funeral in Soweto. We were addressed by Ruth First, who cut a striking figure with her dark hair and flashing eyes. She was an impressive speaker, strong on fact and analysis. She referred to Lilian as a role model for all women.

Ruth ran the Centre for African Studies at Eduardo Mondlane University and interacted with the top FRELIMO leadership. Not one who suffered fools easily, she was critical of the conventional wisdom of our Movement, such as the uncritical view of the Soviet Union; the expectation that ZAPU would win the Zimbabwean elections; our support for the Ethiopian government against Eritrea's secessionist struggle.

When I first arrived in London I got on extremely well with her. She often brought me gifts from her travels in Africa, including an ostrich egg from the Sudan, which became a prized possession. Now that I was in the leadership I was forced to defend some positions to which Ruth did not take kindly. I cannot claim to have been exempt from the scathing side of her tongue, which the cautious strove to avoid. On the other hand, I felt she assumed an unrelenting attitude on my part. Yet my strongly felt convictions did not necessarily imply a closed mind, as Pallo Jordan had noted.

Another ANC member working with the Government was Albie Sachs, who was with the Justice Ministry. Sensitive and intelligent, Albie was at home in Mozambique. He spoke Portuguese and had become well acquainted with the local culture. I stayed in his apartment for a while which, with its collection of Mozambican paintings and sculpture, looked like an art gallery. In a couple of weekends before I became immersed in my new responsibilities, I joined him in laying water pipes at a village outside Maputo. He lived an active life and took me to numerous events.

On May Day 1980, John Nkadimeng and another trade unionist, William Khanyile, led a contingent of South Africans, red flags flying, on a massive march through the streets of Maputo. Both Ruth and Albie were present, and Albie suggested our group wear hard hats and carry picks and shovels. We were well received by the onlookers and got special applause from Samora Machel from his rostrum.

Through Albie I made the acquaintance of many expatriates sympathetic to the ANC. Sue and I began recruiting couriers from amongst them for trips to Swaziland and home. We called them 'surfers', a coding metaphor we introduced, indicating the journey from the 'Harbour' (Maputo), through the 'Bay' (Swaziland) and into the 'Ocean' (home).

The comrades we brought over from Angola were based in a large house in Maputo from where we operated. It consisted of offices as well as sleeping quarters and we called it the 'Galley'. It was there that we prepared them for work in the 'Bay' and 'Ocean'. One of the first things I did was have a trap-door cut into the floor so that we could escape into the foundations below. Some years later, after I left Maputo, comrades saved themselves by escaping through the trap-door during a Pretoria commando raid.

I soon made my first of many illegal border crossings into Swaziland. The border was well patrolled by the security forces of both countries. Crossing what we called the 'green border' entailed climbing two sets of fences, which were four metres in height. A no man's land – 40 metres wide – lay between the fences. We generally crossed near the border post between the two countries at the villages of Namaacha on the Mozambique side and Lomahasha on the Swazi side.

Both Pretoria and the Swazis were well aware that the area was a favourite crossing-point, and consequently there was heavy patrolling by the Swazi Army. The immigration officials, too, were vigilant and always on the look-out for suspicious individuals travelling by vehicle. Whenever operations took place at home the border was reinforced. An ANC house on the Namaacha side of the border was demolished by a bomb explosion and several of our residences inside Swaziland were similarly attacked. There could be no doubt that Pretoria's forces were involved.

Namaacha was also a point where both Mozambique and Swaziland had a common border with South Africa. A South African military communications post was situated on a nearby hill, over-looking the strategic frontier. The border ran along the hills of the Lebombo mountain range, wooded terrain dotted with villages and numerous wild animals.

The first time I crossed, I was in the company of Rashid and Paul Dikaledi (Sello Motau), the youngest member of the Senior Organ in Maputo. We were heavily armed and had driven to Namaacha from Maputo. We were met by two MK guides. They were full of wisecracks as we waited for the sun to set. 'It's best to cross after dark,' we were told, 'because there's a change of shift at sunset and the first patrol will only get here in two hours' time.' Then our guides laughed and added: 'That's if the patrol behaves as expected – otherwise get ready to shoot and run!'

We had moved into the bush away from Namaacha, taking care to avoid the FRELIMO patrols, and began crossing the wire with military precision. This involved crawling up to the first fence and climbing over whilst others covered you. Poised high up on the fence, preparing to jump down, it was a tense moment as you expected searchlights to illuminate the scene at any moment. Stooping low and running through no man's land for the second fence was an eerie experience. At any moment gunfire could break out. Finally we were on the Swazi side of the border, moving swiftly into the bush. We paused to catch our breath and look about into the darkness. As I strove to control the adrenalin rush, I felt a surge of excitement at having successfully 'violated the frontier' as the Russians termed it.

Swaziland has only two small towns to speak of – Mbabane, the capital, and Manzini. The latter was two hours' drive from the border, and comrades would often be picked up at a rendezvous point close to Lomahasha. The Swazis had recently taken to setting up road-blocks in the vicinity, so we were having to hike over the Lebombo hills to a pick-up point closer to Manzini.

It was difficult moving in the dark, as we picked our way along stony tracks up and down the hills close to the South African border. Midway through the night we stopped near a village to slake our thirst at a water pump.

'The other side of the fence is South Africa,' our guides told us. Although I was tired I could not resist climbing over the fence and performing a ritual *toyi-toyi* on South African soil: the first time I had 'touched down' since 1963.

After hiking most of the night, and covering some 30 kilometres in hilly terrain, we were picked up in sugar-cane country just before dawn. We avoided a road-block by using a track through the cane fields and then connected with a good road for an hour's drive to Manzini, at the centre of the Kingdom. I noticed a signboard welcoming the visitor to 'the hub of Swaziland' and we were deposited at a safe house.

Swaziland is the second smallest state on the African mainland. It is almost surrounded by South Africa, except for part of its eastern border with Mozambique. A scenic country, it was declared a British Protectorate in 1910 to prevent its incorporation into the Union of South Africa. Very much a part of the South African economy, it was regarded, along with the other former Protectorates of Lesotho and Botswana, as one of Pretoria's 'hostages'.

Many of our comrades were contemptuous of its claim to independent status, owing to its conservative political and social system, and referred to it as a South African 'bantustan'. The Swazi police were zealous about hunting down ANC operatives who, after a spell in jail, were deported to Mozambique. It was said, with good grounds for the allegation, that most Swazi security policemen were in the pay of South Africa and that the 'Boers' were allowed to operate at will against us.

Yet the head of state, the octogenarian King Sobhuza II, had a sentimental attachment to the ANC. He had been made, along with other monarchs of Southern Africa, an honorary member of the ANC when it was founded in 1912. King Sobhuza presided over 600,000 loyal subjects in a traditional society which, outside the towns and the small, modern economic sector, was based on the strict hierarchy of chiefs and subsistence farming around dispersed rural homesteads. There was a constant power struggle taking place around the King, between the traditionalists and modernists. Most members of both 'camps', it was alleged, were corrupt.

The ANC's Moses Mabhida often visited the King from Lusaka and Maputo to clarify our position and to influence Swazi foreign policy. Mabhida – with his Zulu background (siSwati and isiZulu are virtually the same languages), his imposing grey-haired bearing and his intimate knowledge of a similar history and culture – was always well received. Even when Mabhida became general secretary of the Communist Party the good relationship continued.

There were certainly some good elements in the Swazi police force. One of these had been responsible for saving an ANC cadre who had been kidnapped by Pretoria's agents early in 1980. Daya Pillay was a schoolteacher and ANC operative working at the St Joseph mission outside Manzini. I had trained him in London several years before. He had carried out numerous sabotage actions in Durban before fleeing to Swaziland. One night, armed men had burst into his quarters, overpowered him after a fierce struggle, bundled him into a car and driven off.

For a whole weekend the investigating Swazi police officer, together with one of Pillay's fellow teachers, drove along every street in Manzini and its environs, looking for the getaway vehicle – a red Volkswagen Beetle with a dent on the side. They spotted it, partially concealed in the driveway of a house, in the very centre of town. The occupants – two Mozambican refugees and a black South African – were arrested. They were found with false passports and unlicensed firearms. They admitted that they were responsible for Daya Pillay's abduction and confessed that they had handed him over to the South African police at the border fence. The Swazi Government, with ANC backing, forced the South Africans to release Daya Pillay in exchange for his abductors shortly before my arrival in the Kingdom.

I was working with Daya's brother, Ivan Pillay, and his dedicated wife Ray, and they soon took me to visit him at the St Joseph Mission. It was a five-minute drive from Manzini, well into the countryside and off the national road to Lomahasha. We passed a collection of school buildings and workshops for the disabled and parked by a cluster of houses.

It was dusk and I noticed a few people looking anxiously at us, but they relaxed when they recognised Ivan and Ray. Daya, almost a carbon-copy of his brother Ivan, was a slim figure with spectacles and a wispy beard, who spoke in a quiet, serious manner. He had been expecting us and we sat down to a spicy mutton curry he had prepared. His account of the kidnapping was fascinating and gave me an insight into the methods of our adversary.

'Fortunately I had put up one hell of a struggle,' Daya recounted in a calm voice, 'so, by the time I was bundled into the car, a number of my fellow teachers were on the scene. But they didn't dare interfere because the thugs pointed firearms at them. But at least I knew that the police and ANC would be informed and that gave me hope. I felt if they had wanted to kill me, they would have done so on the spot.'

He was driven to the border fence and carried over. Still blind-folded he was driven for several hours and finally taken into some kind of building, where he was chained to a bed. After a while the interrogation started.

'A rough voice called out: "Okay, Daya, we know all about your activities. If you co-operate and tell us what we want to know, you can come out of this alive."'

Daya smiled mischievously: 'So I answered: "If you know all about my activities then what more do you need to know?"' Daya motioned with his hands: 'Clap! Clap! For my cheek I got these heavy blows either side of my head.'

'"*Jou donnerse coolie* [You damned coolie]," another voice barked, "don't play around with us, or you'll end up in the river."

'The interrogation told me a lot,' Daya continued in his quiet, pensive way. 'They knew about operations in Durban over a year ago and nothing much after that. There was an African guy present, who put certain questions to me, and was knowledgeable about that time. I thought I recognised his voice as a former comrade who had been captured and we suspected had been "turned". At one stage I was left alone with him, I think deliberately, and he began trying to convince me that the ANC was useless and the Boers not that bad. "Daya," he said, "why don't you answer their questions, they'll treat you nicely then. You can live freely at home again and they'll give you a house, a car, and protection."

'I took a chance and used the traitor's name: "Tell your bosses to go to hell. I'd rather die than become an *impimpi* [informer] like you!"

'Well, I got a blow for my troubles,' Daya remarked, rubbing the back of his head, 'but the coward abruptly left me and was no longer involved in the interrogation.'

They questioned him the whole day, punching him when he got cheeky or when he remained silent. He found that once he was prepared to sustain some blows the physical violence did not bother him. He realised that they did not want to beat him into an unconscious state. He also sensed they were worried about the international repercussion of his kidnapping. Unaware that his kidnappers had been arrested, he did notice a change in his interrogators. The physical force stopped and he was given better food. He had felt the ANC was raising 'a hue and cry'.

Daya smiled ruefully. 'The most macabre part of the story comes next,' he said. 'Early the next day I found myself being held firmly down and injected in my arm. "There's no cause to worry," a voice said soothingly into my ear, "this is *sommer* (just) to relax you." I immediately realised they were drugging me, probably giving me some truth serum. I let my body go limp so that they would think they'd given me enough. I could in fact feel the effects of a drug but exaggerated my reaction. Two people held me up and began walking me around. I'd read a lot about disorientation as used by the British on the IRA and held on to my consciousness. It seemed to me that I was simply being marched around the hall I was confined in. At last I was placed in a large armchair and questions put to me.

'A string of questions: about our safe houses, our operatives at home, our communication system, our leaders in Maputo and so on. I slumped over muttering unintelligibly and I could sense them straining to catch the gibberish. They thought I had passed out and they dumped me back on the bed. I wanted to laugh. They had initially gone through the rigmarole of walking me around the place, and yet I must have been three paces from my bed.

'They tried the truth serum again the next day – the same procedure. Only this time they gave me less, because they must have thought they'd overdone it the day before. I played the same game again,' Daya sniggered quietly, 'only more convincingly.

'Over the next few days I noticed a marked improvement in my treatment and sensed I was winning. One night I was told I was lucky to be going back to Swaziland. I was blindfolded, driven straight across the border and dropped off outside Mbabane.'

Daya sat back in the house from which he had been abducted, looking as relaxed as if he had been talking about a Sunday outing in the country. If his kidnappers had not been captured, he would not have been with us and it was unlikely that he would have been alive to tell his tale. His experience needed to be closely studied and the lessons drawn for all our operatives. I thought how useful this story would be in our camps. Too many people cracked under interrogation because of shock and confusion. Daya's behaviour was an example of how to resist and outwit the interrogators. Of course if one was not sufficiently committed to the struggle in the first place, and lacked bravery, then no amount of cool calculation would help. His story showed, however, that it was possible to protect our secrets from the enemy. It reminded me of how Eleanor had once outwitted her captors.

While we had our share of traitors and informers, Daya Pillay was an example of the courage in our ranks. He continued to work with us while teaching at St Joseph's, until 1986 when the situation became so bad in Swaziland that only undercover operatives had any chance of surviving. He married a Canadian and settled in Canada.

Swaziland became my main area of operation in those years. I continued to be based in Maputo but crossed the 'green border' many times. On one such occasion I did so together with Zuma, who was as keen as I was to work in the field with our operatives.

It was a cold, wet night on the border. I was carrying a heavy bag with pistols and grenades for our operatives at a time when Pretoria's hit squads were beginning to eliminate our people in the Kingdom. As I came down off the fence my ankle twisted on a rock and I crashed to the ground in no man's land. I lay stretched out, writhing in agony, as Zuma and our guide tried to help me to my feet.

'Should we continue or go back, *umfowetu* (brother)?' Zuma asked anxiously. We were due to be picked up on the road only a few kilometres away from where we were crossing, and we had an important meeting to get to in Manzini with comrades from home.

I tried standing on my foot, thankful that the rain which was pelting down afforded good cover, and insisted that we continue. I hobbled along until we arrived at our rendezvous point. We were thoroughly soaked by the rain and sat shivering in a cold wind for over two hours. It was a wicked night and it became obvious that our lift was not coming. We waited another hour and decided to return to Mozambique. By now my ankle had got much worse. I was in excruciating pain.

Zuma considered for a moment. 'Just hold on to my arm, *umfowetu*, nobody's out in this rain. We'll take a chance and just walk through the village.'

It was a weird sensation, hobbling through the border village which we were always at such pains to by-pass, in driving rain and mist. I made out the shapes of huts, a few shops, a schoolhouse, the police station with rows of staff houses and the customs post – deserted since dusk. It was heavy-going, getting over the fences. When we arrived at our safe house in Namaacha and I pulled off my hiking boot we found my ankle horribly swollen.

I lay in bed, swallowing pain killers, for over a week. A doctor told me that I had torn ligaments which would take six months to heal. Apparently, if the bone had broken, recovery would have been quicker. I attended physiotherapy at the Maputo General Hospital, and walked slowly along the seashore because soft sea-sand is good for an ankle injury. I hobbled about Maputo with a walking stick and astonished John Nkadimeng by jumping the border fence again with the use of the stick. Zuma was always cool and composed. We were driving undercover in Swaziland along a dirt road when the steering wheel became detached from its shaft. We discovered afterwards that someone had tampered with the car. A bridge loomed ahead and on either side a plunge into a river. Zuma's composed efforts to reconnect the steering failed. He nonchalantly applied the footbrake and we stopped off the road just above a drop into the river. '*Umfowetu*' he chuckled, 'we almost drank from the mighty Usutu River today.'

Our military operations were increasing and having great psychological impact. These included rocket attacks on police stations, sabotage operations against power plants, and the blasting of strategic oil installations at the Sasol complex. Fires at Sasol raged uncontrollably for days and the plumes of smoke could be seen as far away as Soweto. While the development of a guerrilla struggle along classical lines was proving difficult in our conditions, our operatives were demonstrating the power of armed propaganda. The morale of the black population rose dramatically. The government of P.W. Botha, under strong police and military influence, became obsessed with retaliatory action.

During the night of 30 January 1981, Pretoria's commandos (Portuguese and Rhodesian mercenaries among them) struck at the suburb of Matola on the outskirts of Maputo. We had several residences in the area, and three were pointed out by informers.

A focal point of attack was a double-storey house in large grounds where Obadi and his operational group resided. It was one of Obadi's units that had struck at Sasol six months previously.

Dressed in Mozambican army uniforms and speaking Portuguese, a group of the raiders engaged Obadi and others in conversation at the front door of the house. Weapons were suddenly pointed, and the occupants ordered out of the house and lined up against a garden wall. The enemy opened fire and several comrades died on the spot. Obadi staggered away with his guts ripped open. An

MK comrade, posted in the loft of the house, opened fire and hit several of the attackers. The enemy evacuated with several wounded, leaving a radio operator behind. He was found dead in the garden with a bullet hole through his head and a swastika symbol painted on his helmet. The words 'Apocalypse Now!' adorned his combat jacket.

Six comrades were killed at a house used by our Natal operatives. Most died instantly in their beds when rockets blasted the residence. Three were well known to me.

One was the group's commander, Mduduzi Guma, whom I had met at the school in East Germany. He was a popular Durban attorney aged 34 whose wife and children lived in Manzini. With him was his friend, Lancelot Hadebe, who crossed into Swaziland the first time with me and who used to cut my hair in the Angolan camps. The third was the young trainee at Quibaxe, known as Ashok, who used to relax in the lemon grove. I learnt that his real name was Krishna Rabilal. He staggered from a blazing room into a hail of bullets. His father came to Maputo and performed Hindu rites at the funeral.

The third residence attacked had nothing whatsoever to do with MK operations. It belonged to SACTU, our trade union organisation. A friend of mine from the early 1960s perished when it too was hit by rockets and machine gun fire. William Khanyile was a trade unionist from Pietermaritzburg who, together with John Nkadimeng, had led our contingent on the May Day march. As a young activist he was a protégé of Harry Gwala, the lion of the Natal Midlands. I had attended some of Harry's Marxist classes with William. William served eight years on Robben Island before joining us in exile. His wife, also an Eleanor, from Kwa Mashu in Durban, and a young son, lived in London and were on close terms with my family.

In all, ten comrades died in the attack. Obadi, whose real name was Motso Mokgabudi, died in hospital one week later. Five were wounded and fortunately recovered. Three were abducted and taken back to South Africa. It was divulged several years later by a captain in the security police, Dirk Coetzee, that one of those kidnapped, Vuyani Mavuso, was executed because he refused to co-operate. According to Coetzee, he was shot and burnt and his remains disposed of in a river.

One of the survivors was Leslie, the Quibaxe defier and the *toyi-toyi* exponent. He was sleeping in a downstairs room at the Natal residence. He described to me how the house was shaken to its foundations as the rockets struck: 'There was smoke and fire everywhere. I rolled off my bed and sheltered under it,' Leslie began. 'A Boer came to the window which had disappeared leaving a huge hole. He fired a full magazine into the room, just spraying bullets all around. I clutched a pistol waiting for them. I heard a voice behind him saying: "*Komaan, laat ons inklim* [Come on, let's climb inside]". But the bloke was nervous and replied: "*Almal is dood* [Everyone is dead]" and luckily they left.'

I wrote a profile of some of those who died in *The African Communist* (under the pen-name of Alexander Sibeko), in which I attempted to pay tribute to their commitment without having full knowledge of their backgrounds – a consequence of the undercover nature of our work. It conveyed a similar message to that in a poem I wrote for Ntima Segole who died at Novo Catengue:

> *... We go to and fro throughout our embattled country or on the continent of Africa, even the four corners of the world, scarcely getting to know each other. A long dusty journey on the back of a truck; a shared room in some out-of-the-way place; brief intervals during some long, drawn-out meeting; maybe on rare occasions a few cold beers and jocular tales well into the night; more often than not, illegal border crossings and close shaves. Such are the occasions of often chance meetings ... of discussing childhood, families, sweethearts, music, poetry, philosophy. Before you know it, someone becomes dear to you. You look forward to seeing them again. Then news of arrest, torture, death. All you have to offer are a few pencilled sketches when what is needed are oil paints and a huge canvas.*
>
> *'The times are sad when it is necessary to be a hero,' wrote Berthold Brecht, 'but these are the times in which we live.' How many unknown and unsung heroes have died in the struggle to liberate mankind? ... [Here] we record some typical heroes of our time ... whose names we can fortunately set down ...*

Karl Marx had observed that 'Revolution advances by giving rise to a stronger and more determined counter-revolution which in turn compels the revolutionaries to seek more effective methods of struggle.' One need not be a Marxist to understand the do-or-die nature of such a process which forces the revolutionaries to find better ways to survive; to organise and return to the offensive. Because of the polarisation of forces and the upward spiral of violence the protagonists are invariably lumped together as being equally responsible by those sitting on the sidelines. This attitude plays into the hands of the status quo because history has shown that the oppressor will never give up power unless compelled to do so.

Far from intimidating us, Pretoria's raids created a stronger resolve. Our new strategy and structures were beginning to pay dividends. May 1981 was the 20th anniversary of the creation of the racist republic. The ANC devised a campaign against the celebrations which combined mass protests and the distribution of illegal propaganda with armed operations. At last we were managing to find the correct combination of tactical actions which inspired both mass mobilisation and the formation of popular, democratic organisations. We could see that, despite the adoption by the P.W. Botha regime of a 'total strategy' onslaught against the democratic forces, apartheid was ultimately doomed.

Meanwhile the toll on our side was heavy. Our chief representative in Zimbabwe, Joe Gqabi, was assassinated by gunmen on 1 August outside his Harare office. In November, the body of a prominent human rights lawyer in Durban, Griffiths Mxenge, was found with over 40 stab wounds. These were the continuation of over 100 deaths in detention and a growing number of assassinations both inside and outside South Africa. It showed that torture and assassinations devised by the security forces were spreading throughout the body politic and becoming part of top government decision-making.

I was in Swaziland on 4 June 1982 when our deputy representative and his wife, Petrus and Jabu Nzima, were assassinated. The night before I held a secret meeting with Petrus, discussing the situation of our undercover operatives in the Kingdom who were coming under increasing harassment from the police. The next morning Petrus turned the ignition key of his car and it exploded.

A couple of months later, Ruth First was killed by a letter bomb in Maputo. This cowardly action showed that Pretoria not only feared the armed combatants of MK but the mind of a brilliant academic, whose major contribution had become focused on the research and analysis of African development. The death of this gifted woman was an agonising blow, not only for her husband and three daughters, but for our entire Movement and the FRELIMO Party. Tributes poured in from all over the world. She was buried in Maputo under a mound of flowers alongside the graves of the Matola martyrs.

Before the year ran out, on 9 December 1982, SADF commandos raided Maseru, capital of Lesotho. Once again informers from within our ranks helped identify ANC residences and 42 people were slaughtered, of whom 12 were Lesotho citizens. Lesotho had been a traditional sanctuary for refugees from as far back as the 19th century and many of those killed were defenceless women and children. The Prime Minister of the country, Prince Leabua Jonathan, had become a thorn in the side of Pretoria and the action was a destabilisation effort to get rid of both the ANC and him.

The pattern of destabilisation provided a clue to the elimination of Ruth First which we did not perceive at the time. As part of its destabilisation strategy of the Frontline States, Pretoria had focused a great deal of attention on Mozambique. The Renamo bandits, the original creation of the Rhodesian regime, had been taken over by Pretoria and developed into an increasing threat against the revolution.

A brutal war was being waged against the Mozambican people. Civilians on buses and trains and in the villages were being indiscriminately massacred in scenes that were to become familiar in South Africa a decade later. Development projects were systematically destroyed and much of the countryside turned into a wasteland. Mozambique faced the prospect of mass starvation. After what must have been a period of agonising debate Samora Machel announced his intention of signing a peace accord with Pretoria. This was a humiliating about-turn for FRELIMO and a tremendous setback for the ANC. It is quite feasible that those in Pretoria responsible for this strategy argued that Ruth's elimination would make its success more likely. The terms of the Nkomati Accord, signed in March 1984, resulted in the enforced withdrawal of the ANC from Mozambique.

I was the first ANC cadre to have Mozambique's doors shut on me. A month before the signing of the Accord I was undercover in Swaziland. In Maputo, ANC houses were being raided for arms and a list drawn up of all those who had to leave. It was agreed between Tambo and Samora Machel that the ANC would be permitted to maintain a diplomatic mission with a dozen cadres. Slovo contacted me and said I should return to Maputo because Tambo and he wanted me to be one of the twelve. I regarded this as a forlorn hope and felt I would be of better service in Swaziland. The leadership insisted, however, and somewhat reluctantly I boarded a flight for the short hop from Swaziland to Maputo. I was in disguise and carried a false passport, which had become a more convenient way of travelling between the two countries.

Checking in at Swaziland's small Matsapa airport, outside Manzini, was an anxious moment. A well-known security policeman was assisting the usual immigration officials in scrutinising the documents of all the passengers. Things were certainly tightening up, I mused. Together with a handful of passengers I waited for the small 24-seater aircraft to arrive from Maseru for the 30-minute trip to Maputo. There were comrades waiting for me at Maputo's Mavelane International Airport. When I arrived Sonny Singh made the mistake of attempting to assist me through immigration, so that the immigration officials realised I was with the ANC. We were told politely that I could not enter Mozambique and had to re-board the plane, which would soon take off on its return journey. A heated argument broke out between my comrades and the officials.

'Oh, the hell with it,' I said to Sonny. 'Let me take my chances on this flight. There's no way I'm going to sleep at this airport for days on end while we haggle with the Ministry of Interior. Tell Slovo I'll be of far better use in Swaziland.'

I quickly purchased a ticket to Manzini and the immigration official made sure I got on board. '*A luta continua*' (the struggle continues) was my parting shot to him, thankful that he at least had not alerted the aircrew to my unwanted status in his country. As the plane took off, I began considering what explanation I could give Swazi immigration concerning my immediate return to their country.

Yeoville Boys' Under 11 Football Team 1949

The author's parents Isadore Kasrils and
René Cohen during their courtship,
Johannesburg, c1930

René Kasrils and her mother Clara Cohen
in Johannesburg, early 1930s

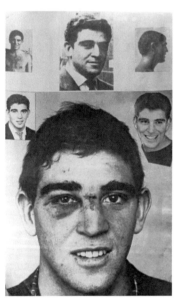

The author's cheek grazed by a bullet after
an encounter with would-be assassins,
Durban, 1961

A collection of photographs of Ronnie
Kasrils taken between 1956 and
1959, discovered in the files of the
Durban security police by Professor
Ian Edwards during his research

Wedding day in Dar es Salaam, 1964

With Eleanor on Hampstead Heath, London, 1972

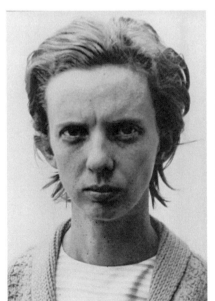

Police mug shot of Eleanor Anderson after a week-long hunger strike in Durban prison, 1963; discovered by Professor Ian Edwards

Eleanor in Dar es Salaam – October, 1963; photo taken at Home Affairs for registration as ANC refugee; hair cut short and dyed black for her disguise after escape from Fort Napier

Ronnie & Eleanor with sons Andrew and Christopher, London, 1970; taken by Eleanor Kasrils using a time-delay camera

Eleanor (39) & Brigid (19) united at last, England, 1975

Outside the Pravda Museum, Moscow; Ronnie with his sons, left, and a guide, right, New Year, 1984

En route to Fidel Castro's guerrilla camp, Cuba, 1987

Kasrils with fellow MK officers Jabulani Jali and Lulamile Dantile (right) who was murdered in Lesotho later that year, Angola, 1986

Members of the SACP Central Committee, Moscow, 1987
Front: Thabo Mbeki, John Nkadimeng, Joe Slovo (General Secretary), Dan Tloome
(Chairman), Ray Alexander, Francis Meli (real name A. Madolwana)
Middle: Sizakele Sigxashe, January 'Che' Masilela, Henry Makgothi, Aziz Pahad,
Reg September
Back: Ronnie Kasrils, Mac Maharaj, Brian Bunting, Chris Hani, Joe Jele

Author in disguise (while undercover) outside a bookshop in Rockey Street, Yeoville,
Johannesburg, 1990–91; magazine poster features an article by himself

© Connie Braam

Some of the author's disguises – 1989–90

Speaking to the Foreign Correspondents Association, introduced by Amina Frense, whilst being hunted by the police, Mike's Kitchen, 1990

Kasrils acknowledging the crowds at an SACP rally at the FNB Stadium, July, 1990

The author and the late Chris Hani at a public meeting in Vosloorus, 1992

Ronnie Kasrils, Joe Slovo (left) and Jacob Zuma, 1993

The author addressing a rally in Port Elizabeth on the 30th anniversary of MK in December 1991; Winnie Mandela in fatigues is seated second row from front, extreme left

Ronnie Kasrils with Smuts Ngonyama to his left, carrying wounded comrade Petrus Vantya (Bushy); Bisho shootings

A delighted Kasrils votes in the first democratic South African election, 27 April 1994 at Duduza on the East Rand

President Mandela and Ronnie Kasrils, deputy minister of defence, meeting Drakensberg Boys' Choir, summit Champagne Castle, Drakensberg Range, 75th Anniversary celebration South African Air Force, 1997

Archbishop Tutu acknowledges the arrival of the author and his wife at the Bisho hearing in 1996

The author and his wife with Kobie Coetzee on board the SAS Protea *during the naval review, 1998*

With Ben Lekalake, a former boxing champion and MK combatant in the ANC office, Johannesburg, 1993; Lekalake had taken part in a protest at Quibaxe camp, Angola

Deputy Minister of Defence Kasrils introduces Her Majesty Queen Elizabeth to World War II veterans at Maitland Cemetery, Cape Town, March 1995, on her inspection of Commonwealth war graves

General G. Meiring, Chief SANDF, Deputy Minister R. Kasrils, Minister Joe Modise,
Parliamentary media briefing, Cape Town, 1997

Alexander Moisseev, the Russian assistant military attaché to South Africa, and the author
during a visit to the Russian destroyer Nastoychivy *in Simonstown, 1997*

Kasrils assists vice-president Al Gore's wife on board a naval vessel bound for Robben Island during a visit in 1997; others: Thabo and Zenele Mbeki, Al Gore and Ahmed Kathrada

U.S. Department of Justice

Federal Bureau of Investigation

Office of the Director   *Washington, D.C. 20535*

October 10, 1997

Mr. Ronnie Kasrils
Deputy Minister of Defense
Republic of South Africa
c/o Embassy of the Republic of South Africa
Washington, D.C.

Dear Deputy Minister Kasrils:

        I met today with Ambassador Sonn to discuss your
understandable concerns and those of other South African
Government officials about false and erroneous perceptions from
the public announcement of the arrests of three Washington-area
residents for conspiracy to commit espionage, including the
charge that two of these individuals provided classified,
national defense information to a person they believed to be an
intelligence officer of the Republic of South Africa. A separate
press release was issued today to once again emphasize and make
clear that neither you nor any member of the South African
Government was involved or implicated in the investigation.

        On a personal note, I deeply regret that inferences
have been drawn from press accounts of the affidavit that you
were somehow involved in this investigation. In concert with the
U.S. Attorney's Office, we made every effort to make it perfectly
clear in our public announcement of the arrests that neither the
South African Government nor any of its officials were involved
or implicated in the investigation.

        In closing, I deeply regret any embarrassment or
difficulties this situation has caused you.

                          Sincerely yours,

                          Louis J. Freeh
                          Director

FBI/DOJ

*Letter of apology from FBI, following their forgery of Deputy Defence Minister Kasrils's
signature on a letter that led to the entrapment of an American spy*

Ronnie Kasrils and Thabo Mbeki celebrate the ANC national election victory at a party at Gallagher Estate, Midrand, June 1999, shortly before Mbeki's inauguration as state president

Deputy Defence Minister Kasrils with British Prime Minister Tony Blair at a medal awards ceremony for British officers for their assistance to the new SANDF, Cape Town, 1998

Minister of Water Affairs and Forestry Ronnie Kasrils and his wife Eleanor with Vladimir Shubin, Professor of African Studies, who had assisted the ANC/SACP during the liberation struggle on behalf of the Communist Party, Soviet Union; Moscow University is in the background, 2002

The author presents Fidel Castro with a copy of an early edition of this book on a trip to Robben Island, 1998

Minister of Defence, Joe Modise and his deputy, Ronnie Kasrils, during a parliamentary session, 1998

Ronnie Kasrils leading 'Jews of Conscience' on the Palestine issue out of the fortified confines of communal thinking, 2001

Kasrils and President Mbeki celebrate the delivery of water and sanitation to a rural village, in 2001

Ronnie Kasrils installed as a Nigerian chief in River State in 2002; with him are Minister Ngalale (left) and a village chief

President Mbeki and Ronnie Kasrils celebrating with Mrs Frida Nzama, the nine-millionth recipient of clean water in July 2002

Drought relief: Provision of emergency water to rural areas during the 2004 drought; Minister Ronnie Kasrils visits a water point in Oribi Gorge, KwaZulu-Natal

Toilet rolls with a message; Ghori Ghosh, Minister Kasrils and Sir Richard Jolly, Chairman of the UN Council on Water and Sanitation responsible for the international Water, Sanitation and Hygiene for All (WASH) programme examine the printed messages produced for the World Summit on Sustainable Development

Kasrils addressing a Palestine solidarity meeting in Pretoria, 2002

© DWAF

Signing the Nkomati-Maputo Agreement on shared river water at the Johannesburg Summit in 2002; from left: Minister White, Mozambique; Minister Kasrils, South Africa; Crown Prince William of Orange looks on

© Bruce Sutherland

The opening of the Water Dome, at the World Summit on Sustainable Development in September 2002; Minister Kasrils with 'water wizards' Nelson Mandela, Salim-Salim and Crown Prince William of Orange

© Amina Frense

Author addressing a Right2Know protest demonstration against Protection of Information legislation, outside Parliament, Cape Town, 2012

FOURTEEN

DISNEYLAND

Swaziland
1984

THE PLANE CLIMBED QUICKLY AND I looked back at the concrete city of Maputo (*cidade concreto*) with its spectacular coastline and harbour. Soon we were flying over the outlying townships, and then the bushveld stretching towards the Lebombo mountains and the mini-state of Swaziland. I looked down at the Namaacha border-post, thinking of the countless times I had jumped the fence with comrades who had since fallen in battle.

We were in Swazi airspace with 20 minutes' or so flying time to Matsapa airport. I needed to have a good reason for immediately returning to Swaziland. I decided to say that, on reaching Maputo, I had received an urgent message that 'my brother' in Manzini had been involved in a serious car crash after dropping me off at the airport. It sounded a farcical reason to me, but I could not come up with anything better.

The Swazi lowveld, with its dry bush and green stretch of irrigated cane fields, gave way to the hills and fertile valleys around the small town of Manzini. We landed at the airport and a handful of passengers alighted – the rest remaining on board for the onward flight to Lesotho.

A large lady in West African dress was struggling to disembark with two young children. I decided to give her a hand, more for the sake of camouflage than courtesy. The same immigration official who had processed me out an hour before was handling the incoming passengers. I handed him my passport, muttering about the family tragedy that had unexpectedly brought me back to Swaziland. He scarcely glanced at me as he began making calculations on a pad. He finally looked up and said: 'You can have 31 days.' At first I could not grasp what he meant and nearly continued blurting out my cover-story. In such circumstances, particularly when dealing with bureaucratic myopia, it is best to take things as slowly as possible. 'I beg your pardon,' I said, 'could you repeat that?'

'I'm giving you 31 days,' he barked back, as though sentencing me to a stretch in jail. 'Visitors are only allowed 60 days per year,' he continued, 'your passport shows you have already had 29 days this year. Therefore all I can grant you is another 31 days.'

'That's fine,' I responded with relief, as he handed back my passport after inserting an entry stamp right next to the exit stamp of that morning. 'Thank you very much.'

Normally someone would fetch me from the airport. There had been no time to alert my contacts, so I caught a taxi and drove into Manzini. The 'hub' of Swaziland consists of a collection of stores along two main streets, with no buildings more than two storeys high; a number of churches and schools; a sports club and showground; a comfortable two-star hotel frequented by South African security police, and a 'no-star' hotel patronised by their informants; a police station; a clinic run by the Nazarene order; and a population of some 30,000 dispersed between outlying townships and some well-to-do suburbs. The latter housed a mixture of schoolteachers, aid workers and business people from abroad and an emergent Swazi middle class. Near the Matsapa airport is a military base, a police school, an industrial area and a low-income housing estate, where a number of South African refugees had resided for years. It was constantly being raided for undercover ANC operatives and local gangsters. It was called 'Beirut', because of the number of gun-fights that had taken place there.

I alighted from my taxi outside the town centre and, after pretending to go into a shop, made the rest of my way on foot uphill to a house in a middle-class area. My soft knocking on a back door was answered by an ascetic, bearded figure with a distinctive Scots accent. His face lit up in a toothy grin:

'What happened? Didn't the plane take off?' he asked. My explanation intrigued him and he puckered up his face in distaste: 'Samora's going to learn the hard way not to trust the Boers, but has he any alternative?'

We analysed the dramatic turn of events in Mozambique while he prepared the evening meal. My friend and his wife had jobs that gave them a lot of free time. I had recruited them in Britain and they had been living in Swaziland for several years, providing a safe house and travelling into South Africa on various missions for our Movement. Their code names were Moses (Michael Stephens) and Aaron (June), his cool American wife. Moses, my contact from Britain, worked as a teacher and found life in Swaziland humdrum, except when I was around because my presence spelt action for him. He could not abide the local expatriate community and had a reputation for being antisocial.

Aaron was attractive and sociable, perfectly willing to carry out the dangerous missions I assigned them. They both enjoyed camping and we had explored the length of the Lebombo range in the east and the border highlands in the north-west of Swaziland, developing many crossing points into Mozambique and South Africa.

Aaron had a university job and, on returning home, thought I had not even departed that day. When she heard what had happened she commented: 'Oh well, at least his nibs over there,' motioning to her husband serving out the dinner, 'will lighten up now you're going to be around for some time.'

There were a number of safe houses I could use in Swaziland, but Moses and Aaron's place was an especially safe retreat because they did not mix in political circles. They lived a quiet life, when they were not off on ANC missions, and we enjoyed passing time playing 'Trivial Pursuit' in the evenings. I surprised them with my useless knowledge of both American and English sporting and literary facts, gained from my childhood passion for comics and the movies. There are questions from the world of cartoon characters under the topic 'Literature' which ask, for example: 'Who is Bugs Bunny's mortal enemy?' When I was able to instantly reply – 'Elmer Fudd' – Aaron's admiration for me knew no bounds.

I had a safe car which was stowed in their garage. Soon after dinner I was on the road to Mbabane, the Swazi capital 50 kilometres away.

The strip between the two towns is the busiest part of the Kingdom. It takes one past Matsapa, the University, the National Stadium, the Parliamentary buildings (silent by day and night because of a Royal suspension), the Monarch's Palace and then along the Ezulweni Valley up a long, steep climb to the cool, damp heights of Mbabane. The Ezulweni is unbelievably beautiful and boasts a weird combination of glitzy hotels and seedy motels; a frenetic gambling arena with casino and one-armed bandits; raunchy strip shows, 'skin flicks' and hot mineral springs named the 'cuddle puddle'; a game sanctuary and golf courses; riding schools and various resorts and chalets within mountain forests. It is an ideal area for discreet rendezvous: between white South African businessmen and Swazi prostitutes; Boer handlers and their covert agents; or ANC commanders and underground operatives. We had a saying that after dark the only cars on the road were ANC and Boers. For those of us working undercover, Swaziland was a capricious blend of beauty and the beast.

The valley sparkled in bright sunlight by day and was dark, moody and frequently under heavy mist at night. The 19-kilometre-long hill, winding up to Mbabane, is extremely dangerous and boasts the record number of fatal accidents per kilometre in the *Guinness Book of Records*. This statistic is exacerbated by the heavy consumption of alcohol in the country, especially by motorists at the weekends.

Because of these features and the topsy-turvy power struggle within the ruling elite, Moses dubbed the country 'Disneyland' – a place of daydream and delusion which could suddenly transform into nightmare. I was always relieved to reach the summit into Mbabane, especially at night, and avoiding the town centre – marginally busier than Manzini – arrived at a second safe house. Knocking at the door, I knew I would be scrutinised through a spy-hole.

'I thought you had left today?' a dark-eyed individual said on opening the door. It was Ebe – Ebrahim Ismail – the senior undercover operative on the political side in Swaziland. Our association of course went back to the 1960s when he had been arrested for sabotage and served 15 years' imprisonment. Like most ex-prisoners he plunged back into the struggle, regardless of the risks. He had joined us in Maputo in 1981 and had been deployed in Swaziland. I helped him set up his safe house and could claim to have taught him to drive in Maputo and to cook in Swaziland.

I reported about the deteriorating situation in Mozambique. We began considering the likely consequences for our network in the kingdom. With the threat of imminent deportation to Lusaka, many cadres were due to slip into Swaziland with instructions to infiltrate home. We would need to prepare for an influx of over 200.

We arranged to meet the military commanders. The commander of the Natal machinery was the impressive Thami Zulu (Muzi Ngwenya). His counterpart on the Transvaal side was an equally tall, erect and imposing individual named Gebhuza (Siphiwe Nyanda). Both were recruited into the ANC a year prior to the 1976 uprising and had trained in Eastern Europe. Thami had spent several years as an officer in the camps and Gebhuza had commanded operations from Swaziland from 1977 onwards. He had acquired a reputation for nerve and audacity and was responsible for many daring operations. Thami had only recently arrived in Swaziland to take charge of a machinery that had lost its capable chief of staff, Zwelakhe Nyanda, the brother of Gebhuza.

Zwelakhe had been shot dead, together with a Swazi student, Keith McFadden, on 22 November 1983 in an assault on an ANC house in Manzini. Every time I looked at Gebhuza, I was reminded of the tall, handsome and self-confident Zwelakhe and had heard that both brothers took after their father, a well-to-do Soweto businessman. Both commanders responded to the news from Maputo in the same philosophical way that all of us did to any reverse. As long as we could devise a counter-strategy there would be no demoralisation, which was why the slogan '*A luta continua*' was so popular in our ranks. No setback appeared to unnerve their generation.

Normally the various structures in Swaziland took their instructions from Maputo. In view of the problems we were facing, we decided to form ourselves into an overall command group and began meeting regularly. Within a week, we were having to contend with the first influx of MK combatants from across the Mozambique border. Our various safe houses were becoming overcrowded. This was bound to create security problems.

We were meeting one morning in a safe house used by Gebhuza when one of his lieutenants, a quiet-spoken bean-pole called Jabu (Solly Choke), interrupted us. 'Problems, problems,' he muttered in undertones to Gebhuza. The latter's eyes opened wide and he intimated we needed to leave at once. At first I did not think the problem concerned us and that he was having to attend to something personally. But he grinned stiffly and said: 'We've got to get out quick. Jabu's just got a tip-off that a raid has been planned on this address by the Swazi police.'

Ebe and I left him to his packing, while Jabu dropped us off in town. Our car was parked at the Swazi Plaza, the main Mbabane shopping mall. We drove a couple of kilometres past the Mbabane golf course, to his modest house in the suburb of Dalrich, where Swazi speculators were putting up modern residences. There were no tarred roads here and the bush encroached up to the boundaries of the homes.

As I negotiated a corner I glimpsed a truckload of soldiers on the main road. As I drew Ebe's attention to this, a second and then a third truck drove by. It looked as though the suburb was being surrounded. We decided to turn around and drive back to town. No sooner had I made a U-turn than we were stopped by a couple of men with rifles who materialised from the garden of one of the houses. They were in shirtsleeves and ties. They demanded to know who we were and what we wanted.

I sensed they were Swazi Special Branch and, looking suitably surprised and irate, but not arrogant, I replied: 'We're businessmen, looking for a house in Pine Valley, but who are you?'

'Police,' was the curt answer. 'Pine Valley's back up the main road.'

'What's going on here?'

'You'll read about it in tomorrow's paper.'

There certainly was a great deal going on. From the main road we could see the soldiers being deployed around the suburb. Back in town we spotted a number of police cars whizzing about. We felt safe enough in our disguises and decided to take stock of the situation over a cup of coffee in a quiet restaurant from where we could alert various contacts by telephone. Ebe needed to see one of our main contacts personally and we decided he would see the individual, who worked in an office nearby, and meet up with me at the Swazi Plaza. As I walked towards the car, I felt I was being followed. I continued walking in order to make sure.

The individual concerned was a young, well-built Swazi, in casual clothing. I had noticed him sitting at a nearby table in the coffee bar and emerge after

I left. I came to a corner, turned left and then immediately crossed the road. There was quite a lot of traffic about, which gave me the chance to look around in a natural way. Sure enough, the young man was still behind me. I was going to have to determine whether this was coincidence or deliberate.

I went into a men's clothing shop and looked through a rack of jackets. My friend had stopped outside and was even squinting into the shop to see what I was up to. On leaving the store, I crossed the road and found he was sticking to me like glue. I needed to get back to my car and pick up Ebe, and could not afford to waste time. This was a situation that required rough tactics.

I walked down a quiet street, turned a corner and waited. Sure enough my friend came sprinting around the corner and almost collided with me. I hit him on the chest with a clenched fist.

'*Pasop jong!*' (Watch out, you!) I exclaimed in Afrikaans. 'If you're trying to rob me you'll get a bullet next time!' I left him, uncertain and shaken on the corner, and walking swiftly away approached the Swazi Plaza.

Rushing up the hill, panting heavily with excitement, was Craig Williamson, the security policeman I had last had contact with in London. I would have recognised him anywhere – the florid complexion, the narrow eyes, the corpulent frame. We had heard from our contacts that he was staying in a local hotel and had been coming to Swaziland on and off to set up a spy network. In fact, we had his room bugged. There is an iron law of counter-surveillance, never to look over your shoulder. I broke it for the first and only time that day. I looked back and Williamson was looking over his shoulder at me. On his part, it was either first-time recognition or he had been alerted to my presence and current disguise. Whatever my view of Williamson, he was an opponent of strong nerve and ability. The sooner I linked up with Ebe and we cleared out of the area, the better.

We stayed the night in Manzini with Moses. The next morning's *Times of Swaziland* had a sensational report of a raid by Swazi security forces on an ANC residence in Mbabane. Gunshots had been exchanged with the occupants, who had managed to flee into the surrounding bush. Several ANC members had been rounded up. Speculation was that these were trained MK cadres who were entering the country in large numbers from Mozambique. The house concerned was just a street away from Ebe's residence and we did not know it was being used by our operatives.

What was more disturbing was the account of how the authorities had tracked down our people. It was an example of crass indiscipline which we could ill afford. According to the newspaper, one of the residents had been to a notorious disco called Club 702 the night before. There he had got into a fight over a young woman and pulled a pistol on her boyfriend. He had left the disco by taxi and got into an altercation with the driver about the fare right outside the safe house during the small hours of the morning, while his comrades were fast asleep.

'The idiot might just as well have left his calling card at the discotheque!' Moses commented as he finished reading the report.

During the following weeks the 'Disneyland' term coined by Moses lived up to its expressive, if at times tragic, character. Within days, a large group of MK combatants were intercepted, crossing the border from Mozambique. A dozen were rounded up and detained at a police station at Simunye in the sugar-cane area. Within no time they had escaped and a massive hunt was underway to track them down in the cane fields.

The *Times of Swaziland*, which normally reported cases of petty corruption, small-town robberies and *muti* murders (when parts of the body are used for 'medicine'), could scarcely keep pace with the dramatic events as a house in Manzini was placed under siege by the security forces. A policeman was shot through the head, possibly by mistake by one of his colleagues, as he approached to check on a report about suspicious occupants. When armoured cars were brought up, the occupants decided to surrender. A couple of our comrades, however, chose to make a break for the bush and gunfire erupted, leaving one of our people dead in his tracks.

We had issued orders that our people should not engage in gun battles with the Swazi security forces and fortunately these were the only fatalities. Thami Zulu and I came under fire outside Mbabane when his car was recognised and Swazi police gave chase. A tyre was hit and Thami, remaining ice-cool, manoeuvred the car off the road and into the bush. We jumped out with bullets whistling overhead and ran as swiftly as we could for a friend's house, which was fortunately close by.

A big problem was finding safe venues for the meetings of our command. In the early period, a number of attempts were made and had to be abandoned because of sudden raids. We tried meeting at picnic spots or by parking in quiet forest tracks. But the army and police were patrolling everywhere, and we just could not manage an undisturbed meeting.

We finally agreed to meet in a secluded restaurant. We dressed in suits, posing as doctors. We drew our meal out and managed to cover a lot of ground concerning the current emergency situation. We were able to linger over dessert and coffee and, to give the meal an authentic finale, I ordered brandies. Ebe, being of Muslim background, ordered a Coke instead, and Thami and Gebhuza said they would have Cokes as well as brandy. Little did I imagine that they meant brandy and Coke.

The wine steward carefully poured three measures of the finest Cape

KWV brandy into the appropriate balloon glasses and watched as I took an appreciative sip. His expression turned to horror as my colleagues, the 'doctors' Thami and Gebhuza, filled their brandy glasses with Coke, said 'cheers', and knocked the mixture back. I tried to explain to them how sacrilegious it was to mix Coke with KWV or cognac, as they sat back with contented smiles.

On another occasion we arranged for Gebhuza to pick Ebe and me up at the Holiday Inn in the Ezulweni Valley. While Ebe and I waited, we talked and sipped drinks by the poolside. I became aware that we had attracted interest when I noticed a couple of white males staring at us from the bar. They were South African SB for sure. Just then one of Gebhuza's lieutenants came to fetch us.

We moved out of the hotel with six heavyweights after us. There were several long lines of vehicles in the car park. Gebhuza's car and a back-up vehicle with bodyguards were 100 metres away. One of our adversaries was trying to cut us off. It looked as though a gun fight was imminent. I put my hand into my pocket and he backed away. They were still behind us, however, as we reached Gebhuza's car, but then they held back. Probably they did not like the look of our boys in the two cars. One of our people aimed an AK-47 rifle at them as we drove off and they ducked behind the shrubs.

Thami's machinery was utilising a contact flat in Manzini. The occupant, coincidentally, was a friend from London called Feivel Cohen who had decided to retire to Swaziland some years previously. Feivel had left South Africa in revulsion over the Sharpeville shootings and had lived in Golders Green. He was a mild-mannered introvert with a dodgy heart who joined the Anti-Apartheid Movement and kept imagining the South African security police were watching him. I advised him to drop out of political activity but was sorry when he left Britain. To my astonishment, I discovered that he was residing in Swaziland and had become a contact of one of the most active of MK machineries. I impressed on Thami and his colleagues that they should not place Feivel in danger, but it was too late.

The army and police surrounded the flats where Feivel stayed and in a night-time raid arrested him and an MK cadre who stayed with him. They were detained in the cells at the Manzini police station, which were by now packed with comrades. Feivel suffered a mild heart attack and was released after a few days. The MK comrade he had sheltered had a cover story which protected Feivel. The latter was able to claim that he did not know of his lodger's ANC connections. Under my prodding, Feivel left soon afterwards to settle in Zimbabwe.

Hysteria in Swaziland was at an all-time high. On a daily basis the media carried news of yet more raids and arrests and implored the public to be on the watch for 'itinerant males', arriving at strange hours at houses which were 'quiet by day and came alive at night'. Mug shots of Gebhuza, Thami and their lieutenants appeared on television and we were having to change our disguises from month to month. The university, which was an ANC support base, was surrounded on several occasions and the students' residences, male and female, searched for fugitives.

The most sinister aspect of the situation was the interrogation of those captured. We estimated that over 100 comrades had been rounded up and were being held in various police stations. They were being illegally removed in pairs by certain members of the Swazi security police, handcuffed and blindfolded, and taken to a secret destination for interrogation. They were given the impression that they were just a stone's throw from the South African border and, if they failed to answer questions satisfactorily, would be handed over to 'the Boers'.

In fact the interrogation centre was a Swazi army base on the old tea-road overlooking the Ezulweni Valley. The actual interrogators were indeed South African security, more than likely the heavy squad we had almost clashed with at the Holiday Inn. Swazi police would put the questions to our comrades but they wore ear-phones and were directed by the South Africans sitting behind glass partitions in a make-shift studio. This was a concession the Swazi Government was making to Pretoria. They could not afford the opprobrium of the OAU by handing our people over, but were prepared to co-operate in this bizarre form of interrogation.

It took a couple of months for the security team to process all our cadres and then they were deported to Tanzania. The most zealous Swazi security officer was an individual called Shiba, who carried out his tasks with great cruelty. He was gunned down from a passing car as he emerged from the police officers' club in Mbabane, after attending a pre-Christmas luncheon in December 1984.

Just after Christmas, Gebhuza, who seemed to have as many lives as a cat, was almost captured in a raid on an Mbabane flat. His right-hand man, Jabu, was arrested as he was parking a car outside the building. Police broke down the door of the flat when the occupants refused to open it.

Gebhuza, and a fellow comrade called Matau, tried to escape via the balcony. Matau fell and broke both legs and several ribs. As he lay, writhing in agony, a bullet was fired through his knee. He was held in solitary confinement, after hospitalisation, and then deported to Lusaka. Gebhuza managed to climb onto the roof where he hid for a day and a night before getting away to safety and reorganising his machinery.

Despite the problems of survival we faced in Swaziland, our structures managed to operate throughout the crisis of 1984. Although over 100 comrades had been rounded up and deported to Tanzania, we managed to infiltrate over 150 into South Africa.

One township after another had erupted in anger against apartheid repression. The initial cause was the attempt by corrupt township councils to increase rates. The police force had tried to come to the rescue of beleaguered councillors and, in their usual trigger-happy way, had opened fire on demonstrators. The fury of the people spread, and there was scarcely a part of South Africa that was not seething with revolt. The situation in the country became even more critical than in 1976. Scores of councillors, regarded by the people as puppets of the regime, were being eliminated, along with the hated *izimpimpi* (informers). The number of MK operations was running at well over 100 per year, being directed at the army and police as well as against communications, power and economic targets.

The major Defence Force base at Voortrekkerhoogte outside Pretoria had been hit by rockets. A powerful car bomb was detonated outside the Air Force headquarters in Pretoria killing 19 people, among them top military officers. The country's power system was being frequently interrupted and the Koeberg nuclear station, about to come on stream, was sabotaged by a powerful explosive device. The capacity of the security forces was stretched to the limit.

In December 1983, the United Democratic Front (UDF) had emerged as a broad, mass-based, pro-ANC organisation mobilising the people. In 1963, the security policeman Dirker had boasted to Walter Sisulu after his capture at the Rivonia farm: 'This will put you back 20 years.' How prophetic his words were. But now, 20 years on, the challenge to the apartheid system was at an all-time high. The ANC leadership in Lusaka issued a historic call to the people of South Africa: 'Make apartheid unworkable and the country ungovernable!' At this time came the news of Billy Nair's and Curnick Ndlovu's release from prison. I heard Billy being interviewed on radio and wrote to Eleanor:

Just imagine it. After 20 years he's still full of fighting spirit. Send him a cable from us both along the lines: 'Congratulations on your release. Share your joy and optimism. We have not forgotten you these 20 years. Looking forward to our reunion.'

I had to slip out of Swaziland in November 1984 to attend a conference of the South African Communist Party abroad. It was held outside Moscow and because of the significant representation we were able to muster it was declared the Sixth Congress of the Party. Moses Mabhida was the General Secretary of the Party and, following the death of Yusuf Dadoo the previous year, Joe Slovo was elected Party Chairperson. I was elected on to the Central Committee.

Moscow under snow, with warm hospitality provided by the Soviet comrades, was a dramatic contrast to the struggle for survival in Swaziland. It was a relief to relax with Party comrades from Lusaka, London, Luanda and many other centres where the Party had a presence. We were able to exchange news of our experiences, and I heard at first hand about a serious mutiny that had taken place in Angola earlier in the year amongst disaffected MK cadres who had been engaged in a government offensive against Unita. I received news and letters from Eleanor and was able to fly to London to visit her for the first time in a year. I felt like a young blade returning to his lover.

Despite the many years I had lived in the United Kingdom I had not qualified for a passport. I had been issued with a travel document for stateless persons instead. This meant that I queued at the aliens' section and faced a rigorous interrogation by the immigration officer on duty. The black book was immediately referred to and I watched as the official thumbed through it to locate my name – no doubt listed as someone to be watched, if not as an 'international terrorist'. The fact that my wife and children were British subjects and that I had resident status in England made it impossible to keep me out. I knew, however, that a button was being surreptitiously pressed and that I would be 'taken apart' at customs.

Inevitably, as I wheeled my luggage trolley through the green 'nothing to declare' zone, a customs official appeared and selected me for scrutiny. On more than one occasion I had been requested to step into the special area reserved for a body search. This means stripping to your underclothes and having every item in your possession minutely checked and all documents photocopied.

Just before departing from Moscow, I had made some hurried Christmas purchases. Time did not allow a visit to more than one shop, so I had bought a variety of watches and clocks for Eleanor and family. The customs man examined each one, carefully weighing the heavy balances of a cuckoo-clock in his hands.

'Not much use as a timing device,' I commented, and received a sour look in exchange. 'They're Christmas presents.'

A Special Branch man appeared on the scene and behaved with copy-book politeness. A number of articles, including some of my lectures and notes on the armed struggle, were in my baggage and he wished to explain to me his right to make copies of these. 'No problem,' I answered. 'You'll find some of this published under my name in a forthcoming issue of the ANC's journal. Maybe I'll use this anecdote in my memoirs one day.'

'Very well, sir,' was the response. 'Just don't publish my name, please.'

Apart from frequent scrutinies by customs at Heathrow airport, I never experienced any problems from Her Majesty's intelligence and security forces.

Channel 4 Television News was in error, however, in 1984, when they transmitted a smear report from South African television. Under the title 'Target Terrorism' the SABC alleged that Joe Slovo and I used Britain as a 'terrorist base' against South Africa. A sequence filmed from a moving vehicle in Golders Green high street showed my home, 'ironically above a health food shop', as the off-camera voice put it. Both Eleanor and Joe Slovo's daughter Gillian received an apology and payment for damages from Channel 4, after issuing solicitors' letters.

After a brief and happy interlude with my family in London, I was soon back in Swaziland. After the deportations to Tanzania, life in Swaziland had the appearance of settling down to normality, with the ruling elite resuming their inner power struggle with a vengeance. Ebe had slipped across the border and was working with our underground network in Durban. The ANC was preparing for a major conference in Zambia in June 1985, and I was waiting for Ebe to join me. He was working with Helene Pastoors, a Belgian national, who was living in Johannesburg after a period of residence in Maputo. After a number of failed attempts to bring Ebrahim across the border, Helene came to meet me in Mbabane.

She picked me up at a rendezvous point and we motored to an out-of-town hotel called the *Forester's Arms*. It was cold and getting dark as we sat by a log fire in the empty hotel bar. Helene was cold and shivered for a while. She was a brave woman, tall and slender with shoulder-length red hair, who had been smuggling arms into South Africa, together with her former husband, Klaas de Jong. I put her initial trembling down to the strain she was living under, although on the surface she was cool and composed.

As she related the abortive attempts to bring Ebe to the border, I grew uneasy. On each occasion they had encountered roadblocks or a strange occurrence which had decided them to retreat.

'Helene,' I asked, 'are you sure you're not under surveillance? Are you using the checks I taught you and Klaas in Maputo?'

Just then a burly South African sauntered into the pub. He did not glance at us and sat at the bar, ordering a drink. He remained for ten minutes and walked out, again without looking our way.

'Strange guy,' I commented. 'The first thing you do when you come into a public place is look around at who else is present. He didn't so much as look our way.' Helene chuckled and said that the problem with 'you exiles' is that 'you see Boers behind every corner'.

'What about him?' I asked, as another single white male, physically strong, shirt sleeves rolled up to reveal well-developed biceps, took a seat at the bar. As the first man had done, he totally ignored our presence.

The story was repeated a third time. After ten minutes and one bottle of beer the customer was replaced, but this time by an impassive black man. We did not wait for him to finish his drink. Although Helene did not agree with me and steadfastly maintained that I 'needed to live in South Africa and get used to being among Boers', she allowed herself to be hustled off.

She was a fast driver, however, and was prepared to follow instructions. Looking back in the gloom, I thought I saw a car following us from the hotel. I told her to step on it and indicated where to pull off into the forest. We took a back road to town. I told her that while I could not be certain, I felt there was a strong possibility that the men in the pub were part of a surveillance team. Ebe was dependent on her and was waiting to be picked up at an hotel in the eastern Transvaal. I told her that we could not proceed with the attempt to get him across that weekend and that she should take great care to check for surveillance.

I used a map to show her what I considered to be a safe crossing at a hill called Mananga Head. I would be back after the ANC conference to link up personally with her and guide Ebe across.

The conference took place at Kabwe in Zambia. It was a great unifying meeting, which confirmed Oliver Tambo as President of the ANC, Alfred Nzo as Secretary General and Thomas Nkobi as Treasurer. A 25-strong national executive was elected as well. Jack Simons, ever the witty cynic, who enjoyed the atmosphere and spirit of the delegates, said to me, when I asked him what he considered the main aim of the conference: 'Ha! We're here as voting fodder. Conferences are all about who is to lead!'

The key discussions centred on the growth of the mass struggle in South Africa and the township uprisings. The need to strengthen the internal underground structures, in both urban and rural areas, was stressed. These needed to be linked to 'mass political revolutionary bases throughout the country' as a way of 'raising the armed struggle to new heights'. Delegates resolved to develop an all-round people's war aimed at the seizure of power. Oliver Tambo, whose health was ailing, pledged that 'his remaining strength would be consumed in the struggle to liberate South Africa'.

There were no illusions about the sacrifices required to overthrow apartheid. On the eve of the conference, South African commandos attacked ten houses in Gaborone, capital of Botswana, murdering nine refugees in their beds – including three women, a child and an old man.

In the same period, four UDF activists from Cradock in the Eastern Cape, amongst them Matthew Goniwe, were abducted and killed.

The murderers were most certainly an apartheid hit-squad. The criminal actions that the apartheid rulers were employing against the ANC in the Frontline States were becoming more and more prevalent in the efforts to suppress non-violent resistance within South Africa itself. The list of UDF-aligned activists who were murdered was growing. Victoria Mxenge, the human rights lawyer, was stabbed to death outside her home in Durban four years after her husband's assassination.

As the Kabwe conference broke up, I received news from Rashid that Klaas de Jong, who was on a mission to South Africa, had disappeared. Rashid asked me to contact Helene Pastoors from the forward areas and warn her to leave the country immediately. We were too late. Both she and Klaas had been detained and were soon charged with smuggling weapons for the ANC. Klaas managed to escape and spent almost two years in the Dutch embassy in Pretoria before being permitted to leave South Africa. Helene served four years out of a ten-year sentence. The prosecution sensationalised her attempts to help Ebrahim leave the country, saying it was part of a high-level 'Operation Mango', so named because of the Mananga Head crossing-point I had described to Helene as a good crossing point.

Ebe narrowly managed to escape arrest. He crossed into Swaziland with Moses and Aaron, who drove him across the border in a secret compartment of an old caravan. He remained in Swaziland to operate from there, while I was called to Lusaka. I had been appointed Head of Military Intelligence of Umkhonto we Sizwe and also served on a Political-Military Council (PMC) responsible for the internal struggle.

Lusaka to the ANC was like Brussels to the European Common Market. There was a proliferation of departments and structures and the inevitable red tape. There the similarities ended, however, for there was no gravy train existence. The ANC leadership and membership lived under extremely modest conditions. At first I stayed with Joe Modise, the commander of Umkhonto we Sizwe, and his wife, Jackie Sedibe, who was on the Military Command with me. Jackie, an attractive and intelligent *mgwenya* of the Odessa generation, was head of communications. They had a small township house in Kabwata, where I slept on a couch in the living room.

I soon managed to find a small flat which I shared with some comrades. One of my first visitors was David Rabkin, who had been living in Maputo after his release from prison at the beginning of 1984. Despite the Nkomati Accord, he had managed to remain in Mozambique as a freelance journalist. He worked with Zuma and Sue and often drove to Swaziland, using his British passport, to maintain contact with our people there. He was on his way to Angola, at his request, because he wanted grounding in some basic military skills. We spent an enjoyable week together, reminiscing about the past and speculating about the future.

It was the last time I saw him. He died in an explosives accident involving a faulty delay-mechanism, on the last night of his training in an Angolan camp. The news reached me in Lusaka as I was on my way to the airport. I was catching a noon flight to Europe for a central committee meeting and I popped into Military Headquarters. Our radio operator had a message for me from our Luanda station. It read:

> *Regret to advise comrade David Rabkin died in an accident last night, 23 November. Please inform his family in London and Sue in Maputo.*

I was stunned, and sank into a chair with my head in my hands. There were so many deaths of lovable friends. A cause such as ours attracted those of high calibre, intelligence, courage and above all concern for people. David was blessed with all of these qualities and was a sensitive and creative person. I thought of Sue's and David's children, of David's mother on her way to meet him for a Christmas holiday with his sister in Harare, and battled to get a grip of myself. Cassius Make, the taciturn, tough fellow member of the High Command, arrived at the office. When I broke the news to him he was as shocked as I was. We set about informing the family and with a heavy heart I departed to catch my flight.

David was buried in Luanda. Joe Slovo and Chris Hani delivered the main orations. Chris, who had become the political commissar of MK, announced that the camp where David had died would be renamed after him. I spoke at a memorial meeting in London, and Raymond Suttner, who had spent several years with David in prison, addressed a secret gathering of comrades in Johannesburg.

By May 1986, I was again in Swaziland. We had been painstakingly rebuilding our structures there. I was sent to encourage our commanders to step up actions in response to the rising mass struggle at home. I had also been recruiting supporters in Europe to provide assistance, especially in terms of setting up safe houses for our hard-pressed cadres. I wanted to check up on the recent arrivals. I flew out with Zambia Airways, using a new disguise and false documents. It was quite a thrill looking down at the Limpopo River, across which our guerrilla groups were operating into the northern Transvaal, and overflying South Africa.

No sooner was I back in Swaziland than things started hotting up. I was reminded of a remark that Kader Asmal, the leading ANC and anti-apartheid figure in Ireland, had made to me at the Kabwe conference. 'Soul brother,' he said, because we got on so well and were enjoying a good tipple of Jameson Irish whiskey together, 'it's good being with you because you're the kind of person things start happening around.' The problem with that kind of observation is its similarity with the Chinese curse: 'May you live in interesting times'.

Both MK's Transvaal and Natal machineries had been increasing their operations. Land mines had been laid in the militarised border zone of the northern Transvaal and also close to Swaziland. Durban had been dubbed 'Bomb City' in the South African press because of the spate of explosions that rocked it. In one of these, the deputy chief of the security police was killed. An attempted attack on the oil refinery resulted in a fierce shoot-out with four MK combatants who fought to the death. Thami Zulu's command had become especially active and, in an attempt to develop a rural base, had opened a guerrilla front across the Lebombo Mountains in the Ngwavuma area of northeast Natal. This area was, in fact, the direct responsibility of Jabu Nxumalo (Mzala). Paul Dikaledi was handling the land mine operations, while Ebe was in overall command of the political underground.

Thami Zulu promised to step up operations. Unfortunately, the TV news soon reported that one of his couriers, a young Swazi student, had been arrested at the Golela border-post with Natal. The car she was driving had a secret compartment loaded with explosives. It looked to me as though the South Africans had prior information, and suspicion fell on one of Thami's lieutenants, but we could not be sure. Of additional concern was knowledge the driver had of one of my longest-serving assistants, 'Vincent' (Pete Smith), a schoolteacher from London, whom I had recently brought to Swaziland. I had brought him out to give special assistance to Ebrahim, but felt that he should be withdrawn. When the Swazi police visited him a short time later to check on his passport and work permit, it put our decision beyond dispute.

Then on the night of Saturday 2 June, two of our operatives and a young Swazi woman were shot dead in a house outside Mbabane. They were Pansu Smith, Sipho Dlamini and Busi Majola. They were found by comrades on Monday morning lying in pools of blood. They had been shot at close range by weapons with silencers. The neighbours had not heard any gunfire. Apart from head wounds Busi, who was Pansu's girlfriend, had bullet holes through the palms of her hands from attempting to ward-off the gunshots. Three white men had been seen going into the house on the Saturday night. They must have been let in by a fourth man, a contact of the comrades from South Africa, who had arrived in Swaziland for consultations with them that Saturday. When I heard that the comrades were prompted to work with him because he had a car and funds, I pointed out an old adage that had much relevance to our situation: 'Beware of Greeks bearing false gifts.'

The day before we made our gruesome discovery, Ebe and I had been meeting a contact at a picnic spot in the beautiful Pine Valley outside Mbabane. While the three of us talked by a sparkling stream, a high-performance red

Mazda drew up nearby. Three white men emerged from the vehicle, and two of them made straight for the river close to where we were sitting. The first greeted us in a frenetic manner, babbling and giggling, and asked whether it was safe to swim.

'Sure,' I said. 'Are you new here? Where are you from?'

'Peru,' he answered, with an unmistakable Latin accent, and hurled himself, clothes and all, into the water.

'He's mad,' the second individual commented, sitting down next to us. He was a lanky, big-boned, evil-looking character, with a Union Jack tattoo on his forearm. Like his friend, he was under the influence of alcohol and maybe drugs.

'Where are you from?' he asked us in an Irish accent.

Keeping my hand close to my pistol, tucked out of sight underneath my shirt, I replied that we worked in Swaziland. 'And what about you?' I added. 'From your accent and your fine tattoo I would guess you're an Ulsterman?'

'Proud of it,' he replied, 'but I had to leave quite a few years ago. Been working in Rhodesia and then I came to South Africa …' He looked back at the third man, who was off-loading a crate of beer from the boot of the car, and, lowering his voice, added: 'You could say I'm on police work.'

The third man arrived and was clearly keen to avoid interacting with us. The Ulsterman lumbered to his feet and, with bowed head and a respectful air, helped him to carry the beer down to the stream. We heard the Ulsterman ask if there was any dagga left for a smoke, and the so-called Peruvian was told to swim over to where they were sitting down.

The third man was clearly a South African. From his appearance, and from the deferential attitude shown to him, I judged him to be a security branch man and most probably the 'handler' of the other two. He was in his mid-thirties, dressed in a casually smart way, had a neatly trimmed moustache, an authoritative air about him and reminded me of Magnum, the popular TV investigator.

Our meeting occurred on the Sunday, the day after the slaying of our three comrades, and the day before we were alerted to their deaths and the sighting of the three white males outside the victims' house. When I received the report I instantly and intuitively thought of the three men at the picnic spot. The alcohol and drug binge fitted with what we knew about the 'spacing out' of hit-squads after such an operation. Had the South African handler been taking the two killers out to unwind after the operation the night before? Were they still around and waiting to strike again? Was the 'Peruvian' more likely a Portuguese mercenary from the former colonies?

I discussed this with Moses on the Monday morning. We decided to go out and investigate. We left his home just before noon, aiming to check every drinking spot between Manzini and Mbabane. We were on the lookout for the red Mazda and aimed to cover a score of watering holes on the 50-kilometre trip. I felt sure that if the trio had remained in Swaziland we would have a good chance of spotting them.

We drove past three possible venues in Manzini itself and one restaurant at Matsapa. At the foot of the Ezulweni Valley, before the posh hotels and restaurants, there is a dirt road branching off to an hotel by the Mantenga Falls. We had a quick look at the car park but there was no sight of the red Mazda. As we were driving back to the main road it materialised around a bend, heading for the hotel. Sure enough, 'Magnum' was at the wheel, the Ulsterman was at his side and a third figure, probably the 'Peruvian', was in the back seat.

'That's 'em,' I told Moses, turning the car about as soon as they were out of sight. When we reached the hotel, the red Mazda was in the car park. We decided Moses would go in alone since they would recognise me from the picnic spot and might get suspicious. I parked out of sight and waited. After some time the three drove by in the Mazda and Moses joined me. We followed their dust trail to the main road and saw them turn left up the valley.

'Christ!' Moses exclaimed, 'what a wild bunch. I came across them at the hotel bar. You're dead right about the big Irishman. What an evil character! What foul mouths he and that smaller fellow have! Everything was "effing" this and "effing" that. The smaller guy was definitely doped to the eyeballs and has a Portuguese accent all right. You could've cut the atmosphere with a knife in there. They were insulting the black staff, who were petrified.'

'What about Magnum?' I enquired.

'Hardly opened his mouth. They refer to him as "Jannie", so he's a Boer all right. He just kept paying for the drinks. Definitely the handler.'

The Mazda sped past the Holiday Inn complex of hotels and began climbing the long hill up to Mbabane. It soon pulled off, however, driving into a motel. We knew there was a bar in the place, and hung back giving the trio enough time to get inside. There was no sight of the Mazda outside the bar, so I drove slowly around the complex, scanning the rows of motel rooms for it. We spotted it outside one of the rooms, with its doors open. I parked in an adjacent row and we could see the Irishman and Peruvian flopped out on their beds.

'Magnum' walked out to the car, closed the doors, and went back into the next-door room.

'Sitting ducks,' Moses muttered, with a nod and a wink. He was all for taking them out then and there.

'No. I'll have to speak to the command here,' I answered. 'This is their turf.'

At a meeting that night with Thami, Gebhuza, Ebe and a comrade called

Thomas who was in charge of intelligence, I gave a report about the three men and we discussed what to do. Thomas had a great deal of information about enemy hit-squads in Swaziland and was able to confirm that the team responsible for the Mbabane slayings was still believed to be in the country. What was more, there was a suggestion that British and Portuguese hit-men were involved. He had a contact working at the motel who would be able to carry out some checks on the men for us. I put forward Moses' line and argued that we should prepare to eliminate the trio.

While we could not be sure they were the same group that murdered our three people on the Saturday night, they certainly fitted into the category of hit-squad. We knew the enemy was preparing further strikes against us, and we now needed to destabilise them. At the least we should seize the trio and question them.

In war it is necessary to act when the opportunity presents itself. We waited for several days while the contact at the hotel obtained bits and pieces of information, all reinforcing the strong suspicions we had of the trio. Most damning of all was a reported meeting they had with a known South African agent. When we finally broke into their motel room, they had vanished.

It was years later, when the scandal of hit-squads was publicised, that I recognised 'Magnum' from a newspaper photograph – the notorious Eugene de Kock, Vlakplaas commander, responsible for gruesome slayings and dubbed 'Prime Evil' by journalists.

The incident of the three men had been a revealing one for me. I found myself on the spot, ready to pronounce on their fate, and to this day feel we should have acted in time. But how does one feel about having to take life? I had never had the slightest doubt that our armed struggle was a defensive measure against the violence of the government. We were forced to supplement mass political struggle by armed action because all avenues of democratic advance had been closed. Oliver Tambo had expressed this succinctly in many an interview: 'There would be no violence at all if we did not have the violence of the apartheid system.'

What of my personal feelings? Up until then I had been engaged in some brief exchanges of gunfire against barely visible foes in Angola or on the South African border. Once, on the wrong side of the fence, a voice had rung out: '*Staan vas!* (Stand still!) My companion and I had instinctively wheeled around, firing from the hip, seen a figure fall, and ran for our lives as bullets whizzed about us. Those were clearly cases of kill or be killed. I learnt that there is no difference between the reflex action of shoot or be shot at in a hot situation, and the more deliberate decision-making required in a council of war. The thought process is simply more prolonged. In my experience none on our side, whether planners or implementers, had any problems of conscience in over 30 years of armed struggle. There has been regret at the loss of civilian lives which, in fact, was minimal. We fought a just war and took decisions on the basis of principle and morality.

That is what, historically, has always distinguished the freedom fighter from the person who serves an unjust cause. Although war is about killing, the logical development, when it is waged by 'those who make peaceful change impossible', is murder and massacre. The government had gone well beyond the bounds and sanctioned the use of cold-blooded murder to uphold apartheid against military and civilian opponents alike. The combatant with an AK-47 and the academic with a pen, the sympathiser and the refugee, the woman and the child, were all regarded as the same enemy. For instance, in the case of the Cradock schoolteacher, Matthew Goniwe, an official instruction was issued by the military brass to 'permanently remove him from society'. Murder and massacre throughout the whole of South Africa and beyond had become the norm for the forces defending apartheid.

Within the next few months we were hit hard by those forces. I worked closely with Thomas, whose real name was Sydney Mbisi. He was a reliable and intelligent individual who had been Oliver Tambo's bodyguard, and he impressed me. Thomas was receiving information from contacts within the enemy's security forces. Just before I departed for Lusaka, he reported that his chief contact was coming to Swaziland on holiday.

'On holiday?' I asked in surprise. 'But Pretoria has just passed a State of Emergency. The police can't cope with the critical situation. How can they allow an important officer to take holiday leave?' It made me very suspicious. I urged Thomas to take care.

He was abducted within a few weeks, in July, when the contact was used to lure him into an ambush. He was detained by the police in South Africa and released without charge the following year. Soon afterwards, he was shot dead outside his home in Soweto by mysterious gunmen.

A second abduction took place soon after Thomas's initial disappearance. Glory Sedebe (alias September) was the intelligence chief in the Transvaal machinery. I had known him for some time but was never too sure of him, owing to his suspect nerve. Some comrades thought he was a coward. There was strong suspicion that he had suffered from a self-inflicted wound at the time of the Matola raid. He reminded me of Bruno Mtolo, the traitor from the Durban sabotage days, and it gave me an uneasy feeling about him.

He had been arrested by the Swazis, and then kidnapped by South African agents from the Manzini police cells, with the connivance of one of the local officers. It is clear that he agreed to work with his abductors, and he became an infamous 'turned' guerrilla. This happened rapidly. Within days of his abduction in August, three of his colleagues were shot dead by South African police at a border crossing-point near Piet Retief.

September had known of the intended crossing. Among those who fell was Tolman Bam, a conscientious young man, whom I had brought with me from Angola to Maputo and the Front Line.

September was again active with the abduction squads in December 1986. Ebe was kidnapped from his hide-away in Pine Valley on 15 December 1986, when gunmen broke into the house while he was watching television. Abducted at the same time was a young Swiss couple whose 'crime' was nothing more than social links with ANC people. Also seized was an old ANC stalwart who had refugee status in Swaziland, Shadrack Mapamulo.

Shadrack, like Ebrahim, had been one of my MK comrades in Durban in the 1960s. He had served a 15-year sentence on Robben Island and joined us in Swaziland in 1980. He was a polite, soft-spoken and considerate person with a placid nature. He had been a factory worker and trade unionist and was pleased to learn, when we first met in exile, that the ANC had declared 1980 'The Year of the Worker'.

He was astonished when I added that the 1980s should be declared 'The Decade of the Worker' if we wanted to be liberated by 1990. 'But surely it's not going to take that long?' he objected. Being in exile since 1963 had led me to adopt a patient approach in such conversations and I responded, 'Shadrack, I'm not prepared to guess when freedom will come. All I'm prepared to say is that on 1 January, in the year 2000, I will meet you outside the Durban City Hall at noon and take you out to lunch.' Tragically the promise was impossible to keep. When they came to Shadrack's small Matsapa flat in the middle of the night his wife, a nursing sister, was on duty at the local hospital. He locked his two children in one of the rooms and attempted to barricade the front door. Shots were fired by the abductors who carried him, wounded, to a waiting vehicle. He bled to death on the way to the border and his body was abandoned at the fence.

December 1986 was a particularly tragic month for us. In Maseru, a hit-squad using silencers murdered seven of our people in an attack on two houses. Among those killed were two of my Angolan students, Nonkosi Mini, alias Mary, and Lulamile Dantile, alias Morris. Nonkosi, the daughter of the executed hero Vuyisile Mini, had survived the Novo Catengue bombing. Morris was found dead, seated in a car, a bullet through his head. Also executed in cold blood were Leon Myers, an MK operative, and his wife, Jackie Quinn. They were found in their house, having apparently opened the door to someone they must have known and trusted. Their baby was found alive, clutching its mother. Once again it was a clear case of an infiltrator having betrayed them all.

I was in Lusaka when all this news came through. I thought back to my last conversation with the comrades in Swaziland at the end of June and how I had urged a pre-emptive measure against 'Magnum' and his friends. I wondered how Moses was feeling about these latest events in his 'Disneyland', especially the kidnapping of Ebrahim, whom he had got to know very well after helping him cross the border.

Years later, while writing this book, I received a letter from my old friend Moses who was back in Britain with his family:

> *There are constant reminders of you in our humdrum daily existence. Yesterday the newspapers announced that 'Roy of the Rovers' was finally laid to rest. We thought that would have been a suitable topic of conversation in days gone by – the competing influences of USA versus UK comic characters on white South African culture. Aaron first heard of Desperate Dan, Dennis the Menace and all their friends during a game of Trivial Pursuit at the safe house on the hill. You will be flattered to know that every time we see Desperate Dan on the [post office's] first class greetings stamp, we are reminded of you.*

Moses was the code name of Michael Stephens from Scotland, who sadly died some years later in Britain after a short illness, survived by his wife June and daughter Monica.

FIFTEEN

MK's 25th ANNIVERSARY

Angola and the Front Line
1985–87

THE GOVERNMENT'S POLICY OF USING brute force to quell resistance was a failure. The ANC declared 1986, the 25th anniversary of MK, as the 'Year of Umkhonto we Sizwe'. The slogan 'Every patriot a combatant! Every combatant a patriot!' reflected the combination of mass struggle and armed action. The State of Emergency, assassination of activists, shooting of protesters, raids into neighbouring states and destabilisation of the region could not quell the wave of resistance, nor solve the contradictions inherent in apartheid.

We were recording over 150 operations by MK combatants annually. There were operations that went unrecorded because we were out of touch with many units. The regime failed to remove our undercover structures from any of the forward areas, including Mozambique and Swaziland. Killer raids into Lesotho failed to eliminate the ANC presence there. In response, in January 1986, South Africa blockaded the landlocked country and instigated a military coup against the Prime Minister, Leabua Jonathan. The deportation to East Africa and Zambia of scores of our people followed.

Despite the sealing of borders, the flow of young recruits into MK camps continued. Significantly, however, a greater number were being trained inside the country. Apartheid spokespersons attempted to scoff at the achievements of the armed struggle, claiming we could never get beyond low-level armed propaganda actions. What they sought to conceal was that we were in fact succeeding in our main objective of locating armed resistance amongst the mass of our people (although our success was more with urban rather than rural inhabitants). For every one operation launched by MK combatants, there were scores carried out by a mobilised population. The degree of resistance forced the government to admit that, between September 1984 and April 1986, over 800 policemen's homes were attacked and extensively damaged.

The popularity of the ANC, MK and the SACP was at an all-time high and the funerals of activists like Matthew Goniwe, regarded as heroes fallen in battle, were turned into victory celebrations. The banners of the outlawed organisations were defiantly on display. Priests were prepared to march behind the red flag of the Communist Party as well as the banners of the ANC. Vast crowds of *toyi-toyiing* youth praised the deeds of Umkhonto we Sizwe. The apartheid regime, lacking legitimacy among black South Africans, was palpably losing its grip on the country.

In fact, the government's strategy of brute force to quell resistance had failed. So too had their constitutional adaptations, which established a tri-cameral parliamentary system, of separate White, Coloured and Indian chambers. This racist system lacked all legitimacy and was totally discredited. But we did not realise the extent of the regime's crisis. At a time when the position of P.W. Botha and his so-called securocrats – the influential security establishment – appeared unassailable, doubts about preserving the system were growing. This started within the ranks of the ultra-secret Afrikaner Broederbond, the elite circle of Afrikaners that provided the intellectual leadership for apartheid. Niel Barnard, head of apartheid National Intelligence and Kobie Coetsee, government minister, began secret talks with Nelson Mandela in prison, about possible negotiations. Waging the armed struggle from exile had been extremely difficult. Ours was a protracted struggle, and simply keeping the ANC intact had been a considerable achievement. The role of Oliver Tambo was of singular importance. He led by example, through sheer hard work, self-sacrifice and above all his integrity. He was respected and loved by all.

Our country lacked favourable terrain in which to develop guerrilla struggle. Our combatants had to operate in small units, of twos and threes. Our enemy was powerful, had considerable resources, a well-trained army of half-a-million, and a social base of five million well-armed whites to rely on. With a sophisticated communication system, the security forces could reach any part of the country in a short time. They tightly controlled the farm labourers and rural population, making our attempts to link with them very difficult. And everywhere they had an army of informers.

Our resources were minuscule compared to apartheid South Africa. We operated out of shoe-box-sized offices, and from distant guerrilla camps. Even our leaders lacked administrative training and experience. We had to compensate for our limitations through the commitment of our members and the massive support of our people, backed by international solidarity. Yet MK operations were increasing all the time and the mass struggle was rising in intensity.

In December many of our leaders gathered in Angola to participate in the 25th anniversary celebrations of Umkhonto we Sizwe. Together with Johnny

Makhathini, the ANC's representative at the United Nations, who had guarded Rowley Arenstein with me back in Durban in 1961, I was allocated to Pango camp, renamed the David Rabkin Training Centre.

It was only the second time we had been together in almost a quarter of a century. We had organised a street protest in Durban on the eve of Johnny's departure from the country in 1962, and in all those years he had represented the ANC internationally. As a result of my undercover role, our paths had hardly crossed. Now we were both dressed in military uniform, certainly much thicker around the waist with the passing years, and it was a pleasure introducing him to camp life.

As the midnight hour passed, we greeted 16 December by firing tracer bullets, flares and rockets into the night sky. From Quibaxe, 15 kilometres away, came a similar response. It was quite a fireworks display and Johnny had the unaccustomed joy of blazing away with an AK-47.

Pango had become our main camp in the Quibaxe area. It was filled with young recruits from the township uprisings which continued to engulf South Africa. Many were in their late teens. They were enthusiastic and militant. Johnny was fascinated by their accounts of the street fighting at home in which Molotov cocktails and stones were used against the firepower and armoured vehicles of the security forces. At the same time he was not in agreement with some of the methods of 'rough justice' being used against collaborators. One of these involved placing a tyre filled with petrol around a victim's neck and setting it alight. It was called 'the necklace'.

While understanding the frustration and anger of the people, particularly with those seen as traitors and 'sellouts', Tambo and the ANC leadership unreservedly condemned the practice of 'necklacing'. Johnny argued with the youngsters about its cruelty and was surprised to find how vigorously they defended it.

'Give us guns and we will eliminate the *izimpimpi* [informers] nice and cleanly,' one young girl who was called Portia (Phila Ndwandwe) responded at our table during the celebratory lunch. Not quite 18 years old, she had impressed us that morning by delivering a stirring speech on behalf of the trainees. 'Yes, comrade Makhathini, necklacing is cruel, but it's helped us put the traitors to flight and turned the townships into no-go areas. What the *izimpimpi* have done to the people is even more gruesome.'

Johnny relied on the moral argument but failed to convince the young comrades. His intelligence, warmth and decency, which were general qualities of the ANC leadership throughout the decades, and which had impressed the international community, could make no headway in this situation.

I had come to know the new generation pretty well, both from the camps and the Front Line, where I had been engaged in some tough discussion about so-called 'hard' and 'soft' targets. I knew that one had to get away from simply the moral argument, which was regarded as academic by those who were daily on the receiving end of bloodshed and betrayal.

'The trouble with necklacing,' I began, 'is in its spontaneity and facelessness. Can you really be certain who has shouted out: "That one is an *impimpi!*"? It could be an agent provocateur who levels the accusation. It means that necklacing can easily become a method used by the security forces to sow confusion. It is the same with attacks on civilian or "soft" targets. It gives the enemy opportunity to discredit us. That's why we stress the need for disciplined operations, against clearly defined targets.'

Johnny applauded my contribution. The young girl remained sceptical. My concern proved prophetic. Especially after 1990, indiscriminate acts of terror by racist provocateurs increased.

Pango had been the scene of a vicious mutiny in May 1984. At dawn on 16 December, we held a solemn ceremony at the graves of eight comrades who had fallen during the mutiny. At the root of the sole mutiny in MK's history was the problem which had confronted us from the time of our first training camps. Frustration with the long delay in returning home, together with manipulation by enemy agents, could produce a volatile situation. I had seen this on a small scale in Quibaxe in 1977 and only learnt from others of the events that took place in Angola in 1983–4, while I was in Swaziland.

In fact, there had been a general deterioration in the running of our camps from 1980. The transfer of many top cadres to the forward areas left younger, inexperienced people in command. Without senior leaders to supervise them, they lapsed into negative practices. A gulf developed between administration and the rest. Some commanders began the unacceptable practice of allocating for themselves the best supplies, while the rank and file went short. Authoritarianism flourished, and with it excessive punishment and the use of informants. The security department acquired the name 'Mbokodo', meaning grinding stone, and became extremely unpopular. Mzwai Piliso had to spend more time in Lusaka. It was felt that some in the leadership relied too much on the reports of commanders. As it turned out, some of these were enemy agents, like Kenneth Mahamba, who became commander of Quibaxe for a while. The deteriorating security situation accentuated problems.

Nomava Shangase, the rotund and cheerful doctor at Quibaxe, died when the driver of the truck she was travelling in lost control and it careered over a precipice. The driver survived by jumping to safety. I thought of Sinatla when I learnt there were suspicions that there had been tampering with the driving mechanism.

The standard of training dropped, with many of the instructors inadequately prepared by our own people in Angola. The best cadres were being sent straight home, directly from training abroad.

I had heard, with regret, that a macho tendency had reappeared in the training. We had adopted many ZIPRA (ZAPU's guerrilla army) practices, which glorified lengthy *toyi-toyiing*, with full pack and weapons, and rigorous survival-training in the bush.

By 1986, with a mature command in place, and Chris Hani as commissar, the situation changed for the better.

The background to the mutiny was the growing security threat posed by South African-backed Unita forces. Jonas Savimbi's units had been spreading throughout the countryside from his Jamba stronghold in the south-east. By then, our main training base had been established at Malanje, over 500 kilometres east of Luanda. The area, which we termed the 'eastern front', had come under severe pressure from roving Unita bands. A combined 1000-strong detachment of MK and FAPLA (Armed Forces of the People of Angola) was formed to flush out the bandits. MK's popular and highly respected Regional Commander, Timothy Mokoena, was Chief of Staff of this force, which included some 400 MK combatants who had completed training. At first our cadres were keenly motivated by the need to keep our supply lines open, secure the area for the Angolan people, and gain battlefield experience. They acquitted themselves very well, inflicting heavy losses on Unita in several engagements and flushing them out of the area.

By the end of the year, the enemy had been driven south from Malanje, across the Kwanza River. Here the terrain suited the insurgents. They had developed bases over the years in this area. When our forces attempted to pursue Unita across the Kwanza, they fell into several ambushes. Many FAPLA and nine MK soldiers died in these engagements.

An indication that agents were beginning to exploit the situation was evident when Radio South Africa, the SABC's external service to Africa, began prematurely referring to a mutiny in MK's ranks.

The objective of sweeping Unita out of the area had been achieved, however, and it was agreed that MK would revert to a defensive role. This meant the majority of cadres would return to our camps.

This arrangement did not suit many of those who had begun to voice dissatisfaction. Without exception, these were cadres who were tired of camp life. Among them were many who had been deployed in the Frontline areas but had been sent back to the 'rear', as Angola was called, because of indiscipline or failure in their missions.

'Let's fight our way south into Namibia and then South Africa,' was one naive but popular cry. Others suggested they find the means to get to Luanda and demand of the leaders that they be sent home to fight. A good half of the MK contingent began exhibiting signs of defiance and refused to obey commands. They began displaying an attitude of non-cooperation by randomly firing their weapons into the air. The Kimbundu name 'Mkatashini', meaning 'a tired soldier', came to characterise their mutinous conduct.

By the beginning of 1984, the disaffected troops had commandeered trucks to travel to Luanda and put their demands to the leadership. They took control of a transit base outside the capital at Viana, where they seized weapons and elected a Committee of Ten to negotiate on their behalf.

Chris Hani entered the Viana camp unarmed and, in an impassioned speech, implored the mutineers to surrender. He was unsuccessful. In the end, the Angolan Presidential Guard stormed the camp and disarmed the occupants. About 30 ringleaders were held at Luanda prison for investigation. Half spent 13 months in prison before being released. The rest were transferred to the Security Department's detention centre at Quatro near Quibaxe.

By March 1984, approximately 300 mutineers were sent to Pango, which had become a transit camp. Pango was cleared of all cadres to make way for the new arrivals. They were placed under the charge of a small administration and security group. The command had a security unit of a dozen comrades. The leadership, in a spirit of reconciliation, decided to deal leniently with the mutineers, hoping to rehabilitate them.

There was a dangerous element within the Pango group, however, which simply gave the impression of regretting their actions. On 14 May they made their move and overran the camp.

There was a furious battle when they assaulted the dugouts where the administration slept. The logistics chief died in the battle and the commissar staggered off into the bush, severely wounded. The mutineers found him in the bush the next day. He had been shot in the stomach and pleaded for water. One of the mutineers, Mgedeze, responded by shooting him in the head.

The mutineers killed eight comrades, including the commissar, in their seizure of the camp and immediately executed six of their own number who refused to join the uprising.

Timothy Mokoena assembled a crack force and within days recaptured the camp. Fifteen mutineers and one of Timothy's men died in the battle. A tribunal was set up to try the ringleaders. Of those found guilty, seven were immediately executed by firing squad on the sports field at Pango.

Mgedeze, who had murdered the commissar in cold blood, managed to flee with over 100 others during the battle to retake Pango. They were gradually rounded up in the bush and surrounding villages where they sought to hide.

Mgedeze, petrified of being captured, committed suicide, using the murdered commissar's pistol.

By December 1986, Pango had been restored to its role as a training base for short-term courses. Quibaxe had become a transit camp, and Johnny Makhathini and I drove in convoy along the bumpy roads to join ANC leaders Gertrude Shope and Thomas Nkobi in a 16 December rally there. There had been a great deal of construction at the camp since the early days. A concert was performed on an impressive stage. Morale everywhere was high and MK had recovered well from the 1984 mutiny. Movement of cadres home had been stepped up, owing to the growing capability of the underground.

About 80 detainees were being kept at a nearby detention centre called 'Camp 32' or 'Quatro'. The latter name is the Portuguese word for 'four'. 'Number Four' was the term for the old central prison in Johannesburg and so its Portuguese equivalent became the name for the ANC's detention centre in Angola. It had been converted from plantation buildings into a detention centre by our Security Department in 1979. Even I, as Regional Commissar, was not then aware of its existence.

Becoming Head of Military Intelligence had given me the possibility of visiting the place whose inmates remained under the jurisdiction of the Security Department in Lusaka. I had been there with Chris Hani on at least two occasions. In the company of the three senior leaders I drove there as part of the December 16th activities. Although it was a mere three kilometres through thick bush from Quibaxe camp, the journey by vehicle was 20 kilometres along a winding dirt track.

Chris Hani was there ahead of us. He had been appointed to officiate at Quatro over the days of celebration. He had intervened to stop the Pango executions because he abhorred capital punishment. He always preferred to take a conciliatory approach to questions of indiscipline and tended to give the accused the benefit of the doubt. By nature he was a soft-hearted individual but was undoubtedly also influenced by his own personal experience. In1969, after serving two years' imprisonment in Botswana in the wake of the Wankie battles, he had been subjected to disciplinary proceedings in Lusaka. This arose out of his public criticism of organisational shortcomings and the conduct of some leaders. He was vindicated by the decisions of the Morogoro Conference later that year.

The question about how to contain and punish enemy agents had become a serious problem by the 1980s. Many MK cadres had a similar attitude to the people at home. Spies and traitors did not deserve to live. The leadership did not share this view and had always striven to rehabilitate those elements. As the struggle intensified, however, and enemy agents became more numerous and dangerous, the complexities increased.

The Security Department under Mzwai Piliso had been set up to screen the new recruits and weed out the infiltrators. They saw themselves as defenders of the organisation. There had been shocks in 1981, particularly in Lusaka, when an enemy network was uncovered, revealing that many seemingly bright and promising cadres were in fact successful infiltrators.

At first these agents were accommodated in the jails of the host country. As the number of proven and suspect agents mounted, it became difficult to cope. Quatro was opened in order to process those who were suspect and rehabilitate those who were guilty. Some among us argued that spies should simply be deported to other African or Western countries. The problem was that they acquired information useful to the enemy and could be redeployed.

The ANC was not a government. We lacked resources, the mature personnel and means to thoroughly investigate those under suspicion. The process of handling suspects proved a particular problem due to the vast distance from home and lack of internal structures capable of checking on individuals' stories. The Security Department could not adequately deal with the workload and consequently the number of cases mounted. In some instances those under suspicion were held for several years. Circumstantially there might have been strong suspicions about the individual but factual proof was often lacking. In this situation, the senior leadership clearly and painfully opted for caution. My understanding was that the heavy responsibility and dangerous consequences of error meant they could not take a chance. We were not running an election campaign in Hampshire or Kent but a struggle against a ruthless enemy who was determined to wipe us out.

Later, when all inmates had been released, most returning to South Africa, many alleged they were ill-treated and beaten. While there have been exaggerations, particularly by those closely involved with state security, the ANC has conceded that abuses did take place. At no stage, however, were such allegations directly raised with the leadership at the time. Perhaps those of us who found time to visit Quatro were naive to believe that all of the warders or security officers were going to behave correctly when news of apartheid atrocities reached them. It is regrettable that inhumane treatment took place in the name of the ANC, even though this was infinitesimal when compared to the crimes of apartheid.

There were many debates within the leadership on the vexed issue of the detentions. A desire for leniency was hamstrung by the cycle of assassinations and massacres we faced, both within South Africa and in the neighbouring states. James Stuart, an NEC member, had headed a commission investigating the situation and strongly recommended reforms. These recommendations and our other demands were not implemented, however, owing to problems of accommodation and the constraints leadership felt about the hazards of releasing individuals who could harm our organisation and people.

One such individual was Robert de Souza, who had been studying in the USA. He was a confessed enemy agent who was claiming that one of my operatives in Harare was a spy. De Souza had won the approval of ANC leaders in the USA, including Johnny Makhathini, when he led a hunger strike at his college against investments in South Africa. He visited South Africa during his vacations and, en route, had met up with Chris Hani in Harare. The latter gave him an information-gathering task to perform but De Souza was actually part of a mission to assassinate Hani. De Souza, however, slipped up and landed in ANC custody instead.

His confession made fascinating reading. He told how he had been recruited by the security police and assisted in obtaining a scholarship to the States. He gave information about his apartheid handlers in the USA and how he had compiled information about the ANC presence and anti-apartheid activists in that country. Under the direction of his handlers, he had become involved in protest activities, but they were alarmed when his hunger strike made too positive an impact and had to restrain him. During one vacation, he had worked voluntarily in the London ANC office, making photocopies of every fax that passed through his hands. As is usual in such de-briefs, he gave a list of persons he either claimed to know were Pretoria agents or individuals he suspected.

I met him in an interview room in Quatro with his case handler present. Where investigations of a detainee related to operatives in the army or political structures, it was sometimes possible to gain access. The Security Department was often reluctant to allow this because 'outside' interference could be detrimental to their ongoing enquiries. Joe Nhlanhla, who had taken over security responsibilities from Mzwai Piliso, had informed me in Lusaka of De Souza's allegations and agreed that I should have a hand in de-briefing him.

De Souza was an anxious individual, wordy in his explanations, with a desperate expression in his dark eyes. He stood uneasily before me, in khaki shirt and shorts. I called for a chair so that he could sit down.

I got him to take me through his entire story, from recruitment to detention as a spy, without showing my overriding interest. We came back to his allegations about his undercover contact in Harare. I placed a number of photographs of various women, including the alleged enemy agent, on a table and asked if he could identify anyone. Sure enough, he identified the MK operative Angela Brown as an enemy agent. This was a tried and trusted operative of Rashid's whose real name was Louise Colvin. 'How did you come to know that this woman is working for Pretoria?' I asked.

187

'My handler told me that if I ever got into problems with Zimbabwe security I should contact her,' he replied.

'How would you contact her?'

'I could phone her or just go to her house.'

'Any passwords or code terms for the introduction?' He paused and his eyes wandered and he finally said:

'Well no. I would just introduce myself and she would know about me.'

The room was quiet and De Souza watched anxiously as I sat in silence for a while.

'You know what I find odd?' I finally announced. 'Your handler is normally very professional. We know a lot about him. Yet he reveals the identities of two important operatives to each other. Rules of security for the enemy, as for our side, require a cut-out procedure in such a situation. In his shoes, I would have provided you with a safe phone number and a way of calling up a blind meeting if you needed assistance. Well, I suppose the security police must be slipping up ...'

I dismissed De Souza, reminding him that it was only honesty on his part that could help him. Afterwards I talked with Chris, telling him that I was unimpressed with the allegation. Within an hour, De Souza was requesting to see me again.

'I lied about that woman,' he declared. 'I implicated her and a lot of those people in America because my interrogators here kept demanding the names of other agents. They said I would never get out of here unless I identified others, and that I must provide names of people working for the Boers or the CIA.'

'Were you beaten at all?' I enquired.

'No, but I was threatened. I was told that unless I co-operated I would die because a Boer spy didn't deserve to live.' He spoke in a rush of words, his eyes wide with fear, and he continued: 'Shooting takes place at any time here. We hear it at night and we're told that agents have been executed.'

It was a relief to clear the female operative in Harare, whom De Souza had been prepared to consign to a fate similar to his. I had always stressed that confessions obtained under duress could not be relied upon. Whatever might be thought about interrogation methods in communist countries, I found that Soviet and East German training emphasised the need to depend on brain work and not beatings to arrive at the truth. Detainees, however, were in the hands of young and inexperienced cadres, who were susceptible to being swayed by circumstance. Many individuals handed to them were already implicated in heinous crimes, including the rape and murder of local peasant women and massacres at home.

What the ANC lacked was a control procedure, capable of preventing personal abuses. The lack of adequate facilities, inexperience in coping with the problem, the geographical dispersal of leadership and long lines of communications, all within the context of a life-and-death struggle, led to the abuses that took place.

It might sound easy to suggest, as I have, that a benevolent approach could work. The argument for tolerance has not been made easier by the subsequent behaviour of some of the former ANC detainees. I believe that a benevolent approach could have worked, but those dealing with the detainees might disagree. A newspaper reported that De Souza shot his wife and friend soon after returning home in 1990 when the ANC freed the Quatro detainees. Some resumed their activities for the security police on their return.

Another detainee I was interested in seeing was a self-confessed lieutenant in the Security Police, 26-year-old Olivia Forsyth. As an undercover operative, with a British passport, she had infiltrated student circles in South Africa, betraying the trust of scores of her anti-apartheid friends. At the end of 1985, her cover intact, she appeared in Harare as a research journalist for a bogus British company.

Her initial contact with ANC members, Howard Barrell and Garth Strachan, appeared to be moving according to plan. She was clearly shaken, however, when she was interviewed by the ANC's chief representative, Reddy Mazimba, a shrewd, no-nonsense member of the Security Department. His suspicions were aroused when she applied to attend an ANC conference in Tanzania. Clearly rattled by the questions he posed, and possibly fearing impending arrest by the tough Zimbabwean Security Branch, she quickly sought out Garth Strachan and confessed to him. She explained that her mission was to infiltrate the ANC, but claimed that her experience in student politics had brought her to the point of genuinely desiring to join the organisation. She was sent to Lusaka to report to Mzwai Piliso, at that time still the head of Security and Intelligence. She wanted to operate as a double agent.

Mzwai brought me in on some of the discussions with Lieutenant Forsyth. I had received Garth's reports about her from the time she first made contact. Before she confessed to him, we discovered that the company she claimed to represent was phony and that there were suspicions about her in student circles.

We sat under an umbrella by the side of a pool at a motel outside Lusaka where she was being accommodated. An attractive brunette, nervously puffing away at a cigarette, the police lieutenant peered at us from behind fashionable sunglasses. Apart from the chain smoking, she maintained a tight control of her nerves as she attempted to convince Mzwai and me that she was genuinely pro-ANC. The self-control she maintained produced a taut expression and excluded passion. In this respect she reminded me exactly of Craig Williamson's emotionless impersonation of a 'leftist' which, in short, was unconvincing. She struck me as being equally cold and calculating.

I asked her to remove her sunglasses, which she did with slow deliberation, as though she was being unmasked. She blinked in the harsh sunlight and looked at me with impassive eyes, set in a blank face.

'So how do you propose to play this double act?' I asked her.

She spoke in low, measured tones and recommended we send her for training to East Germany or the Soviet Union so as to impress her superiors, and then place her in an important sounding position in Lusaka. 'Perhaps ...' she volunteered, drawing coolly on the cigarette, 'given my journalistic background, Thabo Mbeki's information and publicity department?' She would be well placed to provide Pretoria with any disinformation we wanted.

She had nerve all right but her naivety astonished me. There was no question of us trusting her. Mzwai decided to send her back to South Africa on an information-gathering task. The mission would show how useful she could be. Her handlers promptly threw her back at us. I was not in Lusaka when she returned some days later. She explained that her chiefs were so keen to persevere with the infiltration attempt that they had fabricated a story that she was being sought by the police and had to skip the country. I had been encouraging Mzwai to risk using her in a double-agent role, so as to learn more about our rather faceless adversary in Pretoria. Mzwai was not up to playing such games, which take up a lot of precious time. After consultation with his department, he decided to send her to Quatro.

She had lost weight and the khaki uniform was too big for her. She was pale, but the expressionless face I had seen in Lusaka was softer and more relaxed. I met her with Chris Hani and she had no major complaints about her conditions. She had written a poem about an MK woman, Marion Sparg, who had been sentenced to 25 years' imprisonment in South Africa for planting bombs in police stations. It was a sensitive and well-written poem.

We discussed her situation and she maintained that she was genuine in her change of allegiance and that she could still work for us back home.

She shared a large cell with six other female detainees – one a mutineer who had been particularly cruel, and the rest enemy agents. We made a strong representation in Lusaka, first getting the support of Joe Modise and Military HQ, that the women at least should be removed from Quatro. The leadership agreed and all, including Olivia Forsyth, were transferred to safe houses in Luanda.

SIXTEEN

TURNING POINT

Angola, Zambia, Botswana, Cuba
1988–89

THOSE YEARS IN THE FRONT LINE, with an AK-47 always under the bed and regular changes of address to keep one step ahead of death, were indeed Desperate Dan stuff, as Michael Stephens had put it. The following years proved as hectic and tumultuous.

As Chief of Military Intelligence, I had created a Central Staff in Lusaka. It was composed of a talented group of young men and women who had recently trained in the Soviet Union and Cuba, specialising in army intelligence courses. Some had served in MK combat units, and others were former conscripts from the South African Defence Force. The head of our data-processing group, a gentle and lucid young man called Bill Anderson, had served with the South African army in Namibia and Angola in 1975–6. As a 21-year-old conscript, he witnessed the systematic torture committed by the South Africans against the Namibian civilian population at a time when guerrilla activity was growing. Immediately his tour of duty was over, and prior to his next call-up, he left South Africa for England where he exposed the SADF's atrocities in Namibia to the *Guardian*.

Posing as the director of an agricultural research project, I rented a house off a quiet Lusaka road for Bill's unit. We were ready at a moment's notice to switch wall charts for rural Zambian scenes, should the landlord arrive for a visit. Strict security was maintained at the location, which was known only to Joe Modise and Chris Hani.

The greatest proportion of intelligence comes from published material. Since South Africa is a modern, industrial country, we were able to acquire information covering almost its entire infrastructure. This included everything from road, rail and power networks to national key points and strategic objects. Pretoria's predilection for propaganda provided rich pickings from a range of

191

military and police literature. One of our most important tools was the complete breakdown of the SADF's Battle Order provided by Rocklyn Williams working at Voortrekkerhoogte. This deals with the disposition of units, and from this starting point – reinforced by agents on the ground – we sought to keep track of where the enemy forces had been, where they were at present, and where they were going to next.

The SADF, as a largely citizen conscript force of the white population, relied on a call-up system of its trained contingent. Many of these part-time soldiers were disenchanted with defending apartheid and we were making contact with them. We established a communication system, involving telephone-answering machines, many in quiet English locations, and simple codes for contacts to report promptly on their call-up and movement.

We had maps, photographs and diagrams of virtually all the SADF's bases. Rocky had even succeeded in lifting large-scale wall charts from the operations rooms at Voortrekkerhoogte and the Army Battle School at Lohatla in the northern Cape.

Another major prize was a complete set of the country's topographical maps in large scale. Jack Hodgson and Eleanor had started buying these in the 1960s through Stanfords in London. We had succeeded in keeping them reasonably up to date. For economic and security reasons, many white-owned farms in the north-west Transvaal border region were unoccupied. Bill Anderson hit on the idea of plotting these farms on our maps.

The first step to locating unoccupied farms was the current telephone directory. Every entry in the phone books for the rural areas along the borders which had a farm name as an address was entered on an index card. The second step was locating these farms on our maps. Thousands of index cards were shuffled and reshuffled until we believed we had located every farm with a current phone number.

Our theory was that farms without telephones were unoccupied, and we sought to verify this. We subscribed to the *Farmer's Weekly* and local country newspapers, scanning the ads for farms for sale. We sent operatives driving and hiking in these areas. They posed as would-be purchasers, gathering information and taking photographs and filming the landscape. After months of diligent work, Bill and his team produced a mapping system with infiltration routes across the borders, which made the optimum use of uninhabited farms and favourable terrain. We sent in reconnaissance units along these routes and discovered that it was possible virtually to reach Pretoria from Botswana by sticking to the bush.

Apart from opening up many more routes, this discovery enabled us to make a conceptual leap. Many casualties took place near the most convenient border crossing-points, at taxi and bus ranks, or when using transport for pick-ups to reach the urban strongholds. We urged that wherever possible infiltration should be on foot, and that comrades should hike through the bush for at least three nights, resting by day unless they were going to base in the countryside. Such an approach would enable us to increase the rate of infiltration and, possibly for the first time in 25 years, solve the problem of trained cadres vegetating for long periods in the camps and transit houses.

The unrest at home continued unabated. Military HQ had formulated an infiltration programme based on our information, called 'Operation Zikomo'. The word means 'Thank you' in Nyanja, and was a salute to the hospitality and support received from President Kaunda and the Zambian people.

One of the first combatants infiltrated had been responsible for the Christmas 1985 shooting of Shiba, the Swazi policeman in the pay of Pretoria. His name was Raymond Molapo, alias Clement. He arrived in Lusaka mid-way through 1985, after deportation with a batch of comrades from Swaziland to Tanzania. I did not know what he looked like and arrived at a transit house in search of him.

'There's com' Clement,' I was told after enquiring, 'washing over there.'

I turned and saw a slightly-built young man splashing his naked torso at a garden tap, his trousers rolled up to the knees. The real-life person did not fit with the mental picture I had built of this daring young man. He dried himself with a towel and, as he hung it up on a line, I ambled over to talk with him.

We shook hands. I looked into the face of a composed man with clear, serene eyes. He described in a soft voice how he had 'taken out' Shiba without needing to justify the act. Shiba had managed to fire off a single shot before falling. Clement showed me where this had entered his hand and exited at the elbow.

'Fortunately the left hand, the hand that cradled my AK. But it's okay now.'

What he was interested in was the common urge to get back home to fight. He enquired about the possibilities. 'I've expressly come to see you about that,' I answered. 'We're making some useful progress developing safer routes back home, off the beaten track. We're looking for comrades who will keep away from public transport and rest up in the bush during the day. But we're waiting for the funds so that we can provide at least 2000 rand to keep comrades going for a while, once they get to their operational bases.'

'I don't need much money,' he replied quietly. 'I have people at home who will look after me. As long as I'm supplied with weapons, I'll be able to operate.'

I was deeply impressed by his composure and lack of demands. I immediately recommended him to our operations chief. He was part of a stream of combatants that were infiltrated into the country over the next year.

Recorded MK operations rose to 135 in 1987 and 247 in 1988, the highest in our history.[1] Over a third of these attacks were on the police and army. Reported security force captures of MK combatants decreased after 1987. In 1989, with MK operations still running high at 144, the number killed and captured was 75. This figure, at a time when infiltration had increased, was an indication of the safer routes home, the improved capacity of the underground, growing links with rural people, and of security support for operatives. We were proving that, despite the difficult conditions, MK had the capacity to overcome the errors and weaknesses of the past. The armed struggle, as waged by MK, was promising to become far more effective in the 1990s. This was one of the factors that affected the thinking of the regime, when the country's rulers decided to opt for a negotiated solution. Clement's unit on the East Rand was one of the most active. He was involved in numerous gun-fights with the police. He accounted for the deaths of over a dozen before falling in battle himself. He died with a young woman called 'Zoya' in a Bonnie-and-Clyde-style ambush. Only they were not motivated by personal gain.

Prior to Bill Anderson joining me in Lusaka, much of our research was conducted from London. Until 1987, Bill worked from a flat behind King's Cross station. To the neighbours, the mild-mannered young man was a polite tenant, notwithstanding a propensity for playing rock music late at night. Inside, however, the two largest rooms had been converted into a virtual operations centre. The walls – and even the windows – of one room were completely covered in chipboard, on which were tacked maps and deployment charts. Map cabinets and drawing boards filled the room. The second room contained filing cabinets. Bookshelves, filled with the latest military journals from South Africa and elsewhere, lined the walls. When Army Commander Joe Modise visited, he insisted on inspecting not only the work, but also the living area, to ensure that the beds were made properly and the level of tidiness met with requisite military standards.

Our work on the enemy's armed forces was like piecing together a very large jigsaw puzzle. It took years to construct. Every name, unit and base mentioned in any South African military or police journal was indexed and cross-referenced. Telephone books for the whole country were scoured for obscure references to security force numbers. Deserters from the SADF, disillusioned mercenaries and members of the Special Forces were debriefed. Documents were received from our operatives within the SADF. A particular coup was obtaining the SADF telex directory, which not only listed every unit but also, through shared lines for encrypted messages, pointed to key organisational relationships between units. Another was the operator's manual for the military intelligence's computer system. As the jigsaw took shape, we were confident that we knew almost everything we needed to know of the deployment of military and police forces throughout the country, from command structures down to platoon level. This information was used to prepare mini-manuals for operational commanders in the field and to ensure that, from 1987 onwards, most units were provided with a thorough briefing of enemy deployment and tactics in their area of operation.

Target intelligence was another key area of work. Potential targets were identified for their political and strategic significance. Preliminary map work was done to ascertain the terrain and nature of surrounding areas. Reconnaissance operatives would then be instructed to conduct surveillance, and their reports, photographs and sketches combined into target profiles for the Operations Department of MK.

Our operatives were from a varied background: MK cadres infiltrated into the country to build intelligence networks; conscripts; cadres who volunteered for service in the Permanent Force of the SADF (one of whom managed to graduate from the elite Military Academy in Saldanha Bay); journalists; town planners; university lecturers 'spotting' among their students; sympathetic foreigners working in the region; and a number of shadier characters, who were kept at arm's length, but tested on carefully selected tasks to ascertain their true loyalties.

Intelligence on the SADF's conventional ground and air forces was also pieced together. While of some use to our own guerrilla forces, this data was invaluable to our allies in the Frontline States. We closely monitored the development of the SADF's weaponry which, despite advances in certain areas, suffered enormously from the international arms boycott and the shortcomings of South Africa's industry – particularly with regard to the production of modern aircraft. We predicted that the airforce's newly unveiled Cheetah jet fighter – which was an effort with Israel at upgrading a French Mirage series – would be no match for the Soviet Mig-23s.

We also got wind of the development of a Pilotless Reconnaissance Vehicle (PRV), based on an Israeli model. It had an on-board TV facility that beamed pictures back to a monitoring site. Bill drew up a portfolio of this radio-controlled spotter aircraft as early as 1983, and we distributed it to our Frontline allies.

No sooner had I passed on a copy to the Mozambican military, than a PRV appeared over Maputo in April of that year. There was consternation in the streets as it was spotted flying over the city. Comrades from the ANC office, off Avenida Mao Tse-tung, took up positions on the roof of the building, with steel helmets and AK-47s. People ran for shelter, because the week before South African aircraft had bombed and strafed the Matola suburb in search of ANC victims – killing four workers at a jam factory instead.

I looked up into the clear blue sky, half-wanting Maputo's air-defence system to open fire and half-wanting the pilotless plane to fly harmlessly out to sea. The PRV was an expendable metal shell with a pair of wings and communication system. There were eyes across the border closely monitoring and recording its progress and just waiting to pin-point the flashes of ground fire they expected to erupt. 'Don't shoot,' I murmured to myself, when suddenly there was a vapour trail overhead and a sound like thunder as a rocket hit the drone. To the sound of cheers – including my own – it plummeted into the Indian Ocean. Oh well, I mused, at least it had provided the missile batteries with target practice, even if they would now have to change position.

The battle for Cuito Cuanavale in south-east Angola, which began in October 1987, was an example of the most significant information we were able to provide our allies. We were systematically monitoring the programme of celebrations that the SADF had planned for its 75th anniversary in 1987. One of the highlights of the year was to be a large-scale conventional exercise in July at the Army Battle School at Lohatla in the northern Cape. Such divisional exercises had previously been used as acclimatisation practice, and a launch-pad for the army's Citizen Force, conventional brigades, to engage in aggression against Angola.

I studied the information with Bill at our Lusaka house. It was May 1987 and I was due to visit Angola.

'This is going to interest our Angolan comrades, Bill,' I said, 'but apart from alerting them, how much emphasis should we put on a possible invasion?'

Bill thoughtfully ran his fingers through his hair: 'Depends on the situation up in Savimbi's neck of the woods. The Boers have been into southern Angola continuously, usually using 32 Battalion. Maybe with this July deployment they'll take the opportunity of something bigger and send in their brigades.'

By the time I was meeting Colonel Antonio Jose Maria, chief intelligence officer at the Angolan President's residence, overlooking the ocean outside Luanda, I had made up my mind.

Giving him the information about the SADF's July exercise, I said we believed an invasion of Angola from Namibia was imminent. We were in the Colonel's air-conditioned office and he was keenly interested in my news. We had been liaising for two years, exchanging information about Unita and the SADF. In his late thirties, he was a scholar and an athlete, had studied at a Catholic seminary, and cut a dashing figure in camouflage uniform and green beret.

Seated behind a large desk, operational maps of Angola on the walls, he peered shrewdly at me from behind a pair of spectacles and declared in fluent

English: 'Let me tell you – we are presently preparing for an offensive against Unita in the south-east, in the direction of their Jamba base. What you tell us means that the South Africans are engaging in a build-up too. Thank you for this timely warning.'

During this period I was frequently visiting our main training camp near Malanje, over 500 kilometres east of the capital. The cool, interior highlands were a welcome break from Luanda's humidity. To save time travelling, I would hitch a lift on the Soviet transport planes which were making daily flights all over the country. Because of the Unita threat we would abruptly descend in tight circles from a high altitude on the airport, which was defended by Cuban units. Mig-23s were constantly harrying Unita forces still ensconced across the Kwanza River. I once spent an interesting day observing Angolan pilots taking off and returning from their sorties.

A small colony of Soviet specialists, some with their wives, were based in two bougainvillaea-festooned villas in the lively, though run-down, town. They trained MK radio operators who ran our communication station in Malanje, which linked Luanda with Lusaka. They also trained and supervised our instructors at our main camp, 60 kilometres away, near a collection of mud huts that went by the name of Caculama village.

The situation in our camps had improved since the negative period of the mutiny. Soviet instructors were assisting in the training programme. This raised standards, and released many of our most capable people for the home front.

I would sometimes spend a night at one of the Soviet villas enjoying a home-cooked meal – very much like Yiddish cooking, with borscht, black bread, salami, pickled cucumber and tinned sardines to accompany an appetising main dish – washed down with plenty of vodka. I particularly relished a visit after a week's trip to Caculama, and looked forward to relaxing in a small wooden *banya*, or sauna, which they had built near our communication centre. There we would sweat out the dust and grime of camp life, tone up tired muscles by swishing our bodies with eucalyptus branches, and rehydrate by drinking freshly brewed Georgian tea and a spot of vodka.

They were officers there on two- or three-year stints of duty from Moscow. I knew a couple of them from my trips with Modise or Chris Hani to the Soviet Union. We often talked of the economic problems their country was facing and they debated this with a stoicism and ironic wit.

'*Tovarish Khumalo*,' a tough tactics instructor with benign eyes said to me in a thick Slavic accent, 'the only way for us to get production moving is by going into the factories with our AK-47s and telling our workers to get off their backsides.'

Before I could respond, he leant forward on the wooden bench in the *banya*, a twinkle in his eye, and added with a deep chuckle: 'But that's why we teach that the army is secondary to the party and must not interfere with the political line.'

Despite the dry enervating heat of the *banya*, a fierce debate erupted, and continued over dinner, concerning the root causes of the economic problems. Apart from the lack of productivity – said to arise from the over-protection of labour – the chief culprit was defence expenditure. The war had taught Soviet people a harsh lesson. Soldiers or civilians expressed a deep desire for peace. I did not come across a Soviet officer who was happy that the defence budget was so huge. Calculations were made regarding the enormous cost of defending the USSR against Nato's Cruise and Pershing missiles. The same tactics instructor, adroitly doing his sums on a calculator, estimated that the Soviet Union had to spend ten times as much in defence of its extensive land borders against Cruise Missiles than the West's outlay on defence.

'Then there's the question of the scientific-technological revolution,' an instructor called Boris added. 'We might be pioneers in space and in certain military spheres, but in society in general, in agriculture and industry, we are lagging way behind. We made a grave error in the 1960s when we deliberately decided against investing in the new computer sciences. We've paid out a fortune in "importing" this knowledge from the West.' The Russian use of irony is never far from the surface. As Boris mouthed the word 'importing', he raised his eyebrows and smiled wryly. He was of course referring to the smuggling of such equipment.

I told them of how, in 1979, after two years in Angola, I had visited an amusement centre in London with my young sons and first seen the latest computer games. The boys had knocked up impressive scores on 'Space Invaders' and, when Andrew completed his round, a computerised voice had announced that he had achieved the highest score for the month.

'Next day,' I told my Soviet hosts, 'I came across a full-page advert in the London *Times*, inviting youngsters with computer-game skills to consider the advantages of a career in the Royal Air Force and to write in for particulars. Quite an advantage for the military.' It was my way of saying 'why the hell don't you place your space achievements at the disposal of the rest of society?'

My story elicited further irony from Boris. '*Da* [yes],' he shook his head, 'and our boys don't even know what a photocopier looks like when they come into the forces.'

I laughed with him over the mention of the photocopier. He had been present at a training centre for an MK group when Modise and I had visited Moscow the previous year. It had taken several days to get some documents photocopied, because of the bureaucracy, and Modise had joked that maybe such a machine was regarded as 'a secret installation'. We always found that Soviet comrades were able to laugh at their deficiencies.

My reading of Marxism taught me that socialism was meant to be an advance on the capitalist economic system.

Lenin summed this up in a statement that appealed to me: 'The socialist revolution must prove its worth through its labour productivity.' Khrushchev's 1961 expectations about outstripping the West by 1980 had been rash indeed. But I had never anticipated that the Soviet economy would slow down.

It was particularly when one discerned the shortcomings of the economy that one's belief system was challenged. What troubled me was how the West had come, in the late 20th century, to develop technology ahead of a socialist system whose productive forces should have by now led the way. It was easy to rationalise, however, that we had simply underestimated the resources of capitalism and overestimated the stage socialism had reached – at that point in time anyway.

It was also easier to be impressed by the communist rhetoric, the revolutionary heritage and past achievements, than perceive the ineluctable problems within the system. The October Revolution of 1917 had certainly transformed a backward Czarist Empire into a mighty world power. What only emerged later was that, at a certain stage, development misfired and the attempts to create a socialist society had been fatally distorted.

Much faith was placed in Gorbachev's reforms. Those we worked with in the army and Party remained, at that stage, optimistic and unstinting with their assistance.

Our best Soviet friend was a comrade we worked with over the years in Moscow, who first represented the Afro-Asian Solidarity Committee and then the Central Committee of the Party, named Vladimir Shubin. He was a bear-sized man, with a booming voice and bone-crushing embrace. Although of my age group, he was like an uncle to us all and particularly fussed over the health of older leaders like Moses Mabhida and Oliver Tambo. He had a razor-sharp mind and memory, an amazing grasp of South African developments and an impressive sense of what was correct – whether in politics or life. I used to wonder whether he owed the latter quality to a Russian peasant heritage or Marxism. For Shubin, no task, whether big or small, was too much trouble. Some of us affectionately referred to him as 'Tovarish Mozhna', meaning 'Comrade Possible'. He never refused a reasonable request, but nodding his large head thoughtfully, would reply: '*Da ... da ... mozhna ... mozhna* [yes ... yes ... possible ... possible].'

Contrary to Western perceptions during the cold war, the Soviet Union did not control or direct us. Images of vast numbers of Russian conspirators burning the midnight oil in the Kremlin, formulating scenarios to capture South Africa, were laughable. That is not to say that, as fellow revolutionaries, they did not share with us their historic experiences and ideas on how to overthrow a dictatorship. Shubin was part of a small team of comrades you could count on one hand who catered for us – and this mainly involved military assistance, educational studies and humanitarian aid. The Soviet Party naturally had close ties with our Party, and would have been delighted to see socialism triumph. But it did not manipulate the SACP, nor did it require the SACP to act as an intermediary with the ANC. The ANC obviously benefited from the relations that had existed between the USSR and the SACP. Then, in 1963, Oliver Tambo travelled to Moscow with Kotane to negotiate the first training arrangements in the Soviet Union for the ANC. Moscow provided similar facilities to liberation movements where no communist party existed as intermediary. Travel assistance, medical attention and the provision of certain amenities were other forms of contribution that they, and other socialist countries, provided without any conditions being attached. I never came across or heard of a situation where strings were attached to assistance we received, as Party or ANC, nor influence directed away from the primary goals of an independent, non-racial and democratic South Africa. During the period of exile we were able to take advantage of the facilities in socialist countries to hold conferences and meetings of the Party in safety, without cost.

We held the sixth congress of our Party at a centre outside Moscow in November 1984. The meeting had started off as a conference. The last congress of the party had taken place at an underground venue in Johannesburg in 1962. Gatherings during the intervening years had passed by as extended meetings of the central committee or special conferences. During a break in proceedings, I met Shubin, who headed a back-up team catering for our needs.

'Tell me,' I asked, 'how many delegates were there to the first Congress of your Party in 1903?'

'Thirteen, including Lenin,' he replied.

'We've got 40 delegates here. I'm going to submit a resolution terming this a congress. Much more prestigious for the history books, don't you think?'

'Good idea,' he chuckled. 'One of the underground Latin American parties had a congress last year in a Volkswagen.'

The Congress kept us firmly on the path of armed struggle, and pledged to build both the underground and emergent trade union movement.

The camp at Caculama had once been a ZAPU base. It covered an extensive area in the bush and accommodated up to 500 trainees. These were the 'young lions' of the township, who continued to pour out of South Africa to join MK. Chris Hani had become MK's chief of staff and we often addressed the camp together. Possessing an imposing and cheerful bearing, he was the most energetic of us all at Military Headquarters. He constantly visited our camps and worked tirelessly to facilitate the homeward movement of cadres. He was an inspirational force, an extremely warm and caring human being with many fine qualities, including an infectious sense of humour. What amazed me most, however, was his memory of cadres' names, his intimate knowledge of their personal situation and his concern for their problems. This was no mean feat when personnel were constantly changing, arriving, departing and reappearing, sometimes after many months, if not years. There was always a long queue of comrades waiting to raise their concerns with him, which kept him busy round the clock wherever he went.

It was close on 25 years since I had first worked with him in Tanzania. It was fascinating to see how he continued to grow in stature. He was in his element in the camps and had worked hard to restore the morale of the army. 'That period of the mutiny,' he told me as we discussed the present high spirits in Caculama, 'was the most difficult and exacting I've ever lived through.' He was an easy person to relate to. We talked about his personal feelings when Pango camp was retaken and the summary executions began.

'Those mutineers behaved savagely. When we saw how they had slain some of our people in cold blood I was as mad as the rest of us. After seven were executed and I thought of another 20 awaiting the firing squad – some I'd known as young recruits in Lesotho who had clearly been misled – I felt we must stop. I appealed to Tambo in Lusaka, over the heads of the local commanders who were determined to press on with the verdict of the tribunal.'

He clearly enjoyed the discussion, cherishing the opportunity for reflection and to put views about complex problems under the microscope. 'Such a pity life's grown so hectic we scarcely have time for contemplation. The likes of you and I ...,'and he chuckled characteristically as he was about to make a personal observation, 'are basically soft-hearted, we're the conscience of the movement, along with comrades like Slovo and Pallo. That's why neither of us could bear to allow those women to languish in Quatro.'

The condition at the ANC detention camp at Quatro was another issue that constantly bothered him. Later on, back in South Africa, he was to give a frank interview on the role of our security structures.

'Yes there was a culture of intolerance, but those who were critical of that culture were leading Communist Party members. Never again ... should we give [unchecked] powers to the security ... [We must] avoid the sort of thing that happened to a very small extent to the ANC and a very large extent within the security forces of the regime.' Together we addressed the Caculama detachment and received a rousing welcome on the parade ground. Hani's rich voice boomed out as he gave an extensive briefing on the situation at home and exhorted the cadres to make the most of their training. He was able to tap into their personal emotions – hopes, anger and fears – and relate convincingly to the suffering of the people at home, drawing on his own upbringing in the destitute village of Cofimvaba in the Transkei. He peppered his address with witticisms and, to roars of delight, ridiculed the apartheid government and its surrogate forces.

One of the young trainees in the camp was my son Andrew who, after a period of teenage uncertainty about his parents' national identification, had worked as a printer for the ANC in London and then requested to join MK. Chris Hani had known him as a kid in London. Andrew, popular in the camp under a pseudonym that hid our relationship, was brought to our quarters for a private chat one evening. The three of us reminisced about those times. Chris was in great form, his ringing voice and hearty chuckle resounding around our dugout. He reminded Andrew of a scare he had inadvertently given him and his younger brother, when they returned home from school ostensibly to an empty house, and found him sitting alone in our kitchen in an experimental disguise.

'Those years after the Rivonia arrests in 1963 and the Soweto Uprising in 1976 were the most difficult period,' Chris said, 'but we kept going and now nothing can stop us.' Turning directly to Andrew he chortled: 'How can we be stopped when even a little cockney kid like you has become a young lion!'

Andrew was to see action, accompanying the MK convoys to our camps as a sentry. Unita activity increased in the north-east, in an attempt to draw forces away from Cuito Cuanavale. MK casualties in 1987–88 were the heaviest in our history. We lost 100 cadres in a dozen ambushes on the road from Caxito to Quibaxe. But we inflicted far heavier casualties on Unita in return.

Timothy Mokoena was often to the fore in the engagements. His leg was shattered by bullets in one of the actions, but fortunately he was able to recover in a Moscow hospital. We lost many fine young people in those battles to keep the logistics routes open to our camps.

Among them was the son of the Njobes, a couple devoted to the ANC, who lived in Lusaka. Also to fall was Dr Hugo, a medical doctor who had graduated in the Soviet Union. His real name was Thamsanqa Fihla, and he could have taken up a career anywhere in the world, or returned to South Africa. But he insisted on serving MK in the camps. The fact that we were able to sustain such heavy casualties, without loss of morale, showed just how well MK had recovered from the disturbing mutiny of 1984. Many of the negative conditions that gave rise to the mutiny had been overcome. Timothy Mokoena was of the view that the speedier deployment of cadres to the home front made a major difference.

By the time I left Angola the FAPLA offensive against Unita in the south was getting underway. But my mind was absorbed with my own task of infiltrating into South Africa a specially prepared unit based outside Malanje.

We had been preparing the unit in a eucalyptus forest outside the town. It consisted of four white males, three of whom had been living in London. Their commander was an engaging, gritty character called Damien de Lange who had been an instructor in our camps. The London trio had dodged conscription in South Africa, become involved in anti-apartheid activity and volunteered to join MK. They were excellent swimmers and camped by a lake in which they exercised daily. We were thinking big and, among other things, hoped to use them to sabotage harbour installations and shipping.

In Malanje itself, Damien's girlfriend, a feisty and attractive red-head called Susan Westcott, was undergoing training as their radio operator. She was being prepared in the use of a compact apparatus that would link the unit with Lusaka. We had found that some of our intelligence information was of no use to the dispersed township and rural units. Modise was looking for a specialised group, safely ensconced in the white areas, to operate under Lusaka's direct control.

While I flew to Lusaka and then south to Botswana the four followed in my tracks – all incognito, using false documents and disguises. Susan flew to England to be disguised by Eleanor and enter into a marriage of convenience with a friend of Eleanor's which would enable her to undergo a legitimate name change and a new British passport – prior to setting up house in South Africa. The marriage was then annulled.

Meanwhile, several brigades of the Angolan army pushed south against Unita into the country's most remote wilderness, known to the former Portuguese colonial rulers as Cuando Cubango – 'the land at the end of the earth'. From its Namibian bases, and along the Caprivi strip, the SADF was gearing up to support its Unita surrogate. The Seventh Division exercised in the northern Cape close to the Botswana border and on the route to Namibia. Our telephone system in England was buzzing with warning signals from SADF troops engaged in the mobilisation.

Vincent, who had changed identity after his transfer from Swaziland, had prepared a safe house in Gaborone. Within a week of leaving Malanje we had Damien's unit assembled under its roof.

The plan was to fly the unit to Lesotho from where they would descend the Drakensberg Mountains as a climbing party and slip into one of the Natal nature parks. A contact would meet them at a hotel, and they would later link up with Susan. Heavy snows had fallen over Lesotho and their departure was delayed. Then the Batswana couple from whom Vincent had rented the house unexpectedly returned from abroad. They gave him a month's notice while they stayed with relatives, but were constantly dropping by. They were obviously disconcerted to find their home filled with bearded white males who might be mercenaries bent on destabilising Botswana. Vincent explained that we were a group of friends from Britain who were touring southern Africa. I was introduced as a publisher and the couple brought over a knowledgeable friend who grilled me on every facet of the profession. 'Vince,' I said, 'tell your landlord you're taking your pals off on safari. We'd better be on our way.'

We had a second-hand Land Rover, and for months Vince and I had been reconnoitring routes westward through the Kalahari desert and then south to the remote northern Cape border with Namibia. We loaded up with supplies and weapons and dodged the roadblocks, permanently mounted by the Botswana Defence Force along the solitary national highway that runs like a spine along the country's eastern border with Zimbabwe and the Transvaal. This was the main MK infiltration route, and comrades often started by slipping across the Zambezi River by boat near Livingstone. Joe Modise had instructed me to investigate the Kalahari as an alternative.

I was at my happiest in the field away from headquarters and the interminable meetings. After being holed up in the Gaborone house, everyone in the vehicle was in high spirits and I was soon hooting at gaggles of ostriches showing us their heels along the dusty roadway. Botswana is a sprawling, dry country with scattered villages. The haunting Kalahari desert stretches endlessly westwards from the handful of towns along the north-south highway.

We struck camp on the edge of the desert, near the diamond-mining town of Jwaneng. As dusk descended and we were enveloped in a star-studded sky, relaxing with mugs of coffee around a camp fire, the banter was carefree and confident. Some days later, back in Gaborone, I read in the local newspaper that Pik Botha, South Africa's Foreign Minister, had visited the Botswana Prime Minister's brother in Jwaneng on the same night as we were camping nearby.

Late the following afternoon, after a full day's precarious navigation along interminable sand tracks churned up by huge cattle trucks, and stopping at times to admire the ghostly salt pans shimmering in the desert heat, we arrived at a remote point on the border previously earmarked for a crossing. The dried-out bed of the Molopo River forms the southern frontier with South Africa, a well-constructed border fence running alongside it. The scrubland of the area is supplemented by a fringe of bush along the rivercourse which provides additional cover and we parked the vehicle a kilometre from the crossing point. We were a couple of hundred kilometres north-west of the Army Battle School at Lohatla and I wondered how the Seventh Division was getting on with their exercise. If they were going to reinforce the units on the Namibia-Angola border, they would be over-flying our position within weeks, as well as using the Upington-Windhoek highway south of us.

Meanwhile, I led my own invasion force through the scrub and thorn trees to the crossing-point. We lay on our bellies in the fading light and watched through field binoculars as a police vehicle drove along a gravel road on the South African side.

'That's the last patrol,' I told Damien and company. 'The odd farmer will still drive by during the early evening hours and that's it.' As soon as it was dark we moved off and began slipping over the fence. I left Vincent on the border with an AK-47 to cover us and, keeping low, escorted the unit half a kilometre up to the gravel road. We were armed with AKs and grenades and were ready for any eventuality. I placed two empty cans of Coca-Cola at the side of the road some 40 metres apart, by way of a signal for a vehicle that was due within ten minutes. I had contacted an operative in Johannesburg with whom I had worked out such a pick-up in an emergency. There was no way a unit could safely hike the 600 kilometres to Johannesburg in this terrain. We had no contact with the local people, although after the 1990 lifting of the ban on the ANC, I discovered how militant the people of the Northern Cape, and other rural areas could be. We deployed in two groups and waited.

Long before it arrived, we heard the whine of an engine. Everyone crouched low as headlights appeared and in a cloud of dust a farmer's van sped by. I was pleased since we could do with a little traffic as a screen for our own vehicle. It arrived within minutes, coming to a halt by the second can. I had a word with the driver while the four scrambled inside. As the vehicle disappeared I wished that I too was travelling to Johannesburg. For days I had been considering accompanying the group to their destination – at least for the weekend – figuring Modise would not get to know. In the end, discipline prevailed over a desire to face the odds with the unit.

The fluctuating fortunes of the struggle against apartheid saw a spiral of tragedies crowned by an epic success, at the close of the 1980s.

While I was on the Botswana border, two of my colleagues, Job Tabane, alias Cassius Make, from MHQ, and Sella Motau, alias Paul Dikaledi, the youngest member of our Maputo command, were murdered by a hit-squad in Swaziland. Paul picked up Cassius at the Matsapa airport from where they were followed and ambushed near the university.

A close friend, Jeremy Brickhill, a member of ZAPU, was seriously injured but escaped with his life when a car bomb was detonated next to him in Harare in October 1987. The perpetrators were a group of Rhodesians in Pretoria's pay. They were arrested after carrying out other atrocities in Zimbabwe. One of these involved hiring an unsuspecting chauffeur to drive a taxi, with explosives packed in the boot, up to the front-door of an ANC residence in Bulawayo. The luckless driver was blown to pieces when those who had hired him detonated the bomb from an observation point. The occupants of the house fortunately escaped with minor injuries.

The pattern continued into 1988. In January, one of Modise's closest young aides, Jacob Molikwane, alias Biza, was shot dead in a vehicle near Francistown on the Botswana border. On 28 March, our Botswana Regional Commander, Charles Makoena, alias Naledi, who had survived the Pango mutiny, was shot with three innocent Batswana women when raiders attacked and burnt his house in Gaborone. Shortly before this, on 19 March, the ANC's representative in France, Dulcie September, had been assassinated by a gunman on the doorstep of her Paris flat. My younger son, Christopher, had been staying with her only a few weeks earlier. The world was shocked at the live TV footage of Albie Sachs, miraculously semiconscious with one arm severed, being dragged away from his bombed-out vehicle in Maputo on 7 April.

News of the assassination attempt on Albie reached me while I was on a visit to Cuba with Modise. We had been visiting trainees and holding talks about further assistance from Cuba which, despite its economic problems, was prepared to render assistance in the spirit of internationalism. It was a stimulating place to visit and retained a fizz and a zest 30 years after the revolution. One captured this irrepressible panache at the exit from the Museum of the Revolution where there was a 'Thank-you' sign to the revolution's prime recruiters – Batista and Reagan.

Cuba is only 90 miles from Florida. Before the revolution it was virtually run by the Mafia. Apart from the export of sugar, the other sources of foreign currency were gambling and prostitution. The polite saying is that Fidel made a revolution in the USA's backyard. The popular saying is that it took place up their rectum.

The island lived with the ever-present threat of invasion from the USA. On the outskirts of Havana, or wherever else one drove, members of the People's Militia were to be seen, engaged in defensive exercises on the beaches, roads and fields. Apart from the regular armed forces, and the militia, there were the committees for the defence of the revolution. These were organised on a neighbourhood block system. Because most of the younger people were mobilised through other structures, these committees were mainly composed of the older generations. On a subsequent occasion I was in Havana on the anniversary of the foundation of the committees. Together with Joe Slovo I was taken on a grand tour of the city, to visit the street committees, engaged in festive celebrations. Seemingly on every street there were parties. There was dancing and dining, with rum flowing. The staple dish, *caldosa*, a traditional thick broth, was warmed all night in a huge pot on a fire in the street, as nourishment for those manning the watch. Most impressive was the spirit of the older people, who knew what it had been like under the Batista dictatorship. They well knew what benefits the revolution had brought.

As they shouted their 'Vivas!' and sang their revolutionary songs, I caught the eye of a grey-haired woman, who reminded me of Vera Ponnen. She had been in the Party during the dark days of that mafioso, Batista, she explained. Her own sister had been a plaything for an American gangster who once owned half of Havana. And she would kill any Yankee soldier who dared invade her fatherland. Not for the first time, I noted that the most steadfast revolutionaries were women. And then, the next moment someone was shouting: 'Ruth First! Ruth First!'

It was an excited man in his sixties. He had heard that members of the SACP were present in his street. He too was a communist from the old days, who had met Ruth First at a youth festival in eastern Europe, just after the war. Joe Slovo was amazed, as was the Cuban who discovered that Ruth's husband was present. We accompanied the man to his house, where he showed us his scrapbook. There was a newspaper article in Spanish about the Cuban delegation's trip, and a photograph of Ruth, aged about 20, posing with the Cubans.

There was no mistaking the strength of feeling for the revolution, and the natural joy exhibited by the people. Most impressive in terms of social gains were the health facilities. Cuba, with a population of only 11 million, graduated over 3000 doctors a year, and was regarded as a super-power in the sphere of health. Every neighbourhood boasted a white, two-storeyed house, the residence of the local doctor, who had consulting rooms on the ground floor, and an apartment upstairs. Each neighbourhood doctor catered for some 100 families. Fidel Castro took a great interest in health care. Recently, our interpreter told me, he had become involved in raising the quality of life of the aged. He visited old people's homes, and encouraged the inmates to lead a more active life. He coaxed them out, I was told, to travel around and see the island's beauty and achievements.

With the collapse of Cuba's major benefactor, the Soviet Union, and the USA's sanctions and ban on trade, the island would face its severest crisis ever. With petrol severely rationed, the citizens and even the army would resort to using bicycles and the horse and cart would make a comeback in the 1990s.

Cubans are great carnivores. My predilection for fish prompted the interpreter to remark that it was a pity Cubans were unlike me, because the seas around were so well-stocked. Surely the current crisis would remedy that prejudice. On my trip with Modise, in April 1988, we were told that the alligator colony of the swamps was being preserved as a reserve stock of food in the event of critical times.

Cubans can tighten their belts and know how to live on the edge of danger.

The entire population appeared ready to defend the revolution. When they shouted '*Patria o Muerte! Venceremos!*' (Fatherland or death, we will win!), one sensed they meant it. But what they were facing then in addition to the USA's enervating economic squeeze, was a danger more undermining than that of a battlefield. Cubans have a tradition of internationalist solidarity that goes back to before the Spanish Civil War. They look to internationalist assistance in their hour of need.

One of our appreciative comrades said that never in his life had he visited a country where the coffee, the cigars, the rum, the revolution and internationalism were so strong.

Modise and I had a chance to exchange notes about our respective struggles with members of the Farabundi Marti Liberation Front of El Salvador, regarded by the Cubans as among the most creative and self-sufficient guerrilla movements. They were struggling against a US-backed military dictatorship and had developed a people's militia, armed with home-made weapons, to reinforce their more advanced guerrilla detachments. This militia helped to link the guerrillas more effectively with mass struggle. The combination of fighting units greatly interested Modise and me. I had been arguing for just such an approach, given the insurrectionary mood in the townships, and our need to offset the lack of classical guerrilla conditions by situating the armed struggle within the people themselves. As Amilcar Cabral of Guinea-Bissau had stated of his compact, flat country: 'The people are our mountains.'

When we recounted our many years of struggle from exile, the Salvadorians were impressed. The leader of their delegation, a cultured intellectual with a Mexican-style moustache, paid tribute to MK's tenacity and commented that the protracted nature of our armed struggle from exile, without the advantage of a friendly border, was a unique achievement. He explained that they had only once despatched a large group abroad for training. But because re-infiltration proved so difficult, the trainees became demoralised and ended up as students in the Scandinavian countries.

Eleanor was able to fly out from London to join me for a rare holiday. On her arrival we attended a state banquet hosted by Fidel Castro for President Chissano of Mozambique, successor to Samora Machel, who had died in a suspicious air crash thought to have been contrived by South Africa. As we waited with Modise to be presented to the uniformed Fidel and his suave guest of honour, Chissano, I could not take my eyes off the Cuban leader.

He was an impressive-looking individual with a powerful and erect bearing. As we shook hands and I prepared to exchange greetings, Fidel's attention was distracted by Eleanor as she greeted Chissano, the Frelimo activist we had known as a young man in Dar es Salaam in 1963–5. 'Oh, you know each other,'

Fidel said, and called on his official photographers to take pictures of our group. Alas, we never saw any copies.

While Modise visited South African students on the Isle of Youth, where Fidel had once been imprisoned by Batista, Eleanor and I were taken on an unforgettable four-day tour of Granma province. The region is named after the boat from which Fidel's initial force had landed in December 1956 after setting sail from exile in Mexico. We were accompanied by a Cuban friend who had liaised with the ANC in Angola from 1977, Angel Dalmao.

Dalmao came from a small town in Granma province and had suggested the trip. The area was the most undeveloped in Cuba, but rich in revolutionary history. It was here that the indigenous Indian chief Hatuey had fought the Spanish conquistadors and been burnt at the stake after refusing to be converted to Christianity. 'Is heaven inhabited by Catholics like you?' he had asked his captors. When they answered that it was, his spirited reply was: 'Then that's a place I don't want to go to.'

We landed in the small capital city of Bayamo. It was here that the 'Padre de la Patria' (Father of the Nation), Carlos Manuel de Cespedes, after freeing his slaves, raised the banner of revolt against Spanish rule. I reflected on how different South Africa's history might have been if the Boer settlers had followed the Cuban example, and made common cause with our indigenous people against British colonialism. Possibly it was their Catholicism that made Cuba's Spanish settlers less racist than the Calvinistic Boers. Catholics might burn you at the stake, but they gave you the option of becoming one of them, regardless of colour. The result in Cuba is a population that is extremely mixed, and naturally interacts.

To the revolution's detractors, Fidel Castro is an aberration of history. Our tour showed that his July 26th Movement was rooted among the people. We traced the footsteps of Fidel and Che Guevara from the 'Granma' landing site into the foothills of the Sierra Maestra, where their incipient guerrilla force developed and grew. We changed from jeep to mules and began a trek along precipitous mountain tracks through sub-tropical bush to Fidel's command post at La Plata, some 1,500 metres above sea level.

Fidel's quarters were maintained intact, with a rudimentary workplace and sleeping quarters on a raised platform in the bush. A trapdoor provided an emergency escape route. Within the dense foliage of a nearby hilltop was the rebel radio station that had broadcast to the people. I discovered from our guides, who were former guerrillas, that the mountains had been a sanctuary for militant peasants who had fought the large landowners before Fidel's arrival. The peasantry was the social base out of which the rebel army grew in the Sierra Maestra. I recalled heated debates in London in the late 1960s over Regis

Debray's theory that guerrilla movements could initiate a national uprising without the prior political preparation of the masses, starting from an isolated base and spreading like a patch of oil. The physical experience of the actual environment, with an insight into the social context, was worth volumes of books.

I recalled South Africa's terrain. Our mountain ranges were bare, and bereft of the forest that carpeted the Sierra Maestra. All parts of the country were easily accessible to the security forces. There were no remote areas such as this. Neither did we have a peasantry in the classical sense. The bantustans occupied 13 per cent of the land and were easily manageable wastelands. Fidel had achieved his revolution, from the base we were visiting, in three years. Our armed actions had been an on-off affair since 1961. Batista had been a tin-pot dictator compared to the powerful government in Pretoria. What we had in common with the Cubans was a determination to struggle. I was envious of Fidel's mountain fortress. I sensed, however, that the key reason for the limitation of our armed struggle was that we had not linked with our rural people, as Fidel had, and did not fully appreciate the role they could play. We spent too much time in Maputo and Lusaka arguing over structures, instead of developing links with the countryside.

We visited Dalmao's home in one of the coastal towns. We had refreshments with his parents and extended family, who shared the modest, wooden house of his birth. Everywhere we found a proud people. Away from Havana, the economic backwardness which the revolution strove to overcome was obvious. I remarked to Dalmao that such a trip gave one a greater appreciation of the difficulties, and the sacrifices, Cuba made by giving aid to other countries. That aid was not only military. Cuban doctors, teachers, engineers, builders and agricultural specialists worked all over the third world.

The modest way of life in the countryside was also Cuba's strength. The farming people were satisfactorily clothed and purposeful. The resourcefulness of the country might have been a factor in enabling Cuba to survive. Other socialist countries with a thriving agricultural base, such as China and Vietnam, were showing greater adaptability to current problems than the USSR did. Crucially with them, as with Cuba, the Party was in control of the reform process.

After bidding farewell to Eleanor, I flew with Modise to Luanda. We arrived at the end of April, after an 18-hour flight with a stop on the Cape Verde Islands. The distance underlined the effort of maintaining Cuban troops in Angola. We were immediately back in the hurly-burly of the struggle.

Stopping over in Luanda, I visited Olivia Forsyth, who was being held in a safe house belonging to the Security Department. She was being well treated and was translating Afrikaans articles from military and police journals. We were working on a possible exchange of her, and other agents, for MK comrades on death row in Pretoria – Robert McBride among others. She was very chirpy when I suggested we take photographs of her, and rushed to her room to put on make-up. She wrote a letter to her mother which we also tape-recorded. She still insisted she would be prepared to work for us as a double-agent but I shrugged it off as it was no longer an issue.

Just a couple of days later I was in Lusaka seeing Tambo at his living quarters, a small bungalow in the grounds of State House. For years he had to keep changing his accommodation, for security reasons, and had only recently agreed to become a guest of the government on the insistence of his close friend, President Kaunda. I was accompanied by Chris Hani and Steve Tshwete, who had become army commissar. We presented Tambo with the Forsyth material and suggested ways to effect a possible exchange. Tambo looked a trifle confused. 'Is this the woman in the British embassy?' he enquired.

'No Chief,' I answered politely, puzzled at what I thought was his vagueness, 'this is the police lieutenant we had at Quatro. Who's at the British embassy?'

'There's a woman who fled to the British embassy this morning from one of our houses in Luanda. I've just received the news.'

He was referring to Forsyth all right. She had obviously planned her escape well in advance. Taking advantage of a lapse in the watch, she had climbed over a garden wall and, crouching in a sympathetic neighbour's car, was driven to the British Embassy. As the news sank in, the usually loquacious trio from Military Headquarters were at a loss for words.

Tambo did not seem to notice how deflated we were. We trooped back to our car without a word. As we drove off we began to titter in embarrassment and then open laughter rang out. She had certainly pulled a fast one on us.

'I still stand by our decision to pull her out of Quatro,' Chris maintained, defiant to the end, with Steve and me laughing at him.

When Forsyth returned to South Africa, after spending six months in the British Embassy, exaggerated claims were made by her Security Branch superiors about the success of her mission. This was to offset the humiliation of her capture and the important information she had given us. Like her one-time mentor, Craig Williamson, she had cool nerves and considerable courage, but we had never been taken in by her because of her bloodless lack of passion for the anti-apartheid cause, to which she claimed to have converted. Infiltrators have the problem of finding a convincing balance between tight self-control and exaggerated passion. In the end, however courageous they are, a person should be judged according to the cause which they serve.

During the week of Olivia Forsyth's escape I received another blow. Damien de Lange, Susan Westcott and Ian Robertson were arrested at a rented house in the village of Broederstroom north of Johannesburg.

The experience of the unit, in almost a year's activity, in which they carried off several operations, illustrated the tensions of undercover life. It made me ponder about the wisdom of having put such a group together. They had been beset with personality difficulties, arising chiefly from the immaturity of Paul Annegarn and Hugh Lugg, and a loss of nerve on Hugh Lugg's part. Both had been highly recommended by London comrades and had impressed their trainers. Once in South Africa, however, Annegarn had developed an arrogant and uncommunicative attitude. He began failing in his duties and came to be regarded as a 'spoilt child' by the others. After attempting to desert the unit, he was brought back to Lusaka and sent to Angola for a year, where he participated in camp duties. He maintained that he wanted to return under cover to South Africa, but we sent him back to London instead.

When Annegarn first went missing, the unit was thrown into disarray. This seems to have particularly unnerved Lugg who, after subsequent brushes with the police, was – unnoticed by the others – on the point of a nervous breakdown. He began phoning Eleanor at our home in London in an endeavour to contact me, against all the rules of security. This was brought to the attention of the unit who had a heart-to-heart talk with him. Early the next morning, while they were sleeping, Lugg stole out of the house and not only surrendered to the police but led them back to the others.

At the subsequent trial of his former comrades, Lugg gave evidence for the state. He maintained that he had feared being killed by De Lange or sent to Quatro by me. It appears that he had become paranoid under pressure and had disintegrated as a personality. Damien, Ian and Susan were sentenced to prison terms of 25, 20 and 18 years, under the infamous Terrorism Act. A hue and cry was raised in the press about the fate of Annegarn, who Lugg suggested must have been executed by the ANC. Annegarn, after being sent back to England, linked up with Lugg and claimed that De Lange and I had meant to execute him. The fact that he had remained unharmed in Angola for a year made this allegation unconvincing.

Pik Botha, the Foreign Minister, seems to have been fascinated by the case. He attempted to communicate with Lusaka on Susan's radio and obviously learnt from Lugg's full confession that we had been close neighbours that night in the desert when he was visiting Jwaneng. He was incensed that we had managed to smuggle an SAM rocket missile to the unit – handed to Damien over the Botswana fence by Vincent – for intended use against the air force. Later he made a formal complaint to the Angolan government. Earlier that year he alleged I had a hand in an attempted coup to overthrow Lucas Mangope.

Pretoria had always tried to get the Thatcher Government to act against the ANC presence in Britain. They had an ally in Andrew Hunter, the right-wing Tory MP for Basingstoke. On a visit to South Africa, Hunter had surprisingly managed to visit Susan Westcott while she was being held in pre-trial isolation. At the time her Johannesburg attorney, Peter Harris, had been trying unsuccessfully for six months to see his client. Claiming to have received information from Susan about an ANC 'terror cell' operating in London, Hunter made widely reported allegations in the House of Commons which sought to link the ANC with the IRA.

Under the banner headline, 'MP Names London Terror Cell' an *Evening Standard* (3 November 1988) front-page story ran:

> *Leading members of the ANC who have been trained by the IRA are openly walking the streets of London and recruiting potential terrorists, a Tory MP has claimed. Mr Andrew Hunter named three 'ANC activists' as operating from homes in North London ... and he called on [the] Home Secretary ... to consider deportation.*
>
> *Hansard quotes the MP as saying: 'Is it not just as much against the national interest that ANC executive member Ronnie Kasrils walks the streets of London recruiting terrorists, at least one of whom has come from the ranks of extreme Irish republicanism? Also that Timothy Jenkin from his flat in Tufnell Park is using expertise he has got from the IRA to partly assemble bombs which are sent to Lusaka and then on to South Africa to maim and kill the innocent? From a flat in Golders Green, Ronnie Kasrils' wife Eleanor orchestrates terrorist activities in South Africa.'*
>
> *The MP said the police and Government were fully aware of the three as he had given a detailed dossier on their activities and IRA links to Mrs Thatcher earlier this year. A senior detective, denying Mr Hunter's claims today, said: 'Obviously we keep tabs on people like the ANC but we do not believe there is any truth in the allegations.'*

Eleanor, who first saw the story over a stranger's shoulder in a pub, issued a statement through our attorneys denying the allegation and declaring:

> *I challenge Mr Hunter to remove his cowardly cloak of parliamentary privilege and to make his statement outside the House of Commons. I can assure him that when he does so he will be faced with immediate proceedings for defamation. I will be more than happy for a British jury to decide which of us is telling the truth and which of us is lying. I have no doubt whatsoever that I will be vindicated.*

Hunter failed to respond to Eleanor's challenge. The Broederstroom trio first appeared in court in February 1989, three months after Hunter's allegation. Susan Westcott denied that she provided him with any information at all. When he appeared at her detention cell, she was suspicious about the unusual nature of the visit and refused to talk to him. If Susan Westcott was telling the truth, as I believe, then one can only conclude that Hunter's allegations were based on information provided by the South African authorities.

Right-wingers like Hunter could not accept that people in Britain, whether South African or British, were prepared to assist in the struggle to overcome apartheid. What was frustrating to the likes of Hunter and Pik Botha was that the British Government and Scotland Yard were only concerned that no terrorist activities should be committed in Britain. The use of telephones, the mail and research from Britain did not amount to terrorism. The press variously reported Scotland Yard as stating: 'We are aware of these people ... and they are not involved in terrorist activities' and there was 'no evidence of any alleged meetings with the IRA'.

The only person I ever recruited of Irish origin was Sean Hosey. Hunter's attempt to link him to 'extreme Irish republicanism' exposed his political illiteracy, for Hosey was a member of the British Young Communist League which consistently opposed the IRA's tactics.

In fact, Eleanor and I, along with the ANC members in general, enjoyed protection from Scotland Yard. From the time that a hit-list of leading apartheid opponents in Britain was discovered in 1987 we had received advice and protection. Far from being a 'terror nest', our Golders Green home had often been the scene of convivial chats over tea with Scotland Yard officers. They came at our behest. If a suspicious parcel arrived in the post, or Eleanor had received threatening phone calls, or there were suspicious callers to our front door, they answered her call and arrived to check and offer advice. We had been reared in a climate of almost paranoid suspicion of Western intelligence agencies. We found in Scotland Yard seemingly polite if guarded attention.

At the time Eleanor was having her battle with Andrew Hunter, I was back in Cuba, with a delegation headed by Joe Slovo. Notwithstanding some of the setbacks we had received, the situation in Southern Africa had radically changed in favour of liberation. We were in the operations room of the Cuba Ministry of Defence and no less a personage than the commander-in-chief, Fidel Castro, was briefing us on the military situation in southern Angola. There had been a remarkable victory over the apartheid army which, in his words, meant that 'The history of Africa will have to be written as before and after Cuito Cuanavale.'

Fidel pointed out, on a huge table-top model of the region's topography,

214

the drama that had unfolded. Against Cuban advice, the Angolan forces had repeated previous abortive attempts to advance on Savimbi's Jamba stronghold in the remote and undeveloped south-east corner of the country. At first the offensive had progressed well, with FAPLA gaining the upper hand and inflicting heavy casualties on Unita. Then in October 1987, with their logistics lines over-extended, FAPLA's advancing 47th Brigade, attempting to cross the Lomba River, was destroyed by South African forces. Catastrophe followed as several other brigades retreated in disarray, under SADF ground and air attacks. Some of the remnants fell back on the simple landing-strip across the river at Cuito Cuanavale and were swiftly reinforced by a small contingent of Cubans from Menogue, over 150 kilometres to the north-west.

The South Africans were far too cautious, Fidel observed through an interpreter. They could have overrun Cuito Cuanavale there and then with no problem, and shifted the strategic situation in Angola overnight, but they held back, awaiting reinforcements.

His explanation was riveting. The SADF version was that they had simply advanced as far as the river Cuito because it was the next feature of the terrain, in an otherwise flat bushveld, which could provide a holding position.

In fact the SADF were intent on taking Cuito Cuanavale because it would have opened up the interior of the country to domination by Unita and split Angola in half. This was an objective they had long sought for their surrogate. For months they relentlessly pounded Cuito Cuanavale with their powerful 155mm G-5 howitzers and sought to capture it with their ground forces, but their final attack there was repulsed on 23 March 1988. That was the historic day when in the words of SADF Colonel Jan Breytenbach the last major attack on Cuito Cuanavale was 'brought to a grinding and definite halt' and the Unita soldiers who were used as front-line cannon fodder by the racists 'did a lot of dying that day'. He continued: 'the full weight' of firepower 'was brought down on the heads of the [SADF's] Regiment President Steyn and the already bleeding Unita'. The heroic defence at Cuito Cuanavale proved a decisive turning point. With SADF forces entrapped there an entirely new front was opened by the Angolan-Cuban forces.

By April of 1988, 40,000 Cuban troops had been deployed alongside FAPLA and SWAPO units, not only at Cuito Cuanavale, but at strategic points along a 1000-kilometre front. This extended from the Atlantic port of Namibe along the railway line, through Lubango and Cassinga in the south-west, and on to Menongue and Cuito Cuanavale in the south-east. The South Africans had concentrated their forces around Cuito Cuanavale which were isolated as Cuban, Angolan and SWAPO troops advanced in the west, under superior air cover, on to the Namibian border. The task was accomplished by May 1988.

A further masterstroke was the record-breaking construction by Cuban workers of an airstrip at Xangongo – barely 100 kilometres from the Namibian border and the strategic dam above the Ruacana Falls on the Cunene River. Fidel, chewing thoughtfully on the end of his spectacles – a habit he had developed since giving up smoking his famous cigars – showed quiet pride in this singular achievement. The Atlantic border provinces of Moçamedes and Cunene in the south-west had been liberated after years of being an uncontested playground of the SADF. Cuban- and Angolan-piloted Mig-23s had convincingly demonstrated their superiority over South Africa's aged Mirage fighters and now the vast network of SADF bases in northern Namibia was within their reach.

The death-knell for the SADF was sounded on 27 June 1988. A squadron of Mig-23s bombed the Ruacana dam and its nearby Calueque installation, cutting the precious water supply to Ovamboland and its key military bases, as well as a strategic bridge. I had heard that on the completion of the mission one of the Cuban pilots had executed a neat victory roll over the Ruacana dam and its now vulnerable defenders. Again Colonel Breytenbach's opinion is revealing: 'With a lack of foresight the South Africans had allowed the bulk of their available combat powers to be tied down on the Cuito Cuanavale front', which he avers 'should have been regarded as a secondary front'. Fidel used a boxing analogy for us: 'Cuito Cuanavale in the east represented the boxer's defensive left fist that blocked the blow, whilst in the west the powerful right fist had struck – placing the SADF in a perilous position.'

The Cubans could easily have tightened the noose around the South Africans at Cuito Cuanavale. The SADF had shown a fighting tenacity which the Cubans respected. They were resourceful and often tactically creative but made strategic blunders and were outwitted. Chester Croker, the US negotiator, was of the opinion that the South Africans 'confused military power with national strategy'. Fidel Castro was not looking for a bloody encounter which would have cost many lives on both sides. Neither were Pretoria's generals. They could afford casualties even less than the Cubans.

All parties to the conflict now showed a preference for a diplomatic solution that had opened up as a result of the changed strategic situation. Pretoria had to face the reality that the cost of hanging on to Namibia was now beyond its means. International pressure for a settlement had become irresistible. The SADF was forced to withdraw from Angola and by 1989 from Namibia. The Cubans then withdrew from Angola and MK camps were relocated to Uganda. The only reason the Cuban military was in Angola was to safeguard that country from aggression. For MK an alternative base in Uganda was quite acceptable given the enormous gains made for Africa's liberation. Fidel declared that 'the history of Africa would have to be written as before and after Cuito Cuanavale'. Nelson Mandela affirmed that the battle was indeed 'a turning point for the liberation of our continent and my people'.

The glaring deficiencies of apartheid's war machine, a result of the arms boycott, created a crisis for P.W. Botha's 'total strategy' doctrine. From as early as 1986 a reformist trend had become evident within Afrikaner ruling circles. Apartheid was in crisis, as a result of black resistance and MK action, which brute force could not crush. International isolation and internal unrest was placing tremendous strain on the economy. Pretoria had problems rescheduling its foreign debt and investment was drying up. Nothing could prevent change from coming. The reformists within the system argued that the only chance of survival was by managing and controlling the pace and extent of change. With defeat in southern Angola, the power and influence of the SADF hawks and the hardliners within government declined.

A switch to a reformist strategy, and a flexible new leader, President F.W. de Klerk, took place. This led to the lifting of the ban on outlawed organisations and the release of Nelson Mandela.

PART III

HOME
1990–93

SEVENTEEN

FUGITIVE

Johannesburg
25 July 1990

AFTER MY WALK IN YEOVILLE, TO make sure that I had not picked up a 'tail' at Jan Smuts Airport, I met my underground contacts.

Mac Maharaj and Gebhuza were in charge of the Vula Project inside the country. They had both been working in exile and then in 1987 had disappeared from sight. It was rumoured that they were in the Soviet Union, Mac supposedly recovering from a long illness, and Siphiwe Nyanda (Gebhuza) studying at a military academy. Only Tambo, Slovo, and a handful of others, knew the truth.

Mac and Gebhuza had successfully built underground ANC structures and were at last providing the kind of leadership that had been absent for many years. They had a variety of disguises, safe houses and identity documents to assist them in their work. A computerised telephone communications network, using encoded messages, developed by Tim Jenkin and Ronnie Press in England, kept them in close touch with the external leadership. They were also in contact with Mandela in prison, and with the leaders of the internal democratic movement.

It was challenging work, but even before I had joined them at the end of March events began to speed up. On 2 February 1990, De Klerk lifted the ban on the ANC, PAC and SACP. The following week Nelson Mandela was released. By the beginning of May a delegation from Lusaka joined Mandela and other internal leaders for talks with the government in Cape Town. The basis for negotiations was established and the government granted temporary indemnity to the entire National Executive Committee based in Lusaka. This enabled the ANC to begin setting up its offices and legal structures in the country. Maharaj and I received instructions to secretly leave South Africa and report to Lusaka or London from where we would publicly return to the country.

Gebhuza, who was not a member of the NEC, would remain in place. He would continue to supervise the underground and await further developments.

With him was our communications officer, a young woman called Janet Love, who had also been based in Lusaka.

I departed by way of Jan Smuts once more in my businessman's disguise. I shed my false identity in Europe and reappeared in London in my regular persona. There was great excitement in Golders Green as the family discussed the dramatic turn of events and the prospect of our return to South Africa. Our sons, Andrew aged 24 and Christopher, 22, were amused when Eleanor and I debated where we would settle. Eleanor was opting for Durban, while I held out for my home town, Johannesburg. When Eleanor suggested Cape Town as a compromise – the praises of which had been sung by the likes of Albie Sachs, Wolfie Kodesh, Pallo Jordan, Jeremy Cronin, Sue Rabkin and the Buntings – I was dismissive:

'Those Capetonians forget to mention that all the beauty is difficult to appreciate during the howling winds of summer and incessant rain of winter.'

Within 48 hours I was winging my way back to Johannesburg to participate in a meeting of the NEC. Eleanor had a good job at the London College of Fashion and would serve out her contract. With the situation in South Africa not yet clear, we decided, in any case, to consider a permanent family move at a later stage.

For the second time in six months I entered South Africa through Jan Smuts Airport. Over the years I had dreamt of a victorious home-coming. Only Penuell Maduna from our legal department was there to steer me through immigration and drive me to the ANC office. But I was not complaining: it was the years of steadfast struggle that had forced the government to begin opening the doors.

Within a month, I was chairing a meeting, preparing for a public rally at which the SACP was to be re-launched. It was a chilly winter evening, 25 July 1990, and the rally was a mere four days away. In the middle of the meeting, my radio pager began bleeping. The message on the tiny screen jolted me: 'Lara down with food poisoning. Check your health. Contact you later – Jackie.' 'Lara' was Mac Maharaj. 'Jackie' was Janet Love, who had remained in close contact with Mac and me in Johannesburg. The reference to food poisoning informed me that Mac had been arrested and that I was similarly endangered. There was no point in hanging about. I handed the chairing over to a comrade and made my exit.

Although it was early evening, the streets in the so-called Golden City were already deserted. Offices and shops were shut and barred, and there was little traffic. Even at the best of times the city workers hurry home to the white suburbs and distant black townships as soon as the day's work is over, leaving the central business district eerily forlorn under its neon-light glow.

Zipping up my leather jacket and wrapping my scarf around my neck, I kept my head down, walking as briskly as possible to my car, trying not to betray my haste. I had parked several blocks from the meeting place. Over the past two weeks I had been living with a foreboding of disaster.

Now, preparing to cross the deserted streets and looking out for oncoming traffic, I checked whether I was being followed.

Any hope of returning to normality appeared to be dashed once more. I was back in the shadows. I felt alone and vulnerable. As if to taunt me, a newly-daubed slogan on a wall read: DON'T MISS THE PARTY– 29 JULY! A red hammer and sickle made it clear whose party should not be missed.

There seemed to be no tail. Now I was peering ahead, checking for anyone who might be waiting to waylay me. It was comforting to see my car, which was not known to the police. For the month I had been working at ANC head office I had parked it in a city car-park. Not even my colleagues knew what car I was driving. My safety was now, apart from a few other key factors – like a change of appearance and a safe house – dependent on driving a 'safe' car.

As much as I would have liked to jump in and drive off, I strode past the car, crossed the road, circled the block and came to it again – quite sure that the situation was normal.

The motor started like a charm, but I still could not relax. Perhaps I was being watched from a distance? I moved off at a reasonable speed, driving carefully. I timed one traffic light perfectly and slipped through just as it changed from green to amber. No one behind tried to jump the red to keep up with me. It was still possible that I was being tailed along parallel streets. I took the turn off to the motorway that rings Johannesburg and quickly picked up speed, being very careful to keep within the 120 km speed limit. I slackened off, allowing the traffic to overtake me. After a while, satisfied there was absolutely no tail, I was able to relax and consider my next move.

I travelled east, on the southern side of the city, with the skyscrapers to the left and the chain of mine dumps to the right. The highveld air was cold and thin. A sign on a disused mine dump declared it the property of 'WAR GAMES'. Perched on top of another lunar mound stood a drive-in cinema.

Mac's arrest was not unexpected. Both he and I had known we were in danger. Just a fortnight before, Gebhuza had been arrested in Durban. He was now in detention with about ten other Vula comrades. The security police and government had kept quiet about it. Mandela had been discussing the matter with De Klerk, seeking to defuse the situation and secure their release. It was pointed out to De Klerk that the Gebhuza group had been in place before the lifting of the ban on the ANC. Like other underground structures they were awaiting developments at the negotiating table before emerging. Mac and I knew it was just a matter of time before they linked Gebhuza to us, but we felt they would not want to jeopardise the negotiation process by raking up the past.

With Mac's arrest, however, it appeared that De Klerk was about to embark on a hard line. It looked as though he and his police chiefs were going to play up the red bogey on the eve of the Party's launch. We had no way of ascertaining how strong the influence of the security forces over him might be.

I needed to get to a safe place for the night. I had in mind a couple of friends in suburban Johannesburg. But they had young children who would not yet be in bed. Better to get to them after 8 p.m. when the children would be asleep and not see me arrive. The police did not normally mount their roadblocks on the motorway that circles Johannesburg. I felt safe, looping round the city, killing time.

EIGHTEEN

RUNNING ON EMPTY

Durban
Mid-July 1990

THE SENSE OF IMPENDING DISASTER that July had begun, as it happens, on Friday the 13th. Mac had come to my newly acquired office in the ANC building, well groomed, but looking weary behind his spectacles. 'We've had bad news. Gebhuza and a few others were arrested in Durban yesterday.'

As the shock sank in, he told me that he and Janet had spent the night clearing several safe houses of incriminating material and warning their occupants, sympathisers from abroad, to leave the country. They were known to Gebhuza and, even if he refused to talk, as we hoped and expected, security rules applied. We could not take chances. There was also the likelihood that our computer system and records had been seized by the police. There were a dozen questions I wanted to put to him, but Mac broke in: 'Can you get a clean car? We need to get down to Durban right away. I'll fill you in as we go.'

I had miscalculated the capacity of the car's petrol tank. With Maharaj in a deep slumber in the passenger seat next to me, I noticed that the fuel gauge was dangerously low. The flat highveld landscape – the long grasses bleached white by winter sun and night frost – stretched away to the horizon. The Free State town of Warden was still a dozen kilometres distant. We were running on empty.

The last thing I wanted was to break down with an exhausted Maharaj in the car. In the event, our luck held out – the vehicle lurching the last few metres to the first filling station in Warden. It was a typical *platteland dorp* (country town), with its Dutch Reformed Church, rugby ground, police station, grain silos, butchery, liquor store and streets of smart houses. Such *dorps* had benefited from apartheid largesse whilst black needs were ignored. The dilapidated, mud-and-tin shacks of the black township were, as usual, a couple of kilometres away.

With a full tank, we were soon zipping down the Van Reenen's Pass into the rolling hills of Natal. In former days, before the motorway, it used to take a good eight hours from Johannesburg to Durban. Now with a powerful engine, and a watchful eye for the speed traps, it takes an easy five.

Natal was already a tense region in July 1990. A six-day war had erupted in Pietermaritzburg. Buthelezi's tribally based and conservative Inkatha, determined to hold on to homeland power doled out during apartheid's heyday, had clashed with followers of the ANC. We by-passed the scene of Eleanor's 1963 escape, where many refugees from the conflict were living in church halls. In no time we were in Durban.

Despite the winter season, it was pleasantly warm, with a sub-tropical vegetation that is more African than elsewhere in South Africa.

Billy Nair, whom I had worked with in the 1960s, and Moe Shaik, head of Vula's intelligence structures, briefed us on the recent arrests. Billy and I had linked up secretly soon after his release from prison in 1984. When I entered the country on the Vula project it was to find him part of the Durban structure. Now he was looking tense.

It was Moe who gave the report. Things had started going wrong the previous weekend. Two operatives, Charles Ndaba and Mbuso Tshabalala, went missing. At first it was thought they were engaged in a task outside the city but, when on Wednesday they failed to appear at a meeting, it was obvious that something serious had happened. It reminded me of the disappearance of Bruno at Kloof all those years before, and my near fatal procrastination.

Moe's voice was strained as he described their hectic attempts at damage limitation. They had tried to warn all those in possible danger, and began cleaning out the safe places known to Charles and Mbuso.

'Yesterday, Thursday, the axe fell. Everything started going wrong at once. The catastrophe centred on the Knoll.' The Knoll was our main safe house, in an Indian suburb of Durban, and should have been the first place evacuated.

Several comrades were staying here and Gebhuza was trying to house them elsewhere. Then Susan, one of Gebhuza's aides, disappeared. She had removed computers from the Knoll that morning. Gebhuza, who was meant to link up with Moe, failed to arrive at a rendezvous and did not respond to the frantic messages sent out to his pager. By dusk there was still no word from him or Susan. Moe decided to go in person to the Knoll. He drove over with a comrade, who had originally rented the place. Moe parked the car down the road and watched through binoculars. All was quiet as the comrade approached the house and knocked on the front door. It opened and ... 'Yissis!' Moe could not suppress a nervous smile – 'One second he was there and the next thing he had disappeared. Like being swallowed alive, man!'

We sat and analysed what had gone wrong. We concluded that the police had arrested Charles and Mbuso, capturing them at the weekend. Both knew of the Knoll and must have been forced to reveal the address after several days' interrogation. Despite the changing situation, we had no illusions that the security police would stop using their standard methods of extracting information. By Thursday morning they must have raided the Knoll, arresting whoever was there. Thereafter they would have laid in wait and arrested any visitor. It was a matter of speculation whether Gebhuza and Susan had been arrested at the house, or followed and detained elsewhere. We wondered whether the computer disks were at the Knoll, but Moe said he thought Susan was working on them at her safe house.

'Let's hope they kept them encoded,' Mac broke in. 'There's over two years' worth of Vula communications and reports there.'

That consideration cast even more gloom over the proceedings. Billy observed pertinently that the unbanning of the ANC had fostered a climate of laxity. Those in the underground had become complacent. We all accepted joint responsibility for the failure. No single individual was to blame but I could not understand how Mac as Vula commander had allowed such incriminating material, coded or not, to remain in the country. And whom did he think he was kidding in the hope that the disks were encoded? Once in the hands of state technicians they would not remain encoded very long! Damage limitation tasks were divided among us.

Sunday afternoon, our tasks completed, Mac and I surfaced to attend a public meeting which would also serve to explain our presence in Durban. The hall was full to capacity and we received a standing ovation. It was inspiring to be among our people and I was pleasantly surprised to discover that my role in the city in the early 1960s was remembered.

First thing Monday morning, we left for Johannesburg. The morning newspaper carried a report of the Sunday public meeting. We amused ourselves with the thought of the Durban security police discovering in the press that we had paid their city a visit. We were more right than we realised. We learnt later that Gebhuza was being driven up to Johannesburg by the police that very morning for further investigations. They had been unaware of our weekend activity and, when they had arrested Gebhuza on the Thursday, their first demands were about our whereabouts.

They had not arrested Gebhuza at the Knoll. He had called there early in the morning to check on those present. At that point everything appeared normal, but the house was under surveillance. He was followed and forced off the road some kilometres away. He was yanked from the car and pinned to the ground, pistols held to his head. Voices had demanded:

'Where's Mac? Where's Ronnie?'

Gebhuza was astonished by this incessant demand. The Durban security police, after learning about our previous presence in the country through the arrest of Charles and Mbuso, were unaware that we were no longer underground.

'But they've been granted indemnity,' Gebhuza had protested.

None of this was known to us that morning as I stepped on the gas and we headed for Johannesburg. Mac and I lapsed into silence, each pondering the uncertainties we faced. I had a sense that, despite the full tank of petrol beneath us, we were still running on empty.

NINETEEN

PACK YOUR BAGS, ROZENKRANZ!

Johannesburg
17 July 1990

WHEN THINGS ARE GOING AWRY THE last thing you want to do is show people you are anxious. The day after we returned to Johannesburg it was business as usual for me at the ANC office, while Mac participated in a press conference with Slovo, concerning the Party's impending re-launch.

It was going to be a day full of engagements. First I had a meeting at the ANC office. Then I was due to visit comrades at Pretoria Central Prison. That evening I was due to speak at the launching of the newly formed Yeoville branch of the ANC.

During an early morning departmental meeting, my pager began bleeping. While the chairperson eyed me disapprovingly, I squinted at a message which read: 'Rozenkranz is back in town.' A coded telephone number was provided.

The message meant my day was going to be even more hectic than I had thought. I had been anxiously expecting the message because 'Rozenkranz' – a joke term for a lively pair of women whose code-names were 'Roz' and 'Kelly' – were going to have to get out of the country fast. The two young women were supporters from abroad who had provided me with a safe house in Durban. After my departure for London in June, we decided to close down the place and release them to return to their North American home if they wished to go. They had asked me if it would be in order for them to take a trip around the country and decide later. I had agreed and told them how to reconnect with me at the Johannesburg office. Since the Durban arrests I had been fretting about their safety. One of the arrested comrades knew them – although not their real names. I excused myself from the meeting – the chairperson looking even more disapprovingly at my antics – and hastened from the office block in search of a safe phone.

'Hellooo,' Roz answered cheerfully from a Hillbrow apartment block. 'I

229

guess that's our pal Gene, the singing cowboy.' She was a great one for a leg-pull. 'Gene' was one of my code-names, and the quip about the singing cowboy was because of my fondness for Gene Autry's hit from the late 1940s: 'Don't fence me in'. I immediately arranged to meet her at a quiet café.

Roz was sitting at a table, her close-cropped head buried in a novel. Despite the cold she wore a skimpy red T-shirt, a blue denim skirt and a pair of flat sandals.

'Isn't it chilly enough for you?' I asked as I joined her.

'Well it's sunny outside,' she retorted.

'How's Kelly?' I asked. 'Did you have a good trip?'

'Oh yeah, sure, we had a swell time. Kelly's fine. She's at the laundromat. Say, how come you never sent us to the Drakensberg before?' Roz was a great enthusiast and her penchant for the outdoors had been very useful. I had recruited her in London and she had been working for us for several years providing reconnaissance data on the border areas. What she could not photograph, her companion, Kelly, her young daughter who was a talented artist, would draw. We had built a false compartment behind the back seat of their car and, as Roz would say, 'it was a cinch' for them to smuggle weapons from the neighbouring states. When I was based in Lusaka I used to meet them periodically in Botswana or Swaziland to receive reports and allocate tasks. Now I sensed that the police were moving in and was sad to have to let them go.

I briefly told her about the Durban arrests, that even now the police could be on their trail, and that I wanted them to leave the country that evening.

'Now wait a minute,' Roz said, a defiant note creeping into her voice, 'why should the arrest of Mr Adonis endanger us?' She gave nick-names to everyone – preferring them to our code names – and 'Adonis' was the arrested Siphiwe Nyanda (Gebhuza), who was quite a lady's man.

'Okay Roz,' I said, knowing I was going to have to be patient, despite the urgency and the fact that I had to be at Pretoria Central Prison within the hour. 'True, he does not know your real names, and you could be Canadians or US citizens. And he wouldn't be inclined to give you away or anyone else, for that matter. But as I've told you before, you can never bank on anyone in detention not talking or co-operating with the police in some way.'

Roz wanted to butt in and I motioned to her to bear with me: 'Hold on a moment. I'm coming to the point: Our pal knows you vacated the Durban house. If he has to choose to give the police something – maybe to hide more sensitive information – he just might decide they can have that address. Now once they get to the house it is possible to pick up your trail ...'

'How?' she protested. 'There's nothing there!'

'Your car,' I replied. 'The landlady, the neighbours ... any of them can be expected to remember the registration leads to ...'

'Which leads to Grace!' she cut in triumphantly. 'Haaa! You've forgotten about Grace. Whoopee! We're in the clear!'

'Sorry, Roz, I haven't forgotten about Grace ...' Grace, another American, had been with her briefly a couple of years previously, and we had bought the car in her name. They had resided in Johannesburg.

I said: 'Grace used your Jo'burg address at the time when she registered the car. And – in case I need to remind you – although that house was rented in her name, you were on friendly terms with your neighbours, who knew ...' Here I paused for dramatic effect because this had been a bone of contention between us, and she was now to pay the price for it: 'who knew,' I continued, 'that you were registered at the university for a drama course.'

I paused to let the implication sink in. 'Yeah. I see,' she said flatly.

'So they check university registration and discover little old Roz is really Miss World,' she said. 'So, how long do you think it could take them to come up with my real name?' she asked, a touch of nervousness creeping into her voice.

'Adonis was arrested last Thursday – five days ago,' I answered.

'They've got plenty of other things to follow up. I don't believe your trail will be the immediate priority – as important as it is – but we can't take chances. Let's say Friday they got on to the Durban house. If luck's with them, they immediately trace the owner – you remember how difficult it was to locate that peripatetic guy. And if luck's still with them he remembers the car's registration. But if not him, then some smart-alecky neighbour with a good memory comes up with the goods – because, you see, we don't monopolise the good luck.'

I was in full flow now and continued: 'Next step, no problem. Their computer dutifully turns up Grace's name and your Jo'burg address. This could be late Friday but then things go a little slower for them. Durban security must contact Jo'burg security to follow it up. Delays come in here because the Durban big shots must decide on the further course of action. That takes time, what with reporting from the interrogators to operational command, who are assessing and sifting all the data and having to make all sorts of sensitive decisions. Maybe they want to send their own Durban specialists up to Jo'burg, or maybe they opt for speed and request Jo'burg command to send someone out to check your old place for them. Probably they get on to the house agents first to check the records. They find that Grace vacated the place 18 months ago. They're concentrating on locating her. Checking if she's still in the country and, if so, when and how she left. They're also interested in the new occupants. They don't want to go busting into the place, since it might be our people who simply took over from Grace. So over the weekend they put it under surveillance. Begin tapping the phone. Discreetly checking the neighbours. Making innocent enquiries at the house itself.

'Ja ...' I said, nodding my head, more for my benefit than hers, as I became surer of the time-frame, 'ja ... that must take them the weekend and even into Monday. At the earliest, if they think this should be their priority and they're raring to go, they decide to call on the occupants to check by direct interview. So maybe Monday evening when people get home from work, or maybe this morning before the occupants start the day's routine.'

Roz was wide-eyed. 'This morning? You mean this morning? Spooky-wooky!'

She composed herself and sat up, instead of slumping over the table as she had been since I arrived. Now she looked straight at me, and took up the assessment:

'Okay, let's get this straight. The cops are lucky and trace me to Jo'burg. They start quizzing folk. They try the landlady. Nothing there. She was permanently "out to lunch" – never knew what time of day it was.'

Next she considered what prospects the police might have with the neighbours: 'Biggest bunch of itinerants imaginable. One or two were my buddies of a sort. Not the kind who are going to gladly talk about me to strangers.'

I got impatient and she conceded: 'Okay, so luck's still running with the Gestapo and one of the neighbours does blurt out that I was studying at the university. And they don't have to threaten to pull out his finger-nails because one mean look from them, and his vocal apparatus mouths the words – Drama Department. A routine enquiry, and up pops my real name.'

She grabbed her throat with both hands and pleaded: 'Giv'it to me straight, Gene? How much time have we got?'

I realised how much I would miss her sense of humour: 'In our scenario, the earliest the police begin to interview the residents at the Jo'burg house is last night. This morning they begin to interview the neighbours. In fact round about now. They'd have to strike gold but if they do they could begin their enquiries at the university this afternoon. Which means, buddy, that the sooner you depart the better.'

With Roz agreeing that 'discretion was the better part of valour', I spent a few minutes making final arrangements and getting her into the correct frame of mind. Once I had got her to see the danger of delay I needed to get her, and through her Kelly, into a confident frame of mind. Our hypothesis meant the police would have had to hammer away at Adonis about the trail to my safe house in Durban, prioritise the Grace clue, and reach Roz's identity by a succession of swift and lucky breaks. It was possible, but probably unlikely, that they would be in a position to approach the university drama department that day with a description of a young woman in her thirties, who spoke with an American accent, whose real name they were unaware of because it had been concealed from her neighbours, and whose stated address was fictitious but who, it was believed, had registered for a course with them in February 1989.

'I believe, Roz, that even with expert work on their part, we still have a couple of days' leeway. But no time for complacency,' I said, in a businesslike tone. 'Get bookings for the first available flight out this evening. Get your car off the streets. I'll move it somewhere safe later. Be ready by 5 p.m. I'll pick the two of you up then for the airport. Go pack your bags, Rozenkranz!'

By noon, I was outside the doors of Pretoria Central Prison. Peter Harris, a human rights lawyer, was waiting for me. We greeted one another and he told me he hoped we would be admitted soon. After five minutes he grew impatient and, using an intercom system, managed to conjure up someone.

He complained about the delay. There were apologies from inside, which surprised me, and with a hissing of hydraulic air the huge door lumbered open. We passed into an ante-chamber. A warder was operating the door and it hissed closed behind us after he manipulated a lever. Peter explained to me that the elaborate system and other security procedures had been established after the escape in 1979 of Alex Moumbaris, Tim Jenkin and Stephen Lee.

Before we proceeded further, we handed in our identity documents. Peter explained who we were and the purpose of our visit. We were ushered through a walkway to check whether we carried hidden weapons and told to wait.

There was a lump in my throat as I contemplated the fact that, had I not escaped in 1963, this would have certainly been my home for 20 years. Even as I was thinking of the past, however, another part of my brain was recoiling from the notion that I might still land up in the place.

We were told that the prisoner we wished to see was ready. More hydraulic hissing and we passed into a passageway, across polished floors, through barred gates and were ushered into a room.

There, in an olive-green prison uniform, stood Damien de Lange, who was serving a 25-year sentence. We threw our arms around each other. He was looking fit and well, and I told him that in his uniform he would be the envy of the comrades in the camps. Damien beamed broadly. He knew olive green was the colour worn by the Cubans and the uniform most sought after by MK cadres from Angola to Tanzania. We had been informed that we had 45 minutes for the meeting, which to my surprise was a 'contact visit' – the first Damien had been allowed in two years. I congratulated him on his recent marriage to Susan, whom I was also hoping to see, in the nearby 'Women's Section'. He showed me his wedding ring and told me that they had received a congratulations card from Eleanor.

A sergeant in the prisons service sat monitoring our discussion. I remarked that there appeared to be a good attitude on the part of the officials in the place. Damien was clearly on top of the situation and chuckled, 'These guys are on their best behaviour now because ... *dit is die nuwe Suid-Afrika* [this is the new South Africa],' he said, mimicking F.W. de Klerk.

He, and all the prisoners I managed to see that afternoon, were most concerned to find out what the negotiation process was going to mean for their sentences. I also had a visit with Damien's co-accused, Ian Robertson, and two prisoners who were on death row. They were Mthetheli Mncube and Zondi Nondula. They had been sentenced to death for operations on the border in which policemen had died. We talked through an intercom system, peering at each other through a glass screen.

I told them that the leadership was insisting they be released as part of the pre-conditions for meaningful negotiations. I promised that, if necessary, we would wage a mass struggle to achieve this demand. While I wanted to leave them with a feeling of hope, I took care to avoid raising their expectations about an early release. I urged them to concentrate on their studies. The government was likely to drag its feet, 'using you prisoners as pawns in exchange for concessions from us which we might find difficult to make.'

The highlight of the visit was seeing Susan. We sat at a small table, after I had given her a bear hug – and one each from my wife and sons who all knew her – with a wardress in attendance.

I was surprised to find her looking quite glamorous. She wore well-tailored beige trousers and winter jersey over a shirt. Her hair, a striking red colour, was styled. Her fingernails were well manicured.

'They're okay to us,' she replied cheerfully. 'In fact they prefer us to look good, perm our hair, grow our nails, even encourage us to wax our legs. Like them.' She laughed. The warder tried to look indifferent, but certainly was not the hard-faced, *verkrampte-* (conservative-) looking Afrikaner woman of yesteryear.

'They think if we look glamorous, we'll stop being communists. But I'm going to turn this one here into a Marxist-Leninist first,' she said, playfully wagging her finger at the woman.

Before I departed Susan managed to give me a piece of information that made the hair on the back of my head stand on end.

'Do you remember that hippy pal of yours?' she said to me, without changing her tone. 'You know, the trans-Atlantic one?' She meant Roz, whom she could never have guessed I had been with that morning.

'Sure,' I replied, all ears. 'She would have loved to be at your wedding.'

'Well, the Slug once saw her,' she continued, and I realised that she could only be referring to Hugh Lugg, the colleague who had betrayed them. 'He did a beautiful drawing,' she continued, 'a really good likeness for Bobby [the police]. I know because Bobby showed it to us and asked if we knew who she was. But of course none of us did.'

My mind racing, I hugged her goodbye, parted from Peter and sped off for Johannesburg. It was already after four. On one occasion Roz had delivered weapons to Damien. Lugg, who was an artist, must have spotted her.

Roz and Kelly were packed and ready to go. Both looked glum. Kelly had a present for me, a drawing of a singing cowboy on a horse, strumming a guitar. It was a hilarious likeness, right down to my bushy eyebrows.

Roz was hefting up the baggage and hassling us to the door. 'Gene, you're gonna kill me. The plane leaves in under an hour.'

During the drive to the airport I told them about my prison visit, and Lugg's drawing of Roz, but said it did not make any difference to our plans. It simply meant they would be in worse trouble if captured.

We screeched to a halt outside the international departure terminal at Jan Smuts Airport, with little time to spare. A porter loaded their baggage onto a trolley, and they rushed to the check-in. A policeman on duty motioned to me to take my motor to the car park. I raced back to the check-in five minutes later. I wanted to watch them depart in safety. There were plenty of passengers about, with queues at numerous check-in points. But to my surprise there was no sign whatsoever of Roz and Kelly. I could not believe it. I looked again – more carefully – running my eyes slowly around the hall. I moved from one position to another, in case they were being obscured by a knot of people or a pile of baggage. I ran to a position at the end of the hall, from where one could see passengers going through passport control. But there was no sign of them anywhere. I doubled back to the point where I had dropped them. If they had arrived too late for checking in – and we had cut it very fine – they would be waiting for me there. Then a porter came by whom I thought had handled their baggage. But I could get no confirmation from him.

With a fresh idea in mind, I strode back to the check-in. If Roz and Kelly had boarded their flight I could verify it there. There were a dozen positions and very few passengers around now. I approached the attendant at the central computer point, telling him I was late, and wanted to know if my two nieces had departed.

He manipulated the computer keys, checked through the flight list, frowned and tried again. And then, making my blood run cold, informed me that there were 'no such passengers' on the flight I had given him.

All of a sudden it dawned on me. Roz – the tricky devil – would have deliberately misspelt their surnames when booking the tickets. Like getting a ticket issued in the name of 'Herman' instead of 'Sherman'. So if the authorities were examining flight lists for 'Sherman' they would overlook 'Herman'. Normally at the check-in counter your passport is checked against your ticket. The slight change of name would not create a problem – in those days at any rate – if any queries arose.

I explained that 'my nieces' had booked their tickets by phone and that their names must have been misspelt. I suggested the names he should check under. He did as I asked, and again stared at the computer screen. He looked up at me and said: 'There could be something here. But I need to go over to counter five. The attendant there might be able to confirm.'

I turned to follow him and stopped abruptly. Standing near counter five was the security policeman I had had experience of in London and Swaziland – Craig Williamson. It was rumoured that he had resigned from the service. Now there he was, as pink and corpulent as ever, talking to a group of people who had 'Special Branch' written all over them. The computer attendant was trying to attract my attention.

I was worried Williamson might look my way even though I was wearing fake spectacles and had a cap pulled over my eyes. I slipped behind a pillar, no longer interested in the computer, convinced Roz and Kelly had been detained and that Williamson was there to interrogate them. It looked as though the police were much quicker and smarter than I had imagined.

Now that I was managing to slow my pulse rate down, I noticed that Williamson was carrying a shoulder bag as well as a standard briefcase. At least one of his companions also had a shoulder bag. There were a couple of suitcases being handed in at the check-in counter. Williamson's companion with the overnight bag was a distinguished-looking individual with grey hair and spectacles, whom I thought I recognised. As I searched through my mind I recollected newspaper photographs of a Brigadier Erasmus who headed Johannesburg security police. He had been photographed with Olivia Forsyth, after her escape from Luanda. Just then he sauntered past me to the public telephones.

I followed him and picked up a telephone at a position next to his. But he failed to make a connection, so I learnt nothing. He soon rejoined Williamson. To my relief they bade farewell to their friends and caught a flight for London. For the first time I found cause to hope again. It appeared that their presence was a coincidence. I hoped that somehow I had missed Roz and Kelly's departure.

I headed back to my car, trying not to be too late for the meeting of the Yeoville branch. The meeting was taking place at Barnato Park school in Berea, as no suitable venue had been found in Yeoville. There was a good mix of comrades present. I started my address by saying: 'Today has been a most unusual day for me. I have been to two places I had always aimed to keep away from and the experience has been most pleasant. This morning I visited comrades at Pretoria Central Prison. Their morale is good and we must make sure that they get released as soon as possible. My sister used to attend this school – an all-girl school in those days, and of course whites only. The male chauvinist that I was in those days would have been appalled at the thought that one day I would be speaking here. I must say it is a pleasure ...'

After I concluded my speech there were questions and a few business items. The meeting broke up at 11 p.m. All the time I was hoping to receive a message from Roz and Kelly on my pager. We had arranged that once they arrived safely at their destination, a mere hour's flight away, they would page me. All it took was an international call to the pager company. But the little instrument on my belt remained mute.

I was exhausted when I got into bed that night. My friends should have arrived at Harare around 7.15 p.m. A call could have been expected soon after that, if they had been able to telephone from the airport. By 8 p.m. they should have booked into an hotel. By 9 p.m. I could reasonably have expected a message to get through to me. Now it was midnight. Despite the departure of Craig Williamson, I was again tormented by the fact that they could have been apprehended at Jan Smuts. I was haunted by the image of the two of them, in separate cells, being interrogated under harsh lights by mean and sadistic brutes. I tossed and turned all night, and only seemed to doze off in the very early hours of the morning.

I was awakened by the bleeping of the pager. In an instant I had the light on. I noticed it was getting on for 6.30, and read: 'Rozenkranz had a safe journey.' There was a coded phone and room number. Soon a familiar voice was cooing: 'That must be Gene, the singing cowboy ...'

She was quickly explaining that they had been rushed through check-in and passport control in under five minutes. 'We tried to delay, but they said we would miss the plane.' She was sorry about not phoning the night before, but apparently the line had been down.

'Rozenkranz,' I said, 'one day, hopefully soon, when everything's okay, you guys have got to come back.'

Sadly Roz was not able to return. She became fatally ill in San Francisco and died within a few years. Shortly before her death she received a letter of appreciation from Nelson Mandela, President of a democratic South Africa, praising her for her contribution and courage.

Roz was the code name of Hope Edinburgh, widow of South African journalist Charles Blumberg, who had worked for me as an intelligence operative before his death in London in 1986. Hope is survived by her plucky daughter Emunah, whom I had given the code-name Kelly.

TWENTY

MIKE'S KITCHEN

Johannesburg
18–26 July 1990

THE MORNING OF 18 JULY, I drove back to Jan Smuts airport. This time I was in a motorcade comprising the entire leadership of the ANC, led by two motorcycle outriders. We were going to welcome Nelson Mandela, who was returning from a trip to the USA with his wife Winnie. It was a special occasion because it was also Mandela's 72nd birthday.

I had last seen Mandela – the one and only time – at the Durban MK meeting in 1962, just before his arrest. He was leaner, his hair had turned grey, his features were furrowed. But he looked remarkably fit and well. He appeared less taciturn than he had been as the 40-year-old leader of our guerrilla army, the so-called 'Black Pimpernel' of that period.

I scarcely had time to wonder whether he would remember me, when my hand was in his firm grip and he was saying: 'How are you, boy? Still a military man, I hear. But you've put on weight. You'll have to come jogging with me.'

I was surprised, too, that Winnie also remembered me, as we embraced. When I expressed my surprise, she laughed, eyes sparkling, and said: 'Hell, we've been following the antics of all you guys for years. It's kept us going.'

The next week passed rapidly. Preparations for the relaunch of the Communist Party absorbed a great deal of my time. There was a three-day meeting of the ANC leadership, under Mandela's chairmanship, which prepared our approach to the next round of talks with the government, due to take place in Pretoria on 6 August. At this meeting we took the historic decision to suspend the armed struggle, in order to demonstrate to the government our commitment to a negotiated settlement. The duty of formulating the resolution fell to Thabo Mbeki, Joe Slovo, Mac Maharaj and myself.

We were closely in touch with the situation in Durban, where Billy Nair had also been detained. Mac and I were half-expecting to be pulled in too.

239

Then, we learnt that the Foreign Minister, Pik Botha, had briefed members of the diplomatic corps on the uncovering of a so-called 'Red Plot' to foment an armed uprising, as an alternative to negotiations. I was by no means surprised when the blow fell and Mac Maharaj was arrested on Wednesday 25 July. The moment the page message came through to me I realised that, had I been at the ANC building that afternoon, my own arrest would most likely have occurred as soon as I left work. Fortunately I was chairing the meeting of activists preparing for the impending rally when Janet Love had alerted me to Mac's arrest and I slipped away into the shadows again, taking my car on a trip around Johannesburg to a safe house.

I completed a full circle of the sprawling metropolis of Johannesburg, and left the motorway near the Eastgate statue of a gold digger. It was an hour since I had received the signal about Mac's arrest, and I headed for my friends' home. Their children would be asleep by now.

I cruised past the house which was in a leafy, residential area. Like the town centre, the white suburbs became deserted after dark. Houses were transformed into prisons, with high walls topped by razor wire, doors with intercom systems, and signs warning would-be prowlers to 'Beware' because ferocious dogs and armed security companies – a touch of an alarm button away – guarded the establishment. Paramilitary signs such as 'Armed Response', 'First Force' and 'Sandton Sentry' were as common as swimming pools and jacuzzis.

I circled the block and passed the house a second time. There were no cars outside the front gate nor any strangers in the vicinity. I parked the car around the corner and slipped into the house.

Unlike the neighbouring houses, this gave no sign of a fortress mentality, only the excited yelping of a dog as I approached the front door and rang the bell. The door was opened and a small terrier began begging for attention. His master gave me a friendly greeting.

'Are you alone?' I asked.

'Sure, just Sarah and me.'

I followed him into the kitchen where his wife was busy cooking.

'Have you eaten?' she enquired. 'There's enough to go round. It'll be ready soon.'

The three of us sat down while my friend, an acerbic writer code-named Errol, poured drinks. He handed me a stiff Scotch which I downed in one gulp. 'I needed that,' I announced. 'I'm on the run again.' Errol whistled and Sarah raised her eyebrows as I added: 'Mac's been arrested.'

I filled them in on the latest developments. They had been working with me from before their marriage, having both studied in Britain. They had given me assistance after I had slipped into the country for the Vula project. I had often put up with them, sleeping the night in a spare room. They had even named their dog after me on account of his shaggy eyebrows. He answered to the name of 'Max', the code name they had originally known me by in London.

Both Errol and Sarah had a fine feel for the political situation. They were not known as 'leftists' and had excellent contacts with members of the press, diplomatic corps and the *verligte* (enlightened) wing of the ruling National Party – the 'yuppie wing' as Errol called them. I had often relied on Errol's and Sarah's intelligent insight to help me find my feet in the complexities of the newly unfolding situation. This was useful, given my long years in exile. They helped me a great deal to readjust to the changed conditions.

The immediate problem on my mind was whether to honour an agreement I had given, to speak at a luncheon the following day of the Foreign Correspondents Association (FCA). We discussed the risks this could entail and, on the other hand, the enormous advantage to our movement that could be gained by my setting the record straight.

'You'll have the international hacks eating out of your hand, just through your impudence at showing up at their luncheon,' Errol suggested, grinning broadly.

'The wires are going to be buzzing tomorrow morning over Mac's detention,' he continued. 'After Pik Botha's briefing to the dips, which we can now see was aimed at covering the regime's back, ahead of this stupid act, De Klerk and Company will launch a propaganda offensive aimed at smearing the Party and weakening the negotiating position of the ANC.'

Sarah, following attentively, a beam on her face too, raised a finger:

'You'll beat them to it,' she chuckled, 'by getting your version across before theirs. Remember the maxim: the first version of the news is the one that makes the impact!'

By 1 p.m. the next day, Thursday 26 July, virtually every foreign journalist in Johannesburg appeared to have gathered at Mike's Kitchen, a smart restaurant converted from an elegant, old mansion in the suburb of Parktown. Having been dropped off by Errol in a side street, I sauntered over, casually dressed, trying to look as composed as possible.

I was greeted by John Battersby, chair of the Foreign Correspondents Association, and Amina Frense, his deputy. They thanked me for honouring the invitation, looking more concerned than I did. They led me along a garden path, Amina holding my hand reassuringly, and we entered a dining room filled with journalists. Over 50 pairs of eyes turned to me.

'We're grateful to Ronnie Kasrils for showing up,' John began, by way of introduction. 'I needn't stress that this is not going to be one of our usual luncheons. Following Mac Maharaj's arrest yesterday evening, and speculation concerning a so-called Red Plot, the FCA does not want to delay Ronnie for too long.'

Before I began speaking, John asked what I would like to drink. I ordered a large Scotch.

After the tension of the previous fortnight, I sensed I was going to enjoy hitting back at the government, and particularly the security police. Since there were many accounts of my appearance at Mike's Kitchen, including international TV coverage, it is possible to let the journalists do the talking. Shaun Johnson's report in the Johannesburg *Weekly Mail*, of 27 July, captured the flavour of the occasion.

Accompanied by a photograph labelling me the 'Red Pimpernel', and under banner headlines: 'Fugitive Ronnie Kasrils scoffs at state's conspiracy claims' and 'The Red Plot Mastermind slips cover for a chat ... and a whisky', Shaun reported:

> *'I'd better stand next to the window,' said Ronnie Kasrils – arguably the security police's most wanted man of the moment – as he audaciously emerged from 'underground' to address journalists yesterday.*
>
> *With the police apparently hot on his trail, the senior ANC executive member, former intelligence chief, and Communist Party member ... decided ('adventurously', by his own admission) to break cover and publicly denounce the government's 'Red Plot' revelations of this week.*
>
> *It was surely the most extraordinary scene ever witnessed at Mike's Kitchen ... Kasrils surprised journalists by honouring a longstanding undertaking to address the Foreign Correspondents Association: he arrived at the restaurant despite intense speculation that he was the next man in the police crackdown.*
>
> *Kasrils, visibly tense but smiling and joking, asked for a double whisky as he entered an anteroom of the restaurant ('don't drown it in water'), and apologised for not being able to sit down and have a 'leisurely lunch. I'd hoped I could stay long enough to have a vegetarian cutlet ... but now I think I'd better scram in a few minutes.'*
>
> *Kasrils said the police had wanted to take him at the same time as Maharaj, but that he'd been 'a little lucky, just as I was when I escaped arrest in 1963.'*
>
> *Asked whether he would flee the country in order to avoid what seemed like certain arrest, Kasrils said he had been in exile for long enough. 'This time I don't want to leave. I'm enjoying it here ... if they arrest me, that's okay – we have nothing on our consciences to be ashamed of.'*
>
> *He said: 'I will be doing my best to keep avoiding them, to keep putting the message across. That's why I decided to come today ...' As the intensive*

question and answer session drew to a close, Kasrils again apologised for having to leave in a hurry and said he looked forward to seeing the journalists 'next time. I don't think this nonsense will last long.'

On his way to a waiting car, he was again besieged by reporters in the grounds of the restaurant. As the throng gathered a middle-aged lady and a child eating lunch under an umbrella came to see what the fuss was about.

'Who are they talking to?' asked the child. The woman consulted one of the journalists and then returned to the child, aghast. 'It's a communist,' she said. With that Kasrils was gone.

Another of Shaun Johnson's accounts concentrated on the substance of my argument under the heading: 'The Communist Coup Saga ... "Just like the worst kind of oldstyle red-baiting," says Kasrils'. He reported, in summarised form:

Senior ANC leader Ronnie Kasrils confirmed yesterday that Umkhonto we Sizwe had continued to infiltrate cadres and weapons into South Africa during the pre-negotiation period, but strongly denied that this went against the spirit of peace moves. Kasrils added that the government's allegations of a 'communist-inspired insurrectionary plot' was 'Red-baiting of the worst order'.

For most of the luncheon an unmarked helicopter hovered high overhead. It followed a Mercedes the FCA had arranged should ferry me away. I managed a last-minute switch under the trees in the restaurant grounds, however, and disappeared.

TWENTY-ONE

PARTY RALLY

Johannesburg
29 July 1990

ON SUNDAY 29 JULY, THE SOUTH African Communist Party, founded on 30 July 1921 and outlawed in 1950, was relaunched at a public rally at a football stadium outside Soweto.

I had been a Party member since 1961. There was no way I was going to miss the occasion. Besides, I felt that by making an appearance I would be honouring the Party tradition of steadfastness in the face of repression.

Throughout its history our Party had been fighting for the interests of the working people and demanding democratic rights for all. Whatever our opponents said about communism and about the Party, I was convinced that we had tremendous support.

An air of drama was added to the historic occasion by the growing controversy surrounding the alleged 'Red Plot'. The security police had been leaking information to the press about their Vula breakthrough, including their knowledge of MK infiltration into the country, weapons smuggling and the existence of numerous 'safe' houses, their uncovering of computer print-outs, and allegations of a 'London terror connection' which it was claimed would cause 'great embarrassment for both Margaret Thatcher and Nelson Mandela'. Because it suited their purpose better they sought to give the impression that Operation Vula was a Communist Party, rather than an ANC, project.

They clumsily sought to fuse the Vula operation with an SACP conference Mac and I had participated in towards the end of May, shortly before we secretly left South Africa. This was called the Tongaat Conference, after the small town on the Natal coast where it was held. The topic of discussion centred on the unbanning of the Party, and how the Party should function once we had legally re-established it. A group of some 20 people – underground members and key sympathisers in the public mass movement – attended.

A police allegation that Slovo had been at the Tongaat meeting, where they claimed he said the SACP would not be bound by a ceasefire agreement, dominated the news. Then, on the eve of the Party rally, De Klerk insisted that Slovo be withdrawn from an ANC delegation that was due to meet the Government in the coming week. The security police were making a stupid error, and so was De Klerk for believing them.

'Slovo was nowhere near Tongaat,' I told Errol and Sarah. 'He was back in Lusaka and will be able to prove it.'

The police had obviously got the complete minutes of the Tongaat conference. They had come across a participant there named 'Joe'.

'And you want to know who Joe is?' I asked my friends. 'Gebhuza – Joe was one of his code names.'

It was Gebhuza, 'Comrade Joe' in the minutes of that meeting, who had expressed the point of view that a ceasefire should not be binding on people who had to defend themselves. He was specifically referring to people in Natal – many not even ANC supporters – who were subject to attack by Inkatha warlords because of their refusal to pledge loyalty to Buthelezi.

While the security police had shown efficiency in rounding up the Durban group, some of their deductions were incredible. 'They came across the name Joe,' I observed, 'and ping, a globe lights up with Slovo's name.'

'You need to go and see Slovo, and convey to him the gist of our discussion,' I said to Errol. 'It will help him deal with the allegations in his speech at the rally. And do tell him I mean to be present.'

The British connection was dragged into the controversy by a Johannesburg Sunday newspaper, on the very morning of the rally. It alleged that documents captured in Durban showed that the British government's hospitality was being used as a cover to train members of the SACP and ANC 'in violence' in London. It provided me with the clue as to why Craig Williamson and Brigadier Erasmus were on a London-bound flight the previous week.

The report continued: 'Observers said that if Mrs Thatcher was convinced the documents were genuine and regarded the allegations as serious enough, Mr Mandela might either have to condemn the conspiracy or perhaps face expulsion from his organisation's most important international base.'

Despite the lurid allegations of a 'terror base' on British soil there was no response from Mrs Thatcher. The British government was taking a sober view of the developments. While it was true that the Vula project had established a computerised telephonic link using a coding system between South Africa, London, Amsterdam and Lusaka, this was not a breach of British law. I had undergone a crash course in operating our computer programme in London, under Tim Jenkin. For practical experience I had participated in receiving and transmitting encoded messages from South Africa and Zambia through the telephone system in the United Kingdom.

The South African press, with few exceptions, generally fell for the disinformation. Exhibiting all the signs of collective amnesia, they treated the government revelations as though a liberation struggle had never taken place in the country. What they failed to comprehend was that the Vula project had originated more than two years earlier. The ANC, with negotiations barely underway, had made it clear that the underground would remain in place for the time being.

The fact that Maharaj and Gebhuza had secretly entered the country prior to, not after, the unbanning of our organisations could not, on intelligent reflection, be construed as sinister. Whilst preparing to suspend the armed struggle, the ANC made it clear that it would only be abandoned once a new constitution was in place.

By the time I slipped into the soccer stadium near Soweto on a cold, winter's day, a jubilant crowd some 50,000-strong had assembled. I arrived in disguise and was spirited into the players' dressing room to change for the occasion. I emerged from the players' tunnel in my red Party T-shirt – hammer and sickle logo and 'Build the Party' slogan across the chest – with a scarf in the ANC colours of black, green and gold, over a leather jacket to keep out the icy chill. The cold weather did not deter the exuberant mood of the crowd, sections of which burst out cheering as I was recognised crossing the sun-bleached pitch to the stage where the leadership was assembled.

I shook hands with Mandela, Slovo and Sisulu, seated at the front of a large platform. They were surprised, but delighted, at my appearance. I took my seat next to a score of colleagues as a choir led the crowd in singing the 'Internationale'.

The massive assembly – men and women, young and old, black and white, but predominantly African working class (a huge contingent of miners in hard hats among them) – greeted the Party at its first public rally in 40 years with the moving refrain:

> *Arise ye prisoners of starvation,*
> *Arise ye toilers of the earth,*
> *For reason thunders new creation,*
> *It's a better world in birth ...*

Cheryl Carolus, a gritty young leader from the Western Cape, began introducing the Party leadership. Behind us were draped the massive banners of the ANC, the SACP and Cosatu (the trade union congress); a tapestry of black, green, gold and red. When it was my turn to stand and salute the crowd, Cheryl introduced me by saying:

'Well, even I did not expect to find the next comrade here today. Because the police have never been able to catch him, the press are calling him the Red Pimpernel!'

Nelson Mandela stood to address the huge rally, a forest of Party, ANC, trade union, civic and student banners from all corners of the country. In a hard-hitting speech he paid tribute to the SACP 'as a dependable friend who respected the ANC's independence and policy'. Rejecting the 'Red Plot' allegations as an 'insult', the ANC leader called on the government not to erect new obstacles to negotiations by 'whipping up anti-communist hysteria'. To the crowd's delight, he made it clear that the ANC would not give in to government pressure to drop Joe Slovo from the next round of talks. Citing the history of anti-communist campaigns throughout the world, Mandela said that those in government who regarded themselves as democrats should learn the lessons of history: 'The banning of the Communist Party in 1950 was but a prelude to the suppression of all democratic opposition in our country.'

Addressing the issue of the SACP-ANC alliance, Nelson Mandela stated that in his experience, 'the SACP had never sought to impose its views on the ANC', and added: 'The ANC regarded the SACP as a dependable friend and would fight for its right to exist.'

To cries of 'Viva the SACP!' and 'Forward with Socialism!' the General Secretary of the SACP, Joe Slovo, in a smart grey suit – his red socks mischievously showing – rose to address the crowd.

After delivering a moving tribute to the Party for the part it had played in 69 years of struggle, Slovo proceeded to demolish the Government's 'Red Plot' allegations:

'We know what's behind the poisonous offensive against us ... because the peace process has many enemies and some of them are right around De Klerk himself. They feed him a diet of ghastly lies and distortions about our Party. They aim to drive a wedge between the SACP and ANC. They are clearly more interested in anti-communist manoeuvring than in bringing about peace,' he said.

The allegations rested on a 'three-fold lie':

'Lie number one is that I participated in the Tongaat meeting on 19 and 20 May. Their immigration records will show that I left South Africa for Lusaka on 14 May and returned on 21 May.

'Lie number two is that I told the Tongaat meeting that the SACP would not be bound by a ceasefire agreed to between the ANC and the Government: I have never said anything of the sort, at any meeting, anywhere.

'Lie number three is that the Operation codenamed "Vula" was an SACP project to build up its underground structures as a new anti-peace negotiation plot. They know perfectly well that it was an ANC underground project dating from 1987 and there had been no mention at Tongaat about bringing in weapons, as is shown in the meeting's minutes.

'Government allegations of a Communist conspiracy are an attempt to "rubbish" the Party. It is they who forced us to work in the cellars and shadows. Even now they are trying to force us back into the underground cellars.'

As Slovo finished a major and historic speech, high above the stadium heavy rainclouds were gathering, and a police helicopter circled for the umpteenth time. I began to wonder, a little nervously, whether I would be able to return to the safety of 'the cellars'. Slipping into the stadium unnoticed was one thing, getting out quite another.

I conspicuously joined other leaders and guests in a motorcade of a dozen cars, driven on to the stadium field to ferry them to the Mandela home nearby. I jumped into a car carrying Ahmed Kathrada. A couple of minutes from the stadium, police cars forced Kathrada's driver to the side of the road. They searched the car and the boot and reported on their walkie-talkie: '*Die donder is nie hier nie*' (the bugger's not here).

I was in another car speeding off in the opposite direction. I had got Kathrada's car to stop momentarily in the motor tunnel under the stadium, slipped into the players' dressing rooms, pulled a cap over my head and stuck a false moustache under my nose. I was going to miss the celebration at the Mandela home, but that could not be risked.

According to one journalist: 'The incidents [at Mike's Kitchen and the Party rally] further fed the reputation returning guerrillas have, in the past decade, built for [Kasrils] among township activists. The hunt continues, despite repeated police statements that no warrant of arrest had been issued for Kasrils – a nice irony, which took local journalists almost a week to pick up, given that no warrants have been necessary for political detainees since before Kasrils joined Umkhonto nearly 30 years ago.'

TWENTY-TWO

NO FIXED ABODE

South Africa
August 1990 – December 1993

'EVEN NOW THEY ARE TRYING TO force us back into the underground cellars,' Joe Slovo had declared at the Party rally. I was back in the shadows, but being on the run in the South Africa of 1990 was much easier than in the former periods. Many more individuals, emboldened by the changed situation, were predisposed to provide assistance to fugitives like me. The morning after the Party launch found me reading the press accounts on a sun-filled patio. This was a far cry from the converted stables at Kloof in 1963, which more accurately reflected Slovo's turn of phrase.

Not that the tension and dangers were entirely absent. This was brought home by an account of Mac Maharaj in shackles, surrounded by security policemen, surprisingly given permission to attend a relative's funeral. Photographs showed him looking grim but unbowed. It was a strange period. In the old days it would never have been permitted to attend a funeral. The detention of my old comrade Billy Nair worried me most of all, because yet again he was in custody while I evaded arrest. The consolation was that given the government's need to get negotiations underway the detentions were not expected to last longer than a few months.

While some colleagues in the leadership were suggesting I retreat to Lusaka for reasons of safety, I had been told by Mandela, Sisulu and Slovo that I should simply 'lie low' for the time being.

There were several tasks, in any event, that needed my attention. These included linking up with others on the run like myself, assisting them with 'safe houses', and providing funds for survival. The lifting of the ban on the ANC and SACP had not meant that our underground networks had been dissolved, and these required supervision. Our contacts were reliable and extensive and I was able to move around the country. I seldom slept in one place for more than

249

a week at a time. Accommodation ranged from homes in affluent suburbs, to township lodgings and rural homesteads.

Since I normally only moved out of doors after dark, there was time to relax during the day. It was pleasant catching the winter sun in a back garden while reading the morning newspapers and listening to radio news reports. I made productive use of the time by working on memoranda to the leadership or articles to political journals, and by catching up on reading.

I began writing letters to the press, giving my address as 'No Fixed Abode', and giving telephone interviews where a defence of the underground was required. At that time the editor of one of the more serious newspapers, *Business Day*, was Ken Owen. He ran a column which was fiercely combative, from a right-wing liberal perspective. He attacked the ANC and the Communist Party with the same vehemence that he criticised the governing National Party. While South Africa desperately needed an open society, I found in Owen's polemics the same blind intolerance – when it came to communism or, for that matter, majority rule – of which dogmatists on the left were often guilty. I liked the fact, however, that he was prepared to open a debate and showed a sense of humour. I was looking for an opportunity to cross swords with him and found what I wanted when a reader criticised the media for being 'utterly unreliable in its coverage of crucial issues affecting blacks'.

The main issue cited was the so-called Red Plot. Owen ran a comment under the reader's letter in which he declared: 'We do not believe these criticisms apply to *Business Day* which reported the affair with balance and responsibility. We invite an examination of the record.'

I responded to his invitation and wrote a letter which was published under the heading: 'Editor's column is utterly unreliable.' I congratulated the newspaper for an editorial which (after some days of hesitation) had decided that the security agencies had deliberately 'falsified information' concerning the so-called 'Red Plot'. But I supported the reader's allegation:

Ken Owen's column contains an appalling statement which is neither balanced nor responsible, and illustrates that its author suffers from Red Plot paranoia of the most extreme and dangerous kind. He writes that the launching of the SACP will make it easier to identify communists and continues: 'We know now that the serpent exists, and we have a starting point from which to trace its length. We look for the connections that reach from the SACP into other political organisations, into welfare groups and into the human rights struggle, into the unions and into the legal profession, into the media and religious lobbies, and into all branches of civil society.'

This must be one of the most chilling prescriptions for anti-communist witch-hunting ever written and is a throwback to the time when the late and unlamented Senator Joe McCarthy haunted the USA with his un-American hearings – the harmful effects of which the country is suffering from to this day.

Ken Owen's statement is more ironic from someone who ostensibly champions individual rights, democratic freedoms and open society ... Your reader is right after all. Business Day or Ken Owen's column at least, is utterly unreliable in its coverage of crucial issues affecting blacks.

Another controversial editor, who showed that he had a sense of humour, was Johnny Johnson of *The Citizen*. It was a notoriously right-wing newspaper and it often carried inspired leaks from the security forces. According to a report in the newspaper, I learnt that I was supposedly present at a police raid on the offices of Cosatu, the trade union movement, the previous day. A full and erroneous description of me appeared in the report. I thought I would have some fun:

Your intrepid reporter should be congratulated for 'spotting' me during the police raid on Cosatu's offices ... too bad the police were so slow to respond to his alarums, but in compensation they have, according to your report, a video recording of me amongst the spectators ... which is something to go on I suppose ...

There are just a few small errors in your report which I would like to correct ... On the day in question I was not wearing the bright green rollneck shirt described – it was in fact yellow and crewnecked. Neither was I clad in an overall covered with patches of brightly covered material. I had on a green tracksuit and a black headband with matching Adidas jogging shoes (Yes! an ANC colour combo).

As for referring to me as 'diminutive', your reporter must be confusing me with my father who was admittedly of slight stature. Since I am over 80 kg (I refrain from giving the exact weight because why should I make the task of the police any easier?) I think you would agree that the descriptive term employed is a wee bit inaccurate?

Finally, I did not 'sidle off', after becoming aware that the Citizen *reporter was observing me, and 'disappear around the corner ...' That was impossible because at the time of the raid I happened to be in a kosher restaurant in Doornfontein dining on pickled herring and potato latkes ...'*

On a more ominous note, at the end of August 1990, the government withdrew the temporary indemnities it had granted earlier in the year to Mac Maharaj, Chris Hani and me, while extending those of our colleagues in the leadership. It was stated that our conduct had 'not been conducive to peace'. While security sources and sections of the press attempted to project us as 'hawks' seeking to 'undermine peace efforts', the ANC accused the government of 'souring the air'.

Through the press I expressed doubt about De Klerk's integrity and questioned his intention. I said his 'indemnity was not worth a tuppence' and added: 'Mac Maharaj had indemnity and was arrested. This was a flagrant breach of trust. I was given indemnity and they hunted for me, Chris Hani has had his indemnity removed because they don't like what he is saying. De Klerk is using indemnity like a blackmailer uses threats.'

The removal of Mac's indemnity was academic since he was in detention. Hani was in the Transkei at the time and was safe as long as he remained there, because of its 'independent' status as a bantustan. I slipped into the territory to consult with him and we agreed that I should remain in the Johannesburg area to be close to the leadership. Like Maharaj we supported the negotiation process and rejected the notion that the Movement was split between 'hawks' and 'doves'. The fact that on the eve of Mac's detention, when the ANC's National Executive had met and suspended the armed struggle, the sub-committee that drafted the resolution had consisted of Maharaj, Slovo, Thabo Mbeki and myself was proof of this.

Under pressure from Mandela to release the prisoners, the authorities, at the end of October 1990, decided to charge Mac Maharaj, Billy Nair, Siphiwe Nyanda (Gebhuza) and six others for 'attempting to overthrow the government by force'. Bail, with stringent conditions, was set at a total of R300,000. Several of those detained had been brutally treated. They believed that Charles Ndaba and Mbuso Tshabalala had been killed, probably during interrogation soon after capture. The two had disappeared without trace.

Within two weeks of this twist in the Vula saga came the dramatic November announcement by the police that they were hunting me and my companions, that we 'were armed and dangerous', and that there was an unspecified reward on our heads.

The photographs that were shown on television appeared in all the major newspapers. Among those listed with me were Janet Love and Charles Ndaba. The ANC officially stated that the police warning was tantamount to an incitement to kill us on sight. In fact, several returned MK exiles had been assassinated in mysterious circumstances. The attempt to criminalise us could not, therefore, be taken lightly. The ANC referred to us as 'highly disciplined members' who had announced our support for the peace process.

The photograph of Janet showed an attractive young woman with a hint of impishness in her smile. It was strange that the police had waited four months after the arrest of Maharaj to issue wanted notices about Janet and myself.

I was soon meeting Janet. We both concluded that the inclusion of Charles in the police hunt was a sinister ploy. It appeared to us that the announcement was, among other things, a smoke-screen to absolve the police of responsibility for his disappearance. They were trying to wash their hands of him and Mbuso on the grounds that they had never been in custody.

Whatever the case, Janet and I had to live undercover lives, with the 'armed and dangerous' tag hanging over our heads for another eight months.

By March 1991, the state's Red Plot saga collapsed in anti-climax, charges were suddenly dropped, and Mac and the others were freed. There was silence, however, about those who were in hiding and the reward on our heads. Then in June, just before the ANC's first national conference in the country since 1959, the Vula fugitives who were at large were indemnified.

At a press conference at Nelson Mandela's home a dozen operatives who had been in hiding surfaced and were reunited with Mac, Siphiwe and others who had been detained. Welcoming our indemnification Mandela said at the press conference:

'All ... associated with Vula and the underground in general were acting on the instructions of the ANC. They displayed exemplary qualities by refusing to be panicked by the detentions and relentless search by the security forces. They kept cool heads, maintained their discipline, and stayed at their posts. Today, I am pleased to take this opportunity to present them to the public and I welcome them to the overt, legal structures of the ANC.'

For those of us whom the state had attempted to depict as 'armed and dangerous', this was a welcome endorsement. Mandela went on to raise his deep concern about the fate of Mbuso Tshabalala and Charles Ndaba, demanding a full and satisfactory answer from the state.

Mandela took the opportunity once again to stress that Operation Vula had been aimed at relocating the external leadership of the organisation inside the country, from well before the lifting of the ban on the ANC. It was not an SACP plot to seize power by violent means. He added that the project had not been inconsistent with the search for a negotiated settlement.

The press was keen to interview me, seeking anecdotes about my year on the run as the Red Pimpernel. The London *Times* reported that I had 'evaded arrest with aplomb and a variety of disguises'. A popular black paper observed that 'he brought a touch of romantic adventurism to his escapades'. There was a serious side to my apparent 'derring-do', however, for by my public appearances and statements I believed I demonstrated the possibility of outwitting the security forces. As the London *Observer* noted, 'he liked to tweak the noses of the police.' On one occasion two traffic policemen kept me company as I waited for a breakdown lorry to tow away my car on a motorway. On several occasions, dressed as a rugby or soccer fan, with a 'VIP' sticker on my windscreen, I had been waved through heavy traffic to reserved parking. My closest shave came when officers looking for a stolen car unwittingly arrived at one of my hide-outs. I put the kettle on, explained that they had the wrong address, and they left after a cup of tea.

After almost a year of evading the police, and some months of undercover activity before that, it was pleasant to be 'in from the cold', with the hope of resuming normal life inside the country. Since 1963 I had been without a fixed abode in the country of my birth. Now I could consider the possibilities of setting up home in South Africa with Eleanor again.

I had no illusions about the normality of South African life. MK cadres were returning from exile, without a red carpet, uncertain of prospects, accommodation and employment. They were having to depend on the ANC to deliver the goods. My travels in the country laid bare the poverty and degradation in which millions were living. I had written to Eleanor about how, standing on a hill outside Durban, looking into the squatter area of Inanda, I had felt it was a glimpse into 'Dante's inferno'. Women were labouring up the hillside out of a smoke-filled gully to fetch water from taps in a neighbouring area.

Around the cities were run-down townships with scarcely any amenities, and squatter shacks housing millions of the hungry and unemployed. It did not surprise me that crime was soaring, war-lords were proliferating and secret forces exploiting the situation to destabilise the black communities, through a wave of violence aimed at the ANC and its supporters.

Pik Botha boasted that South Africa's blacks were far better off than those in the rest of the continent. This might have applied to the approximately 25 per cent, out of the total black population of 32 million, who were in employment of some kind. As for the rest, I saw worse conditions of deprivation, over-crowding and lack of amenities than in Harare, Maputo or Lusaka. And in those poorer countries, people at least had the dignity of being free. I made it clear in the interviews I gave that if De Klerk wanted to win people's trust he had to move towards a fully democratic constitution that enfranchised blacks, and not aim at perpetuating white domination in some new form.

At the ANC's National Conference in July 1991, I was elected to the NEC, and at the SACP's equivalent Congress in December, I was voted onto the Central Committee. It was gratifying to receive a popular endorsement from thousands of delegates who attended those two historic events.

Times certainly were changing. A photographer at the ANC Congress caught me sandwiched between diplomats from Britain and the USSR. From the Soviet side was Vladimir Shubin, a friend of long standing, and Alexi Makarov, who had been our interpreter at the military school in Odessa. One of my colleagues, spotting us posing for the picture, remarked: 'I see it's taken the combined forces of the KGB and MI6 to catch you.'

'Not at all,' I replied, 'I've been recruiting them.'

I later received as a gift, from one of the British diplomats, Anthony Rowell, a copy of Baroness Orczy's *Scarlet Pimpernel*. It was a nice touch.

After being forced by the liberation struggle and international pressure to release Mandela and other political prisoners, unban organisations and begin the negotiation process, it was the De Klerk government that played a well-prepared double game.

On the one hand, there was the dragging-out of talks, as the ruling power sought a negotiated solution on its terms. On the other hand, the movement's perception was that the government strategy was aimed at whittling away ANC influence through violence against its supporters. The government hoped to demoralise our support base by showing that the ANC was incapable of protecting its people.

The state-inspired violence typically relied on other forces. Among these were Buthelezi's Inkatha and Mangope's brutal Bophuthatswana army.

Then there were the invisible forces. Apartheid had spawned a reservoir of murky elements, black and white, ultra-right or plain criminal, home-grown or foreign, who would act for mercenary reasons or simply out of hate. The army and police were past masters at organising covert activity. They had years of experience in destabilising the Frontline States, kidnapping and assassinating opponents, and providing secret aid to insurgents such as Unita and Renamo.

Documentary proof was to show that they had trained, armed, and financed members of Inkatha as early as 1986. An 'Inkathagate' scandal revealed direct police funding for Buthelezi rallies, to boost his support. Inkatha supporters were involved in up to 70 per cent of political violence on the Witwatersrand in the three years from July 1990 to July 1993, according to the Human Rights Commission. Almost ten thousand people had died in the three years since the lifting of the ban on the ANC in February 1990. The figure was 18,000 for the period since 1985, the year when Inkatha began trying to protect its Natal 'turf' against the ANC-aligned United Democratic Front.

Random terrorist attacks with automatic rifles, knives and spears on train commuters, reminiscent of the early actions of Renamo in Mozambique, accounted for hundreds of deaths and injuries.

In 1989 the operations of a 'Civil Co-operation Bureau' (CCB) run by the military had been uncovered. The CCB employed despicable thugs who were responsible for the intimidation and murder of many apartheid opponents inside and outside South Africa, from the time of the total strategy period.

In fact, a low-intensity war had been waged against the ANC's support base. An ANC incapable of coping with the violence, so it was calculated, would lose its prestige as a liberation movement, allowing the so-called forces of the centre, under the leadership of an affable De Klerk, to gain ground. It is a doctrine which enabled an authoritarian ruling class to reform without losing power. It had worked, to varying degrees, elsewhere in the world, notably in Latin America and parts of Asia.

The strategy also sought to soften up the Movement, co-opt the so-called moderates and isolate the militants and the communists. Our mass action had been presented as the brain-child of frustrated romantics and revolutionaries who wished to scuttle the negotiations. Joe Slovo and Mac Maharaj had confounded this theory by becoming key negotiators. Chris Hani and I made it clear that we supported a negotiated solution.

As it happens, I attended the first round of multi-party negotiations as a delegate for the Party, from January to May 1992. The forum was known as Codesa, the Convention for a Democratic South Africa. As I arrived, one of the MK *mgwenya* in our security team quipped: 'Quite a long road from Odessa to Codesa.'

It was fascinating to meet our old enemy, eyeball to eyeball. I participated in a commission dealing with the 'levelling of the political playing fields'. On the government's team was Niel Barnard, then still head of the state's National Intelligence Service (NIS). I knew that he had been a key figure in the change of direction towards reform. He had begun sounding out the imprisoned Mandela as early as 1986.

We got to know one another over a cup of coffee. He intimated that he knew all about me from his files. He indicated with his hands that my file was a thick one. I responded in similar vein, only making the thickness of the file I had on him much bigger than the one he had on me.

Two of the government's most obdurate negotiators were in the same commission: Kobie Coetsee, the Justice Minister, and Hernus Kriel, Minister of Law and Order. Neither was budging an inch, whether on the issue of the release of the remaining political prisoners, in the case of Coetsee, or on that of police culpability in violence, in the case of Kriel.

They reminded me of my Afrikaans schoolteachers. Direct and stubborn, but not without dry humour. They were no fools, understood what they were after, and stuck to their guns. During a break, which came after their delegation and those on our side had smoothed the way for progress of a kind, I asked them whether they knew what was being said about our co-operation.

'That the Government and the communists are allies?'

'*Nee* (No),' I replied, '*dat die regering en Vula hardloop met die bal* (that the government and Vula are running with the ball).' Vula? They were taken aback. I rattled off the names. Mac Maharaj was co-head of the overall administration. Janet Love worked at his side. Pravin Gordhan was a co-chair of the Management Committee. Moe Shaik headed the Indian Congress delegation in our commission.

Coetsee and Kriel saw the irony. They had presented Vula as an operation designed to scupper negotiations. I met my old mentor Rowley Arenstein at the talks. Well into his seventies, he had become an Inkatha supporter but represented a minor Indian party from the discredited tricameral parliament. Political differences aside, it was a tender moment meeting him.

I had no problem about entering negotiations. From MK's inception we wanted to force the government to talk. But we had to be careful not to fall into a trap. It is not in the nature of a ruling power to hand over power voluntarily. The answer to their determination to control the pace of change and confine it within acceptable boundaries is the mobilisation of our people. We had to involve the popular forces in the process, and guard against isolated negotiations between elites. If there had been differences on our side, it was not between negotiators and insurrectionists, as the press would have it. It was over striking a correct balance between talk and mobilisation, and the timing of the latter. Unless we involved the people in the process, we would not swing the balance of power in favour of democratic change.

There had not been fundamental differences within our leadership. That was the reason why the split in our ranks, which our adversaries had hoped for, failed to materialise.

As intelligent as our adversary was, I witnessed a startling and dangerous hangover from their past in our negotiation commission. We offended Hernus Kriel by laying a great degree of responsibility for the violence in the country at the door of the police.

His patience running out, he declared that he was going to take the 'gloves off', and expose those of us sitting there, who pretended to have 'lily-white hands'. One of his police generals, Andre Pruis, handed him a file. As he thumbed through it, I wondered which of my 'crimes' was about to be tabled.

'On 5 December 1991,' he began in a schoolmasterly way, 'the Communist Party had a meeting in a Hillbrow Hotel at which a number of statements were made.' I remembered the meeting.

'At that meeting,' Kriel continued smugly, 'Walter Sisulu said that for every person killed in the townships ten policemen should die. Chris Hani said:

"If the government fails to integrate MK with the SADF, we will go to war." And Jay Naidoo, secretary of Cosatu, said: "Once we have power we will ban Inkatha."'

He shut the file and looked triumphantly around at the delegates from 19 organisations. My hand was up and the chairperson allowed me to speak.

I told the gathering that I needed to correct Minister Kriel. There had, indeed, been a meeting on the date indicated, at the Park Lane Hotel in Hillbrow, to be precise. It was a cocktail party for the press and international guests, hosted by the SACP on the eve of its national congress. Hani spoke, but only to welcome everyone. Sisulu and Naidoo had delivered messages, but only on the following day, at the opening of the congress, at a totally different venue.

The press had been present and could attest to the fact that neither of them had made anything remotely resembling the statements alleged by Kriel.

'It is apparent that the police informant was either drunk at the time, or deliberately lying, probably both.'

What was most ominous about the episode was that Kriel had clearly believed his information. It was a rare insight into the kind of misinformation that in the past had led to the detention, torture or even assassination of an individual.

During the coffee break, I gave Kriel some friendly advice. His statement was defamatory, and could lead to litigation by Sisulu and the others. After the adjournment he withdrew the allegations.

The first round of negotiations deadlocked at the end of May 1992, when the government and its supporters refused to budge on key constitutional issues. They rejected an ANC package based on an elected Constituent Assembly, for which we had generously conceded an unprecedented 70 per cent majority requirement for constitution-making decisions. The government created the deadlock. Their demand was an unacceptable form of minority veto.

With the resumption of multi-party negotiations in 1993, the ANC displayed magnanimity and statesmanship by offering a government of national unity, for a five-year period, after the country's first-ever one-person-one-vote elections. These elections were now set to take place on 27 April 1994. Ominously ultra-right wing Afrikaner forces attacked and temporarily occupied the conference centre without resistance from the police. And Inkatha-aligned hostel dwellers went on the rampage and clashed with people on the East Rand during July, after the election date was announced. Almost 600 died.

The obstacles in the way were formidable. An amalgam of conservative and ultra-right wing forces, centred on Buthelezi's Inkatha and the Afrikaner die-hards, demanded forms of federalism and confederalism to protect their narrow interests.

The end of 1992 had seen dangers mounting. Our names circulated on death lists, and plots to kill Hani and Slovo abounded. The chief of the army, General Meiring, accused Chris Hani, Siphiwe Nyanda and me of distributing weapons to the township self-defence units. A document, falsely linking Eleanor and me to the IRA, was submitted to a hearing, involving allegations against the security forces.

The Inkatha Youth Brigade passed a resolution aimed at Chris, Mac, Siphiwe, Modise and me, holding us responsible for the deaths of their members, and specifically targeted us for action. The assassination of Chris Hani during Easter 1993 shocked the country to the core, and was a cruel expression of the depths to which those opposed to democracy were prepared to sink. Within a fortnight of Chris's death, Oliver Tambo passed away as a result of another massive stroke.

There have been terrible losses. But this has also been a time of trying to put some of the pieces of disrupted lives back together. Ebe and I visited the small black township of Mhluzi, next to Middelburg in the eastern Transvaal. We were being shown around by January Masilela, alias Che O'Gara, the commissar from Novo Catengue. He told us proudly that over the years he and 35 others had left Mhluzi to join MK. Eight had fallen in the struggle. One of them, Ruben Mnisi alias Duke Maseko, was killed by the mutineers at Pango in 1984.

We met his mother, who was still grieving. She had been bitter because it took the ANC in Lusaka so long to inform her of Ruben's death. She told us how the Security Branch policemen had attempted to exploit the lack of news. For years they had constantly harassed the family, and unsuccessfully tried to bribe them and turn them against the ANC. They claimed the ANC was concealing his death because we had killed him.

As she spoke, the suffering on her face was obvious. But she needed to talk. There were Inkatha-aligned neighbours who scoffed at the family for wasting their time with the ANC. Ruben had given his life for nothing, they jibed. She thanked us for bringing news of her son. We had confirmed what January Masilela and the other MK comrades had told her. She blessed us and we left.

It has not been possible to console the parents of Thami Zulu. The MK commander I liked and respected was detained by ANC security, and suffering from an illness died within days of his release at the end of 1989. Suspicion fell on him after his Natal machinery suffered many casualties. An autopsy showed that within twenty-four hours of death he had mysteriously ingested a poison associated with Pretoria's hit-squads. I do not believe he was a police agent. That and his death remain a riddle. Certainly, enemy agents within our ranks had acted to silence him.

I drove with Eleanor to the outskirts of Pietermaritzburg, looking for Fort

Napier. 'Behind the railway lines,' someone had directed us. It was a run-down neighbourhood, with rows of lower-income, 'white' housing. At last we found the security walls of the establishment. Behind were stately gum trees. We drove until we came to an entrance. Eleanor had lapsed into silence, the knuckles of her clenched fists showing white.

Several guards loitered at the entrance. The massive gates were open. Buildings inside looked dilapidated. 'Can we drive in?' we enquired. 'Are there still patients here?' The guard looked bored, gave us the go-ahead, and said one wing still functioned. Nowadays, most patients were accommodated elsewhere.

The place was run-down, with overgrown gardens. The red-brick structures were turn-of-the-century. A water tower, with a look-out post, dated back to Fort Napier's earlier military status. From the windows of one building, a few black patients stared vacantly at us. We drove along a road, searching for the lock-up that had housed Eleanor, and the patient who cried for her 'sweet baby, Jesus'. How long had she been trapped there, under sedation?

'Stop here,' Eleanor commanded. Neither of us talked much. I followed her around a single-storey building, older and more dilapidated than the rest. All the windows were heavily barred, and had wire meshing over them. It was impossible to see inside. The place looked as if it had been unoccupied for years. There was a formidable wooden door in the front. Round the back, Eleanor stopped by a smaller door.

She gave an involuntary shiver. 'This is it. This is where I came through. It was left unlocked for just one minute by that sympathetic nurse.' One minute, almost 30 years before. She was reliving it as though it had been yesterday.

How many people had suffered in those wasted decades of police state rule in the lock-up that was South Africa?

We thought of the woman who had risked everything by unlocking the door for Eleanor. We thought of Babla Saloojee, who had taken us to the border, only to die in police detention. We thought of so many others among our comrades who had spent years in prison or fallen in the struggle. How safe were we now? And how many more were going to die before the country was free?

We drove down to Durban, to a reunion with her parents. Our sons, Andrew and Christopher, would be present. They were arriving from England to spend Christmas with us. It was impressive how effortlessly they fitted into a South Africa in the throes of tension and change and we were very proud of how they could adapt. But then they were familiar with so many members of the Movement, leaders and rank-and-file, and had grown up in the ANC Young Pioneers corps where they learnt the freedom songs and struggle history. Andrew had joined MK and served in Angola. Christopher worked in London with struggle stalwart Denis Goldberg and then as a back-room boy for Mannie

Brown's 'Secret Safari' agency which smuggled weapons from Mombasa through Lusaka and into South Africa.

TWENTY-THREE

GOING FOR THE GAP

South Africa
7 September 1992

ONE MOMENT I WAS RUNNING, MY comrades with me. The next instant, without warning, the soldiers opened fire. I instinctively dropped to the ground.

We were in an open field, having run through a gap in a fence and across the road. We were without weapons or cover. Like my companions, all I could do was flatten my body into the earth, keep my head down and hope by some miracle to survive. The shriek of bullets cut through the air above our heads. It seemed to go on endlessly. How many behind us were getting killed?

As the first fusillade died down, Bushy, my bodyguard, lying five metres to my right, cried that he had been hit. Only feeling the heat of the wound (the pain would come later), he thought it was a rubber bullet. As I began to crawl towards him, the gunfire broke out again, as angry and prolonged as before, and I froze where I lay. The sinister whirr of projectiles overhead, followed by four dull thuds, made me realise with horror that they were firing grenades as well.

The shooting was unbelievable. The soldiers were crazy. When would they stop? Could I help Bushy? The gunfire continued endlessly.

It was 7 September 1992, and I was at the head of a huge march trying to gain access to the small town of Bisho, the artificially created capital of the Ciskei bantustan. A parched enclave in the Eastern Cape, the Ciskei homeland had been set up by Pretoria, was funded by Pretoria, and its troops were trained and armed by Pretoria. It was ruled by an aspirant strong-man, Brigadier Oupa Gqozo, who had seized power in a military coup in 1990. A pint-sized individual with an outsized military hat, he cut a figure of ridicule. But his ruthless suppression of any opposition was real enough.

The ANC and its allies had decided on a peaceful march to Bisho, where we would hold a people's assembly and demand political rights in the territory. To do so we had marched for an hour in blazing heat, along a road from the nearby

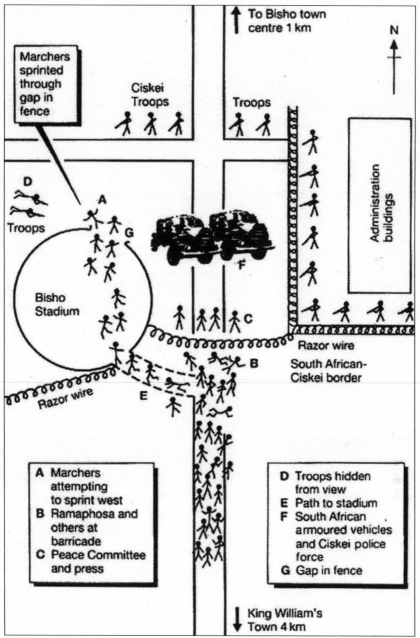

Marchers sprinted through gap in fence

To Bisho town centre 1 km

N

Ciskei Troops

Troops

Administration buildings

D

Troops

A

G

F

Bisho Stadium

C

Razor wire

South African-Ciskei border

B

Razor wire

E

A Marchers attempting to sprint west
B Ramaphosa and others at barricade
C Peace Committee and press

D Troops hidden from view
E Path to stadium
F South African armoured vehicles and Ciskei police force
G Gap in fence

King William's Town 4 km

The march on Bisho, 7 September 1992. The situation at the border when Ciskei troops opened fire.

white South African hamlet of King William's Town, northwards up a hill to reach the nominal border. Over 80,000 people, mainly from the destitute villages and dormitory townships of the area, had rallied behind our banners.

Half an hour before the shooting broke out, the leadership of the march despatched me to check the situation ahead. With a few companions I had motored up the hill, lined by thorn bush and gum trees. The border was normally marked by a simple signpost at the roadside reading, 'Ciskei border'. As with most of the bantustans, there was no border or passport formality. That day, coils of razor wire had been strung out, along the border and across the road, preventing further passage north. Behind the wire was a blockade of South African armoured vehicles, and behind them a contingent of the Ciskei police force. Three hundred metres behind the police were lines of Ciskei soldiers by a radio station. There were more over on the right, along a ridge. They guarded administration buildings adjoining the road on the east side. South African and Ciskei military helicopters buzzed overhead.

There were also rolls of razor wire strategically placed to channel the march leftwards along a side path, into a sports stadium, about one hundred metres west of the road. The stadium, situated on the border, had been the venue for a rally at the end of a similar march, exactly one month before. Only then there had been no razor wire. On that occasion the soldiers had formed a barrier along the road and, after hours of parleying, the marchers had been allowed to enter the stadium to hold the rally.

But the reign of terror in the Ciskei had continued unabated. Widespread violence, intimidation and killing of people living under Gqozo's rule made life unbearable. The decision by the ANC's regional leadership to march into Bisho itself, to hold a people's assembly there for 24 hours, to raise the demands of freedom of speech and association, had been publicly endorsed by the national leadership. Ahead of Cyril Ramaphosa, Steve Tshwete, Gertrude Shope, John Gomomo – the President of Cosatu – and numerous other leaders, I had been despatched to the region to assist with the organisation of the event. For days before the march I had toured the impoverished villages and townships, with Chris Hani, listening to the people's grievances, observing their simmering anger, registering their appeals for action to get rid of Gqozo. These were the rural people we had failed to link up with during the years of armed struggle. Now, their fighting spirit was impressive.

The press and TV cameras were in position behind the razor wire barricade on the road. They stood alongside Dr Antonie Gildenhuys and John Hall, leading officials of a national Peace Accord Committee that had been formed with the hope of curtailing the country's spiralling violence. They were present to assist in keeping the proceedings peaceful. Although they were aware our objective was

Bisho, they hoped we would hold our event inside the stadium.

I told them I could not assure them of that. But I emphasised that ours was a peaceful march, that we did not intend using violence against the soldiers. And I requested that they restrain the Ciskeian soldiers from opening fire. But Gildenhuys, Hall and a group of their observers remained at the razor wire, facing the oncoming march.

The Ciskei soldiers and officers, the most senior of whom were whites seconded by the SADF, remained unsupervised behind their backs.

Gildenhuys and Hall awaited Ramaphosa at the head of the march. They wanted an opportunity to talk. I told them that our aim was to get to Bisho and hinted that I was not sure we would have 'that sort of time', but that Ramaphosa would soon be with them.

Taking my leave, with the head of the march less than 15 minutes behind us, we drove along a track into the stadium. We immediately noticed that a ten-metre-long section of the outer fence of the stadium, on the north side, had been broken down. My companions explained that this part of the fence had been flattened, by the mass entry of the people, during the previous march. Two hundred metres beyond the opening were the soldiers.

The gap in the fence offered a route into Bisho. 'Going for the gap' in South African rugby parlance is to seize the opportunity – to go for the opening in your opponent's defence. It looked like the way to go.

To the left were open, seemingly unguarded fields. If we turned west, in that direction, we would move away from the soldiers. We had received information that some were sympathetic to us. Others were wavering. It seemed as though they were deployed to guard the radio station. By not charging in their direction, by giving them a wide berth, we would avoid confrontation. Once we had bypassed them, we could change direction and move northeast into the town.

We found it strange, however, that the security forces had not repaired or sealed the gap in the fence. What was odd was that the well-intentioned Gildenhuys and Hall, I suppose through ignorance or an oversight, had not mentioned the opening, and encouraged us to enter the stadium. It would have needed no instruction for any of our followers, once inside the stadium, to march on to Bisho through the gap. We wondered whether we were looking at a deliberately laid plan by the Ciskei forces to lure us into a trap. We dismissed that possibility too easily.

Many months later, in the context of the ongoing negotiation process, I had occasion to speak to a senior SADF officer. According to him, what Gildenhuys and Hall failed to convey to us was that the Ciskei troops had been deployed earlier along the length of the razor wire. Their officers were going to make it clear that any attempt to cross the border would be met, after due warning, by force of arms. But the Peace Committee intervened and instructed them to fall back so that we could have use of the stadium: a stadium with a yawning gap in its fence.

According to some sources, the Ciskei command, with no time to repair the fence, had deployed soldiers over 100 metres to the west of the gap, hidden in a trench and behind shrubs. If so, we were unaware of their presence, as they lay directly in our intended line of advance to the left.

Was it a deliberately laid ambush? Or was it, as my SADF source suggested, a last-minute bungle?

Driving back down the hill gave a magnificent view of the march: a solid phalanx of people, 50 or 60 abreast, snaking back down the road, and swelling all the time. It was a dense mass of humanity, people of all ages and types, from urban townships and rural villages, the majority dressed in sneakers and colourful but tattered T-shirts. They were in lively spirits, eager to get to the destination, but disciplined and responsive to the instructions of the khaki-clad marshals who controlled the march. I had been on countless marches, throughout South Africa, during the previous year. There were regional language differences. But the hopes, the humour, the mood, the demands were common. People wanted an end to poverty and suffering. They wanted basic human rights and freedom. They wanted an end to white rule and the corrupt bantustan system. They wanted, in areas like the Ciskei, the right to free political activity and an end to violence. We were using peaceful mass action to reinforce our demands for democratic change at the negotiation table, and for a climate of free political activity.

The people sang and joked in the heat, alternating between *toyi-toyiing* and slowing to a pace more suitable for the elderly. At the head, mingling with the leaders, were priests in robes, marching behind the red flags of the SACP and the banners of the ANC and Cosatu. The priests joined with other firebrands, taunting Gqozo 'the puppet', and De Klerk 'the puppet master'. Their chant '*Viva Tixo!* [God]' blended with 'Viva ANC! *Phantsi* [down with] Gqozo! *Phantsi* De Klerk!' But it was Steve Tshwete who struck a real chord in a speech at the outset of the march. That day, he said, we would 'drive the pig from the barn'.

I reported to the leadership on the situation at the border. It was unanimously agreed that we 'take the gap' in the fence. Cyril Ramaphosa would proceed with a section of the marchers to the razor-wire barricade, and negotiate for the march to proceed along the road into Bisho. At the same time the main column of the march would move into the stadium, and immediately proceed through the opening in the fence and on to the town. I was asked to lead that column, with Chris Hani and a number of regional leaders such as Smuts Ngonyama and Linda Mti.

As the second fusillade died down, Bushy cried for help again. Those of us out in the field lay still, faces down, not daring to move until we were sure the firing was over. Another plaintive cry came from Bushy. How long could I ignore him? I began crawling to him, at first tentatively, as a few last rounds of gunfire echoed across the field.

He was in distress, but managed to tell me that he had been hit on his right side by a rubber bullet, he thought. I gently rolled him over, to find his shirt and trousers sodden with blood. It was a hard-nosed bullet that had hit him, leaving a gaping wound in his stomach. Still crawling, I began dragging him back to the stadium, some 40 metres away. Others came to my assistance and we carried him through the fateful gap in the fence, and through a channel leading into the playing arena.

The dead and injured were being attended to by our first-aid workers. At a glance I counted five bodies, already shrouded in blankets. A young man was in his death throes, a hole in the side of his head. His companion desperately administered the kiss of life, while the dying man's legs twitched uncontrollably. A score of wounded were receiving treatment. I commandeered a car for Bushy. He was losing blood fast and would only survive if he was swiftly transported to hospital.

Bushy's real name was Petros Vantyu, and he was 29. He had trained in Quibaxe and was arrested inside South Africa in 1988, later benefiting from the indemnity for political prisoners. Just a few days previously we had visited his parents' simple homestead in a remote village. He was not able to visit often, and they had been happy to see him. His young nephew was just beginning to kick a ball around, and Bushy promised the child that he would return to teach him to play soccer.

I turned to assist with the wounded. A young woman was writhing in pain, her leg shattered by bullets. I gave her water which she drank ferociously. More vehicles were arriving and we swiftly evacuated the wounded.

I reassembled with the leadership back on the South African side of the border, to assess the situation. Everyone was subdued and shocked, but miraculously no leader had been hit. Ramaphosa had come closest.

The soldiers had first opened fire on those of us charging through the gap in the fence, killing one of their own number in the process. The firing had spread to all sectors. People inside the stadium had been shot. Ramaphosa, and those with him at the razor-wire, had come under fire. Gildenhuys, Hall and the press corps had dived for cover, together with the leadership of the march. Two marshals had thrown themselves over Ramaphosa to protect him. The crowd along the road, back into South Africa, had been mercilessly raked. Twenty-eight died, many at the border. Some of these died later in hospital. Over 200 were wounded. Four people had their spinal columns severed and would be paralysed for life. Later an official investigation revealed that the first fusillade had lasted 90 seconds, the second a full minute. It seemed a lifetime. At least 425 rounds were fired, and probably double that number.

Just before the shooting began, *The Independent* correspondent noted that the South African police in their armoured vehicles had suddenly driven off from their position at the barrier. This, and their massive deployment in King William's Town, pointed to their complicity in the massacre. There was no way that Gqozo could have risked the shootings without Pretoria's permission. A distressed Ramaphosa laid the blame right there: 'We blame De Klerk for this. The Ciskei is the creation of the apartheid system and it is responsible for the atrocities committed in its name.'

The crowd had shown bravery and discipline. Most, under the guidance of the marshals, had dropped to the ground. It was mainly people attempting to run away who were hit. The majority retreated down the road. The SADF and police had thrown up a roadblock, cutting the majority of the marchers off from those of us who remained. We amounted to about 5000. After some deliberation, we decided to remain on the hill overnight, to hold a vigil for the dead and to show that we would not be intimidated.

I had a foretaste of the South African media reaction to the massacre, when members of the press descended on me, to ask whether my 'sprint through the gap' had been an individual breakaway from the main march. Yet, from the onset, it had been made plain that our objective was to hold an assembly in Bisho itself.

That evening I put aside the foreboding that I was going to be made a fall-guy, as I helped organise our followers for a cold, wind-swept night on the bleak hillside. It was Chris Hani who became the soul and spirit of the remaining crowd during the aftermath. I moved with him from one camp fire to another, as he engaged our followers in spirited banter. Gqozo was the butt of their bitter humour. It was rumoured that he had never been circumcised, a Xhosa tradition which marked the attainment of manhood.

'Don't worry, commander,' a villager told Chris, 'we're going to circumcise that boy Gqozo yet.'

The next day, Archbishop Tutu and the Reverend Frank Chikane, of the South African Council of Churches, arrived to pay homage, to pray and lay wreaths. By noon we broke off the vigil. Chris and I were at the head of several thousands of our followers, as we began the five-kilometre march back to King William's Town.

We jogged down the hill, past heavily armed South African security forces. The white residents of the neat town stood silently at their gates. We sang '*Sing amaSoja kaLuthuli*' (Sing soldiers of Luthuli), and reached a stadium that was filled to capacity. Tens of thousands cheered our arrival. These were the destitute people of the Ciskei, an area known as the Border from the time of the frontier wars with the Cape Colony. Neither the British nor the Boers had quelled their spirit. And neither could Gqozo.

A last-minute bungle? Or a carefully laid ambush? I could not be sure. To stand up, the first version required some explaining. Were there troops beyond the gap in the fence deployed in ambush formation in a ditch, as some ANC members believed? If it was not a carefully laid and timed ambush, then what was the explanation for the sudden evacuation of South African police at the border just minutes before the firing?

What was incontestable was that throughout the period of our heightened mass action – launched on 16 June 1992 and reaching a high point in August with massive marches on Pretoria and other centres – the De Klerk government had been attempting to turn the mass action against us.

This became obvious, too obvious, on the very day after the 16 June launch of the campaign. On 17 June, 43 men, women and infants were murdered in Boipatong, an ANC-aligned squatter camp. For some hours, armed men from a nearby Inkatha-supporting hostel had gone on the rampage through the camp. The security forces had refused to respond to calls for help. In the days following the massacre, and in the subsequent trial, much evidence emerged of security force complicity in the attack.

But the first official reaction from the side of the government was that the massacre 'was caused by the ANC's mass action campaign'. When this failed to wash with the media, the government fell back on the tried and tested 'black on black' violence theme.

Then, on 18 June the National Party announced it was beginning a recruitment drive in the black townships, and on 20 June De Klerk actually travelled to Boipatong as a 'peacemaker'. But the strategy backfired badly at the time. Rather than being hailed as a saviour, De Klerk was hounded out of Boipatong. This precipitated further shooting by the police, and more civilian deaths. But the government did not abandon its strategy.

When we planned the Bisho march, we reasoned that we had marched 120,000-strong on Pretoria itself in August, the march had gone off peacefully, and the security forces had acted in a restrained manner. Our error of judgement, in planning the Bisho march, was to assume that in the presence of the international press and observers from the Peace Committee, the Ciskeian forces would not dare open fire. We had assumed that Pretoria would counsel Gqozo against such an option.

The difference between the Pretoria and other mass marches in August, and the Bisho march, was that, in the former, it was the SADF and SAP that carried direct responsibility for law and order. In substance, the same applied in the Ciskei, but superficially, we were up against black troops in the nominally independent Ciskei Defence Force. We miscalculated in believing that De Klerk would not allow Gqozo to go ahead with a massacre. We probably underestimated the temptation in Pretoria to play, once more, the 'black on black' violence card.

At the time I believed we walked into a deliberate ambush. But even if this were not the case, hardly had the gunfire died down, than the next broadside was unleashed in the form of a disinformation war, and there was certainly nothing non-deliberate about it.

Just as with Boipatong, so at Bisho, the official spokespersons of the government immediately blamed the victims for the massacre. An hour after the shooting, the government-controlled Radio Algoa was putting out a story 'that a group had broken out of the stadium and rushed at Ciskeian soldiers, firing as they came. The Ciskeian soldiers then acted in self-defence and shot back.' On the government-controlled television news that evening, the news-reader said, incredibly, over footage of the shootings: 'From the pictures, it's obvious how difficult it was to determine exactly where the shots were coming from.'

There were too many international observers, Peace Accord officials and journalists, who had personally come under fire from the Ciskeian troops, for this kind of disinformation to remain credible. But, in the days and weeks that followed, the propaganda war continued and I found myself a prime target.

While the anger of the victims, and the black community, was aimed at Pretoria and Gqozo, the South African government was quick to blame the ANC, and particularly the communists. De Klerk alleged that mass action, not suppression of human rights, was responsible for the violence. Mass action raised dangerous emotions, and was unnecessary because the door to negotiations was wide open. To their credit, the British Foreign Minister, the Australian Prime Minister, and the US Secretary of State for African Affairs, all laid blame where it belonged, with Ciskei troops and ultimately with their military and political mentors in Pretoria. However, sections of the media, national and overseas (particularly the right-wing British press), took up De Klerk's refrain. Chris Hani and I became the main targets of attack. As had been the case during the Vula 'Red Plot' hysteria, there were calls for the ANC to get rid of the communists in its ranks.

The idea of using direct action was seen as a sinister communist monopoly. Ignored were the facts showing that the decision emanated jointly from the ANC's regional and national echelons, the trade unions and the Party. Ignored was the fact that there were places in South Africa where no freedoms existed, and that demonstrations were the only form of peaceful political activity open to the vast majority of South Africans, who still remained disenfranchised. Chris and I were accused of using the people as cannon fodder, even though we and the rest of the march leadership were in the forefront, and came under fire personally.

The invective against mass action was hypocritical. Those who railed against it had been the first to applaud the demonstrations in eastern Europe in 1989. The students in Beijing's Tiananmen Square were regarded as heroes. It was the Chinese government that was condemned, for crushing the students with tanks, not the leaders of the demonstration. In South Africa the victims were to blame.

As someone whose name had become synonymous with mass action, and who headed the charge through the fence, I found that the searchlight fell firmly on me. I was accused of a reckless disregard for life, for having no thought for the law, peace agreements or the safety of those who followed me. The government-appointed Goldstone Commission, while strongly condemning the Ciskei soldiers, recommended without proof that the ANC censure me, together with the organisers of the march, for the decision to lead demonstrators through the gap in the fence. The fact that the ANC rejected this recommendation made it clear that the decision was a collective one and that I was carrying out an instruction. But it did not deflect the criticism. Nor did the fact that Mandela went on record to defend the role of Hani and myself, and affirmed that we were loyal and disciplined members of the ANC.

I had been asked, on the Bisho hill, if I had any regrets. 'One cannot regret what one does in good faith and in the best judgment of the collective leadership,' I had answered, digging deep into my conscience. 'Casualties take place all the time ... We cannot regret trying to go forward.' My words were used, by some sections of the press, to give the impression that I was unconcerned about the loss of life.

In fact I was deeply distressed. My political involvement had been precipitated by the Sharpeville massacre. Now I was being held responsible for triggering a similar massacre. I shared the grief of every family that had lost a loved one. The fact that I had not acted on my own, that everything I did was within the decisions of my organisation, and decided on in consultation with my fellow leaders, gave me strength.

But it was still a deeply distressing period for me. Without doubt we had made an error of judgment. We had underestimated the cynicism of our adversary and paid heavily for it in lives lost.

The trauma of the actual massacre was one thing, the sustained character assassination was another. But there was one huge compensation. There was no doubting who the people held responsible for the atrocity. The massive crowd at the funeral of the victims, and those at memorial services throughout the country, depicted Gqozo as the 'Butcher of Bisho', and De Klerk as his accomplice. Handwritten placards declared: 'Hands off Ronnie.' I had received many messages of solidarity from around the country, but it was particularly gratifying to be warmly received in the Border region itself.

I had travelled from Johannesburg to the Border region for the funeral on the same plane as the Reverend Frank Chikane. He was escorting the head of the World Council of Churches, Dr Emilio Castro, who delivered the main sermon at the funeral.

I had become increasingly struck by the positive role of Christians in the struggle for freedom and dignity. During my time as a fugitive, I had found sanctuary and real friendship among South Africa's Christian community. As Dr Castro spoke, I found myself moved and fortified:

'The tyrants always try to blame the leaders of the people for the massacres,' he declared. 'Don't let them do that!'

I visited the injured in hospital. Bushy was recovering and, like the others, was in fighting spirit. He would be able to play football with his young nephew after all. The woman to whom I had given water was on traction, her entire leg in plaster. She was a modest peasant woman from one of the villages. She smiled shyly at me, as I asked how she was. I joked about the amount of water she had drunk, lying there wounded in the Bisho stadium. Overcoming her initial shyness she told me she could have drunk a bucketful. '*Qabane* [comrade], you were nearly killed. I saw your green shirt, and wanted to run with you. Then I was hit. The pain in my thigh was unbearable. Later, when you were giving me water, and calmed me down, I realised I would live.'

I wanted to remain there, with her and the others. My bodyguards were motioning that we had to leave for another appointment.

I said farewell, wanting to hold her and comfort her for the violence that had been done to her. She murmured words I could hardly hear: '*Qabane*, don't worry, we're going to make those killers pay. We will still liberate Bisho, and the whole country.'

I realised that it was me, not her, who needed reassuring.

'Leaders come and go, but the masses are always there,' J.B. Marks used to tell us. There will be mistakes and setbacks, and some of us will not survive to see freedom. Those who hold the reins of power, regardless of their slogans and their political colours, must understand that unless they serve the interests of the people, they will never succeed.

With the passing of time I have come to the conclusion that the violence of the time was beyond De Klerk's control and that die-hard elements within the security forces were responsible.

PART IV

FREEDOM AND GOVERNMENT
1994–2004

TWENTY-FOUR

GENERAL ELECTION

April 27, 1994

THE FIRM BELIEF OF THE WOMAN wounded at Bisho that the Ciskei and the whole of South Africa would be liberated, was fulfilled in just over 30 months.

The tragic deaths at Bisho were not in vain. Mass action helped break the deadlock in the negotiations, even though the killings continued into 1994 at over 100 per month, mainly in Natal and around the Witwatersrand hostels.

With an interim constitution in place, we threw ourselves into mobilising for South Africa's first-ever democratic elections. For months we lived, breathed and dreamt nothing but the election campaign, which the ANC Alliance contested under the slogan 'A better life for all'. We had an army of natural organisers, men and women of all ages, who were steeled in the struggle and whose roots were amongst the people. We engaged in voter education, staged road shows, door-to-door campaigns, house meetings and people's assemblies where the leadership answered questions at grass-roots level. It was clear that there was tremendous support for the ANC and we would win as long as the elections were free and fairly contested. Conservative and ultra-right wing white groups, together with the homeland leaders, formed an alliance to boycott the elections and the constitutional process, and there was often the threat of disruption.

Our activists bravely took our campaign into hostile areas such as right-wing towns, the bantustans, and Inkatha-contested hostels and areas of rural Natal. Undeterred by the Bisho massacre, ANC campaigners raised the prospect of marching on Ulundi, the capital of Buthelezi's KwaZulu homeland administration, and Mmabatho, capital of Mangope's Bophuthatswana bantustan, to demand the right of unhindered political activity. Jacob Zuma showed how to get our message across by donning traditional dress to lead our followers in exuberant Zulu dancing at election rallies. At headquarters we had discussed the need to challenge Inkatha's claim to be custodian of Zulu culture,

275

just as Zuma was doing. I debated the issue with Pallo Jordan who was not disposed to pandering to such tradition. Popularising ethnicity could take hold and open a Pandora's box and Zuma was straddling a fine line. When we could not come to an agreement he jocularly suggested we toss a coin to decide. I suggested we throw the bones instead.

With confidence and expectations rising, a popular uprising broke out in Bophuthatswana in March 1994. Mangope, like his ally, Oupa Gqozo, was resisting free political activity. He sparked mass protest when he announced his refusal to allow the elections to take place in the territory. A retired SADF general, Constand Viljoen, who had become active in Afrikaner right-wing politics, and headed a committee of former military and police generals, attempted to organise armed support for Mangope. Eager to respond were members of Eugene TerreBlanche's neo-Nazi *Afrikaner Weerstandsbeweging* (AWB) who drove hell-for-leather to the rescue in a convoy of vehicles and trucks. After terrorising the population of Mmabatho, and nearby Mafeking, randomly shooting many black people for good measure, they fled in panic as soldiers of the bantustan army revolted against Mangope and came to the defence of the people. Three of the raiders failed to escape when soldiers fired on their vehicle. As they lay wounded in an aged Mercedes-Benz, an angry black policeman summarily executed them in front of the television and press cameras. It was an ignominious end to a hare-brained undertaking. The image of white men dying at the hands of a black man dramatically destroyed the myth of white supremacy and symbolised the end of an era that had lasted for centuries.

The anti-election alliance collapsed. Constand Viljoen's group, disillusioned by the AWB's riotous lack of discipline, was converted to the constitutional option after talks with the ANC, and decided to participate in the elections. Viljoen established a *Vryheidsfront* (Freedom Front) to establish Afrikaner support for a Volkstaat, a homeland where they would govern themselves.

Reading the writing on the wall, and not wanting to go the way of Mangope, Oupa Gqozo announced the dissolution of the Ciskei Government and accepted the electoral process. Only the IFP remained intransigent. Their brinkmanship resulted in 53 deaths when a belligerent Inkatha march ran out of control in the Johannesburg-Soweto area a month before the elections. Eight marchers died when a mob, largely of migrant hostel dwellers, attempted to storm ANC headquarters whilst the police held back, and were repulsed by armed security guards. Then, with exactly a week to go, the IFP leadership performed an about-turn and decided that participation was the wisest course. The democratic process had proved irresistible.

There was a last-ditch bombing outrage by white racists on the eve of the election, which left shattered bodies on the streets of downtown Johannesburg, just around the corner from ANC headquarters. But the resolve of the disenfranchised did not waver.

Along with millions of South Africans I will never forget the country's first-ever democratic election which took place on April 27, 1994. As Eleanor and I awoke early that morning we felt tense, excited and infinitely lucky to have survived the years of struggle. We washed and dressed as though preparing ourselves for an event akin to our own wedding, nervously hoping there would be no last-minute hitch, relieved that the noises from the streets were subdued and peaceful.

I put on a favourite shirt I had worn on countless demonstrations throughout the country, but not at Bisho, as a good luck omen, despite being scornful of superstition. With us was our eldest son, Andrew, who had joined us from England. Christopher, our younger son, working for the *Morning Star* newspaper in London, voted at the South African High Commission. My mother, aged 86, had voted for the ANC the day before under special arrangements for the elderly.

The expectation of the sceptics that South Africa would be plunged into an apocalypse proved groundless. In a massive turn-out – the vast majority voting for the first time in their lives – black and white, rich and poor, young and old, patiently queued for hours under the hot African sun, at polling stations in the black townships, urban suburbs and rural areas.

Eleanor, Andrew and I cast our votes in Duduza, one of the townships east of Johannesburg. We were escorted to the polling station by ANC campaign organisers. One had lost his arm during the struggle while throwing a hand grenade that had been booby-trapped. He was part of a local group of nine, all killed or maimed through entrapment by an agent provocateur. It was a grim reminder of betrayal and death at the height of the conflict.

As we queued to vote I strove to remember every comrade I had known who had fallen in the liberation struggle. They had sacrificed their lives for universal franchise and equal rights. Casting our precious vote was like a tryst with them. Placing one's cross on the ballot form, next to Mandela's picture and the symbol of the ANC, was a lifetime's fulfilment.

The ANC won by a landslide, taking 62.7 per cent of the vote. Not quite the two-thirds majority required to write a new constitution on its own. But even if that target had been reached, we would still have sought a broad consensus in the spirit of national unity and reconciliation, which had been a hallmark of ANC policy since its establishment in 1912.

De Klerk's National Party received only 20.4 per cent of the vote. Substantial numbers of middle-class whites voted for the liberal Democratic Party, and many Afrikaners for the Freedom Front with its hankering for a Volkstaat.

The Inkatha Freedom Party only did well in its home base, the re-named province, KwaZulu-Natal. It was predominantly rural people under the direction of conservative chiefs who voted for the IFP, whilst the province's urban black voters generally chose the ANC. Inkatha failed elsewhere in the country, only mustering regional support.

The Pan Africanist Congress, whose emotive espousal of black exclusivity proved to have little appeal, received a paltry 1.25 per cent. Bantustan puppets, such as Gqozo and Mangope, did not even feature as a blip on the electoral screen, confirming just how discredited they were.

The result was a triumph for the policy, organisational capacity and commitment of the ANC and its allies. These were consistent factors throughout the decades of struggle, and the reason for the ANC's overwhelming popularity and the vote of confidence it received.

There was national euphoria and exceptional relief at the outcome, for in fact it was the democratic process that had triumphed. Apartheid as a system was dead and buried, even though its consequences would remain for a considerable time. Mandela's inauguration as President took place in the gracious setting of the Union Buildings, Pretoria.

Immediately after he took the oath, six Air Force fighter jets flew overhead, trailing smoke in the colours of the new national flag. A huge roar rang out from the throng of thousands, even though all the pilots were certainly white. A black man from the once-embattled townships captured the mood and the change in relationship, by raising his fist to the sky, and declaring in Afrikaans: '*Ons vir jou Suid Afrika!*' ['We're for you South Africa' – a line from the old national anthem.]

In a throw-back to my schooldays I bumped into a bemused Gary Player in the VIP section, where stalwarts of the liberation struggle sat down to lunch with the country's well-heeled elite who were palpably anxious to be accepted. As I wondered whether South Africa's golfing maestro would remember me, he clasped my hand like a long-lost brother and told me how kind my mother had been to the neighbourhood kids. I had developed an antipathy towards Gary Player during the exile years when he was referred to as 'South Africa's unofficial ambassador' on the international golfing circuit, and regularly played exhibition matches with apartheid strongmen like B.J. Vorster, a particularly odious prime minister who, during the Second World War, had been interned for his pro-Nazi activities. As we celebrated our common citizenship, I wondered what kind of a test our new policies would pose for his patriotism.

Accompanying Mandela at the swearing-in ceremony were his two deputies: the immensely gifted Thabo Mbeki who, in his mannerisms, reminded me more and more of Oliver Tambo, and a lack-lustre F.W. de Klerk.

On the basis of proportional representation, and in terms of the negotiated interim constitution, the ANC was entitled to eighteen cabinet posts, the NP six and the IFP three.

Amongst the newly-appointed ANC Ministers with whom I had been closely involved during the years in exile were Joe Modise – Defence; Joe Slovo – Housing; Alfred Nzo – Foreign Affairs; Mac Maharaj – Transport; Pallo Jordan – Telecommunications; Steve Tshwete – Sports; Kader Asmal – Water Affairs and Forestry; and Nkosazana Zuma – Health.

All the new ministers effortlessly exchanged their liberation struggle portfolios for their new responsibilities. The bywords for the tough years of struggle in difficult and changing situations were courage, commitment, resourcefulness and integrity, which does not mean to imply that they were not human beings with both strengths and weaknesses. The leadership could not have had better preparation. Modise and Nzo were well suited to their new posts. The former had been involved in military affairs as long as the most senior SADF generals, and the latter had skilfully represented the ANC in more countries than the apartheid regime had a presence. Joe Slovo, an advocate by training, had a natural inclination towards justice, but readily took up the difficult challenge of building the houses that were so desperately needed for the disadvantaged. Dullah Omar, a courageous struggle lawyer and most impressive thinker with a calm manner I admired, became Justice Minister.

Nkosazana Zuma was married to Jacob Zuma who was strategically deployed to build the ANC in his home province of KwaZulu-Natal, where he used his diplomatic skills to seek common ground with the IFP to curb the bloodshed. Nkosazana had worked with Jacob and me in the underground in Swaziland, whilst practising medicine, and had somehow managed to bring up four young daughters. Now she was Minister of Health and determined to ensure that the poor were provided with health care. My respect for Jacob Zuma increased at his decision to focus on provincial politics. A national cabinet post would have been his for the taking.

Aziz and Essop Pahad, friends from my London days, became Deputy Ministers: Aziz of Foreign Affairs and Essop in the office of Thabo Mbeki. They had a relationship with Thabo stretching back to post-graduate studies at Sussex University in the 1960s. Together with Jacob Zuma, they had given Oliver Tambo and Mbeki vital assistance in the initial, sensitive contacts that paved the way for fully fledged negotiations with the former regime. Assisting in that process had been Joe Nhlanhla, ANC's dedicated security head, who became Deputy Minister of Intelligence and, in effect, chief of South Africa's new intelligence services.

Apart from Dullah Omar there were several cabinet appointees who had been active in the internal, mass-based movement and trade unions without which victory would have been impossible. The romance of exile and armed struggle had tended to overshadow their efforts, as it and imprisonment had concealed the remarkable contribution to a negotiated solution that Mandela had painstakingly been edging towards from the mid-1980s in parallel with Tambo and Mbeki. Decades of struggle had produced a tried-and-tested leadership capable of combining a whole range of methods and tactics, and synthesised the experience of prison, the internal mass contingent, the underground, armed combat and exile. Mac Maharaj, Steve Tshwete and Jacob Zuma had experience of all these categories.

Amongst the internally-based group were talented and brave individuals such as Cheryl Carolus, Alec Erwin, Patrick Lekota, Trevor Manuel, Popo Molefe, Valli Moosa, Sydney Mufamadi, Jay Naidoo and Cyril Ramaphosa.

Key organisational and government posts were in their capable hands, along with a young crop of former MK members I had shared many a tense moment with. These included Sankie Mthembi-Mahanyele who had taken shelter in a railway culvert when our camp in Angola had been bombed; Jeff Radebe, a former Robben Island prisoner; Lindiwe Sisulu and Penuell Maduna whom I had worked with in Swaziland; Geraldine Fraser-Moleketi, Gill Marcus, Mathews Phosa, Tito Mboweni and Joel Netshitenzhe who, amongst others, had proved their mettle in exile.

Geraldine – petite and tough-minded – had trained in our Angolan camps in 1981. She was 21 then, but looked far younger than that. A Cuban instructor, amazed at her waif-like appearance, remarked that the ANC was bound to triumph since 'those Boers are driving even children to take up arms'. She became a deputy minister at the age of 33 and a full cabinet minister two years later.

Gill Marcus had tirelessly produced ANC publications from an office in London and worked closely with Yusuf Dadoo. She narrowly escaped death when a bomb, planted by apartheid security police with links to Craig Williamson, blew up the premises in 1982.

Mathews Phosa, a lawyer who wrote poems in Afrikaans, became Premier of Mpumalanga. We had worked together in adjacent Mozambique setting up a network of underground cells in his beautiful and fertile home province, which we code-named Orange Orchard.

Tito Mboweni, born in 1959, worked at our underground headquarters in Lusaka as a researcher after obtaining a post-graduate degree in economics at a British university. Like many others of his generation he toiled away quietly and impressively to emerge, at a young age, as a government minister of exceptional talent. The press was fascinated by his forename, assuming he was named after Marshal Tito, the Yugoslav leader. In fact it was the diminutive of the Titus of biblical origin.

Youngsters like Tito and Joel Netshitenzhe (who trained as a guerrilla in Angola and who emerged as one of our brightest intellects, becoming an aide in Mandela's office) were of the generation of black children that Dr Verwoerd, the architect of apartheid, had preached 'must forever remain hewers of wood and drawers of water'. He had added: 'What is the use of teaching them mathematics when they are never going to need to use it?' Now they were running the country.

On a family note our elder son, Andrew, would make a name for himself as a popular TV and musical artist amongst the black youth whilst a very talented Christopher would work at the South African High Commission in London as media officer and speech writer. Brigid and her family settled down in Cape Town and Eleanor reconciled with her parents. After all, with the ANC becoming the governing power we were now quite respectable in their eyes. Irrespective of that, Eleanor was a loving daughter with a kind nature who had it in her heart to forgive their past deceit. Ironically, and proving to be an unresolved heartbreak for her, mending a rift with her own daughter proved insoluble. Alas, life rarely ends with a perfect outcome.

TWENTY-FIVE

MINISTRY OF DEFENCE

I WAS APPOINTED DEPUTY DEFENCE Minister under Joe Modise. There is no denying the sense of honour one experiences on receiving such news, or the surge of surprise. Although we had always maintained that freedom would come in our lifetimes, we had been acutely aware of our vulnerability. Hence picturing oneself as a deputy minister, at the time we were operating out of bush camps and underground basements, would have been venturing into the realms of fantasy.

The Ministry of Defence was situated in a top-security, ultra-modern building on the outskirts of Pretoria owned by Armscor, the arms procurement agency. Because of its reflective glass facade MK intelligence referred to it as the 'Crystal Palace'. SADF officers called it 'Battlestar Galactica'. Cynics in the new era, who felt the military was incapable of change, dubbed it 'Jurassic Park'. The SADF had been an empire unto itself and the Minister its front-man in Parliament. The time to commence with change had begun, even if it was a little like David confronting Goliath. The Ministry was minuscule, situated along a solitary passageway within a monstrous complex. We had a staff of some 20 secretaries and clerks on loan from the military. Almost 2,000 people in the rest of the building served the needs of Defence Force headquarters and Armscor. I discovered that my salary and even the petty cash account in my office was paid for by the Defence Force's Chief of Finance.

As soon as Modise and I took office we requested the personal files of the staff we had inherited. We planned to carry out an audit to see what immediate changes could be made. Replacing the gung-ho, militaristic paintings from the Magnus Malan era in our swish new offices was high on the agenda but could wait. The senior civil servant in the Ministry, a brigadier with the title of Military Secretary, replied to our request for files in an unperturbed manner, explaining that his own file was several volumes thick. His response would have done credit to the BBC Television series *Yes, Minister*, which satirised the power relationship between government and civil service. We immediately countered by saying the curriculum vitae would do. Of course we were very keen to see our own files but these had been conveniently destroyed – or so we were told. I personally went through the data-base at Military Intelligence HQ. Cueing in the names Tambo and Slovo produced hundreds of pages of their statements and speeches. Personal data that once had been painstakingly collected about them, or anything else of significance, had been wiped from the computers and said to no longer exist. This was not particularly helpful in terms of confidence building.

We had not expected things to be easy. Making policy – the executive function – was one thing, but implementing it – the management role – quite another. The new government having taken political office, but with an inherited (predominantly pro-National Party) civil service and security apparatus – the result of concessions in the negotiated settlement – still had to take control of state power and ensure that public servants became representative of the population and loyal to democracy. The taking over of the state structure, rather than smashing it, was a departure from Marxist revolutionary theory most ANC and Communist Party militants had imbibed since embarking on the armed struggle in the 1960s. Given the choice, we preferred a peaceful democratic transition, in which the olive branch of reconciliation and a measured approach to the transfer of power would avoid bloodshed and conflict in which the ordinary people would suffer the most. This position was in fact borne out by the MK Manifesto which declared at the inception of the armed struggle in 1961, that we hoped our actions would bring the Government and its supporters to their senses before matters reached the desperate stage of civil war.

There is a view that had the Soviet Union continued to exist we might have followed a more confrontationalist approach. The fact is that from the time of the SADF's defeat at Cuito Cuanavale in 1988, both the Soviet Union and Cuba encouraged us to seek a negotiated settlement. The ANC itself, as early as 1987, discerning a positive shift in the balance of forces, resolved to intensify the armed and mass struggle whilst preparing for the possibility of negotiations. The passage of time has helped to clarify events. The changes in the Soviet Union under Gorbachev clearly led the Western powers to regard the ANC as less of a revolutionary threat to their interests than beforehand. Their intelligence services had remarkable insight into Soviet weaknesses and the impending crisis of socialism – which has been confirmed by Markus Wolf, former East German intelligence chief in his book, *Man Without a Face* – and they accordingly influenced De Klerk to negotiate a settlement.

The civil servants in our ministry were extremely courteous and it became clear that their major concern was holding onto their jobs. For their part they were amazed to discover that the former 'terrorists', now in charge, had a pleasant demeanour. This was in sharp contrast to their previous chiefs who surrounded themselves with pomp and ceremony and, by most accounts, were arrogant and aloof. Some lowly civil servants – gardeners, tea-makers or messengers of many years' service – had their first-ever experience of the head of state or a minister shaking their hands and enquiring about their work.

I heard from Kader Asmal how, on his first day at the Ministry of Water Affairs, he had popped into the messengers' room where an old white retainer was struck so speechless with disbelief by the unprecedented visit, that his cigarette had hung forgotten from the corner of his mouth as he clung onto Kader's hand in gratitude. Mandela effortlessly set the standard and it was normal for him to shake the hand of every member of a choir after a performance.

There was no escaping certain rules of protocol. On the second day of being chauffeured to the defence ministry, my newly allocated bodyguard politely requested that I wait for him to open the door before alighting from the vehicle. It was not only a question of etiquette but of security. While it would have been preferable to dispense with formalities and maintain the common touch, government cannot function without established procedures. Its representatives cannot simply go walkabout and flaunt potential security hazards. Modise and I were the object of death threats. The defence force, which was responsible for our security, was bound to take these seriously. It was interesting observing our protectors, former MK and SADF members, working together and becoming friends. One of them was Vusi Mpela (alias Lazzie) who had been my student in Angola, and had served by my side in Swaziland and again at ANC headquarters in Johannesburg.

Taking these threats seriously meant accepting the instructions and presence of bodyguards. It was disrespectful not to, even though it was embarrassing, at first, being constantly accompanied by a pair of bodyguards in public – as discreet as they were. Although people in the streets and shopping malls, whether black or white, were inclined to cheerfully greet me, this was not always the case. On one occasion I happened to be alone in an hotel reception area when I found myself being stared at, long and hard, by a decidedly unfriendly-looking individual. As recognition dawned he approached me with a scowl on his face and, pointing a finger at my chest, said it was a pity he did not have his gun with him. He was an immigrant from Poland, he claimed, and like Janus Walus, the assassin of Chris Hani, hated communists. I got rid of him by demanding his name and threatening to call the police. I always kept my security team primed about my movements after that.

The press followed our movements closely. The media developed a bee in their bonnet about former revolutionaries jumping on a so-called parliamentary gravy-train. The facts did not bear this out when compared with former parliamentary benefits. ANC MPs, who were starting their parliamentary careers from a zero savings base and no property or pensions to speak of, accused the media of exhibiting a racist bias and resenting their new earning power.

Ken Owen, editor of the *Sunday Times*, spotted me being ushered out of a car and printed some sarcastic comments about even 'Red Ron' being chauffeured around in a 'luxury limousine'. In fact the vehicle was nothing more spectacular than a Nissan Maxima I had purchased with my ministerial allowance. And if I had not, the allowance would have been heavily taxed. Owen had one of his reporters ferreting out the cost of refurbishing government residences for the new ministers. New curtains in my home were said to have cost the taxpayer R71,000. The actual cost was R17,000. A three-bedroomed government residence was described as my 'mansion'. After I wrote a letter of complaint, Ken Owen was gracious enough to publish an apology for 'the error – and the hyperbole' (*Sunday Times* – 2/04/95). When he retired both Essop Pahad and I were invited to his farewell banquet. As infuriating as he was, we both had a sneaking admiration for him. I suppose it was because he was an honest-enough street fighter like ourselves.

Tackling the press was often a diversion from my tasks, but I enjoyed engaging with them. As a public figure one had to be stoic about the slings and arrows. I am a firm supporter of a free press. What has been infuriating are the inaccuracies and professional short-comings which are a product of the apartheid years. John Carlin, the British journalist, once wrote that I preferred taking the offensive, as was my preference in football, and his comparison pleased me – more for the soccer analogy than anything else.

Tackling the standing army was a formidable challenge. We had to sensitively manage the tension between change on the one hand, and maintaining stability on the other, always bearing in mind the importance of the military as the ultimate force on which state power rests. Many of our supporters, including ANC MPs, wanted to see a more radical approach and were deeply suspicious of our former foe still seen to be in military command. We took our cue from Mandela who often remarked to the ANC leadership that we should not behave as if we were dealing with an enemy whom we had defeated on the battlefield. 'Implicit in this warning,' Pallo Jordan had observed, 'is that the enemy is still strong and might well have unexhausted reserves of power and energy that he could marshal against us.' (*The National Question in Post 1994 South Africa*, a discussion paper, November 1997.) The extent to which the former 'enemy' might be prepared to mount an open or covert challenge to the new democracy, given conditions such as the break-down of law and order or a major economic crisis, was a question that could not be lightly dismissed. Nor could we rule out such forces plotting to destabilise government from within and without or engineering a crisis. These were practical possibilities. At the same time we also needed to avoid exaggerating the potential threat from the ultra-right or indeed falling prey to fabricated threats. Both could hold government hostage to pressing on with transformation. Apartheid's security services had developed an industry based on the dissemination of disinformation and bogus threats. Damaging rumours, with no basis in fact, are still spread to undermine confidence in government or destroy an individual – and in later years some elements within the ANC were to become increasingly susceptible to such destabilisation.

Our success in a new historical era depended on being able to develop a better standard of living for the poor and disadvantaged majority of the people, deepening the democratic changes and transforming the state. This was the biggest obstacle to any would-be organisers of a coup d'état who, with the irreversible demise of white minority rule, would have to appeal across colour lines for legitimacy and support. Coup leaders in history such as Spain's General Franco or Chile's General Pinochet required considerable social forces for their support as well as international encouragement. White supremacists were isolated, demoralised and in disarray. With the overwhelming support of the majority of the population for the ANC, as well as universal international approval, the threat of armed revolt receded.

The apartheid-era generals were accustomed to having their way with the politicians – their influence in the 1980s having been excessive – and a firm resolve, together with civil control, would be required to get them to implement the more strategic decisions and change their mind-set. MK-SADF negotiations had gone well, however, and Modise in particular established a positive rapport with 'Kat' Liebenberg, the affable SADF commander. 'Kat' was down-to-earth, unpretentious and the only SADF general to express to me, over a relaxed drink, remorse about some of the things the military had been required to do. We were disappointed that he was due to retire.

Mandela appointed General George Meiring, former chief of the army, as the commander of the new South African National Defence Force (SANDF). A tall, erect figure, with a sour manner and strong will, he had commanded South Africa's forces in Namibia between 1983 and 1986. Inclined in the past to mixing politics with soldiering, he had alleged at an army parade in 1992 that Chris Hani, Siphiwe Nyanda and I were arming underground units. We trusted he would co-operate in the interests of the defence force and the country.

Meiring's appointment did much to settle the anxiety of conservative elements both inside and outside the military, amongst whom he commanded considerable respect. Although he hinted to Modise and me that there were some individuals who were not altogether happy about my appointment, there were many younger officers who we soon discovered proffered the contrary opinion.

The full-time section of the apartheid defence force, the old SADF, was 70,000 strong. Conscription had accounted for another half-a-million white males in the part-time service. We abolished this unpopular practice, opting for an all-volunteer system which would include both regular and part-time units. The first task which confronted us was the historic step of integrating seven former adversarial forces into the regular component of the SANDF. These were MK and APLA (which was the PAC's armed wing), the SADF and the four armed forces of the former bantustans – Transkei, Bophuthatswana, Ciskei and Venda.

After the voluntary demobilisation of thousands of MK combatants, many of whom were tired of military life or preferred careers in politics or the private sector, 13,000 chose integration into the new defence force, together with over 7,000 former APLA cadres. The bantustan forces amounted to 11,000 military personnel. A further 2,000 members of the former KwaZulu self-protection units were later added. The combined figures meant that the former liberation fighters were greatly outnumbered in the new defence force. There was the need for systematic progress to avoid them being 'absorbed' by the old rather than 'integrated' into the new. There was also the likelihood that some would lose their jobs if they, like all military personnel regardless of background, were unable to prove their ability. Government policy was to downsize a civil service bloated by apartheid patronage. The military, which had expanded due to the integration process, would have to reduce in number and adapt to peacetime budgetary requirements.

The first thing we did was announce the appointment of nine former MK officers as generals. The old guard had hoped we would settle on three. In fact one such officer, in convivial mood over a few brandies and Coke at a *braaivleis* [barbecue], enthused that with the largely white officer corps and black troops we could become the best army in the world. This attitude was not uncommon and I believed that changing this mind-set was our biggest challenge.

By March 1997 the number of black generals appointed was 15, although one had died (Petrus Tshikeshe alias Julius, the camp commander at Novo Catengue who had demonstrated for me how a 'staff rider' rode the trains) and three had reached retirement age, including Lambert Moloi – MK's operations chief. General Siphiwe Nyanda became Deputy Chief of the Defence Force, and General Gilbert Romano, Deputy Chief of the Army. General Themba Masuku, our chief doctor in Angola, became head of the military's medical service and the first black service chief. Other generals were Godfrey Ngwenya, formerly known as Timothy Mokoena or 'Bra T', the MK commander in Angola, and Mojo Motau, a young deputy chief of Defence Intelligence.

Also appointed to the senior ranks was the country's first-ever woman general, Refiloe 'Jackie' Sedibe, who had trained with me at Odessa and who was one of MK's most senior figures. She was married to Joe Modise who was unfairly attacked by the political opposition for alleged nepotism. In fact it was I who had fought for her rank on the grounds of her ability. Rashid, the MK operative who had once dived into the swamp at our Funda camp outside Luanda during a mock air raid, and whose real name was Abubaker Ismail, became a general and was appointed chief director of Defence policy. Jackie and Rashid had served on the MK High Command in Lusaka. Three outstanding officers from the old Transkei Defence Force were made generals.

The white generals originally numbered over 40 and there were over 130 brigadiers, which were far too many for peacetime requirements. Through early retirement and rationalisation, the number of these officers steadily decreased. We introduced an affirmative action programme to create a force more representative of the population. Within three years of integration, 70 per cent of the defence force was black with the number of black officers increasing from less than 1 per cent in the old SADF in 1994 to over 22 per cent in the new national defence force. Modise announced that this black officer corps, which numbered 2,200 men and women by 1997, constituted a strategic base from which to achieve greater representivity.

A civic education curriculum was also introduced, and a culture and value system reflective of South Africa's newly won democratic principles inculcated. Reflecting a paradigm shift from the past, a non-aggressive defence posture had been adopted, the military budget having been slashed by over 60 per cent since 1989. South Africa also became one of the first countries in the world to destroy its stockpile of anti-personnel landmines.

Time has been required to provide former guerrilla combatants with the qualifications for regular warfare. There was some impatience with this process so I could not but be impressed when I learnt from an admiral of the Indian Navy – erudite and philosophical like so many of that country's officer corps – that it had taken India almost a decade after independence from British rule in 1947 to appoint its own army, air force and navy chiefs.

Whatever ideological concerns the old guard might have had with transformation, the essential factor uppermost in the mind of the individual officer was to retire gracefully, comfortably and hopefully with a medal and a handshake from Mandela. The ANC cleverly anticipated this during the negotiations. Joel Netshitenzhe coined the term 'sunset clauses', which broke a deadlock in the talks and guaranteed the jobs and pensions of the old public servants. I disagreed heatedly with Joe Slovo, who too readily adopted the idea but must admit the carrot appears to have worked – for the time being at least. For some of the former order the pension proved mightier than the sword. On the other hand, not everyone was willing or ready to retire and the bottom line for many was quite naturally a struggle to preserve job and career. And there can be nothing more bitter than such a struggle.

None of this could make the change-over easy or smooth or rule out the antipathy of some old-time bureaucrats, who would battle to retain control. A sergeant or junior officer in any military institution, let alone the higher ranks, can make life extremely unpleasant for a subordinate. There were consequently several protests by former MK and APLA members regarding administrative delays, perceived racism, the use of Afrikaans, application of the outdated military disciplinary code, and disputes over allowances, pay and ranking. One of these involved a march on the Union Buildings in the middle of the night, in which I joined President Mandela to listen to their grievances, and attempt to deal with their frustrations.

Many complaints have not been easy to prove or resolve. We had our share of disciplinary lapses in MK, so we could not take all criticism at face value or defend unacceptable conduct. But there had been an almost Prussian-type emphasis on 'order' in the former SADF which, with the application of harsh discipline, had sometimes provoked protest among the white conscripts. This emphasis was in contrast to the idea of 'fairness' in MK's culture, which was preferable in all volunteer forces – including modern, professional armies – and was not inimical to the development of good discipline and morale. At the same time it was made abundantly clear by Modise that neither racism nor lack of discipline would be tolerated in the new SANDF. He also emphasised that he would judge the performance of all officers on their attitude to transformation.

It was only to be expected that the defence force, as a microcosm of society, would exhibit the negative prejudices afflicting the white population of the country. More so, in fact, given the weight of its authoritarian hierarchy, culture and tradition. The problem was that those in the driving seat were predominantly whites from the old force, with possibly only a minority able to recognise their own ingrained bias. Many were predisposed to uphold the norms of the past and hang on to their jobs at all costs. I learnt that one white officer's view of integration was that it had to be suffered, but after completion the defence force would 'shake the dandruff out of its hair' – by which was meant getting rid of unwanted MK/APLA 'riff-raff'.

We emphasised not only substituting some white faces for black, but transforming the entire defence culture and ethos and assisting all members to build a common trust and cope with change. We drew on experts from civil society such as Laurie Nathan, director of the Institute for Conflict Resolution. Laurie, a former anti-conscription campaign leader and one-time bête noir of the old SADF, won the respect of military officers through his contribution. One of Laurie's favourite anecdotes for his military audiences was the American tank commander's forthright statement: 'I don't care if you are black or white, gay or straight. If you can zap a tank, I want you on my team.' What was encouraging was the number of white officers displaying a positive and professional attitude to change, a desire to co-operate with the new order and work with their black colleagues. It was encouraging to find such individuals transferring their loyalty. The military secretary, Roelf Beukes, was one such officer and he was promoted to general after returning to his arm of service, a clear signal that those with the right attitude had good prospects, irrespective of race or background. There were many other examples. Differences between people are likely to dissolve once they become involved in tackling shared tasks. But they must have a mutual stake in the success of the outcome with an unrivalled driving power and political will to make things work such as the ANC at that time. This was the so-called 'win-win' formula that had underlaid the successful political negotiations between former adversaries in South Africa. Unfortunately not everything can be resolved to everyone's satisfaction since there are simply not enough jobs to go round. There were therefore bound to be some losers although the aim was to provide acceptable retrenchment packages and assist military personnel to re-enter civil society.

Our whole approach was in marked contrast to that of the National Party after it came to power in 1948. The civil service was grossly inflated to become a repository for National Party supporters. Senior officers who had distinguished themselves during the Second World War, both Afrikaans and English speakers, were purged by F.C. Erasmus, Minister of Defence and notorious Anglophobe. They were replaced by far less qualified individuals. The episode was known as the 'Midnight Ride', because despatch riders delivered dismissal notices late at night.

Erasmus left a legacy of bitterness which is still encountered to this day, particularly within the regiments of the former Citizen Force. Led by Modise, the MK command had met representatives of these units before the elections when they were relieved to learn that we had no intention of dissolving them. Their leader was Colonel Ian Deetlefs of the Natal Carbineers. Modise promoted him to brigadier and put him in charge of a new Part Time Forces system.

It was gratifying redressing the wrongs of the Erasmus era. One of these involved the disappearance in 1945 of a naval lieutenant, George Arthur Heard, who mysteriously vanished whilst on shore leave in Cape Town. For years his wife Vida had unsuccessfully claimed a war widow's pension, granted under the Smuts government in 1947, but annulled by the National Party in 1948 on the grounds that he had not gone missing in action.

George Heard, a journalist before enlisting for wartime service, had publicly campaigned against the pro-Nazi movement in South Africa and exposed their links with the National Party. He had aroused their ire and received several death threats. There was strong suspicion that he had been murdered by the Nazi Ossewabrandwag and his body disposed of.

I came to learn of the story through a personnel officer in my ministry, a naval captain. Together we strove to put things right, which meant the captain patiently working through the red tape and undertaking numerous trips between Defence and Finance Ministries. It was with great satisfaction that we finally received a cheque which we posted on to Vida Heard, aged 93, still in good health and living in Britain.

I was totally surprised when George Heard's son, Tony, came to thank me. Former editor of the *Cape Times* and an opponent of apartheid, he was working as media officer for Kader Asmal. He had not wished to personally intervene in the matter because of his connections with our government. In gratitude he presented me with a copy of his book, *The Cape of Storms* (Ravan Press, Johannesburg, 1991), his personal history of the apartheid years. A chapter in the book deals with the disappearance of his father. Tony inscribed a message to me in the book which made me feel my job was worthwhile. He wrote:

> *With my warmest appreciation of your successful and most energetic efforts in closing the final George Heard chapter and for the recognition extended to Vida Heard over George's war record against Nazism.*

I was most grateful for the accolade. Running the defence function in peacetime is basically a struggle to maintain an adequate budget. Praise is a rarity. The likes of Kader Asmal were bringing joy to the impoverished masses by laying on clean water to millions. I told Tony he had made me feel just a little like Kader did every time he turned on a new tap.

One of my first military engagements was a visit to the regimental headquarters of a part-time unit, the Transvaal Scots in Johannesburg.

As I entered their impressive establishment I searched for a witticism to break the ice. Mentioning how good it felt coming in through the front door, when for years I had plotted slipping in surreptitiously through the back on a spying mission, generally did the trick. I was met by a group of burly officers smartly kitted-out in traditional Scots uniform. As drinks were poured at a bar adorned with regimental trophies, a fierce-looking fellow with a handle-bar moustache caught me totally off guard by enquiring if it was true that I had been schooled at KES, which was the popular acronym for my old school, King Edward, just up the road.

I was almost bowled over, said yes, and asked what school they had attended. Jeppe High, they replied – KES's arch-rival.

When I told them that my father had attended Jeppe they were delighted, as though that partly made me one of them. I never used my planned witticism. Instead I proposed a toast to one of Minister F.C. Erasmus' failures, which had been an attempt to ban Scottish kilts being worn in the defence force because they were 'foreign uniforms'. I heard in response that his wife had established a factory manufacturing regulation uniforms which, not surprisingly, prospered.

The evening developed into a most convivial one. When my hosts heard of Eleanor's Scottish ancestry they volunteered to have a piper play a traditional tune over the telephone for her. We followed that up with a similar telephone call to her mother in Durban for good measure.

Whilst maintaining these former citizen force units, we are encouraging the creation of regiments with an African tradition and nomenclature. One has in mind hypothetical names such as Shaka's Light Infantry, the Oliver Tambo Regiment, and the Soweto Rifles – having a ring which should help attract black youth to the new defence force.

The name *Voortrekker Hoogte* was to be changed by Modise to *Thaba Tshwane* – The Tswana Hills.

A particularly festive event enjoyed in the company of our former foe was the Rugby World Cup Final, when South Africa beat New Zealand at Johannesburg's Ellis Park in 1995. Modise and I watched the encounter in the company of General Meiring and other senior officers, as guests of Llew Swann, a businessman who hosted us in his company's box. There was an outburst of passion and patriotism throughout the country that seemingly made the ideal of a rainbow nation possible. I had sensed this before the match on my way to the stadium through downtown Johannesburg. The applause from inner-city blacks for the typical white rugger supporters making their way to Ellis Park was an eye-opener. So too was the sight of Mandela, in his Springbok jersey, triumphantly hoisting captain François Pienaar's arm aloft after the final whistle – and the entire country erupted. Modise and I unreservedly shared in the joy – although along with most Africans soccer was our preferred game – and we were willing to be photographed as front rank forwards in a mock rugby scrum in Swann's box. There was little emotion from most of the white generals as though they distanced themselves from the exuberance.

Sport reflects a country's character. Subsequent unfortunate developments under Rugby's chief administrator, Louis Luyt, starting with the shock dismissal of the enlightened François Pienaar from the team, and developing into Luyt's arrogant attitude towards President Mandela and Sports Minister Steve Tshwete, illustrated a Volkstaat determination that rudely stated: 'Pasop! This is our territory.' Former MK members in the defence force argued that this attitude existed in the military. If this was so, then those concerned, in whatever sphere of the country's life, were wilfully jeopardising the golden opportunity of reconciliation so generously offered by Mandela and the ANC.

Only one player of colour, Chester Williams, had featured on the Springbok side but the entire country – and their number one fan Nelson Mandela – were solidly behind them. I often made the point to the military that unless the rugby team – and the defence force – became truly representative of our population such support would wane.

Despite my reputation of always being happier on the barricades, I was not uncomfortable with formal state functions. When Queen Elizabeth visited South Africa, I escorted her around the Maitland Cemetery with its section of Commonwealth war graves. 'Red Ron proud to have met Queen' was the inevitable press report headline. Such occasions are not without their hazards. I arrived at the cemetery a good half hour before the Queen, to be confronted with a list of a dozen veterans to whom I was expected to introduce her. So I spent the next 30 minutes studiously avoiding eye-contact or chit-chat with anyone as I repeated names, ranks and associations in my mind.

Eleanor later remarked that I had looked somewhat transfixed as I awaited the Queen's arrival and when I explained why, we were seized by a fit of the giggles.

We later dined on the Royal yacht *Britannia* with Mandela and a bevy of other invitees. The Queen amused her guests with her wit and ability to tell a funny story. I also met her daughter, Princess Anne, who visited a military assembly area for MK integration outside Pretoria, and was impressed by the interest she showed and insightful questions she posed. Anyone involved in public relations or diplomacy knows how taxing such occasions can be and – communist or not – I could not help but admire the professionalism of the royals.

In contrast to our *Britannia* visit, Eleanor and I were guests on a Russian warship, the *Nastoychivy*, which docked in Cape Town. Whatever has changed in the former Soviet Union the Russians continue to honour those who served in the war. A group of South African seamen who had participated in the dangerous wartime convoys to Murmansk had somehow been traced. Medals were presented to the veterans and traditional toasts of vodka were drunk. I inspected the guard of honour, made up of smartly turned-out young cadets. They presented arms and waited for my greeting.

I had been informed that the word *tovarish* [comrade] was still in use in the armed forces. I barked out in Russian the parade ground greeting I had first heard in Odessa 34 years previously: '*Zdraviya jelayem tovarishi kursanti!*' [Good health, comrade cadets!]

We were accompanied by Alec Erwin, our Trade and Industry Minister, his wife, Annie, Brigadier Ian Deetlefs and his companion, Beverley. Many more toasts were drunk before the ladies got us safely home.

On another memorable occasion I was able to call up the South African navy at remarkably short notice for Thabo Mbeki when he hosted the US Vice-President Al Gore and his wife, Tipper, on an official visit. Mbeki was taking the Americans to see Robben Island, the former penal settlement some 6 kilometres off Cape Town, where Mandela and other political prisoners had been incarcerated. Helicopters were standing by to fly the party across the water, when it was learnt that top US representatives were not permitted to travel by such means in a foreign country. After Al Gore's security team examined one of our naval ships from stem to stern we set sail. It was an extremely pleasant and relaxed occasion, notwithstanding the deeply felt emotions experienced by Al and Tipper Gore when they viewed the small cell where Mandela spent the first 18 years of his 27-year imprisonment.

With us was Trevor Manuel, our Minister of Finance, who had been necessarily strict over the defence budget allocation. Our navy had suffered as a Cinderella service during the days of apartheid militarism when the focus had been on air and landward defence to the north. The few warships in service were reaching the end of their life span. Trevor was proving particularly tough regarding our attempts to purchase new ships, which we argued were needed because of our long coastline, almost exclusive dependence on the sea for trade and important maritime interests (and consequently the need to maintain a navy for seaward defence and projection) if South Africa was to play its anticipated regional role.

Eleanor managed to snatch a picture of Trevor on the ship's bridge, resplendent in the captain's cap, which I had mischievously placed on his head. On visiting his ministerial office some time later I was amused to discover that he had perched the photograph on a model of a 17th-century ship he had received from a seafaring nation. I could not miss the opportunity of pointing out that our naval ships were almost that old.

Modise and I met President Chissano of Mozambique over a working breakfast and the first thing he had asked was when we were getting our new ships. He was worried, along with leaders of the region's other littoral states, by the increasing poaching of fishing resources and, with no navy to speak of, looked to us for assistance. Another visitor to South Africa was the much-respected former President of Tanzania, Julius Nyerere, whom Eleanor and I had often waved to as he drove past us in the streets of Dar es Salaam. Nyerere had no hesitation in urging South Africa to assume leadership responsibilities in Africa which a modern navy would contribute to.

At a time when the country urgently needed houses and hospitals, and with no conventional threat of war on the horizon, there was no question that the government needed to spend more on social needs and less on defence. Modise had the responsibility, however, of maintaining a balanced defence capability. We argued in parliament that the future was unpredictable, that we were bound by the constitutional imperative to provide for the defence of our sovereignty and territory, and that we needed to guarantee a safe and secure environment for economic growth and development, not only for South Africa but for the region. Although the media reduced the debate to one of 'guns or butter, houses or corvettes', we projected the argument as one of 'defence and development'.

My passion for the navy's case had inspired the Air Force Chief, General Kriel, to refer to me as 'The Admiral' and I suppose I lived up to the name for I was always available to take important visitors to sea. One such was Portugal's socialist President, Mario Soares. I was one of hundreds of well-wishers who had shaken his hand at his country's London embassy in 1974, shortly after the dramatic armed forces uprising in his country against dictatorship and colonial rule. He couldn't possibly have remembered me but recounting the event made a deep impact on him, and he marvelled at the twists and turns of history which had us meeting again, under totally different circumstances, over 20 years later. I had the pleasant task of transporting him by helicopter onto the deck of one of our naval vessels lying off Cape Point. We would then round the southern tip of the Cape Peninsula in the manner of the famous Portuguese navigators, Bartolomeu Dias and Vasco da Gama, who had rounded the Cape and opened the sea route to the East Indies.

We alighted on deck and had to immediately stand to attention as the ship's band struck up our national anthems. There was the usual huge sea-swell off the Cape and the two of us had a desperate battle striving to maintain our footing, let alone a stately bearing, as the band played on and I gritted my teeth knowing just how long the new South African anthem was. There was also the usual heavy fog and although we could tell Soares that we had rounded the Cape it would be a disappointment for him not to see land. Fortunately the fog lifted and the sun broke through, if not at Cape Point itself, at least a few nautical miles up the coast. I took the responsibility of pointing out the approximate southern tip to him, somewhat tongue-in-cheek, but to his evident delight.

Another interesting encounter at sea was with Kobie Coetsee during our navy's 75th anniversary celebrations. He was a former Justice and Defence Minister whom I first knew from the Codesa talks, where he had been a tough negotiator. I had got to know him better in Parliament after his appointment as President of the Senate – a post which appeared to soften his demeanour. I discovered that Mandela had a soft spot for Kobie, who had been the first government minister to initiate the dialogue with him in prison that helped pave the way for negotiations. Clearly Mandela had discovered his soul years earlier.

With a host of invitees we were on board the SAS *Protea* from where Mandela was taking a review of South Africa's naval fleet and warships from 13 participating countries. Eleanor and I enjoyed Kobie's company, out in the middle of Cape Town's famous Table Bay, finding in him a genuine warmth we would once have found impossible to believe in a former senior government official. He had recently retired from the Senate and told us how he was enjoying his first months of retirement on his Free State farm.

Just in time for the occasion we had renamed our ships, which had previously borne the names of former defence ministers, including Kobie Coetsee's. Mandela was pleased that ships named after apartheid-era die-hards such as P.W. Botha and Magnus Malan had been renamed after African warriors – the SAS *Shaka* and SAS *Makhanda* respectively – but hesitated when it came to Kobie Coetsee. It was evident that he not only held Kobie in high esteem but regarded his role in having broken the impasse of the apartheid era as vital. I was able to explain to Mandela, however, that we had taken a decision in principle not to name any of our ships after living persons. He understood and asked me to explain this to Kobie to avoid any embarrassment.

Kobie had no problem with my explanation. As the ship that had once borne his name, renamed the SAS *Job Maseko* (after a Second World War hero who sank a German ship in Tobruk harbour), sailed past the *Protea*, President Mandela proudly waved his cap in salute and Kobie and I waved in unison. We grinned cheerfully at one another and Kobie Coetsee appeared so relaxed and happy that I sensed him sighing in relief at having got rid of all his past baggage. It might have been the roar of the wind and the sea, and the foghorns and whistles of the passing ships, but I fancied he cried out, '*Totsiens!* Goodbye to all that.'

We were able to arrange, through the ANC, a hero's visit for Alex Moumbaris and family. It was his first return to South Africa since his dramatic escape from prison. He was refused entry as persona non grata by immigration officials at Johannesburg airport when he arrived. The stalemate was only resolved when a hot blast was administered down the telephone to the immigration chief who imagined he was still operating in the old South Africa. We hosted a private banquet for Alex at the military command's Cape Town headquarters – the historic Castle, which dates back to early Dutch rule.

There were some individuals I chose to avoid. One such was Andrew Hunter, the Tory MP, who had always sought to link the ANC with the IRA, and who in 1989 had used British Parliamentary immunity to accuse Eleanor and me of running a 'London terror cell'. During a visit to London I received a message of congratulations from him and a request to meet which I ignored. What has emerged are admissions by an apartheid dirty-tricks unit, called Stratcom, that they had planted disinformation in the House of Commons about ANC-IRA links. They knew well enough that if you throw enough mud, it sticks. Brian Walden, a television commentator and former MP, launched a weasel-like attack on President Mandela in a BBC programme accusing him of, amongst other things, constantly praising the IRA, Colonel Gaddafi and Saddam Hussein (*Private Eye*, December, 1997 and *Walden on Heroes: Nelson Mandela*, BBC2, 03/02/98).

I enjoyed being shown around Britain's Parliament by Bob Hughes, Labour MP and Chairman of the Anti-Apartheid Movement and an old friend. Pointing out the historic sword's-length division between the opposition front benches in the House of Commons, he recounted how when he, as a new MP, had been shown where he could sit, he had gestured to the Tory benches opposite and remarked: 'So that's where the enemy sit!' 'No!' he was emphatically told by a Labour cabinet minister on the government front benches, 'that's where the opposition sit.' And gesturing behind him to Labour's back-benchers where Bob sat, the minister added with feeling: 'That's where the enemy sit!' In time I came to understand how true this was to become for the ruling ANC and the descent into vicious in-fighting for personal power and positions that unconstitutionally deposed sitting President Thabo Mbeki in 2008 in favour of Jacob Zuma. This saw the resignation of the Pahad brothers, Sydney Mufamadi, Terror Lekota, Alec Erwin, Thoko Didiza, Phumzile Mlambo-Ngcuka, myself and others in protest. That episode with the endemic corruption and cronyism that set in is a book for future consideration.

The tension between the Executive and the Legislature, between Ministers and MPs of even the same party, should be a healthy one. There are times when one inevitably experiences the hot breath of rivalry down one's neck, and Bob Hughes's anecdote comes to mind. The nature of competition is that it keeps one on one's toes and that is not at all a bad thing if it is part of a healthy democratic process.

Aside from the bitter ANC inner-party struggle of the future, what we needed to contain in 1994–99 was tension within the military, where leadership needed to be shared between the newly integrated forces. The country could never accept the continuing domination of white ex-SADF officers. Generals Romano and Motau were due to become chiefs of the Army and Military Intelligence in July 1988, and Siphiwe Nyanda was in line to succeed General Meiring as Chief of the SANDF on his retirement in April 1999. Accepting such promotions would be a test of the professionalism and loyalty of former SADF members.

An old revolutionary who was impressed with our handling of the military was Fidel Castro. It was my honour to escort him to Robben Island, as I had Al Gore, on one of our naval vessels. He had spent two years himself as prisoner of the dictator Batista, also on a penal island, and his respect for South Africa's liberation struggle and efforts to transform the country was considerable. Comparing Mandela's incarceration to his own left him deeply thoughtful. It was cold, with a heaving sea, as we sailed back to Cape Town. I supported him on deck as the boat plunged and rolled. Although he was strong and upright for his age, I quipped as I braced my body to hold him steady, that my action was a gesture of solidarity for the Cuban revolution. After which we decided to go below and sample some fine Cape brandy to keep the cold at bay.

TWENTY-SIX

BACK TO BISHO

September 1996

WHILST WE WERE FORTUNATE TO be able to toast memorable times and new relationships, the crimes of apartheid were not to be forgiven and forgotten. An Act of Parliament established a Truth and Reconciliation Commission (TRC) as a process to uncover the truth and attempt to heal the wounds of the past.

The irrepressible Archbishop Desmond Tutu was appointed Chairperson of the TRC with Alex Boraine as his Deputy. Compassionate, courteous and humane, they led a team of commissioners, legal minds, researchers and investigators. Victims and culprits were encouraged to testify about the violations they endured and the crimes they committed at public hearings throughout the country. The process was based on reconciliation, not retribution. Applicants for amnesty were required to provide full details of their acts to a special Amnesty Committee and show that these were linked to a political organisation and had a political purpose. Culprits who failed to apply ran the risk of criminal prosecution.

The TRC's hearing on the Bisho massacre took place in September 1996, four years after the shootings. This was not for the purpose of amnesty. It was a general hearing to assist the TRC to ascertain the facts of the matter. I looked forward to the opportunity of helping establish what had transpired.

I travelled to Bisho the weekend before the hearing, accompanied by my dear wife Eleanor. Her presence was a great comfort. With the pressures of office she had become even more indispensable to me. I had come to appreciate her soothing manner as 'the calming essence of Eleanor', a term coined by one of her former colleagues at the London College of Fashion where she once worked.

Before the hearing we attended an ANC commemorative rally and placed wreaths at the cemetery where most of the 28 who were killed were buried.

Ironies abounded, one of which was that we gathered at Gqozo's former residence for lunch. It had become the official home of Raymond Mhlaba, who was both Premier of the province and Chairperson of the Communist Party. The residence was a large, soulless building, typical of Pretoria's bantustan constructions. A helicopter landing pad was a short sprint from the main patio, which must have provided some comfort to Gqozo during his beleaguered days as Ciskei's ruler.

Another irony was that it had been my responsibility to instruct General Meiring to settle the claims for compensation of the injured and the families of those killed. One of the claimants was a brave young schoolteacher, Ntobeka Mafa, who was paralysed from the waist down by a bullet in the spine. The settlement of his claim meant that he could afford, amongst other things, to replace his wheelchair with a motor vehicle designed for the disabled. A further twist was that the former Ciskei troops, who had tried to kill me and had been integrated into the new national defence force, sought my advice as to whether to apply for amnesty. I encouraged them to do so.

There were indications from the police investigating the Bisho massacre outside of the TRC process that I might be charged with culpable homicide. This would depend on whether I applied for amnesty, which would indemnify me from such prosecution. When the press enquired whether I would be seeking amnesty, I made it clear that I would not be applying since I had committed no crime.

Gqozo, stripped of power and abandoned by his former masters, had retreated to his farm from where it was said he seldom emerged. He had, however, travelled up-country on at least one occasion when he was involved in a criminal act that led to his arrest. He was charged with illicit diamond dealing and, after standing trial in Kimberly, was convicted and sentenced to a R10,000 fine or two years' imprisonment.

On the day before the hearing commenced, which was a Sunday, we attended a special church service arranged by the TRC. It was an uplifting experience with moving hymns and prayers. One of the highlights was a passionate sermon by the Reverend M.G. Khabela of the University of Fort Hare. His address was entitled 'My father was a wandering Aramaean'.

My biblical knowledge was revived. I listened attentively to the story of the Israelites who, after their bondage in ancient Egypt, fled in search of the promised land. The theme of the address was the need to identify with the suffering of the poor, the downtrodden, the homeless. Some might consider the reaction of an avowed non-believer like myself yet another irony of the day. Communists have all too readily ignored the positive role of genuine religious conviction and its affinity with the struggle for freedom. Marching with priests, many of whom were active in the struggle against apartheid, had its impact on all of us. South African history has been enriched by the involvement of religious figures of all devotions in the liberation struggle.

At the climax of the address, Reverend Khabela used the most sacred phrase of the Hebrews and their affirmation of nationhood:

'Hear, oh Israel, the Lord our God, the Lord is One.' I had learnt the words as a child in Hebrew school and they readily came back to me. I passed the Reverend a note, writing out the Hebrew words phonetically for him: '*Shema Yisrayl, Adonai Eloheinu, Adonai Echad.*'

The hearing into the Bisho massacre was held at the university over three days. The campus overlooked the crossroads and the stadium where the fatal shootings had taken place. When Eleanor and I arrived for the hearing on the Monday morning, we were warmly greeted by Archbishop Desmond Tutu. He had only arrived that morning, but had heard of our participation in the previous day's church service. He consequently raised his hands to the heavens as though in praise of a miracle, which excited the attention of the press photographers.

There was great interest in the hearing and the venue set aside for the occasion was filled to overflowing.

First to testify were a group of victims, and relatives of those who had died. We listened to their moving testimony and relived the tragedy. Without exception they blamed Gqozo and the former Pretoria regime for the massacre.

Typical of the submissions was that of a middle-aged woman, Mrs Buzelwa Mtikinca, from the distant village of Healdtown. She had marched to Bisho with her husband, Cameron, a self-employed builder. They were some way from the stadium when the shooting broke out. Amidst the teargas and the gunfire she found herself on the ground, shot in the leg. Cameron lay injured some way from her. She called to him three times. All he did was raise his hand in reply. Then a comrade who was trying to help her was shot in the leg. Then two others, a man and a young boy, were shot in the head. She was taken to hospital and the next day she learnt that her husband had died.

Ntobeka Mafa gave evidence from his wheelchair: 'We didn't realise immediately we were being fired on. Then the people who were running to the stadium were running back and there were screams of "We are being shot", and some people shouted we should lie flat ... I felt something burning on my side. I fell and when I tried to get up I couldn't.'

When asked by Tutu's deputy, Alex Boraine, whether he had any requests, Mafa asked for a memorial to be erected to those who had died, and for sports facilities for the disadvantaged. A visibly moved Boraine stated: 'You inspire us, you think more about others.'

Cyril Ramaphosa, who nearly died at Bisho, and had been heading the process of writing the country's new constitution, presented the official ANC account of the events.

His was followed by that of Smuts Ngonyama who had run through the gap with me. Their testimony made it perfectly clear that the decision to move on to Bisho through the gap in the stadium fence was a collective one and not the result of an independent decision by myself, as had been reported by sections of the media.

Pik Botha, the former Foreign Minister, arrived after lunch to give his input. He placed the blame for the massacre on the ANC and claimed, that contrary to common belief, Gqozo had not been a puppet of the South African government but was master of his own domain. Although Botha had asked to testify early because of pressing business elsewhere, after leaving the hall he suddenly found ample time to regale members of the media about his political future. The day wore on and Tutu sent me a note enquiring about my schedule. He assumed I had a flight to catch, but was anxious to first take testimony from a final batch of victims. Coming from distant villages they needed to get home before nightfall. I readily agreed since I had no problem postponing my departure until the following day. By the time I was finally called it was already growing dark. I outlined the events and my own role. I stated that I was filled with intense regret that our peaceful march had ended so tragically, and that my heart and thoughts went out to the families of those who died and to the injured.

I accepted in a profound moral sense that I was an element in the events that culminated in the massacre, and that I was still haunted by the thought that perhaps we could have done more to avoid the terrible outcome. But if we had known that the Ciskeian forces would open fire on us, we would never have taken the risks we did. With the benefit of hindsight, some might say that our decision was a tragic miscalculation, but at the time such a possibility seemed improbable to us, particularly since our stated objectives and visible conduct were so clearly non-violent. I posed the question whether we should have taken the risk, and attempted an answer by quoting Gandhi: 'Civil disobedience becomes a sacred duty when the State becomes lawless ... non-co-operation with evil is as much a duty as co-operation with good.' To achieve our end, we were prepared to take certain risks because we believed in the cause of freedom and we could not acquiesce in tyranny or tolerate oppression, the alternative being submission and that was intolerable.

I stated that although the ANC took collective responsibility I did not seek to evade any objective enquiry into my conduct on that fateful day. One aspect of the event of which I was uncertain was whether soldiers were concealed in a trench near the gap in the fence. Whilst not ruling out the possibility of a plan to lure us into a deliberate ambush, which I urged the TRC to investigate, the shooting could have been the result of sheer negligence by the authorities. I finally turned to the role of the Ciskeian soldiers who were mostly young men with little education. They were the product of a system that conditioned them to fear even a peaceful march. They were programmed to believe that we were the devil incarnate.

Two of the Commissioners, Dumisani Ntsebeza and the Reverend Bongani Finca, referred to the Goldstone Commission's recommendation that the ANC reprimand me. I informed them that the ANC had ignored the request. They were particularly surprised to learn that I had not been given the opportunity to answer any questions by the Goldstone Commission.

By the time I had finished, proceedings had gone on well into the night. Archbishop Tutu thanked me. He said it was a sign of the times that a senior government official had been prepared to wait all day, allowing the ordinary people to testify first. He approved of the fact that I was accompanied by my wife and expressed appreciation of our participation in the previous day's church service. It had been a relief to finally give my version of events in public and, with Tutu's sensitive summing-up, I felt a burden lifting from my shoulders.

There was great interest in the following day's proceedings with Gqozo and his former officials due to testify. Eleanor and I decided to stay on for the morning session.

The bantustan-era bureaucrats provided a sorry spectacle as they gave their account of the events. It was obvious that they had been superfluous to any serious decisions. They made it clear that all information about the ANC's intentions and the threat posed by the march had come from South African intelligence officers. Gqozo's former deputy, Colonel Silence Pita, who had a reputation as a strongman – sinisterly silent like his name, it was thought – emerged as little more than a typical bantustan non-entity. He recounted how Gqozo had received a security report on the day of the massacre, to the effect that the ANC's military wing planned to overthrow his government.

Everyone patiently awaited Gqozo's arrival. There were angry mutterings, however, when his attorney arrived and stated that he could not appear that day. He was not in a fit condition to make a contribution, the lawyer explained, since he was suffering from a lack of concentration, a lack of coherence and extreme fatigue. An affidavit from a state psychiatrist was also submitted, stating that Gqozo was suffering from a 'depressive episode' and required treatment.

At that point Eleanor and I had to depart. We missed the submissions of former SADF officers who had been in charge of the Ciskei Defence Force. I had come to know some of them personally. General Marius Oelschig was a career officer integrated in the new SANDF. He prided himself on his professionalism and was an archetypal Prussian-style officer, the sort who had set the standards of the old SADF. Pretoria had seconded him to the Ciskei Defence Force as commanding officer. Prior to that he had been an SADF liaison officer to Jonas Savimbi of Unita.

Oelschig explained to the hearing that his instructions were 'to stop marchers entering Bisho at all costs as that would be disastrous' (General Oelschig's submission to the TRC, 11/09/96). He provoked strong reaction from the spectators when he bluntly stated, 'I believe that the ANC wanted, in fact engineered, the whole incident.' He believed this was supported by the massive presence of the local and international press who, he averred, would not have been there in such numbers if there were not the strong possibility of violence. He went on to recount how a field commander had reported over the radio that his position was under attack. Oelschig explained how he asked for confirmation that the crowd was firing at the troops and storming their position. When this was received he confirmed that the troops were authorised to fire, 'meaning those troops who were in immediate danger'. He realised that the firing spread and was not of a defensive nature. He gave an instruction three times on the radio to cease fire, whereafter firing died down to a few sporadic shots. There was a subsequent intensification of fire again for a brief period whereafter firing terminated. He was unable to say who gave the orders to fire on the ground. He claimed that he did not recall having heard explosions.

Oelschig stated that he was unaware of the gap in the fence. He strongly rejected suggestions that the marchers were ambushed or intentionally led into some trap. That might be true, since it was the only aspect of the ANC version of events that had not been confirmed. But I was amazed by Oelschig's admission that he was unaware of the opening in the fence. For that to have been overlooked by the security forces, claiming to have been intent on stopping us entering Bisho at all costs, would confirm the manifest negligence that I referred to in my submission.

A former MK officer in the national defence force remarked derisively to me: 'And that's the man who insists we meet his standards of competency.' Oelschig has since taken a severance package and retired.

From Oelschig's own admission it was he who gave the orders to fire which precipitated the massacre. He gave those orders when it was clear to any observer that there was no surge of unarmed marchers towards the military lines and that included the group I headed, which was 200 metres distant and racing away from where they were deployed.

One of Oelschig's fellow white officers, a Colonel Schoebesberger, by contrast showed remorse that drew applause. I had met him during the negotiation process and he had given me cause to doubt the ambush theory, claiming that the shooting was the result of panic and insufficient training. Schoebesberger had survived an attempt to blow him up in his car after the Bisho massacre. He was not the kind of conventional SADF enemy we had once supposed. Austrian by birth, he was married to a black woman and socialised mainly with black people.

Gqozo provided testimony at a special hearing two months later. Described in the press as looking drawn, and flanked by two legal advisers, he alleged that the ANC was entirely to blame for the massacre. He added that 'Ronnie Kasrils appeared to be prepared to risk any situation for political gain.' He claimed the action of his troops was defensive in nature: 'A soldier had been shot. An order to fire was given after a report was made of gunfire from within the crowd as well as hand grenades having been used.' (Brigadier Oupa Gqozo's Submission, East London hearing, 19/11/1996.)

It was put to Gqozo that the soldier who was shot was killed by a fellow Ciskeian soldier. There was no doubt because police ballistic reports showed that he had been killed by the same calibre weapon used by the Ciskei Defence Force. There was in fact suspicion that he may have been deliberately shot by the military to provoke the shooting. Gqozo appeared at a loss to accept such a suggestion.

With an exceptionally busy schedule to complete by July 1998, the TRC findings were not expected to be made known for some time.

Several months after the hearing I attended the opening of a new highway, built by the provincial administration, at the fateful intersection in Bisho. Archbishop Tutu was the main speaker and declared that we could walk freely 'because twenty-nine people died here' (the number included the deceased soldier). He added: 'This road is a symbol of coming together – a symbol of healing.'

TWENTY-SEVEN

REVELATIONS 1996–1997

Countless thousands mourn man's inhumanity to man.

Robert Burns

THEY SAY THAT A WEEK IN politics is a long time. After two years of the Government of National Unity, of ground-breaking work in creating new policy and legislation, Cabinet Ministers and Deputies posed for formal photographs at the Tuynhuys offices in Cape Town.

We had civil – if not warm – relations with National Party and IFP ministers as we sought to make the system work. I found De Klerk a polished chairperson of committee meetings. Outside of cabinet, however, in parliamentary debate and on the hustings the gloves came off. Mandela's patience with De Klerk wore thin in Parliament, and he tore strips off his deputy president after the latter had attacked the government for failing to deal with the rising crime wave. Mandela caustically pointed out that De Klerk chaired the cabinet committee on security and intelligence and had a shared responsibility to deal with the crime problem.

Gert Myburgh, one of the National Party Deputy Ministers who had served in previous cabinets, wondered about who would be present in the line-up for the photographer the following year. From past experience, he remarked to me, it took just a single change of cabinet post to produce a knock-on effect that could radically alter the entire picture.

The very next day one of his party colleagues posing for the photographer, the Minister of Welfare, affable Abe Williams, resigned from the cabinet. No sooner had he returned to his office the previous day, than he was confronted by police investigators with a warrant to examine his papers. The matter involved the alleged misdirection of contributions for welfare distribution for which he later served a prison sentence.

Within a week Gert Myburgh suddenly died of a heart attack. It was a strange turn of events. In fact the next official cabinet photograph will be even more different. Midway through 1996, F.W. de Klerk abruptly announced his party's withdrawal from the government in an attempt to make it a more effective opposition to the ANC. The move was clearly provoked by his party's right wing and resulted in a peeling away of his brightest and most enlightened colleagues such as Roelf Meyer, Dawie de Villiers, Chris Fismer and Leon Wessels. The last was the solitary member of the former ruling party to publicly apologise, at that stage, for the sins of apartheid.

The day before De Klerk's announcement one of his more moderate MPs, Sheila Camerer, confided to me that 'the madmen are taking over our party'. It appeared that up until that point De Klerk had no intention of pulling out of government. One of the workers on the Groote Schuur estate, where ministers resided and De Klerk was my neighbour, indicated that his household had major refurbishment plans in the pipeline for a much-loved government residence he now had to vacate.

This uncertain nature of parliamentary politics was not only confined to National Party personalities. Both Winnie Mandela and Bantu Holomisa, on the ANC side, lost their positions as government deputy ministers for flouting party discipline, Holomisa on slim grounds I felt.

We soon became accustomed to parliamentary politics, which is very different from struggle politics. It is advisable, for peace of mind, not to be overwhelmed by a feeling of self-importance or permanence, but to accept that as suddenly as the head of government can appoint one to a senior position, so one can be replaced.

The rules of parliamentary politics are designed to manage differences with reciprocal courtesy and to peacefully resolve conflict. Quite remarkable was the way in which animosity between the ANC and IFP abated, not only between leaders but at the grass-roots level. Clashes between rival supporters began to steadily decline notwithstanding the occasional murderous flare-up in a diminishing number of KwaZulu flashpoints. Prince Mangosuthu Buthelezi, Home Affairs Minister, astonished us with his warm and jocular nature. He soon delighted in referring to me as *Umkhwenyana* – Zulu for son-in-law – because Eleanor was from Durban in his home province. In turn I enjoyed pulling his leg about the communists in his midst, namely Joe Matthews, the IFP's Deputy Minister of Safety and Security, who had once been a leading ANC and Communist Party theoretician, and Rowley Arenstein, my one-time mentor, who died in Durban in 1996.

A week can be a long time in many respects. As I was clearing my desk in anticipation of a rare weekend break with Eleanor to celebrate her birthday, my secretary buzzed me on the office intercom. I was informed that the Minister of Transport was on the line. It was Mac Maharaj, invariably first with the news.

Information was being provided by former security policemen in Durban to the TRC's investigative unit about the murder of ANC activists in KwaZulu-Natal. They were becoming jittery and anxious to avoid prosecution.

Secret burial sites had been revealed and the remains of victims unearthed on a farm near Pietermaritzburg. The remains of a young woman, a bullet hole in her skull, were identified as those of Phila Ndwandwe. Phila was the young MK recruit who had debated with ANC leader, Johnny Makhathini, over the 'necklacing' of informers when he visited our Angolan camps in 1986. She was subsequently deployed in Swaziland from where she mysteriously disappeared in 1988. She had left her infant son with neighbours before leaving to keep a clandestine appointment. She was not seen again. A rumour was circulated that she was a police informer who had for some reason fled back to South Africa. The security police had in fact abducted her, kept her at a secret camp outside Pietermaritzburg in a naked state for ten days and, because she refused to co-operate, she was executed. They had spread the rumours about her.

There were revelations about Charles Ndaba and Mbuso Tshabalala, the Vula operatives, who had unaccountably disappeared in Durban in 1990 just before Siphiwe Nyanda and Mac Maharaj were arrested and I had gone on the run. They had been spotted in the city in July 1990 by an *askari* (a 'turned' guerrilla operating as an undercover agent with the security police) and captured.

Their arrest had indeed triggered the round-up of the Vula operatives in Durban, as we had surmised at the time. As with Phila, their refusal to co-operate with the police also resulted in them being shot. The execution took place at night on the banks of the Tugela River. Their bodies were wrapped in wire mesh, weighted down and tossed into the shark-infested river mouth, never to be seen again.

I spent most of the weekend on the telephone, trying to piece together news and having to respond to press enquiries. The conclusion Janet Love and I had come to at the time when our 'wanted' pictures – 'armed and dangerous' – appeared in the media in November 1990 with that of Charles Ndaba, had been chillingly confirmed. We had reasoned then that his inclusion in the nationwide hunt for us was a smokescreen to divert attention from his possible elimination.

As former security force members came forward to confess, the truth about the gruesome deeds of the past began to emerge. The most notorious case was that of Eugene de Kock, the commander of a security police unit based at a secret farm near Pretoria called 'Vlakplaas'. For them it was all-out war against the 'terrorists'. 'Since they were killing our chaps we would kill them,' was how a former chief of the security police, General Hendrik van den Bergh, had phrased it in the 1970s. Van den Bergh did not consider the state's obligation to the rule of law. For our part, the ANC was a signatory to the Geneva Convention on war and armed conflict.

Because of his cruelty, De Kock came to be referred to by his own men as 'Prime Evil'. They specialised in slaughter of the most horrific kind, emulated by similar death squads throughout the country.

These squads operated with *askaris* who, being former guerrillas, were well acquainted with MK operatives and methods. The technique for 'turning' a captured guerrilla was chillingly simple: Put a pistol to the captive's head with the choice to 'co-operate or die!'

Information provided was immediately acted upon which thoroughly compromised the informant, so that he or she became terrified of ANC retribution. The Rhodesians had used the technique very well, and De Kock and others had served with them.

Hugh Lugg, after betraying Damien de Lange's unit, ended up under De Kock's command whilst Damien became a colonel in the SANDF.

A broken man, Lugg gave evidence in a criminal trial against De Kock, describing the killing of an 'unreliable' *askari* at Vlakplaas as akin to 'a shark-feeding frenzy'. The assault had commenced with De Kock breaking a billiard cue over the man's head and everyone wading in. It ended with the man being smothered by rubber tubing.

De Kock had been arrested and charged with various crimes before the TRC process commenced. After a lengthy trial he was convicted of six murders and scores of other crimes ranging from fraud to conspiracy. He was sentenced in November 1996 to two terms of life imprisonment plus 212 years. He claimed in court that his superiors in the police and government had full knowledge of what he had been doing. He was extremely bitter at having been abandoned by them. He claimed that he was not a racist because he had targeted not only blacks but also whites. Both Joe Slovo and I were on the hit-list.

In the course of the revelations, an affidavit was submitted by an *askari*, Almond Nofomela, describing an attack on June 2nd, 1986, in which three MK members were shot dead in a Mbabane house in Swaziland. It was claimed that De Kock was in Swaziland at the time, in all probability supervising the operation. The victims were Pansu Smith, Sipho Dlamini, and Busi Majola, who Moses and I believed were struck down by the three sinister white men we had suspected and followed. We had referred to the leader as Magnum, who exercised control over the drugged-up duo from Ulster and Peru. De Kock has admitted to shooting Zwelakhe Nyanda, Siphiwe's brother, in Swaziland in 1983.

Two of De Kock's cohorts, Brigadier Jack Cronje and Captain Jacques Hechter, appeared before the TRC's Amnesty Committee and confessed to over

60 politically motivated murders. They later applied for amnesty for a further nine killings, which they said they had previously 'forgotten about'.

In a psychiatrist's report to the amnesty hearing, Cronje was described as coming from a close-knit, religious family background. After completing school he joined the police force because his parents could not afford to send him for further studies. He served with the Rhodesian security forces and in 1983 was posted to Vlakplaas. According to the psychiatrist, Cronje developed post-traumatic stress disorder as early as his Rhodesian days. 'He is convinced about what he is doing,' the psychiatrist reported, 'he knows blacks as his enemy ... He lost his ability to feel, to fear, and became moody and suffered insomnia. He doesn't realise he is sick.'

Captain Jacques Hechter strangled an ANC activist with a piece of wire. The body was doused with petrol with a tyre around the neck and set alight to make it look as though the murder was the work of activists. Hechter told the psychiatrist he could not stand pain and did not like to inflict it. He never shot anyone, but killed with his hands. He did not believe he had killed anyone who was innocent. He was diagnosed as being on the border between neurosis and psychosis.

It was astonishing getting an insight into the make-up of the killers who had terrorised liberation activists for decades. Those who observed their testimony found it difficult to reconcile their deeds with the ordinariness of their appearance. This is a chilling reminder, by the writer Hannah Arendt, of the banality of evil when describing the mediocrity of leading Nazis who had committed unspeakable crimes. It is not that evil deeds are ordinary but that those responsible for the most wicked acts are often so commonplace that you could not pick them out in a crowd. Although, in my experience, virtually every bully shorn of power can look pretty pathetic, an evildoer imbued with power has a sinister aura that can often be sensed a mile off.

One such was a notorious security police interrogator, Captain Jeff Benzien, who had filled activists' hearts with fear. He demonstrated for the Amnesty Committee, with the assistance of a volunteer, how he had tortured his victims by means of the so-called 'wet bag' method to make them talk. He sat astride them and tightly applied a wet rubber bag over their heads to the point of asphyxiation. The process was repeated until the victim was prepared to talk.

The obscene image of a florid-faced and overweight Benzien sweating and puffing whilst re-enacting his favourite method of torture, in the full glare of the press and television cameras, brings to mind the judgment in the trial of notorious Nazi Adolf Eichmann. The degree of responsibility rises up the command structure from the man who uses the fatal instrument with his own hands.

310

Benzien pleaded with his victims for forgiveness. Stripped of the aura of power once endowed by his superiors, he looked like a shabby and pitiful nonentity. The episode brought back to my mind the feelings of anxiety I myself had experienced when the security police were hunting me back in 1963. For years after fleeing South Africa I had recurrent nightmares of being relentlessly pursued. No matter what evasive action I resorted to – in and out of buildings, up and down stairways, along alleys and back streets – in the end I always ran right into the clutches of the Durban special branch, and awoke with a jolt. I experienced these nightmares in the safety of my London home. Once I was back in Africa, more directly in the arena of battle, they ceased.

Whilst many subordinates applied for amnesty, perhaps more out of expedient self-interest than genuine remorse, their subpoenaed superiors became tied up in knots over the meaning of words in orders issued. As one observer reported: 'The higher the rank of the policeman questioned ... the more ambiguous the word'.

Former police chiefs like Johan van der Merwe and Johan Coetzee explained that words like 'eliminate', 'take out' and 'neutralise' could have meant removal from society by 'arresting' or 'detaining'. Consulting a dictionary Coetzee argued that 'eliminate' meant nothing more than to 'remove'. General Joop Joubert, former chief of the SADF's elite Special Forces and one of the few military officers to testify, possibly because he had been named by another applicant, explained: 'I think we should be very careful when we look at the word "eliminate". I can eliminate a person by arresting him. I can neutralise him by arresting him. Each case must be dealt with on its own merits. If you could eliminate a person by not killing him then you could arrest him. I don't think the generally accepted term "eliminate" means "kill"' (*Cape Times*, 9 /11/97). Their subordinates, however, rejected this Alice-in-Wonderland logic, and steadfastly maintained that orders to eliminate an individual had only one meaning and that was to kill.

My old adversary, Craig Williamson, who grew more corpulent and more angry with his former masters by the year, and was streets ahead of the rest in terms of intellect (most likely because of his exposure to anti-apartheid politics), testified that the language of instruction had been deliberately 'all-encompassing'. In an intelligible insight into what had occurred he explained that the former government had sought to keep itself at arm's length from covert operations so that it could deny knowledge or responsibility for such actions.

Williamson continued that 'the operational procedures were designed by people who knew the law, in order to circumvent proof of legal responsibility for the deeds by the upper echelon'. He added that, 'with the benefit of hindsight, it appears that the upper echelons, especially the politicians, were so keen to be at legal arm's length from covert action, that they abdicated their responsibility to exercise close operational supervision of such actions and so lost significant operational control'. Williamson further declared that F.W. de Klerk must have had his eyes closed if he was honestly unaware of covert actions.

I had met Williamson in the back garden of a Johannesburg home, at his request, to encourage him to appear before the Truth Commission. He was meeting me to test the water for his mentor, General Johan Coetzee, a close friend of his parents who had cultivated him as a schoolboy and turned him, for a few short years, into a master spy. Now they were both sweating it out, in disgrace, with uncertain futures. Williamson had written to me, describing the two of us as warriors whose war was over. There was no comparison between those who fought for freedom and those who served in apartheid's ranks and resorted to indefensible actions to do so. Yet I was not overcome with hatred meeting him face-to-face, as slimy as he was, now that the conflict had passed. Now, listening to his sober assessment of the situation, even details of his personal business problems, I felt emotionless. All that mattered was that he be encouraged to co-operate with the Truth Commission.

We could not bring the dead back to life, but at least with the testimony that was emerging we could know what had happened. This was some comfort to the families of the victims and was at last a way of putting the deceased to rest. If we could not punish those responsible, at least they had to be accountable for their deeds. Whilst not a perfect instrument the TRC process has been a phenomenal success, particularly when compared with the limited commissions set up in countries such as Argentina and Chile. It has been hailed as a model for the world.

Another erstwhile adversary who requested to meet me was Joe Verster. He had once served under General Joubert in the SADF's Special Forces. He had been tasked in 1986 with establishing the sinister, Orwellian-sounding Civil Co-operation Bureau (CCB) to wage unconventional war against anti-apartheid activists. The creation of the CCB reflected the growing role of the military under P.W. Botha and the frustration of the generals with their failure to counter the rising tide of liberation. It fell squarely into the category referred to by Williamson of upper echelons keeping at arm's length the killing machines they brought into being so as to protect themselves. This was both cynical and cowardly and a telling indictment of the P.W. Botha–Magnus Malan era. Verster's operations were placed beyond the formal SADF structures. Command and control was vested in him with a covert link to the Chief of the SADF, who from 1985 to 1990 was General Jannie Geldenhuys. In his spare time the general wrote children's books. The Verster arrangement was a prescription for lack of control and responsibility, and undermined military professionalism and legality. It caused irreparable damage to the already tarnished image of the SADF which had, after all, established a positive reputation for itself in the two World Wars. Verster was given inordinate power – the licence to kill combatants and civilians he deemed were enemies of the state, whether they resided inside or outside the country. His recruits were a mixture of hardened paratroopers and reconnaissance soldiers like himself, reinforced by mercenaries, ex-convicts and gangsters. These were the operatives who wielded the instruments of death with their bare hands.

They were conditioned by a lifetime's brainwashing about the threat of communism and the *swart gevaar* (black peril) which they believed aimed to sweep the white man into the sea. Their operations ranged from bizarre acts of harassment, like hanging a baboon's foetus outside the house of Archbishop Tutu, to the assassination and bombings of activists. These are thought to have included the murders of university lecturer David Webster, SWAPO lawyer Anton Lubowski, ANC representative in Paris Dulcie September, the bombings of Albie Sachs and Jeremy Brickhill in Maputo and Harare, the poisoning of MK commander Thami Zulu (Muzi Ngwenya), the possible sabotage of Mozambican President Samora Machel's plane, the parcel-bomb executions of Ruth First and Jeanette Schoon in Maputo and Angola, and the countless elimination of trade unionists and other activists inside the country such as Griffiths and Victoria Mxenge, Matthew Goniwe and Fort Calata.

Joe Verster, like Craig Williamson, was totally disillusioned with the politicians and generals who had used him, and left him in the lurch when he became an embarrassment. Strongly built and bearded, Verster spoke in the grave tones of an individual who had woken in shock to the true facts of life. He had been deluded into believing that the ANC had posed a mortal threat to everything he stood for. Then, overnight, he had seen his chiefs negotiating with us whilst he became an outcast, a pariah, with his career in ruins. He regarded them as bearing a far greater responsibility than himself. Former sworn enemies, like Modise and me, were running the National Defence Force and, according to him, doing a reasonable job. He had come to his senses.

As we talked, I pictured the young Joe Verster, fresh from school, enlisting in the SADF out of a spirit of adventure and naive patriotism. He had excelled in physical activities and unquestioningly accepted the doctrine regarding the communist-inspired enemy and 'threat to Western Christian civilisation'. When he had proved himself to be a fearless and dedicated soldier, he had been approached by the generals to create and lead the CCB. This had entailed giving up his regular force career and his beloved uniform, and going undercover in civilian guise. It must have been an almighty wrench, but he agreed out of misplaced devotion to duty and skewed love for his country. He must have felt immensely honoured to be trusted with the power and funds provided by his superiors and the fact that there was limited supervision or need for accountability. Who was he to have understood at the time that the arrangement was more to protect the generals than to service his own operational needs? The CCB grew into a law unto itself before it was terminated by De Klerk in 1990.

De Kock, Benzien, Williamson and Verster were pawns in the hands of the country's apartheid rulers and generals. Those who were furthest removed, who gave them the unlicensed power to wield the instruments of death and, for a time, covered them in glory, must be held responsible for their crimes. The Eichmann judgment undoubtedly provides the moral guidance.

Growing revelations to the TRC related not only to the years prior to the ANC's unbanning in 1990, but also to the subsequent period. The number of those killed after 1990 had reached the 14,000 mark, with 22,000 injured. This was double the number who died in political killings in the preceding 42 years of apartheid.

Vula operatives Charles Ndaba and Mbuso Tshabalala, and other victims whose remains were unearthed in the Natal killing fields and elsewhere, would be added to those statistics. According to Mathews Phosa, who was present at many of these grim exhumations, an estimated 200 secret graves existed.

Most revelations emanated from the former security police. Few former defence force members were forthcoming. They were a tight-knit circle with strong loyalties to one another, operating according to the 'CRAFT' principle. I was told this stood for 'Can't remember a f...ing thing.' It remains to be seen, however, just how long the SADF skeletons remain in the cupboard.

I had a debate, under the auspices of the TRC, with General Constand Viljoen, leader of the Freedom Front. As chief of the army from 1976 to 1980 and then successor to Magnus Malan as head of the SADF until 1985, he was well versed in the role of the military and its cross-border raids. The topic was 'The Just War Debate and Reconciliation.'

Viljoen had proved popular with the ANC because of his co-operation and perceived honesty, and often received polite applause from our parliamentarians. I respected him and we often exchanged views on defence issues. I was disappointed, however, when he argued in the debate that the ANC's armed struggle did not qualify as a just war. Viljoen was an apparently decent man, but to adhere to such a judgement three years into a democratic state, and after the nauseating revelations concerning the security forces, made me doubt whether some of his generation would ever truly overcome their prejudices.

TWENTY-EIGHT

THREE MONKEYS

Parliament, May 1997

DESPITE THE GRIM REVELATIONS, FORMER President F.W. de Klerk continued to disclaim responsibility on the part of his government. He argued that the atrocities were the work of 'mavericks' and 'rotten apples'.

I declared to the press that the revelation about the Vula pair, Charles Ndaba and Mbuso Tshabalala, was the most compelling evidence yet to emerge, that De Klerk had apparently been involved in a double-track agenda during the negotiations process. One which 'possibly' condoned the elimination of his opponents. I referred to his denunciations of the so-called 'Vula Plot' and the fact that, by his own admission, he had been briefed by his security police chiefs. So how could he plead ignorance? I posed two questions.

If he knew what was going on, as he publicly claimed at the time of the Vula arrests, then it meant he was apparently prepared to allow his opponents to be eliminated by a sinister cabal, and seemingly washed his hands of the responsibility. If, however, he did not know, then he was arguably negligent in the discharge of his duties, because that meant he had not bothered to find out the facts surrounding the fate of detainees in the hands of his security police; more especially at a most sensitive time in the country's transition, when he publicly claimed to be negotiating in good faith. I consequently called on him to resign because of his apparent gross dereliction of duty whilst State President. So too did Mac Maharaj and Peter Mokaba. The latter, a deputy minister, was regarded as an ANC fire-brand who aroused De Klerk's anger by referring to him as a bald-headed criminal whose hands were dripping with the blood of innocent people.

De Klerk responded by threatening to sue us for libel. Instead of proceeding with a lawsuit, however, he lodged a complaint with the Human Rights Commission, a newly established statutory body to protect citizens' rights. I issued a statement that De Klerk had resorted to a stratagem popularly known as 'chickening out'. In fact he placed himself in the ridiculous position of regarding the questions I had posed as a violation of his human rights. For him it was clearly a case of the chickens coming home to roost.

All political parties, the ANC included, were expected to make submissions about their role during the apartheid era to the Truth Commission. The ANC did so on several occasions in which the leadership took collective responsibility for the actions of subordinates, placing our operations within the context of the just war for national liberation we had waged. This was a bitter pill to swallow, for the crimes of apartheid cannot be equated with operations by liberation fighters. We were prepare to swallow our pride for the sake of the TRC process, however, and to accept the moral responsibility for our actions which had led to the death of civilians. This created the grounds for the ordinary MK foot soldiers to qualify for amnesty in respect of all MK operations.

When De Klerk appeared before the TRC on behalf of the National Party, he attempted to evade responsibility for its appalling history. Instead of a simple act of contrition which the TRC and country were looking for, he persisted in placing the blame on the 'rotten apples' within the security forces and refused to accept responsibility for their actions.

When he was forthrightly criticised by Tutu's Commission, his Party responded by attempting to cast aspersions on its credibility and impartiality, and threatened to withdraw from the process. They wanted Tutu to apologise for critical remarks he had made, and Boraine – a liberal who had become as great a hate figure as any white communist – to resign. I joked with Boraine that not only did he look like Joe Slovo, with his flowing white hair and avuncular appearance, but right-wing circles were treating him as such.

The ANC called a snap debate on the issue in Parliament. I was one of four members requested to speak on the ANC's behalf. The National Assembly, the new wing of the old Parliament building in Cape Town, has a classical exterior – a simple pediment resting on white columns, with walls painted in terracotta and cream. It was a white elephant of the apartheid-era constitution and had been built to accommodate the rare joint sittings of three separate houses of parliament – for whites, Coloureds and Indians. It consequently was spacious enough to house South Africa's first-ever democratically elected Parliament. Visitors are bedazzled by the scene. Parliamentarians of all South Africa's racial groups, often attired in traditional, ethnic, modern and informal dress, create a buzz of relaxed laughter and conversation as they settle down to business. Thirty per cent of ANC members were women, so the picture of female representation was impressive.

The Speaker, Frene Ginwala, presided over the Assembly. A striking figure, with silvery hair, always dressed in an elegant sari, she had spent over 30 years in exile. The ANC had 252 representatives in the 400-seat Assembly. Amongst the MPs were Billy Nair, Curnick Ndlovu, David Ndawonde and Ebrahim Ismail, having all survived long jail terms from our 1960s sabotage campaign in Durban. Another MP, before he became an ambassador to Sweden, was Raymond Suttner, whom I had trained in London and, as he liked to put it, 'facilitated his entry into prison'. Then there were the Vula operatives: Janet Love, Pravin Gordhan and Scott Mpho.

De Klerk's National Party had 82 seats. Although there were some black faces on their benches, and a handful of women, the predominant impression was pale, male and stale.

The debate on the TRC issue began in a surprisingly mild way, given the strength of the emotions that surrounded it. Then an Inkatha Party member, M.A. Mcwango, raised the temperature by describing the TRC and Tutu as 'a sensationalist circus of horrors presided over by a weeping clown craving the front page spotlight'. Like the NP, the IFP was unhappy about revelations concerning the past which linked their involvement with violence to the apartheid security forces. In 1994 Judge Richard Goldstone had announced a 'network of criminal activity' linking the South African and KwaZulu police with Inkatha. Uproar broke out on the ANC side of the House and only subsided when the honourable member withdrew his remark.

It was my turn to address Parliament and I began by referring to the story of the three monkeys. The House visibly tensed. You could be ejected if you called a fellow MP a monkey. There was the monkey with his hands over his eyes who could see no evil. The one with his hands over his ears could hear no evil. And the third, with his hands over his mouth, could speak no evil. And to roars of approval from the ANC benches I added that this was how De Klerk was behaving.

The whole world had known of apartheid's atrocities. How could De Klerk not have known? The apartheid regime had spies everywhere. They listened in on telephones. They rummaged through the post. They knew who slept with whom and what you ate for breakfast.

De Klerk had referred to those who had been caught out in their crimes as a few rotten apples. There were whole orchards of rotten apples, I said. De Klerk had publicly proclaimed knowledge of Operation Vula. I reminded the House of the two questions I had posed and of his threat to sue me. He had still not sued me and I challenged him, in time-honoured tradition, to put his money where his mouth was and sue me, saying I would see him in court and the nation would know the truth. I ended by calling on him to do the honourable thing and resign, saying he should be grateful his retirement would be a peaceful one, protected by the very people whom he had oppressed for so long. The former oppressed on the government benches applauded with gusto.

Tony Leon, urbane leader of the Democratic Party, sent me a congratulatory note:

'That was a truly great parliamentary performance. Devastating of your opponents. Well done!'

Justice Minister Dullah Omar later stated in Parliament that he would revoke the truth commission and begin a process of 'Nuremberg-type' trials instead if the National Party persisted in its attempts to destroy the commission and its work. A leading Afrikaans newspaper, *Die Burger*, responded with an attempt at an intimidatory warning: 'Nuremberg also for Kasrils', since I had declined to apply for amnesty with regard to the Bisho shootings.

By the end of 1997 there was still no sign of any intended prosecution concerning my role at Bisho. On the issue of my verbal attack on F.W. de Klerk the Human Rights Commission issued its findings which rejected the National Party's complaint against Maharaj, Mokaba and myself.

De Klerk opted out of politics, announcing his retirement at the end of August 1997, describing himself as part of the 'baggage of the past'. Mandela stated that although De Klerk had made mistakes, he would be remembered in history for his role in making change possible.

It is unique in history for a ruler of an authoritarian state to voluntarily hand over power to the opposition, and there had been an attempt to glorify De Klerk's role. No-one had imagined apartheid would end quite the way it did, but it was no voluntary change of heart on the part of De Klerk and his followers. It was the liberation struggle, in all its rich dimensions, that forced his hand. He bowed to the inevitable to stave off the revolution he feared. In so doing he showed a grasp of the inevitable that eluded his predecessor, P.W. Botha.

I had complimented De Klerk on his courage when I first encountered him in Parliament, and he had replied that there was plenty more where that came from. His career ended, however, because he failed to summon up the necessary pluck to take full responsibility for the deeds of his foot-soldiers.

One such subordinate was a controversial medical doctor, Wouter Basson, who had been a Brigadier in the SADF and was said to be the brains behind apartheid's development of a chemical and biological warfare (CBW) programme. In 1993, he had taken early retirement after a specially commissioned report by SADF General Pierre Steyn prompted a nervous De Klerk to prematurely retire 22 officers. Apart from Basson, most worked for Military Intelligence, including some former CCB operatives who had been recruited after that outfit had been closed down three years previously.

It was strongly suspected that the military's CBW programme, which the SADF insisted was only for defensive purposes, had a special covert section producing sophisticated and undetectable poisons, and bizarre techniques of administering them for CCB-style assassinations. A straightforward method was spiking whisky or beer, which is how it seems MK commander Thami Zulu and others were poisoned. There had been a plot to secretly substitute poisoned pills for the heart tablets Dullah Omar regularly took and another plot to shoot him. The would-be assassin, a hired gangster called Peaches Gordon, hesitated to do so because of the number of regular security policemen, uninvolved in the plot, who closely surveilled Omar. Both Frank Chikane and Conny Braam of the Dutch Anti-Apartheid Movement, became violently ill when their clothing was secretly impregnated with a toxic chemical. I learnt from a reliable source that the James Bond-style equipment included a screw-driver that could inject a lethal poison by simply scratching the victim's skin, and of a scheme to kill a Special Forces officer who knew too much with a device that simulated a venomous snake bite. Apparently harmless substances such as shampoo, lip-balm, roll-on deodorant or chocolate could be tampered with to fatal effect. It appeared that Francis Meli and Solly Smith, senior ANC officials, had probably been poisoned after returning home from exile in the early 1990s – possibly to silence them because it was believed they had direct knowledge of apartheid intelligence agents who had compromised them and whom they could expose.

There were other possible deaths of this kind. One such was that of Mandla Msibi, a strapping and engaging operative in Swaziland, who died mysteriously of a heart attack after taking a drink of whisky in 1980. Mandla was the MK operative who shot Stephen Mtshali, who had testified against Billy Nair and the others in the Pietermaritzburg trial of 1964. Mandla had also tried to hunt down Bruno Mtolo without success.

There was no direct evidence, in the Steyn Report or elsewhere, linking Basson to these allegations. In fact an unavoidable shortcoming of the Steyn Report, given the lack of co-operation by the former SADF, was that it was mainly based on unsubstantiated allegations. I believe De Klerk panicked when he received the Steyn Report because it verified a similar report he had received from the old National Intelligence Service (NIS), headed by Niel Barnard. NIS, and Barnard in particular, had played an active role in pressing for negotiations in the 1980s, and resented the political interference and influence of the generals. So in all probability NIS found a way of recycling its own data back to De Klerk. Members of Military Intelligence, main rival of NIS, were the chief victims of De Klerk's purge. The SADF loathed him for seeking to rein in their power.

Dr Basson was assisting the authorities in fraud investigations connected with the CBW programme and its covert funding through a host of front companies. The South African Government was a signatory to the international agreements against the proliferation of weapons of mass destruction. We were concerned that Basson, a jumpy and eccentric individual who was in financial difficulties and unemployed, should not leave the country or be tempted to provide expertise to questionable clients. We consequently took what we judged was the safest option. This meant re-employing him as a consultant physician at a military hospital, where he could at least be kept under some form of supervision. De Klerk, who was still Deputy President in the Government of National Unity at the time, was party to the decision with Mandela.

Controversy briefly flared when Basson was arrested by police and charged with the production of narcotics. A journalist, Ray Hartley, learning that he had been re-employed by the government – Basson claiming in court he had been re-appointed by the President – interviewed me and was surprised to hear that this was in fact the case. The newspaper ran the sensational headline 'ANC Hired Basson' with the sub-heading 'Amazing admission by Ronnie Kasrils about "Mandrax doctor"' (*Sunday Times*, 23/02/97). But there was nothing amazing about my admission. We had never kept Basson's re-employment a secret and although the newspaper claimed this was a contravention of the public service regulations because he had previously taken early retirement, we were able to show that in fact the necessary permission had been granted.

Suspicions continued to linger about the odious lengths apartheid officials were prepared to go to stave off defeat. These were under investigation by the TRC, and included allegations about the spreading of anthrax and cholera in neighbouring states.

A postscript to the Basson investigations was that an agent had attempted to assassinate Pallo Jordan and myself in London using a poison-tipped umbrella. The plan apparently was to inject us surreptitiously on the streets or on public transport, but when we could not be tracked down the umbrella was tossed into the Thames.

TWENTY-NINE

FBI FORGERY

October 1997

AT THE BEGINNING OF OCTOBER 1997, the FBI arrested three United States citizens on spying charges. They were labelled old-style communists.

Eleanor and I were watching the early-morning television news over breakfast. The report was followed by an announcement that a senior South African government official was involved. Whilst we wondered who the official could be the telephone rang.

It was Thabo Mbeki who calmly explained to me that a letter I had received two years previously from an American woman calling herself 'Lisa Martin' was linked to the FBI arrests.

I immediately remembered the letter which had congratulated me on my book, *Armed and Dangerous* (the 1993 edition). The letter had gone on to provide an elegant Marxist analysis of the post-cold war world. I had received many letters congratulating me on my book, which I normally acknowledged, and recalled responding to the letter in question by way of a Christmas card.

What I learnt from Thabo Mbeki astonished me. The woman, whose real name was Theresa Squillacote, had worked for the Pentagon. The FBI alleged that she, her husband and a friend had spied for the German Democratic Republic during the 1980s. The opening of the GDR's intelligence files after the collapse of that country gave the FBI plenty of leads concerning the trio. They gained even more information by interrogating former East German intelligence officers. The three were consequently kept under tight surveillance. The letter to me, dated 22 June 1995, and my Christmas card reply six months later, were intercepted by the FBI.

The FBI had composed a fake letter purportedly from myself to Squillacote and had forged my signature. The letter requested she meet an emissary of mine in a New York bar. The individual, posing as a South African intelligence operative, was in fact an FBI agent. Gaining her confidence in a so-called 'sting' operation lasting over a year, he apparently induced her to provide confidential Pentagon documents, ostensibly for South Africa.

Thabo Mbeki had received the briefing overnight from our Ambassador in Washington, Franklin Sonn, who had been informed by the US government. I was relieved to find that both he and Franklin were determined to set the record straight about my non-involvement in the case and were requesting an FBI apology. Mbeki's office immediately issued a press statement revealing that I was the South African government official concerned, and explained the fraudulent circumstances in which my name had been misappropriated. The statement emphasised that neither the South African Government nor I had been involved with the alleged spies or the FBI (Press Statement – 7/10/97).

The impression was initially created, it seemed, from unnamed FBI sources that I had handed Squillacote's letter to my government which, in turn, had alerted the FBI. This is not true and the reason for the strong denial from Mbeki's office. Squillacote made no offer to spy for South Africa in her letter to me. Neither did I read anything untoward in the correspondence. Interviewed by Voice of America, I stated that the FBI had jeopardised the trust between two friendly governments by forging my signature on a fake letter to entrap an American citizen. This was absolutely unacceptable by anyone's standards. (Interviewed by VOA's Delia Robertson, 8/10/97.)

The FBI issued an apology of sorts, expressing 'regret as to any embarrassment this investigation may have caused to the SA Government, as well as any official of the SA Government'. I received a personal letter of apology from the FBI's Chief, Louis J. Freeh, repeating the public apology and ending: 'I deeply regret any embarrassment or difficulties this situation has caused you' (dated 10/10/97).

What the FBI patently failed to do was apologise for the disrespect they had shown South Africa's sovereignty. Whilst 'false-flag' recruitment is common in espionage activity around the world, even US commentators expressed astonishment at the forging of the signature and impersonation of a minister of a friendly foreign government. They observed that this was unprecedented in the annals of the FBI's history (SABC Television News, 9 /10/97).

Most South African newspapers concentrated on the 'unconventional tactics' of the FBI. The *Weekly Mail & Guardian* alone showed concern over the principles of the matter. Their editorial comment stated:

> *While the apology represents an achievement of sorts for the deputy minister who, much to his credit, has taken such an outspoken stand on the issue, it points to the continued inability of the United States to understand the*

principle at stake ... the violation of (Kasrils's) integrity represented by
the FBI's act of forgery amounts to an attack on this country ... it seems
symptomatic of a wider contempt shown by the US towards an ally ...
(October 17 to 23, '97).

In the same week the US State Department was calling on President Mandela
not to travel to Libya on the eve of a visit to that country. 'How can they have
the arrogance to dictate to us where we should go or who our friends should
be?' he told a gathering of business people and politicians in Johannesburg.

What I had no problem in accepting was the genuine concern shown to me
by the US Ambassador to South Africa, James Joseph. A political appointee of
President Clinton, he had been a follower of Martin Luther King and was also
an anti-apartheid activist. We were on good terms and he made every effort
to keep me abreast of events. He expressed his thanks that I distinguished in
my media statements between the US government and the actions of the FBI.
President Clinton, of course, has had his own experience of FBI investigations.

Life is full of quirks. I had only recently given James Joseph a copy of my
book, signed 'from a not-so-dangerous deputy minister', when the FBI story
broke. I was saddened that Theresa Squillacote and her companions were
sentenced to so many years' imprisonment. They were entrapped because
they were misled into believing they were assisting a democratic South Africa.
Despite the fact that I had never met her, her fate weighs heavily in my heart
because my name was fraudulently used as the bait.

THIRTY

THE NECESSARY AND POSSIBLE

MUCH REMAINED TO BE DONE. THE ANC has inherited a situation where millions of South Africans lived in abject poverty. Having established a political democracy, we faced the task of improving the people's standard of living and transforming South Africa, in the simple words of the ANC's election manifesto, into a better place for all to live in.

Within the first term of office of a democratic government – after almost 350 years of colonial and racial repression – significant progress had been recorded. Houses, schools and clinics were under construction, water and electricity provided to millions of people in impoverished areas, and land restitution carried out. Immediate steps have been taken to assist the poor and underprivileged. Pregnant women and infants were receiving free health care; over four million primary school children were receiving school meals for the first time whereas when I was a child this was a privilege for white children only; social welfare grants had been extended, and pensions increased whilst fiscal discipline was maintained. The new constitution and bill of rights guarantee human rights and dignity that never previously existed, and economic growth and recovery was underway. The basis for fundamental transformation of the country was being laid and South Africa, previously a world outcast incapable of getting even a school sports team accepted internationally, had become a highly acclaimed member of the global community.

Unfortunately, the attitude of most white South Africans has tended to be bogged down in the mire of the past and their own self-interest in a predominantly African country. Despite the generous hand of reconciliation extended by Mandela, far too many whites were disinclined to embrace the new spirit required for South Africans to overcome the legacy of racism and discover a common patriotism. Many ignored the fact that reconciliation was impossible as long as the majority of black people live in grinding poverty The vast disparities between the haves and the have-nots were a recipe for turmoil and a barrier to coming together. The vast majority of whites stubbornly clung to the privileges of the past and showed little inclination to make the slightest sacrifice that would assist in the redistribution of income from the rich to the poor. Nowhere had this been more in evidence than among the wealthy whites of such places as affluent Sandton, Johannesburg. After years of subsidised treatment at the expense of blacks, they refused to pay increased council rates which would have benefited the neighbouring disadvantaged black township of Alexandra. After decades of silent acquiescence with apartheid they resorted, with alacrity, to middle-class protest and boycott over a rates increase of only a few hundred rands per month against a standard of living that was amongst the highest in the world.

It was not easy to find a white person to admit they once supported apartheid. Most pathetic were those who fraudulently claimed anti-apartheid credentials, giving new meaning to the old adage that after a war strange heroes present themselves. At the same time most whites blamed the ANC for the crime wave afflicting the country, as though crime was unique to South Africa. They blithely refused to acknowledge that the roots of the problem lay in hunger, unemployment and a system that had exclusively served their privileged interests. Unfortunately they appeared to be afflicted by a collective amnesia concerning the appalling situation of misery, conflict, isolation and acute tension that was a way of life for the majority of the population during the apartheid years. 'Packing for Perth' – even Paraguay – and other destinations had become commonplace.

More whites needed to heed the words of Judge Rein, a distinguished war veteran. He addressed a memorial service for Jewish ex-servicemen which I attended at West Park Cemetery, Johannesburg, in October 1995. After speaking of the just war against Hitler and the eradication of Nazi evil, he turned to the miracle of change in South Africa.

Things would get better, he stated, because socio-economic conditions would improve and the crime rate would abate. He admonished the pessimists who had hoarded groceries and candles on the eve of the April 1994 elections and had turned into prophets of doom because South Africa was not yet a country flowing with milk and honey. He asked whether white South Africans had forgotten the sleaze, corruption and jobs for pals of the apartheid years; the billions which went down the drain in the bantustans; the financial looting which had been the order of the day. Corruption had prevailed but with the change in government there was now transparency and boards of inquiry. And he reminded his audience of the other miracle: of the many top people in government who had been tortured and incarcerated for years. Yet there had been no vengeance, no bitterness, no attacks on whites because they were whites. Judge Rein wondered how many whites would have been so forgiving.

In front of the impressive monument to those who sacrificed their lives in the Second World War, he said ex-servicemen knew what it was like to face adversity and never despair in the struggle against Hitler. The indomitable spirit which revolted against dictatorship prevailed and triumphed. He urged his audience to seize the opportunity and participate in building a new country. I warmly congratulated Judge Rein on an outstanding speech, copies of which I hand out to this day.

We had no illusions about the effort required to overcome the age-old chasm between the rich and the poor as we approached the end of a century and the start of a new millennium. Notwithstanding the failure of the first attempts in history to establish socialism and the problems and errors that led to the collapse of the former Soviet Union, I maintain my belief that socialism as the hope for attaining a just and humanistic world is still possible. Only a system based on human need, rather than on private profit and unbridled greed – enabling people to enjoy the benefits of the common wealth they produce – can establish the possibility of eliminating all forms of discrimination and provide education and work for all. But this is only possible if people are prepared to work as hard for society as they are for themselves. This is a noble ideal to which humanity constantly returns reinvigorated by the harsh lessons of history. The vital lesson that ought to be learnt from the attempts to build socialism in the twentieth century is that such a project can only succeed within a dynamic and vibrant democracy.

In assessing the errors and abuses enacted in the name of socialism most communists have focused on the beleaguered nature of the Soviet Union by counter-revolutionary forces for much – if not all – of its existence; the one-party rule and the over-centralised commandist economy that evolved; the consequent stifling of market laws; a dogmatic approach to ideology and the view that the theory was essentially correct but the mistakes lay in the practice. Whatever the drawbacks and failures I am convinced that in years to come humanity will look back to Soviet achievements as a source of profound inspiration.

Experience in government, with all the complexities of the pluralist democracy we had created, has given me a healthy respect for the separation of powers between the Executive, Legislature and Judiciary – the French philosopher Montesquieu's checks and balances that my old school teacher, Teddy Gordon, had drummed into our heads at KES. There had been days in the Ministry of Defence when I dearly wished we had more power but realised how easily one might be corrupted by its unfettered use. The concentration of state power in the former socialist countries, with executive and legislative functions virtually combined in a single body, stifled democracy, allowing for the abuse of power by the Party, its ultimate isolation from the people and a major cause of the disintegration that followed. Although not conceivable in Karl Marx's time parliamentary democracy, if it is authentic and utilised to express the broad interests of the people, can – with grass-roots participation – create the basis for a better quality of life for all. I believed this might well be the platform from which to build socialism in the future in the four simple words that Chris Hani loved to enunciate: 'Socialism is the future.'

Whatever complex reasons lay behind the collapse of the socialist model of the twentieth century, and these will be debated for centuries to come, the liberation struggle in South Africa had given us a fervent commitment to the rule of law and a system of democracy that is both representative and participatory. The struggle had also given us a belief in self-sacrifice, in leading by example, in courage, determination and revolutionary morality whatever the odds.

It struck me that Cuba and Vietnam, as small as they were, had managed – as had China where one third of humanity resided – to keep alive a model of socialism because they were rich in those qualities. Those were qualities we referred to as the subjective factor, which were personified particularly by the life of Che Guevara and other communist heroes. In contrast the apparently more powerful Soviet Union under Gorbachev had crumbled. As problematic as the economic conditions had become, there was a fatal loss of confidence and will by the leadership which failed to modify the Soviet system and instead opened it up for liquidation.

I made this point at a meeting in Johannesburg commemorating the thirtieth anniversary of Che Guevara's murder in Bolivia. I addressed the gathering together with an old friend, Angel Dalmao, who had once escorted Eleanor and me around Cuba, and had become Cuba's ambassador to South Africa. Present were representatives of over 300 Cuban doctors who were working in largely remote rural parts of South Africa where we faced a chronic shortage of doctors because most South African doctors preferred to work in the cities – a weakness for the flesh-pots evident in our Movement and the emergent black elite. The presence of Cuban doctors was a result of the initiative of Health Minister Nkosazana Zuma, and they rendered their service in the finest tradition of Cuban internationalism.

Change depends in the final analysis on what is possible in specific historical circumstances – on objective factors. A socialist revolution was both necessary and possible in Russia in 1917, followed by phenomenal economic growth and the heroic defence of socialism against imperialist intervention during

1918–1922 and against Nazi Germany's awesome invasion in 1941. But in retrospect it appeared that the conditions to sustain an alternative economic model to global capitalism had failed to materialise. Whether this was as a result of a failure to compete with global capitalism (part of the objective factor) or a surrender of will (the subjective factor) is a debate which will last for a long time. Whilst a socialist model is a necessity if our planet is to eliminate hunger, war and exploitation and the obscene gulf between wealth and hunger – for capitalism has always failed in this respect – it has suffered a tremendous setback with the collapse of the Soviet Union.

What we may achieve in South Africa, or anywhere else, is constrained by both what is necessary as well as possible in the world today. The next century will show whether there is a sustainable alternative to global capitalism which will overcome the hunger and poverty of two-thirds of humanity. History has shown that people will always strive for a better life and will unite in action. I believe that the twenty-first century will see a revival of the socialist alternative in creative new forms and alliances, harmonising the subjective with the objective conditions on an international scale.

Thabo Mbeki, ever the rational strategist, made this profound observation during the mid-1980s in Lusaka:

> We must, by liberating ourselves, make our own history. Such a process, by its nature, imposes on activists the necessity to plan and therefore requires the ability to measure cause and effect; the necessity to strike in correct directions and hence, the requirement to distinguish between essence and phenomenon; the necessity to move millions of people as one man to actual victory and, consequently, the development of the skill of combining the necessary and the possible.

Were we able to combine the necessary with the possible as Mbeki had once observed in the 1980s? Lenin had something else to say about the outcome of a struggle for national liberation and the path of social and economic development thereafter. 'The socialist character of the outcome,' he said, 'would depend on the strength of the organised working class.' Our liberation struggle had achieved its zenith in overcoming apartheid rule. With an advanced economy, modern industrial development and superb infrastructure, an industrial working class with a rich tradition of struggle and trade unionism, not to mention what then was a mature communist party, our hopes were high that South Africa would demonstrate to Africa and the world a dynamic advance in revolutionary social progress. Our optimism, however, tended to overlook the vast resources and tenacity of a powerful capitalist system and its ability to seduce and corrupt an emergent new elite should we stray from our noble principles and objectives and especially from our commitment to serve the people and not ourselves.

Kwame Nkrumah had stated after Ghana's independence that first came the political kingdom and then the economic. We had always criticised the disconnect in the concept. Political without economic independence would see the political power weakened in the ability to serve the people. The way we had achieved political power in South Africa with compromises regarding the sanctity of private property – particularly of the heights of industry and finance, mining resources and land ownership – and postponing key economic goals of the Freedom Charter held serious dangers. The need to break the back of apartheid rule, however, presented by the possibility of negotiations, rather than a costly and bloody insurrectionary path, was a most tempting option – too good to be ignored.

THIRTY-ONE

PASSING THE BATON

December 1997 – April 1998

There are those who struggle for a day and that is good;
There are those who struggle for a year and that is better;
And there are those who struggle for twenty years and that is better still.
Then there are those who struggle all their lives and they are the ones we
cannot do without.

Bertolt Brecht: 1898–1956

JOE SLOVO REMARKED TO ME TOWARDS the end of 1994 that very few people in history had enjoyed the unique privilege of serving in a liberation struggle and then in government, as we had.

Sadly, this was just a few weeks before his death at the beginning of 1995 after a long battle with cancer. An emaciated Joe, who worked in his Ministry to the end, received the ANC's highest award, the Isitwalandwe medal, from Mandela at the ANC's 49th National Conference in Bloemfontein, in December 1994. Joe was buried at the Avalon cemetery in Soweto.

In a brave funeral oration, his widow, Helena Dolny, referred to Joe, the human being, and his passion for 'wine, women and song'. None of us revolutionaries, inhibited by political correctness, would have dared cut it so close to the bone. There was a hoarse, approving roar from the Soweto poor, packed in dense ranks, as near to the graveside as possible. The response stood out as a moment of sheer Brechtian expression.

I know what Joe with his delightful sense of humour would have said to me about the FBI forgery: 'What's a good Jewish boy like you sending Christmas cards for, anyway?'

We buried Joe, Oliver Tambo, Chris Hani, Thomas Nkobi, Mzwai Piliso and many more. Most poignant was the reburial of the remains of those who had been secretly killed such as Phila Ndwandwe, the young woman who debated 'necklacing' with Johnny Makhathini in Angola.

We managed to trace Phila's son who had been an infant in Swaziland when she was abducted by the security police. The young boy, named Thabani, aged nine, was taken to meet Phila's father. I cut out a newspaper photograph of a beaming grandfather hugging his grandson and pinned it on my notice board.

I accompanied President Mandela on a journey to Durban. We were attending a memorial rally for the Vula operatives Charles Ndaba and Mbuso Tshabalala, whose remains were never recovered, and those such as Phila Ndwandwe and several others who were being reburied as heroes. Mandela spoke in honour of the fallen, and presented MK medals posthumously to the next of kin – amongst them the brother of Charles Ndaba, the daughter of Mbuso Tshabalala and Phila Ndwandwe's nine-year-old son, Thabani. I thought of the last time I had seen Thabani's young mother, an 18-year-old recruit, full of vitality, in our Angolan camp. He had her high cheek bones and lovely smile. It was a thrilling moment as we held his arms aloft to acknowledge the cheers of the crowd.

At the end of 1997 the ANC held its fiftieth national conference in Mafeking. The 79-year-old Mandela retired as President of the organisation, having previously also announced his intention to retire as President of South Africa in 1999. In his Mafeking speech to 3,000 ANC delegates he handed the 'baton' of leadership – as he described it – to Thabo Mbeki. Thabo was his and the organisation's unanimous choice. If there was a single word written on that baton – and I thought of all the leaders, warriors and unsung heroes through the years – it was integrity.

As a newly-elected National Executive Committee took its place with Mbeki on the platform, acknowledging the thunderous cheers of a united and successful conference that had endorsed ANC policy and leadership, my eyes were drawn to Mandela. Wearing the yellow T-shirt all delegates had received, he quietly took his seat in the audience amongst other retired veterans. It was a snapshot of history and he looked serene.

A few months later a different leadership baton was handed on in unexpected circumstances. The arena was the national defence force. The surprising development resulted from a controversial military intelligence report which General George Meiring presented to President Mandela in February 1998. The report alleged that senior ex-MK officers in the SANDF were involved in a plot to assassinate Mandela, murder judges, occupy Parliament and key institutions and overthow the government prior to the 1999 general elections. Believing such a report stretched credulity to the limits, for these were the officers Modise had announced a year previously would be promoted to the most senior posts of the SANDF during 1998–1999. It meant that they planned to overthrow the very government they had sacrificed to put into power and which was planning to promote them. This would be absurd and irrational.

In fact the report brought to mind scaremongering tactics of the past. Operation Vula had been depicted by the security forces as a sinister 'Red Plot' aimed at undermining the negotiations. Hernus Kriel had presented fabricated information at the Codesa negotiations alleging communist threats of murder and mayhem. What was unclear was whether Meiring – as may have been the case with Kriel – was manipulated by his own intelligence-gathering structures or was privy to their schemes. But Meiring, I thought, was too much the fox to be manipulated.

Within a month Robert McBride, the MK combatant lauded for his bravery by the oppressed and castigated by the old order, was arrested in Mozambique. It was alleged that McBride, who worked for South Africa's Department of Foreign Affairs, had been attempting to purchase weapons from a Maputo gun-runner while on a private visit to Mozambique. A week later a Johannesburg daily newspaper, notorious for the leaks it had carried from the apartheid security services, reported the sensational news of the plot to overthrow the government and linked McBride, and his alleged attempt to purchase arms, to the so-called Meiring Report and the MK generals.

The independent *Mail & Guardian* on the other hand saw the circumstances of McBride's arrest as bearing the hallmarks of a classical sting operation. McBride was arrested with a self-confessed police informant, Vusi Madida, who had introduced him to the Maputo arms dealer, who also turned out to be a police informant. It transpired that Madida was also an agent of the SANDF's Military Intelligence and the sole source of the Meiring Report. It was possibly no mere coincidence that McBride's arrest conveniently provided corroboration for that report whilst it was being considered by President Mandela. McBride's friends claimed in the *Mail & Guardian* that he was investigating a suspected trail linking Mozambican racketeers to South African criminal syndicates. These were believed to be connected to anti-democratic schemes to destabilise the country by elements within the former security forces.

President Mandela coolly referred the intelligence report to a judicial commission of inquiry. The commission, headed by Chief Justice Ismail Mahomed, found the report to be without substance, inherently improbable and fantastic. The procedure whereby it reached Mandela, without the necessary verification and by-passing the relevant ministers and structures, was severely criticised. Meiring had Modise's permission to see the President but, according to Modise's spokesperson, Modise had only been informed by the general of what amounted to a couple of paragraphs of information in a written report that contained 238 paragraphs. Modise had not even been aware of the written report. In an address to Parliament on 21 April, Mandela stated that the findings had placed General Meiring in a difficult position with Modise and the senior military officers by mentioning them in the report. A breakdown of confidence had resulted which compromised Meiring's capacity to perform his tasks. As a consequence Meiring requested early retirement, to which Mandela acceded. This was a year ahead of Meiring's planned retirement. His successor was later announced as General Siphiwe Nyanda, the MK commander once known as Gebhuza, detained in 1990 over the so-called Vula plot.

Mandela stated that he had full confidence in the former MK officers named in the report. Thabo Mbeki slammed the report as a ploy by old agents of apartheid to get the ANC to act against its own people. Sydney Mufamadi warned against disinformation techniques which had been used in the past to legitimise destabilisation programmes, whilst I described the report at a press conference as 'a long, dirty thumbsuck'. The *Mail & Guardian* observed that the report and the arrest of Robert McBride had backfired on old-guard remnants within the country's security forces whom the government believed could have been involved in a huge destabilisation campaign against the democratic order. If that was so, then those forces were certainly hoist by their own petard.

I look forward to recounting my perspective on the episode when I am able to. I have refrained from doing so owing to my present government position and have utilised public statements to recount the salient facts. Transformation is on track but it would be foolhardy to underestimate its opponents even if they had underestimated the ANC. The balance of forces have radically changed and the adversaries of progress can obstruct but not halt the advance of South Africa's democratic revolution. Looking back now in 2013 I see how foolhardy those words were, ignoring the crucial question of who controls the economy and the extraordinary power of subversion and corruption which that can entail.

THIRTY-TWO

FROM FIRE TO WATER

I STOOD ON THE ROOF OF A RESERVOIR, squinting down a manhole into the dank interior, wondering where the bomb had been placed.

This was within weeks of my becoming Minister of Water Affairs and Forestry in 1999. I had been summoned from my office by news that an explosive device had been discovered at a water works outside Pretoria.

Fortunately the detonator had jolted harmlessly loose from the main charge. The abortive attempt had clearly been designed to coincide with our recent national elections. I instructed my Director-General, Mike Muller, to step up security around the country's dams. Mike was of the new breed of public servants, having run the Beira water system in Mozambique as well as having been an underground member of the ANC.

He cheerfully observed that my new job had almost started with a bang and that the department's engineers would look forward to my assessing their security measures. Given my former career as saboteur the irony did not escape us.

The ANC had won the country's second general elections with a resounding majority, improving even on the 1994 result.

After Thabo Mbeki's inauguration as president, he called the previous ministers and deputies in, one by one, late in the night following the celebrations to inform us of our fate.

Mbeki's demeanour was always on an even keel. His was a quiet statement made at three o'clock in the morning, as he informed me of my appointment. He remarked that 40 years as a soldier warranted a change.

The conversion could be described as 'from fire to water'.[1] Some joked 'from red to green'. I certainly looked forward to delivering the precious resource to the poor and thirsty.

Joe Modise was retiring. At a farewell function he stated that my guerrilla career had provided me with intimate knowledge of the rivers and forests of the region and this should stand me in good stead in my new post. I thought of the times we had infiltrated guerrillas across the borders, and how I once relieved the tension, in a tight situation near the Limpopo river, by reciting Kipling for him: 'The great grey green greasy Limpopo all set about with fever trees.'

My predecessor in the portfolio was Kader Asmal who had become Minister of Education. He introduced me to his old department at his farewell function, presenting me with a water pistol. I filled it whilst he delivered his swan song and, when he was done, pursued him around the stage giving him a fair drenching.

I was soon travelling around the country and becoming acquainted with my responsibilities. I visited forests and irrigation schemes, dams and water-purification plants, and new projects aimed at providing clean water to the millions of people totally neglected during the white supremacy era.

I arrived in the Eastern Cape village of Lutsheko in the foothills of the Drakensberg to a rousing reception from the inhabitants. The matronly chairperson of the village water committee proudly showed me around. Water was being pumped from below ground near a dried-out riverbed a few kilometres away, piped to the village and delivered to taps each no more than 200 metres from every household.

To operate and maintain the system, which included diesel fuel for the pumps and the salary of a maintenance worker, required a contribution of ten rand per household per month – about one US dollar.

The village committee was strict about payment. The small contribution encouraged consumers not to waste water. It looked like a model system and helped me overcome my initial bout of naive horror when I learned that there was some element of cost-recovery. After all, was water not free from heaven? Which it was until the cost of storage, purification, distribution, operation and maintenance was taken into account. The cost of supply rose, as one could point out, because God forgot to put in the pipes and taps.

It was by the dried-out river that I saw some women scooping muddy water from holes they had dug in the ground. I stopped to talk to one of them, with a bundle on her back. The bundle turned out to be a two-week-old infant. Why was she not using the tap water from the village system? I asked. The reason was simple. Her husband was unemployed. The ten rands was needed to put food on the family table. If she had to spend time searching for water, that was money saved. The question of clean water was not an issue. I discovered the same story in other rural areas.

I discussed the problem with President Mbeki and a new policy was formulated. Six thousand litres of water per month would be provided free to every household. For a family of eight this meant 25 litres per person a day. Consumption in excess would be based on a rising, stepped tariff, so that the better-offs would contribute to subsidising the poor. A free basic amount of electricity was also decided upon.

In 1994, at our first democratic election, 14 million rural black people were without clean water, one third of the population. By 2004 ten million people had been reached and the backlog ought to have been wiped out by 2008, ahead of what was termed the Millennium Development Goals – if delivery went according to plan. Unfortunately there is still some way to go owing to problems of service delivery.

It was not only clean water, however, that was needed but also adequate sanitation – decent toilets.

If there were millions of South Africans without clean water in 1994 there were over 20 million without sanitation. Although the provision of piped water was usually the first request of villagers – with electricity, tarred road, school, crèche next in line of priorities – the highly personal business of sanitation had rarely, if at all, been raised. Mention of the fact, all over the world, was something of a taboo. Most rural people made do with a rickety privy or outhouse over an unsanitary pit or simply used the bush.

After a cholera outbreak in KwaZulu-Natal it became clear it was not only clean water that was required. Adequate sanitation and hygiene awareness were needed to keep diarrhoeal disease at bay. Research showed that the simple act of hand washing could reduce infection by 40 per cent. Studies also showed that cholera epidemics were not simply caused by contaminated water. The way infection spread was related to poor hygiene practices.

As the cholera spread, the route followed was along the roads, not the rivers. This indicated that human beings were passing on the strain via hand-to-mouth contact. New outbreaks often occurred after social events where beer and food were shared from communal pots.

The outbreak of 2000–2001 saw over 100,000 cases. That fatalities were kept to 215 deaths attested to the sterling work of Minister Manto Tshabalala-Msimang's health department. I travelled with her to rehydration centres where patients were swiftly restored to health. The outbreak prompted a campaign to build decent toilets in the rural areas. This led Finance Minister Trevor Manuel to dub me 'Minister of Sanitation'. I was flattered, in a book called *The Big Necessity* by Rose George, to be described as one of the handful of politicians anywhere in the world with the guts to take up the sanitation issue.[2]

On one memorable occasion the women of a village spontaneously broke into the national anthem as I inspected their new toilets, proudly painted in the colours of the national flag. 'Standing to attention before a pristine privy' was the headline in a Sunday newspaper.[3]

Whilst over one billion people worldwide were without clean water, those without sanitation amounted to almost two-and-a-half billion. Little wonder that life-threatening, water-borne diseases accounted for over two million global deaths a year, mainly children. This amounted to 6,000 deaths a day, the equivalent of 20 jumbo jets crashing every 24 hours.

A way of addressing the sanitation deficit was urgently required. When I travelled abroad I sought to learn how other developing countries were dealing with the problem. In this I was disappointed, for whilst my hosts were keen to show off their water-resource projects they singularly failed, except in the case of India, to take me anywhere near a rural toilet. It got to the stage where I resorted to feigning the need to 'go to the gents' during rural trips, whereupon I would be whisked off at breakneck speed, sirens blaring, to the nearest modern hotel.

One of the achievements of the Johannesburg World Summit on Sustainable Development (WSSD) in September 2002 was placing sanitation, alongside water provision, squarely on the agenda and aiming to halve those on the planet without such services by 2015.

We owed much to a partnership with the United Nations Water Supply and Sanitation Collaborative Council, which helped developing countries grapple with water-borne diseases. Sir Richard Jolly, Gourisankar Ghosh and Eirah Gorre-Dale directed the Council's work. Their WASH campaign (Water, Sanitation and Hygiene awareness) was launched in South Africa, followed by other African countries.

Aside from tireless work, burning the proverbial midnight oil at the UN Headquarters in New York and in Johannesburg itself, where we plotted our moves and built our alliances, we also managed to have some fun. Sir Richard, who had worked with the late Jim Grant, renowned head of the United Nations Children's Fund, referred to us as 'we few, we happy few, we band of brothers and sisters', elaborating on *Henry V*. He well understood the role of the 'movers and shakers'. We were delighted to be interviewed during the victory of the Johannesburg Summit enthroned on VIP toilet seats at a water-sector exhibition. These did not signify 'Very Important Persons' but 'Ventilated Improved Pit' latrines – specially designed 'dry' non-flush toilets for water-stressed rural conditions.

We found in Nelson Mandela our role model, and he starred in a TV commercial emphasising the need to wash one's hands for the sake of good health. There was no escaping the message. Even the toilet rolls in the Summit washrooms carried the slogans: 'Stand up for better sanitation! Lobby leaders for better loos! Hygiene is not a soft issue! Private moment – Global problem!'

The Summit was an outstanding success. South Africa's team, led by Foreign Minister Nkosazana Dlamini-Zuma and Environment and Tourism Minister Mohammed Valli Moosa, engaged in marathon negotiation sessions. These ensured that the event became a global assault on poverty, successfully linking socio-economic issues with the environment.

I had the pleasant task of playing host at an international water-sector exhibition, housed in a glittering Water Dome which was opened by our three 'water wizards'. They were Nelson Mandela, Crown Prince William of the Netherlands and Salim-Salim, former Secretary General of the OAU. I had the trio turning a water wheel that switched on a neon-lit waterfall.

The Prince enjoyed visiting development projects and I took him off to see a rural water scheme. Introducing him to the villagers, I said that whilst his colour was orange and mine was red, water could unite everyone because it was colourless. I spotted two splendidly dressed women in the crowd, one in orange and the other in red. The audience applauded when I pointed out how close the prince's colours were to mine, and he clearly enjoyed the banter.

The Water Dome was the setting for a special session of a newly established African Ministers Council on Water (AMCOW). An historic agreement on the sharing of the Inkomati and Maputo rivers was signed between Mozambique, Swaziland and South Africa. It gave me the opportunity to refer to Mark Twain's statement that 'water was for fighting, whisky for drinking'. We demonstrated, however, that water could be the catalyst for peace and co-operation.

Led by President Mbeki and Nigeria's President Obasanjo, Africa was seen at the Johannesburg Summit and elsewhere to be contributing to a more equitable global agenda and through the New Economic Programme for African Development (NEPAD) aimed to transform the continent and create a turning point in its history.

I received a rare honour on a visit to Nigeria, being made chief, at a River State village ceremony. The title given to me – '*Emere Nyine Onona 1*' – translated as the Chief of Good Deeds. I was robed in traditional dress, replete with a top hat, with a beautifully attired chieftainess Eleanor at my side.

I was also honoured, alongside Foreign Minister Dlamini-Zuma, with a Cuban award for friendship and solidarity. My old school, King Edward, asked me to act as a patron of its centenary celebrations alongside Ali Bacher, Richard Goldstone and Gary Player. On visiting the school I paused for a drink at a water fountain to discover it commemorated Teddy Gordon, the teacher who influenced my life.

THIRTY-THREE

FROM DARKNESS TO LIGHT

MAX SISULU AND I SUED SEVERAL South African newspapers for defamation after they alleged that we were being investigated for possible kickbacks in the country's arms deal. *Business Day* carried the original story under the headline, 'High ranking ANC members named regarding alleged irregularities in R43 million arms deal'.[1] Whilst at least one of those named admitted guilt there was no truth in allegations regarding Max Sisulu and myself. We were exonerated when all the newspapers concerned retracted their allegations and published front-page apologies.[2] *Business Day's* unnamed source had relied on nothing more than an innocuous request from the public prosecutor's office to a parliamentary secretary, seeking confirmation of the positions we and others connected to the standing committee on defence had held.

The media has a key role in helping expose corruption but needs to do so with due care and responsibility. The ANC government had made it clear that it would not countenance the seeking of wealth, power or benefits through illicit means. Those who erred could not expect to be exonerated because of their struggle credentials. The rule of law would be upheld.

Old comrades were inevitably passing on. Alfred Nzo, Sonia Bunting, Fred Carneson, Govan Mbeki, Wolfie Kodesh, Joe Modise, Jack Simons, Steve Tshwete and Rusty Bernstein, amongst others, were products of a magnificent struggle illuminated by their gifted lives.

My mother passed away at the age of 94. I was grateful to her and my father for influencing me to respect all human beings. I recited the Jewish kaddish prayers at her funeral, which I had not been able to do when my father had died whilst I was in exile.

I had never in my adult life regarded my Jewish origin as guaranteeing uncritical support for the state of Israel. From the time I joined the liberation struggle I had viewed the idea of a mono-ethnic, exclusivist Jewish state as akin to apartheid and an injustice to the Palestinian people. The reservation of special rights for Jews consigned non-Jews to an inferior status and smacked of apartheid's race classification. Israel had come into existence as a settler state through the forceful dispossession of the land of a people who had lived there for centuries. A London friend of mine, John Rose, aptly coined the term 'the hijack state'.[3] If one were to select a statement that best illustrates the making of the conflict it would be, for me, that of two rabbis from Vienna. They visited the Holy Land in 1897, soon after the Zionist Founding Congress in Basel, Switzerland, on a fact-finding mission to investigate the suitability of Palestine as a prospective site for a Jewish homeland. 'The bride is beautiful,' they cabled home, 'but she is married to another man.'[4]

The root cause of the conflict has been that Israel's founding fathers, and leaders to this day, sought to violently dislodge the groom by means of a shotgun divorce. The bloody struggle over the bride continues, and the victims should never be morally equated with those who have violated their rights. The criminals who have abducted the bride aim to chase the legitimate husband away and, if he does not comply, to eliminate him.

This is very difficult for many Jews to concede, given their emotional ties to Israel, the nightmare of the Nazi holocaust, and the threat to the existence of Israel. Whilst the rationale for resettling biblical Palestine as a Jewish state might sound justifiable to Zionists, Erich Fromm, noted Jewish thinker, best characterised the absurd nature of the contention by stating: 'If all nations would suddenly claim territory in which their forefathers had lived 2,000 years ago, this world would be a madhouse.'[5] Who actually lived there two millennia ago is a contested issue. The Palestinians are not simply the descendants of invading Arabs spreading Islam from the 7th century but the indigenous inhabitants who had been there from pagan times, converting to Judaism then Christianity and later Islam. In fact, irony of ironies, they are quite likely descendants of the ancient Hebrews, whilst certainly they have Canaanite roots. The idea that there can be one pure-blooded race spawned by a region that was the melting pot of the world is dubious. (See *The Invention of the Jewish People* by Israeli academic Shlomo Sand).

It was only natural that the dispossessed Palestinians would strive to resist. Failure to redress their just grievances and to suppress them by a doctrine of enforced segregation, collective punishment, humiliation and iron force only generated greater resistance – as South Africa's freedom struggle demonstrated. Consequently the world witnessed, in Israel, the spectacle of a state that aspired to radiate 'as a light unto the nations' descending to the depths of the most brutal of colonial tyrannies. This involved the wholesale abuse of human rights, contemptuous violation of international law and draconian measures such as the punitive curfews and sieges that turned the lives of an entire population into a living nightmare; the endless checkpoints impervious to the pregnant and the sick; the bulldozing of homes; raining of bombs and rockets on inhabited areas; destruction of town centres and refugee camps; the shooting of children; the chilling, non-judicial executions that did not distinguish between the target and his family. Anglican Archbishop Njongonkulu Ndungane of Cape Town observed, after visiting the Holy Land, that the suffering of the Palestinian people made the apartheid years look like a picnic by comparison.

With arch-hawk Ariel Sharon at the helm, the situation had deteriorated to its lowest point. In seeking a military solution he bore heavy responsibility for the deaths of Israelis and Palestinians alike. 'The Palestinians must be hit and it must be very painful,' he blindly raged. 'We must cause them losses, victims, so that they feel the heavy price.'[6]

Whilst focus was often diverted by the desperate martyr or suicide bombings and indiscriminate targeting of civilians – I urged that the causes of the problem needed to be understood. In a letter to *Business Day* I wrote that Israel could learn from South Africa's transformation and warned that unless its government began to act responsibly, unimaginable consequences were in the offing.[7] The letter was published the day before the 9/11 Twin Towers atrocity. The following month I participated in a parliamentary debate and condemned Israel's intransigence.[8] Along with fellow ANC MPs I stated that only a fair and just negotiated settlement, ending the brutal occupation and recognising Palestinian rights to self-determination, would end the violence and ensure the peace and security of both Israel and Palestine, in terms of UN resolutions. Unfortunately an imperial Israel flouts these resolutions with impunity owing to the unadulterated protection and support it receives from the USA.

In the process of an ongoing discourse I experienced greater abuse and vilification from sections of the Jewish community than I encountered from white South Africans during the apartheid years. I argued that being Jewish did not automatically equate with being Zionist or pro-Israel. Neither did criticism of Israel imply anti-Semitism. The legacy of the Holocaust left far too many people in the world woefully silent in the face of Israel's crimes. Since Israel claimed to represent Jews everywhere, I joined like-minded Jews all over the world in declaring that Israel had no right to act in our name in repressing the Palestinian people. As a human being it was incumbent to speak out. As a Jew I felt a double obligation to do so.

A group of 300 South Africans of Jewish origin signed a declaration of conscience formulated by ANC activist Max Ozinsky and myself. We reiterated the growing call around the world for Israel to withdraw its troops from the occupied territories and resume negotiations for a peaceful settlement. Virtually all the signatories had participated in the struggle against apartheid. Some adopted the title 'Not in my Name'.

We were repudiated by South Africa's orthodox rabbis and were castigated by most publicists of the Jewish community. We expected opposition but not the degree of venom and distortion that spewed forth. This was almost exclusively of a personal nature and failed to deal with the issues we raised. I was accused of being uninformed and politically motivated, by the chairman of the Jewish Board of Deputies.[9] This was mild compared to those who libellously labelled us traitors, self-hating Jews and anti-Semites. We were dismissed by the Chief Rabbi as marginalised Jews, and it was pointed out – as if it was necessary to do so – that we were but a small minority of the community.

The 'marginalised' included Nadine Gordimer, the country's leading writer and Nobel laureate; Denis Goldberg who had been sentenced to life imprisonment with Nelson Mandela; Lael Bethlehem, the daughter of the President of the Jewish Board of Deputies; political analysts such as Steven Friedman and Anton Harber; academics, public servants, artists and, among others, Zapiro, the renowned cartoonist.

As for being dismissed as a minority we were accustomed to that accusation, as white protagonists against apartheid. Besides, I responded, were Jews not meant to act 'as the leaven unto bread' – the biblical phrase for a chosen few whose duty it was to show humanity the righteous path?

A liberal rabbi in London, Dr David Goldberg, provoked consternation by describing Israel as the 'last colonial power in the world'. Yet the Board of Deputies of British Jews stated that he was within his rights to speak his mind.[10] I wrote to the South African Jewish Board of Deputies suggesting they adopt a similar position.[11]

When some of my critics called for my resignation and demanded to know why a Minister of Water Affairs and Forestry was pontificating on foreign relations, I referred them to Israel's policy of depriving Palestinians of an equitable share of water and barbarically destroying their precious olive and citrus groves. Particularly odious was the practice of planting forests to conceal the location of hundreds of Palestinian villages destroyed from 1948 onwards – the year of Israel's independence and commencement of its ethnic cleansing operations. On the West Bank the Israeli government allocated half of all water to the one-tenth of the people who were illegal Jewish settlers.[12]

Whilst our opponents alleged that our stance would encourage anti-Semitism, the contrary was the case with Muslims and Christians joining the 'Not in my Name' group in protest actions. At a Palestine solidarity rally in Cape Town attended by thousands of Muslims, I received a standing ovation when I addressed the crowd.[13] Wherever I went, Muslims asked to shake my hand and professed that Max Ozinsky and I had encouraged them to rethink their growing stereotypical conception of Jews as heartless people.

Dullah Omar, my colleague and Transport Minister who, with his wife Farida, joined many of our events, stated that our stance reminded him 'of the small group of whites who stood up against apartheid'.[14]

An important initiative was President Mbeki's hosting of a four-day retreat near Cape Town in January 2002. Present were representatives of the aborted Oslo negotiating group, from Palestine and Israel, meeting with ANC and apartheid-era leaders, discussing what could be learned from our negotiated settlement. The guests were amazed that Mbeki found time to be present for the duration of the proceedings. The Palestinian delegation was led by Saeb Erekat, one of Yasser Arafat's chief negotiators, and the Israeli's by Yossi Beilin, former Labour Party Justice Minister. Avraham Burg, Speaker of the Knesset who attended, has since described Israel as 'a failed society' resting 'on a scaffolding of corruption, and on foundations of oppression and injustice'. Concerning the suicide bombers, he stated that they 'consigned themselves to Allah in our places of recreation because their own lives were torture'. Things could be different, he implored, and 'crying out was a moral imperative'. He appealed to diaspora Jews, as well as Israelis, to 'pay heed and speak out'.[15]

To return to the reference of the Vienna rabbis, it appears that the only feasible solution may be for the protagonists to share the bride. Whether this takes the form of two internationally recognised, viable states or a bi-national, unitary state is for the Palestinians and Israelis to decide. It is the only way they can emerge out of the darkness of conflict and into the light. But do Israel's current rulers, Likud or Labour, really want a solution? Arafat's PLO and the Arab states have on several occasions committed themselves to recognising Israel's right to exist. One would have thought Israel would have long ago jumped at such a golden opportunity to end the impasse.

Most of Israel's leaders unfortunately either wish to impose a patch-work of bantustans on the Palestinians or to implement a final solution: the ethnic cleansing of the Holy Land of all Palestinians. By so doing, they add to the ongoing suffering of the displaced Palestinians, and those living within Israel, but demonstrate that the only just and feasible solution – no matter the time-line – is a single, unitary state of equal citizens.

Although there had been animosity between Chief Rabbi Cyril Harris and myself, the hatchet has hopefully been replaced by the olive branch even if we may not have reconciled our opposing view-points. We met, appropriately, at Nelson Mandela's eighty-fifth birthday celebration in July 2003. The rabbi's wife, Ann, caught my eye with a friendly smile – which helped break the ice –

and he and I had an amicable chat and shook hands.

When Walter Sisulu passed away in May 2002, the ANC asked me to speak at a Soweto memorial service. Thoughts of Sisulu conjured up qualities of kindness and modesty, gentleness and approachability. These clichés ran through my mind as I travelled to the venue. On the way I read a column in *Business Day*, by Xolela Mangcu.[16] He expressed criticism about the homilies that were being published and which implied that other leaders were arrogant, impersonal and ruthless. It made me change my speech.

My contribution was by way of reflection. The first time I set eyes on Sisulu was in 1962, at a clandestine meeting of the ANC Alliance near Chief Albert Luthuli's Groutville farm, as we geared up for armed struggle. He was quiet and serene and together with Moses Kotane steered the meeting and formulated the tough strategy for what lay ahead. The gathering was chaired by Chief Luthuli throughout the night. Before we broke up, Luthuli asked Sisulu to thank the owner of the farmstead on our behalf. I recalled Sisulu voicing our gratitude to a humble Indian sugarcane farmer. It was a seemingly simple task, yet all were glued to his every word. The meeting demonstrated both Sisulu's steely resolve and the gentility of his spirit.

I turned to a story from exile. Relaxing with Sisulu's buddies, Uncle J.B. Marks and Duma Nokwe in Dar es Salaam, with the Mandela-Sisulu leadership languishing on Robben Island. They recounted, over a round of ice-cold beers, how Sisulu was the front man in their ploys to obtain the white man's booze in apartheid South Africa.

It was on long car journeys, busy organising for the ANC, that they chose to have Sisulu with them. He was always well provisioned with *padkos* (food for the road) and a flask of tea by wife Albertina. Uncle J.B. and Duma shared his food, but had no need of his tea. It was when they stopped for petrol and spotted a liquor outlet that they appealed to him. Rocking with laughter, as they told their story, they described how they would point to the store and tell him that was where they wanted their 'tea' from. With his light complexion, Sisulu could present himself as a man of mixed race at the store, where coloureds but not blacks were permitted to make limited purchases. Although he was a confirmed teetotaller he would dutifully oblige. What was revealing was that despite his temperance and seniority, he was prepared to run such errands. It bothered him that he was entitled to privileges denied his comrades.

I came to benefit, like so many, from Sisulu's wise counsel after his release from prison. I referred to the first meeting of the ANC National Executive Committee held in Soweto, in June 1990, a few months after its banning was lifted. During the morning tea break I found Sisulu and a few others taking their ease where the winter sun was warming up an outside wall. Old prison lags well knew such comfortable sunspots and indeed, as I stepped out into the highveld cold, I remembered how as a Johannesburg schoolboy I had behaved just like that during wintertime. There was no space for me against the warm surface of the wall as I stopped to chat to Sisulu. He moved over and guided me to stand beside him so that both our backs were up against the wall. That was the moment that stuck in my mind. Walter Sisulu's life, I told the gathering, was about bringing people out of the cold and into the light, and helping them to stand upright.

As we approached ten years of freedom and democracy in 2004, that was exactly what the ANC government was achieving. South Africa's progression radiated as a beacon of hope to the world.

Writing now, almost ten years since I wrote the above paragraph the gloss has worn off and South Africa, in the eyes of many, has lost its way. Now as we approach twenty years of freedom and democracy in 2014 the challenge for those who govern is to serve the people and not themselves – and that is how we must ultimately be judged. For if we fail to focus all our strength on solving the people's problems we will continue to fall prey to corruption, avarice and delusional theories to explain all our mishaps instead of facing up to reality and there will be an inevitable descent into darkness and decay.

NOTES

Introduction to the Jacana Edition

  1 *Armed and Dangerous* Chapter 25 p. 299, 2004 edition

  2 Professor Sampie Terreblanche advances that view in his book *Lost in Transformation* KMM publishers, Johannesburg 2012, which should be required reading for all

  3 *Ibid.*

  4 *Ibid. p. 73*

  5 *Death of Dignity* by Victoria Brittain

  6 *Amandla!* December 2009

  7 *New York Times,* 9 April 2011

  8 M. Leibbrandt et al, SALDRU, University of Cape Town, September 2010

  9 *Armed and Dangerous* Chapter 23:'Going for the Gap'

  10 *Armed and Dangerous* Chapter 33: 'From Darkness to Light' p. 345, 2004 edition

Chapter 16

  1 Data compiled by the University of Maryland, USA

Chapter 32

  1 I am indebted to the Norwegian Ambassador Jon Bech for the phrase.

  2 *Sunday Times,* 18 November 2001.

  3 *Daily Telegraph,* 26 September 2008, Review by Tom Fort

Chapter 33

  1 *Business Day,* 29 March 2001.

  2 *Pretoria News,* 21 December 2002; *Cape Argus* and *Sunday Tribune,* 22

December 2002; *Business Day*, 19 June 2003.

3 John Rose, 'Israel: The Hijack State', A Socialist Worker pamphlet, London 1986. John was one of the students to act as ANC couriers in 1970. See page 106. His book, *The Myths of Zionism* is to be published by Pluto in 2004.

4 Avi Shlaim, *The Iron Wall*, Penguin Books, page 3.

5 Origin of Palestine-Israel Conflict; published by American Jews for Justice in the Middle East, p.18.

6 Press statement, 5 March 2002.

7 *Business Day*, 10 September 2001, 'Israel Could Learn From South Africa'.

8 23 October 2001. For text of speech see Hansard, 6844–52.

9 *Sowetan*, 24 October 2001. 'Uninformed Kasrils slammed by Jewish Board'.

10 Andrew Johnson, *The Independent*, London, 28 October 2001.

11 Letter to Russell Gaddin, Chairman, SAJBD, 1 November 2001.

12 *Sunday Times*, 20 January 2002.

13 *The Star*, 22 April 2002.

14 *Weekend Argus*, 29 December 2001.

15 Yediot Aharonot, 'A Failed Israeli Society Collapses', 5 September 2003.

16 *Business Day*, 15 May 2003.

INDEX

348